A LEVEL ICT
FOR AQA

Carl Lyon and Jackie Rogers

www.payne-gallway.co.uk

✓ Free online support
✓ Useful weblinks
✓ 24 hour online ordering

01865 888070

PAYNE-GALLWAY

Payne-Gallway is an imprint of Pearson Education Limited, a company incorporated in England and Wales, having its registered office at Edinburgh Gate, Harlow, Essex, CM20 2JE.
Registered company number: 872828

www.payne-gallway.co.uk

Text © 2008 Jackie Rogers and Carl Lyon

First published 2008

12 11 10 09 08
10 9 8 7 6 5 4 3 2 1

British Library Cataloguing in Publication Data is available from the British Library on request.

ISBN 978 1905 292 34 9

Copyright notice

Typeset and illustrated by HL Studios

Cover photo © iStockPhotos

Printed by in the UK by Scotprint Ltd.

Websites

There are links to relevant websites in this book. In order to ensure that the links are up-to-date, that the links work, and that the sites are not inadvertently linked to sites that could be considered offensive, we have made the links available on the Heinemann website at www.heinemann.co.uk/hotlinks. When you access the site, the express code is 2349P.

Ordering Information

Payne-Gallway, FREEPOST (OF1771),
PO Box 381, Oxford OX2 8BR
Tel: 01865 888070
Fax: 01865 314029
Email: orders@payne-gallway.co.uk

Photo acknowledgements

Alamy: pages 80 (POPPERFOTO), 182 (Steven May), 200 (ClassicStock), 281 (Motoring Picture Library)

GettyImages/Home Office: page 175

iStockPhoto: pages 23 (Suprijono Suharjoto), 25 (Brandon Blinkenberg), 28 (Jaroslaw Wojcik), 39, 49 (Norman Chan), 76 (Russell Tate), 80 (Edward Todd), 143, 177 (Yakov Stavchansky), 237 (Petra Kukofka), 271 (Emilia Stasiak), 289 (Alex Bramwell).

microdrones/www.mwpower.co.uk: page 176

Acknowledgements

Every effort has been made to contact copyright holders of material reproduced in this book. Any omissions will be rectified in subsequent printings if notice is given to the publishers.

Page 7 – reprinted with permission from John Gill and www.tiresias.org; page 22 – reprinted with thanks to Opportunity Links - www.opp-links.org.uk; page 26 – reprinted from www.wacom.com.au; page 32 – reprinted with permission from AP Digital Newsletter/theYGSgroup.com; page 33 – reprinted from techworld.com; page 36 – reprinted from physorg.com; page 37 – reprinted from news.com.com; page 40 – reprinted with permission from IP Syndication © The Times April 2007; page 41 – reprinted with permission from CBC.CA Archives; page 47 – reprinted from bottomup.wordpress.com; page 50 – reprinted from eurotechnology.com; page 51 – reprinted from space.com; page 73 – crown copyright PSI License C2007001903; page 74 – reprinted with permission from Ryan Cartwright/ ICT Hub; page 75 – reprinted with permission from USAID Leyland Initiative; page 82 – reprinted from pencomputing.com; page 83 – reprinted from nintendo.com; page 87 – reprinted from ft.com; page 89 (left) – reprinted from Wikipedia GNU Free Documentation License; page 89 (right) – reprinted from searchnetworking.com; page 97 – diagram reprinted with permission from Pat Heathcote; page 99: – reprinted from businesslink.gov.uk; From *The New York Times*, October 24 © 2004 *The New York Times* All rights reserved. Used by permission and protected by the Copyright Laws of the United States. The printing, copying, redistribution, or retransmission of the Material without express written permission is prohibited; Reprinted with permission from PC Advisor; page 104 – reprinted from © Evening Standard; page 112 – reprinted from deseretnews.com; page 116 – reprinted with permission from Amadeus Software Limited; page 118 (above) – reprinted from Sensoray.com; page 118 (below) – reprinted from hearingconcern.org.uk; page 119 – reprinted from peachtreeextra.com; page 122 – reprinted with permission from Richard Craven, SustainIT 2007; page 128 – reprinted from i-newswire.com; page 129 – reprinted from www.parrswood.manchester.sch.uk/school/network.html; page 130 – reprinted from www.tes.co.uk; page 131 – reprinted from thisislondon.co.uk © Evening Standard; pages 134–135 – reprinted from theregister.co.uk; page 138 – reprinted from retailtechnology.co.uk; page 140 – reprinted with permission from Fujitsu Services Limited; page 143 – reprinted from selfemployedweb.com; page 148 – reprinted from phillips.com; page 149 – reprinted with permission from Vanderbilt University Medical Center/Barb Cramer; page 152 – reprinted from selfemployedweb.com; page 154 – reprinted from ford.com; page 158 – BBC/Beatles Abbey Road; page 160 – reprinted from printsolutionsmag.com; page 174 – reprinted from www.extremerfid.com August 1, 2005, with permission. Copyright © 2005 Enterprise Media Group, Inc. All Rights Reserved; page 178 – reprinted from theage.com.au; page 185 – reprinted with permission from Summit Retail Technology; page 189 – reprinted with permission from Ebase Technology Ltd; page 190 – reprinted from IT Reseller; page 192 – reprinted from www.sap.com; page 194 – reprinted with permission from Matthews, K.B., Buchan, K., Rivington, M. and Miller D.G. (2007) Land; Allocation Decision Support System - Climate Change. [online, accessed 30 Oct 2007], http://www.macaulay.ac.uk/LADSS/climate_change.html; page 197 – reprinted with permission from www.tutor2u.net; page 198 – reprinted from computerweekly.com; page 202 – legislation descriptions. Crown copyright PSI License C2007001903; page 212 – crown copyright PSI License C2007001903; page 219 – text and diagrams reprinted from www.ibm.com; page 222 – reprinted with permission from Tony Drewry, Senior Lecturer, page 227 – text and logo reprinted with permission from www.connect2u.co.uk; UWE, Bristol; page 228 – crown copyright PSI License C2007001903; page 229 (left) – reprinted from inderscience.com; page 229 (right) – reprinted from www.comp.lancs.ac.uk; page 230 – reprinted with permission from the Acutest Library as presented on http:///www.acutest.co.uk; page 232 – reprinted with permission from the Acutest Library as presented on http:///www.acutest.co.uk; page 234 – reprinted with permission from The National eProcurement Project with thanks to Wellingborough Borough Council; page 245 – reprinted from itbusinessnet.com; page 248 – reprinted with permission from ICT Hub and Michelle Edmundson; oage 250 – reprinted from Xansa.com; page 252 – reprinted from unisys.com; page 278 – reprinted from csrc.lse.ac.uk/asp; examination questions copyright AQA – see www.aqa.org.uk.

Contents

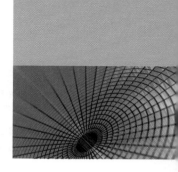

Guide to features

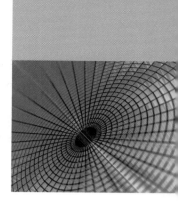

This book has a number of features to help you relate theory to practice and reinforce your learning. You will find the following features in each section.

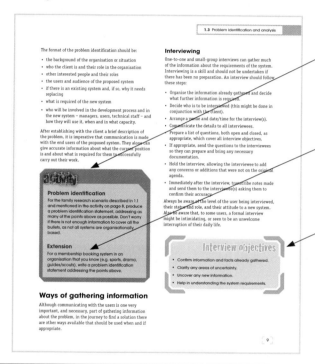

Activities

Activities are provided throughout each section. These can be used to reinforce your learning as you work through each section.

Extensions to activities

These are harder questions in some activities which aim to stretch and challenge more able learners.

Box features

Important details that you need to keep in mind are in these blue boxes. They will help identify particularly vital or interesting information.

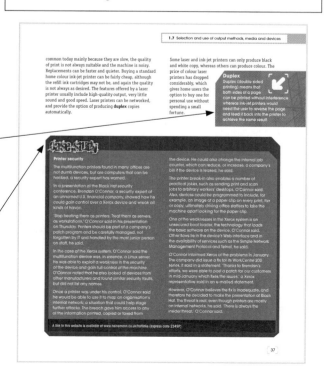

Key terms

Terms that you need to be aware of are summarised in these boxes. They will help you to check your knowledge as you learn, and are a useful quick-reference tool. They are also listed in the glossary at the back of the book.

Case studies

Interesting examples of real situations or companies are described in case studies that link theory to practice. They will show you how the topics you are studying affect real people and businesses.

Exam Café

In our unique Exam Café, students will find lots of ideas to help them prepare for their exams. There are three easy-to-follow steps to exam success: **Relax and prepare**, **Refresh your memory** and **Get the result**.

Relax and prepare

You can **Relax** because there's handy revision advice from fellow students. Students share handy revision tips and experiences to help others feel supported in their new course.

Refresh your memory

Refresh your memory with summaries and checklists. Revision checklists remind students of the key concepts, topics and skills they need to revise for the exam.

Getting started

Guidance about being examined at a new level helps students to relax and prepare for their exam.

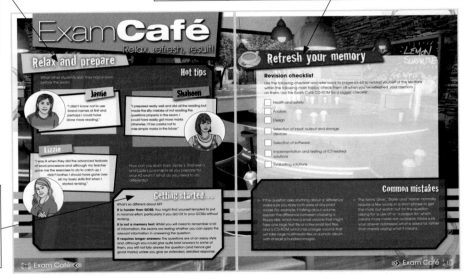

Get the result!

Get that result and achieve your potential through practising exam-style questions, accompanied by hints and tips on getting the very best grades. Sample answers annotated with examiner feedback show students what is expected of them.

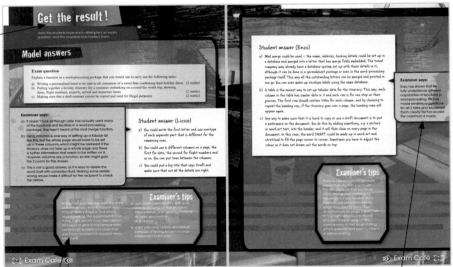

Examiner's tips

Extra advice and tips on exam and coursework preparation are given in these features.

Examiner says

Detailed examiner feedback on a student answer helps students to understand the questions, see what examiners look for and what makes a strong answer – a real help in exam preparation!

About the authors

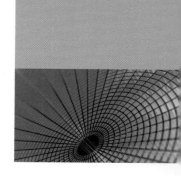

Jackie Rogers

After gaining a BSc in Computing Science way back when, I spent over 15 years in industry in various software system development roles (programmer, analyst, auditor, estimator) before training to be a post-16 teacher.

I then taught mainly 16-19 courses in further education and sixth form colleges for two periods, of eight years and four years, with a four-year spell as an estimating and business assurance consultant with a well-known software house in between. I started examining ICT A level in 1998 and have been involved ever since, for both Computing and ICT and for different exam boards.

I was part of the senior team for the Curriculum 2000 ICT specification and have been a part of the group that developed this exciting new specification. I live in the north-west of England, handy for the exam board offices, with my husband and three cats. My two grown children live nearby.

Carl Lyon

Prior to graduating I worked in the retail and hospitality industry. I graduated in 1997 with a BA in Business Education with ICT and taught Business Studies and ICT for three years until concentrating solely on the teaching of ICT in 2000. After initially setting up the AQA ICT GCE course at my previous school I became an examiner with two established boards and have moderated and examined work on a variety of ICT based courses at various levels since.

In 2004 I became Head of ICT at Shiplake College and graduated in 2006 with an MA in Professional Studies in Education from Northampton University. I live with my wife, Cynthia, and two young children, Paul and Isaac, in Henley on Thames.

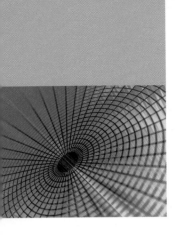

Introduction

My five-year-old neighbour got a digital camera and printer for Christmas. He can take a picture with the camera, attach the camera to the printer, press the right buttons and print a photograph and present it to us. He watches as his dad downloads the pictures from the camera on to his PC, manipulates the images and produces Christmas thank you cards from the children with a photo of the three of them on the front, made up of pieces from three separate photographs. By next Christmas, the five-year-old will be doing this himself.

A 60-year-old friend uses a web-cam and instant communications software to keep in touch with her children and grandchildren who live the other side of the world – she can witness first steps and dress rehearsals for school plays and generally feels as though she is a part of their lives, albeit from 6,000 miles away.

Music, television programmes and films are downloaded to suit people's tastes constantly, free or for a few pence. People upload personal photographs and images to share with their friends and the whole world. They write diaries, web-logs (blogs), thoughts, feelings, lyrics and items of interest and invite comment, discussion and contact, at all hours and with all-comers.

Technology makes it possible to see and hear others whilst using ICT, to interact, play games with and against them, to laugh, cry, share moments and memories with people that may never be met face-to-face.

We live in a digital world, where the technology is available to everyone.

This is **not** what you will be studying when you undertake an AS and A level in Information and Communication Technology.

What you **will** be studying at AS level is the appropriateness of ICT technology and systems to any situation, and how to decide what is the most appropriate to be used. You will be studying how ICT is used in the world of business, how data is collected, organised, manipulated and turned into information; how that information is used and misused, kept and passed on, controlled and kept secure, stored and displayed. It provides an opportunity to study the phenomenal rise in the amount of information that exists in our digital world; how this has arisen, what facilities there are to hold and control the flow, and to what purposes the information can be put.

The two AS sections allow exploration of the practical use of ICT for problem solving in the digital world, and a study of the underpinning knowledge and understanding to do with living in the digital world.

The first section is a practical one, and learning will take place using a variety of technology and different software whilst investigating problems and designing, creating, testing and evaluating solutions. The sections in this book give practical examples, suggested exercises as well as the background knowledge from which appropriate hardware and software choices can be made. Work produced during this process will be taken into the section examination, where some questions will be based on the prepared work. Other questions will be based on other practical activities that you will have done during your study of this section.

The second section is a more traditional theory section, which covers the underpinning knowledge and understanding required of an AS ICT student. It covers general information about ICT, about the people who use and interact with ICT, about how ICT is used to transfer data from system to system, about how data is kept safe and protected (and why), and how ICT is used in many different situations, such as, in education, in publishing and in banking.

When you reach A2, hopefully with a solid understanding of the capabilities and limitations of ICT in the digital world, it is time to study the wider issues – how ICT is used in organisations and businesses both large and small, how new innovations in technology and communications can create better conditions and more efficient workings for all, how organisations cope with large-scale systems and how those systems are integrated into the lives of the people using them. Part of this section is examined using a pre-released case study scenario.

The final section allows a practical opportunity for you to show your knowledge and understanding of one or more of the issues raised in the third section. Working with a real organisation, you will investigate a situation, design a solution to a problem, then show your implementation of the solution by testing and evaluating your work. This coursework section is not necessarily about creating a software application, although that is one of the suggested options, but could be more related to the business use of ICT – a backup strategy and disaster recovery plan, for instance, or the creation of a company security policy. In this section, the product is not the key to success; it is the process that is assessed.

This book aims to give you not only the knowledge that is required to pass the course, but also ideas for practising the skills that are required to produce top-quality practical work at both AS and A2 levels. Example questions follow each section.

In our unique Exam Café you'll find lots of ideas to help prepare for your exams. You'll see the Exam Café at the end of the three externally examined sections. You can **Relax** because there's handy revision advice from fellow students, **Refresh your memory** with summaries and checklists of the key ideas you need to revise and **Get that Result** through practising exam-style questions, accompanied by hints and tips on getting the very best grades.

You'll find an exam café CD-ROM in the back of the book containing a wealth of exam preparation material: interactive multiple choice questions, revision flashcards, exam-style questions with model answers and examiner feedback, and much more!

Jackie Rogers

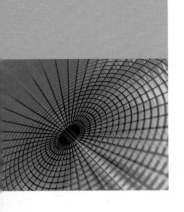

Introduction to the characters

Jamie

Jamie is a popular young chap who has lots of friends and a great social life. He wears the latest teenage fashion (whatever that is) and has an equally cool girlfriend. He passed most of his GCSEs without doing too much reading but didn't achieve any A grades. He did not do ICT at GCSE but he taught himself most of the ICT skills he knows and has built a successful website for his mother's beauty treatment business.

Shaheen

Shaheen lives in the pub her mother and father run and own. She has used the skills she learnt while studying GCSE ICT to make several systems to use within the business. She has a lot of artistic flair and this is reflected in the bohemian style of clothes she always wears. She passed all her GCSEs after working hard for the last year of the course and carrying out all the tasks recommended to her by her teachers.

Lizzie

Lizzie is a lively girl from a Midlands town, attending a large sixth-form college. She got seven GCSEs grade C and above, including a couple of As in her favourite subjects of English Literature and Drama. She's taking Theatre Studies, English Literature and Business Studies at A level, as well as ICT. She is normally 'plugged in' to her MP3 player and spends a lot of time texting her large circle of friends.

Enzo

Enzo attends a local Further Education college in a northern city and has a good circle of friends who came from the same secondary school. He is half Italian and only came to England with his parents when he was 14. His spoken English is good, but sometimes his vocabulary lets him down. He works very hard and did really well in his GCSEs, gaining 10 at B or above. As well as ICT, he is taking Maths, Physics and Geography.

AS Section 1

Practical Problem-Solving in the Digital World

This is a practical section that is assessed by a one-and-a-half-hour examination. During the course of studying for this section, you should be given and make use of opportunities to develop your knowledge and understanding of the development of ICT systems through practical experience in using a range of applications software, hardware and communications technologies in a structured way.

The skills, knowledge and understanding you gain from these experiences can then be applied to the solution of further problems.

The range of applications software, hardware and communications technologies used should cover the processing of text, images, numbers and sound.

Skills to develop include analysing simple problems, designing solutions for those problems, using the most appropriate software, hardware and communications technologies, implementing solutions, testing the solutions and evaluating the systems so created.

You must produce a set of sample work to take into the examination. It is suggested that this work should be about 10–20 pages only. Any more and it would be harder for you to organise your answers in the exam. Any less and there might not be enough material for you to use when answering the exam questions.

This section of the book contains the underpinning knowledge for all the topics in the section, giving you a starting level of skills and knowledge that you can take and, using practical investigation and practice, develop your own skills in analysing, designing, selecting suitable tools, implementing, testing and evaluating a problem solution.

There are three practical exercises that could be used as a basis for the sample work, or as practice in developing the skills required. There is a selection of practice exam questions and some tips on what to revise for the exam.

Finally, the first Exam Café contains plenty of advice from students and examiners, and exam-style questions and answers, with comments as to the standard of the answers given.

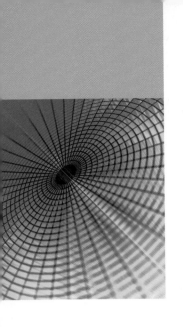

1.1 Learning practically – the use of ICT for solving problems

Problem-solving in any context needs methodical working: having a look at what the problem is, investigating the current situation, deciding exactly what is required, looking at different options for solving the problem, designing a way forward, then putting the solution in place and seeing if it solves the problem in a way that satisfies everyone. Finally, it is useful to reflect back after a while to see if the solution was the best one, or if it could have been improved – is there anything that could be done to make it work as a solution in the long term, or could it be done better next time?

An example of this is the problem of staging a school prom.

The problem could be the size of venue required, the number of people expected to attend, the budget acceptable when turned into ticket price, or the type of event to be held.

Investigation might include seeing how it has been done in the past, available venues on the date required, costs and prices of the elements and choices for event (sit-down dinner, buffet and disco, live band or entertainment, competitions and so on).

A list of requirements would be drawn up with constraints set by various people, such as the organising committee and the head teacher. Different options might be looked at, and a solution put in place that seems to be the best match to the requirements within the constraints. Making sure that it all comes together in time for the prom to take place is the implementing and testing stage.

After the event, the organisers would check back against their requirements. Did it go over budget? Were there balloons on each table? Did the entertainment offer value for money? Any lessons learnt could be kept for the following year so that the organisers didn't make the same mistakes (if there were any) and could use the good practices once more.

Investigating a problem with respect to solving it using ICT can vary from the straightforward use of a piece of hardware or software to provide a solution, to the use of multiple input, storage and output devices, using different methods of communication, to create a complex system with many phases.

An example of a simple problem might be taking a digital photograph of all your 16th birthday presents and including it in a personalised thank you note to everyone that sent you a present, using the mail merge function of a word processor.

Staging a school prom

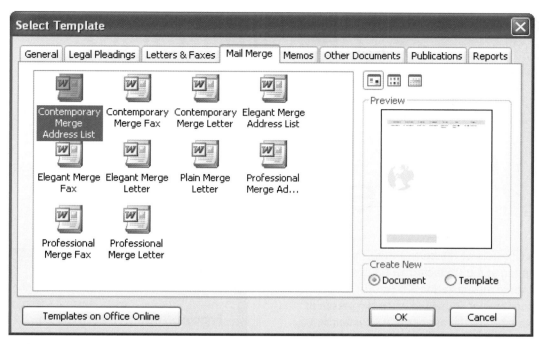

Mail merging your thank you notes

An example of a complex problem might be investigating your family tree. You could use the Internet and other electronic sources to find out birth, marriage, death and census information. You could digitally record the reminiscences of older family members, scan in old photographs and take new ones of houses, places and gravestones, keep a database of all the information, draw up a family tree, use genealogy sites to track down living relatives and use email or web-conferencing facilities to communicate with them. Finally, you could put all of this onto a family website or CD that all relatives can access and possibly add to.

The best way to find out what is the most suitable hardware and software to use is to try out a range of equipment for a range of different purposes and to make notes about which do the job and which don't in any given circumstance. It is easy to know that a mouse does this, and a joystick does that, but unless you try out all choices, you will never be sure which is the best.

Remember some of those old PC games? Games such as Tetris, where you could use the arrow keys for manipulating the objects? Some mobile phone games still work in this way

– there is one called Snake, which would be better with a joystick-type input device, and another called Pairs, which would work so much better with a mouse or a touch screen to pick the pairs and see if there is a match.

If you have been given a task to create a newsletter, for instance, it is easy to learn, from a list of features, which pieces of application software have the capability to create a newsletter; however, without trying more than one of them out, you may not choose the most suitable – other software may have facilities and functions that could make the newsletter so much better.

This section is designed for you to try out many items of hardware and many pieces of software, so that you can start to make informed decisions about the best or most appropriate ones for any given purpose.

It is suggested that you address several different problems during the course of studying this section. The problems can be tailored to meet your individual needs, but need to cover the processing of all of the four types of data – text, numbers, images and sounds – so that you have experienced the full range.

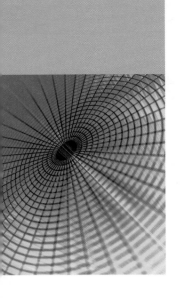

1.2 Health and safety in relation to the use of ICT systems

The health and safety of the human user is paramount when designing and introducing an ICT system. Some aspects are covered by legislation – if certain health and safety issues are not addressed, then the person or company responsible for the use of the ICT system may be liable for prosecution.

There are other aspects of design and introduction that are not covered by legislation, but are required to make the use of the ICT system accessible for all its users. This not only covers the working environment of any person using a computer, but also the ICT systems that they are using. Therefore, system design – input and output design, hardware to be used, and so on – becomes very important.

Ergonomics is associated with the layout of an environment. Workstation ergonomics is specifically associated with the design of the immediate working environment of a computer user.

A workstation consists of:

- the display screen equipment, including software that determines the interface between the equipment and its operator or user, and a keyboard or any other input device
- any optional accessories to the display screen equipment (e.g. web-cam, speakers)
- any disk drive, telephone, modem, printer, document holder, chair, desk, worksurface or other item peripheral to the display screen equipment
- the immediate work environment around the display screen equipment.

Health and safety legislation

The Health and Safety at Work Act (1974) was drawn up to protect all employees, whatever the nature of their work, so this applies to all workers who use ICT systems. It is not only employers who are responsible for safe working, but also the employees themselves. The main duties under the act are as follows:

- An employer has a duty to provide a safe working environment for its employees as far as is reasonably practical.
- An employer must consult its employees if it is to make any changes to the workplace that might affect their health and safety.
- An employer must appoint someone with the responsibility for ensuring a safe workplace is provided and monitoring health and safety issues.
- Employees must take reasonable care of their own safety and that of other employees, and must co-operate with their employer.
- Employees must use any protective equipment provided by their employer.

A 1992 set of regulations (Management of Health and Safety at Work) added further responsibilities:

- An employer must set up a risk assessment process to check the workplace for health and safety problems.
- An employer must provide an emergency procedure and provide information and training on all aspects of health and safety for its employees.

More specifically, the Display Screen Equipment (VDU) regulations (1992) aim to protect users of ICT systems. Under these regulations, the employer must:

- assess the risks arising from use of display screen workstations and take steps to reduce any risks identified to 'the lowest extent that is reasonably practical'
- ensure that new workstations meet the minimum ergonomic standards as set out in the regulations
- plan the work of employees so that regular breaks or changes of activity away from the workstation can occur
- provide an eye or eyesight test to any user who requests one (if the test shows that glasses are necessary, and that normal glasses are insufficient, then special glasses or corrective appliances must be provided)
- provide adequate training in health and safety whilst using a computer workstation.

Such legislation will help to protect employees against computer-related injuries:

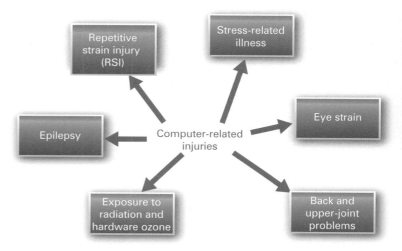

Computer related injuries

However, legislation does not cover people who are not employees, such as students in a school, self-employed people working from home, or leisure users.

Safety procedures

Make a list of potential health and safety problems and suggested solutions for working with ICT systems for each of the following individuals:

- an A level ICT student who spends, on average, 2 hours a day at school and 3 hours a day at home working on a computer
- an unemployed person who spends most of his time either on auction websites or playing computer games
- a self-employed mobile beautician who uses her laptop computer to record bookings and customer details and to keep accounts; the laptop is used on and off all day and she normally spends about an hour each evening at home, completing her 'paperwork'.

It is not only the environment and physical equipment that are important to ICT system users' health and safety, but also the information system or software that they are using.

The design of a system's interface can cover the input devices to be used, the output devices to be used, and the visual and aural interfaces. System interface designers must take into account several factors to minimise any health risks and encourage usability.

Input devices

Input devices should be chosen to enable the user to enter data into the system with as much ease as possible. The use of closed choice options, pull-down menus, default values in entry fields and so on can further ease the input burden on the user. Interfaces that use voice recognition, for instance, can make the interface usable for those unable to type or use a manual input device.

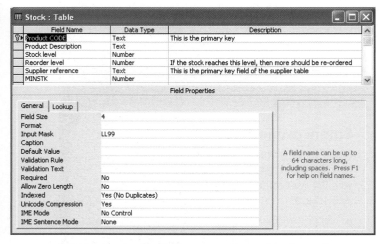

Default values in entry fields can ease the input burden on the user

Output devices

It is not always appropriate to have the output from a system displayed on a screen. There may be too much information to see, in which case the interface may be designed so that the output is printed. Other output options are aural, through speakers or a headset, or sensory, such as with devices being developed for deafblind users (see the case study).

Colour

Bright colours and flashing parts of a screen might induce eyestrain and headaches, or even epileptic fits. Some colours are indistinguishable to users with colour blindness (red/green or blue/brown combinations can cause problems). Contrasting colours may help with visibility.

Text size and font used

The font and its size must be chosen so that any text or instructions that the user needs to read are clear. Text that is too small may affect the eyes, and a complex font may cause frustration and stress. The ability to enlarge text may also be useful for those with restricted sight.

Sound and images

The design should not overload the user with unnecessary sounds and images, especially flashing images. Sounds and images can sometimes distract from what the system is trying to achieve and can also confuse the user.

Help and instructions

An inexperienced user will be able to learn how to use the system, but too much interference from a 'helpful' system could cause frustration, so the ability to 'switch it off' would be useful.

Pathways through the system

Menus and option buttons should enable the user to quickly find where they want to be in the system. If there are too many options, users may get confused; too few and they may not know where to go next. Lengthy navigation to a much-used function will cause frustration.

Consistency

It is useful to the user for the design to have a consistent layout for all screens in an ICT system. This way, they will always know where to look to find certain items of information – such as the date, the system name, and the buttons for 'next record', 'return to menu' etc.

Compatibility

Some software designers use a common user interface design for all their applications, which makes it easier for a user new to an application to learn how to operate it. Functions should work the same as they did before, so that the user only has to learn the new or amended parts of the system.

Interface design for disabled people

1 Read the case study 'Information Technology for deafblind people'.

2 Research the available interfaces for physically and mentally disabled people.

3 In a word-processing package, set up a report template to collate your findings. Use a watermark to indicate that this is a draft report.

- Create a consistent design for each set of findings; you could structure the report by type of disability or by type of device found.
- You should cover at least two different mental disabilities and at least two different physical disabilities.
- You should cover at least four specific-use input devices or mechanisms and at least four specific-use output devices or mechanisms.

Extract from 'Dual Sensory Impairment – Devices for Deafblind People' by John Gill

This case study shows how people who are both deaf and blind can still access ICT systems, and highlights some of the accessibility problems they face.

Access to Information Technology

It was the advent of the personal computer with Braille or magnified visual output that opened up opportunities for a significant increase in access to information for deafblind people. Software for producing large characters on the monitor is relatively inexpensive, but Braille displays have remained expensive.

The DOS text-based operating system is easier for many deafblind people than ones, such as Windows, which use a graphical user interface. However, keeping to DOS restricts the choice of software in that most new software is written for the Windows environment.

Fortunately email systems are predominantly text-based and therefore relatively easy to use with a Braille display. The world wide web is more problematic in that many sites employ graphical representations without an adequate text alternative. The sites which are fully accessible tend to be ones belonging to government departments, and the ones which are largely inaccessible are the popular home shopping sites.

Even with these restrictions the Internet has the potential for significantly increasing access to information by deafblind people. What is needed is a range of affordable user-friendly terminals which provide access for deafblind people who need non-visual output but who do not read Braille.

The basic mobile telephone has been of limited use to deafblind people. However the introduction of Universal Mobile Telecommunications System (UMTS) offers exciting possibilities if the services are affordable. For instance, the ability to transmit pictures of where you are to a service centre and receive textual replies could greatly assist a deafblind pedestrian in an unfamiliar environment.

Related to developments in telecommunications will be radio-based systems for short-range interconnection of both domestic equipment and public terminals. Systems such as Bluetooth have the potential to facilitate the connection of assistive devices to a whole range of equipment. If this technology lives up to the publicity, then deafblind people can anticipate significant improvements for those who wish to live independently.

However, not all technological developments are to the advantage of deafblind people. With analogue television it is possible to obtain Braille output of Teletext which gives basic access to the news. However, digital Teletext is graphically based so this is no longer possible.

A link to this website is available at www.heinemann.co.uk/hotlinks (express code 2349P)

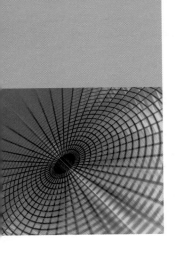

1.3 Problem identification and analysis

Problem identification

Clearly identifying the problem to be solved is the first step in deciding what any new system is to do. An analyst or developer cannot identify the problem without communicating with the people who want, need or will use that system.

The client is usually the person who needs a solution to a problem and makes contact with the person who will provide the solution. This communication will normally provide a brief description of the problem and some of the required outcomes. For instance, a teacher who wants to record his lessons for remote teaching may want a system to record and distribute a set of podcasts to be used.

The user or users will use the system once it has been developed. They may be using it on their own behalf and using the outputs as part of their job, or they may be entering and setting in motion the processing of that data so that other people can use the information that is output. In the podcast scenario, a teaching assistant may be tasked with actually creating the podcasts and organising the access.

The audience can be external to the organisation whose system it is – customers, or remote users of the information. The audience for the podcast scenario would be the remote students, who have downloaded the lessons for remote studying.

Other people who might have an interest in a system include the system commissioner, who may make the final decision on whether or not to proceed with any development on cost/benefit or internal constraints considerations, and the ICT technical, support and maintenance staff who might be involved in installing, amending and maintaining any system.

It is important to find out the skill levels of all the potential users of the proposed system in relation to what they might be asked to do with it. These users may vary from the highest manager, who may be wanting the data laid out in different formats, to the operational staff entering data, to a sole user of a home leisure system – in fact, anyone who might use the system. Finding out what they have done before will enable the analyst to choose the most suitable options, or to recommend specific training for those users.

The format of the problem identification should be:

- the background of the organisation or situation
- who the client is and their role in the organisation
- other interested people and their roles
- the users and audience of the proposed system
- if there is an existing system and, if so, why it needs replacing
- what is required of the new system
- who will be involved in the development process and in the new system – managers, users, technical staff – and how they will use it, when and in what capacity.

After establishing with the client a brief description of the problem, it is imperative that communication is made with the end users of the proposed system. They alone can give accurate information about what the current position is and about what is required for them to successfully carry out their work.

Problem identification

For the family research scenario described in 1.1 and mentioned in the activity on page 8, produce a problem identification statement, addressing as many of the points above as possible. Don't worry if there is not enough information to cover all the bullets, as not all systems are organisationally based.

Extension

For a membership booking system in an organisation that you know (e.g. sports, drama, guides/scouts), write a problem identification statement addressing the points above.

Ways of gathering information

Although communicating with the users is one very important, and necessary, part of gathering information about the problem, in the journey to find a solution there are other ways available that should be used when and if appropriate.

Interviewing

One-to-one and small-group interviews can gather much of the information about the requirements of the system. Interviewing is a skill and should not be undertaken if there has been no preparation. An interview should follow these steps:

- Organise the information already gathered and decide what further information is required.
- Decide who is to be interviewed (this might be done in conjunction with the client).
- Arrange a venue and date/time for the interview(s).
- Communicate the details to all interviewees.
- Prepare a list of questions, both open and closed, as appropriate, which cover all interview objectives.
- If appropriate, send the questions to the interviewees so they can prepare and bring any necessary documentation.
- Hold the interview, allowing the interviewee to add any concerns or additions that were not on the original agenda.
- Immediately after the interview, transcribe notes made and send them to the interviewee(s) asking them to confirm their accuracy.

Always be aware of the level of the user being interviewed, their status and role, and their attitude to a new system. Also be aware that, to some users, a formal interview might be intimidating, or seen to be an unwelcome interruption of their daily life.

Interview objectives

- Confirm information and facts already gathered.
- Clarify any areas of uncertainty.
- Uncover any new information.
- Help in understanding the system requirements.

Questionnaires

If there are many similar users, and there is apparent conflict over some of the requirements and details that are being proposed, then a well-constructed questionnaire might be a fact-gathering or opinion-gathering option.

For ease of analysis, as many questions as possible should be of the closed variety, with a small finite number of options. Such questions are mainly used for consolidating information that has already been gathered from documentary evidence. They will only work if the correct user group has been targeted and there is a control mechanism in place for distributing and collecting the completed questionnaires.

Observation

Sometimes it is only through the technique of observing users doing their existing work that problems can be identified. Often, an unnecessary manual step is taken at a point in a data or information transfer process and is accepted by all users involved without question, and it is only by observing this that the requirement for an automatic method can be seen.

Other environmental or working condition issues that have been raised by one set of users but dismissed by others require observation so that a judgement can be made either way. This could include choices for input devices to be more robust than at first thought, or to propose different kinds of interface for use in the office and for the mobile users of the system.

Document analysis

The client may have plenty of documentation to use in this analysis, or the analyst may have to search around for documents that would help them come up with the requirements for the system.

It is a good idea to include any existing input forms used or reports that are output from a current system. Even something that the client has seen that looks like what they would like in their system will be helpful. This is especially true for multimedia or website systems.

Here are some basic items of documentation that may help:

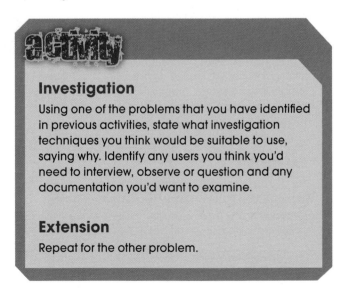

A list of people in each department

An organisation chart, which might help decide on how information will need to flow

Lists of procedures that are followed currently, including steps in the current processing

Basic items of documentation

Sample reports, whether electronically or manually produced

Sample forms currently used, to identify what data is currently captured and to help identify any gaps

Job roles, to help identify the potential users

Basic items of documentation

Any of the above investigation techniques can occur at any time and in any order during the information-gathering phase, and may be repeated as and when necessary to ensure clarification.

activity

Investigation

Using one of the problems that you have identified in previous activities, state what investigation techniques you think would be suitable to use, saying why. Identify any users you think you'd need to interview, observe or question and any documentation you'd want to examine.

Extension

Repeat for the other problem.

Once the investigation is completed, it should be straightforward to make a list of client requirements in terms that they understand. Once this list is complete, it should be taken back to the client to get agreement that this is the comprehensive list. At this point, they may suddenly remember other features or functions that they had not thought of, or may be prompted to do so by the analysis of users' needs.

Requirements are likely to be of various types. Some will be physical or measurable; these are known as **quantitative** requirements. Some will be less concrete, and may be subjective; these are known as **qualitative** requirements. Quantitative requirements can be assessed objectively, but qualitative requirements can only be assessed by the client.

School library system (1)

Some typical client requirements for a school library system are as follows:

Quantitative

The system should be able to:

- hold borrower (student) details and identify which class they are in
- add new students, delete students who have left and amend details for a particular student
- automatically move a whole class to a new class at the start of a new school year
- record book and other item loans
- keep track of what's in the library and what's out on loan
- update the records when an item is returned
- add new items to the library stock
- list which items are out on loan for an individual or a class
- identify overdue items and send out reminder letters
- deal with fines for lost items.

Qualitative

The system should:

- be easy to use for both the librarian and any parent volunteer
- be secure, so no student can get in
- require minimum ICT skills and training
- have clear fonts and colours
- use sounds to get attention, but not be too loud
- look nice with things in the same place
- have clear instructions in a manual
- show solutions to common problems.

A link to this website is available at www.heinemann.co.uk/hotlinks (express code 2349P)

Listing client requirements

1 For either of the problems identified, list five quantitative and five qualitative requirements that you think are necessary for the proposed system.

2 Compare these to those produced by another student and see if you have both understood the requirements in the same way.

Interpreting requirements as input, process and output for ICT solutions

Now the requirements are listed, it is time to identify what this means in terms of the output required from the system, the data that is available for entry into the system and what has to be done to the data to create the outputs required.

Clients tend to think in terms of what they want to see from the system, as this drives how they use the information. This is therefore the starting point when breaking the system down.

From the requirements, identify what outputs are needed. These outputs may be as lists or reports to be printed, as still or moving images to be displayed, as sounds to be heard, or as screens to be displayed. Give each an identity and a title, then identify the elements each output should contain.

School library system (2)

For the school library system, the outputs might start to be listed as follows:

- Rep001 List of Borrowers, tabulated, containing Name, Address, Class, Form tutor, Number of Items allowed

- Rep002 Items on loan for a Class, tabulated, containing Class, Form tutor, Name, Item identity and title, Date due back

- Rep003 Overdue items, tabulated, containing Class, Form tutor, Name, Item identity, Number of days overdue

- Rep004 Overdue letter, one per overdue item, containing Name, Address, Form tutor, Date due back, Fine amount

- Rep005 Receipt, one per fine paid, containing Name, Address, Form tutor, Fine amount, Date received.

From the outputs identified, the next step is to identify the data required to produce those outputs. Some data may already be available and can be entered directly into the system. Other data may have to be calculated using the entered data. For example, the field 'Number of days overdue' is the result of a calculation of subtracting 'Date due back' from 'Today's date'.

The inputs can be mapped onto a series of data entry forms, where any kind of data can be entered or uploaded. In many conventional systems, data is entered into screen entry forms, and these need to be identified in much the same way as the outputs. Less conventional data entry, through non-manual means for video or audio input for instance, still needs to be identified with its elements.

School library system (3)

For the library, examples might be:

- Inp001 New borrower details, one form per borrower, containing Name, Address, Class, Form tutor, Number of items allowed

- Inp002 New item details, one form per item, containing Item id, Item title, Type of item, Other details (e.g. Author, ISBN, Dewey classification, Genre etc.)

- Inp003 Borrow Item, one per loan, containing Name, Item id, Date borrowed

- Inp004 Return item, one per loan, containing Name, Item id, Date returned.

Note that, at this stage, there is no reference as to how the data is to be input or how the information is to be output. Only the actual requirements are listed.

Once the available data has been identified, together with the requirements for information output, then the processes involved to turn one into the other can be worked out.

Any preset calculations are written down. For example, on an invoice, the item price is multiplied by the number of items for each line, then a net total is put into a total without VAT at the foot of the invoice. Any discount calculations can be applied, which may be conditional upon the amount spent. VAT calculations are normally known percentages and are displayed, then added to the net total to give a gross invoice total. This set of calculations might be entitled 'Produce invoice process'.

School library system (4)

Here is an example of a process from the library scenario:

Pro001 Produce overdue items report

Input   – Today's Date

Process – Print report titles

Read through Books on Loan file from start to finish

For each record, check to see if date due earlier than today's date

If yes,

Calculate Number of days overdue = today's date – date due

Write a report line containing class, form tutor, name, item id, item title, number of days overdue

Check there's enough space on page/screen for another line

If not, throw a page, print report titles

(next record)

Output   – Rep003

Inputs, outputs and processes

1. For one of the problems you have been using through this chapter, write out three or more inputs from your list of requirements, three or more outputs and at least one process.

2. Compare these to another student's work and see how they compare – can you understand their process and can they understand yours?

3. Explain their process to a third party and see if they can match it to the requirements.

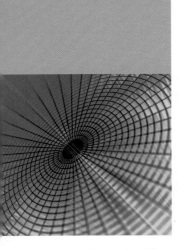

1.4 Design of solutions

There are various design techniques and the one chosen will always depend on the type of problem and the planned method of solution.

At the end of the problem analysis, there should be an indication of the type of solution that is viable. If data manipulation is involved then it is likely that some form of database solution will be chosen. Database design is well documented in other books, so here we will just cover the basics that are appropriate for this level of course.

Web and multimedia solutions have different design concerns. There are normally many elements in constructing either of these types of solution and the trick in designing the solution is to be methodical, so that elements are captured, manipulated, stored and used in a logical fashion.

A text-based application, maybe using word processing or desktop publishing software, or a numerical application, perhaps using spreadsheet software, or any other solution that involves creating an application by using one or more generic software packages, also has design techniques associated with it.

Using the lists of inputs, processes and outputs from the analysis, it should be possible to draw up a picture of the logical set or sequence of events in the system. This can be done using a system outline chart or a system flowchart (which is similar but also shows the sequence of events).

Planning

Common to all solutions is the need to plan what work will be done in what order, so the first thing to do is to create a work breakdown structure (WBS) and a work plan.

The best way to do this is gradually – at this stage, there may be an overall plan that covers the development

Milestone
A fixed point in a plan, often connected with a delivery to the client.

from start to finish in phased chunks. There may be time constraints that need to be factored in, and planning is all about fitting the tasks to be done into the time available. If the client can only meet with the designer on particular days, then these dates need to be put into the plan and time allocated before these **milestones** to do all the tasks that must be completed before them.

A Gantt chart is a good way to show this overall plan. The example opposite shows that the first two phases can be estimated and planned in some degree of detail, but it is too hard to break down the following phases into tasks until the design phase is completed, as the exact number of input forms, output reports and so on are not finally established until then. So 'ball park' estimates are given for the unknown phases. Also planning should be done assuming a certain percentage of time will be allocated elsewhere.

Once design is over, and more detailed tasks can be identified, a new plan for the remaining phases should be made, with estimated times being quoted in terms of hours, rather than whole days. The smaller the task, the more accurate the estimate. This way, any additions or adjustments have a smaller impact on the overall plan, and it is easier to identify whether extra resources are needed to complete the tasks in time for the milestones.

Inputs	Processes
Borrower details	Borrow an item
Name, Address, Class, Form tutor	Return an item
Item details	Produce overdue letters
Item, ID, Item title, Other details	
Loan date	
Return date	
Data	**Outputs**
Borrower details	Display
Item details	List of items borrowed
Loan details	Reports
	List of borrowers
	List of overdue items
	Overdue letters
	Receipts

Sample system outline chart for a school library

Task	Type T(ask) M(ilestone)	Estimated time (days)	Week 1	Week 2	Week 3	Week 4	Week 5	Week 6	Week 7	Week 8	Week 9	Week 10
Analysis Phase												
Research & preparation	T	1	▓									
Meet with client	T	0.5	▓									
Meet with users	T	0.5	▓									
Observations	T	0.5	▓									
Document analysis	T	0.5	▓									
Write up problem ID	T	0.5	▓									
Write requirements	T	0.5	▓	▓								
Check back with client/users week 2, day 3	M	0.5		▓								
Write input/output/processes	T	1		▓								
Analysis Phase total		**5.5**										
Design Phase												
System outline	T	1		▓								
Data design	T	1		▓								
Data dictionary	T	0.5		▓								
Design inputs	T	2		▓	▓							
Design outputs	T	2			▓							
Design processes	T	2				▓						
Write up hardware requirements	T	0.5				▓						
Write up software requirements	T	0.5				▓						
Check back designs with client, week 5 day 2	M	0.5					▓					
Rework	T	1					▓					
Test strategy & plan	T	3					▓	▓				
Design Phase Total		**14**										
Implementation phase	T	15						▓	▓	▓		
Testing phase	T	8									▓	
Install & Evaluate	T	3										▓
Project completion meeting, week 10 day 5	M	0.5										▓
Project Total		**46**	days									

Sample Gantt chart

Data design

If the analysis has been done thoroughly, there should be a list of data items to be entered into, stored in or output by the system, including any calculated data items. This is known as a **data dictionary** and is a necessity for all types of system so that all data resources are identified and labelled.

An example for a desk-top publishing system might start as follows:

Data dictionary

This is typically a table containing information about the data held in the system. The columns will normally hold the following:

- item name (that will be used on implementation)
- description
- data or file type
- size or length
- any validation rules associated with the item
- any relationships to other data items
- any special properties of that item
- any other information about the item (e.g. default value).

Item	Description	Type	Size	Relationships	Properties	Other
P1HT.DOC	Pg 1 header text	Text	34KB	Top of page 1	Arial 32pt	
P1T1.DOC	Pg 1 1st block text	Text	250KB	LHS	Arial 14 & 12pt	
P1P1.DOC	Pg 1 Photo 1	Image	340KB	Middle text 1	1280 x 960	Resize to 60 x 40mm
P1T2.DOC	Pg 1 2nd block text (table)	Text & image	1.6MB	Bottom of page 1		HTML code from www.sss.com/table.htm

Example data dictionary

With such a comprehensive list of data items and where they are to be found, the rest of the design process can be much more precise and accurate. Because of this, the data dictionary should be at least started before embarking on input, process and output designs. Item names need to be those actually used throughout, so a sensible naming system is also an example of good design practice.

Naming systems

First design a folder sub-system for holding all the files for a system together. Here is an example:

Level	Folder name	Contains
0	INF01	All work for INF01
1	INF01 ABC-Posters	All files and documents relating to the ABC Poster System
2	ABC-Plans	WBS, Gantt charts, Diary
2	ABC-Write-up	All documents to be taken into exam
2	ABC-Import	All imported files
3	Text files	All original text files
3	Image files	All original image files
2	ABC-System	Versions of DTP from draft to final
3	Text files	Draft and final versions of text components
3	Image files	Draft and final versions of image components

Example folder structure

The next step is to decide on file names, in such a way that anyone can immediately see either what is contained in the file or where it belongs in the finished product. Calling files meaningless titles such as 'image1' means that a cross-reference list would need to be constructed, or the viewer would have to look at each file's content to determine the one they wanted.

If the poster was full of pictures of dogs, for instance, file names Dog1 or Dog2 would not be helpful. It would be better to name them Red Setter v0, Black Labrador v0 etc., where v0 indicates that this is the original version. Once the original file had been taken and manipulated, then the version number would be incremented, so that it could be seen that a change had been made.

In the above example, Red Setter v0 would be found in the sub-folder ABC-Import/Image files; the Red Setter v1, Red Setter v2 and Red Setter v3 might be found in the sub-folder ABC-System/Image files.

When naming individual data items, it is important to avoid using real words, such as Name and Date, as this can cause run-time problems with some packages that use these words for their own functionality. The easiest way to get around this and still have meaningful data item names is to either add the file name in front of the item name, e.g. Loan_Date or LoanDate, or to add a lower-case letter in front, e.g. mFirstName, mSurname, mDate, etc. This way there will never be any confusion about which field called Date is being referred to.

Designing data entry

Accurate design of data capture forms is essential for a successful system. Armed with detailed file and data information from the data design, it should be a very small step to design an accurate data capture or input form, as all of the information for the data items will be in the data dictionary.

Design should be precise and comprehensive. It is normal to include the name or logo of the company, the name of the system, the title of the input/entry function, plus a reference for the design and, most likely, the current date. And this is before adding any of the data items. Data items should be entered in a logical order, and that order should be specified.

Data items should be labelled, with the entry area being the correct size for the allowed amount of data to be entered. Each entry field should be annotated so that a third party could implement the design. Notes should include:

- appearance (e.g. Arial 14 Bold, Blue)
- display format (e.g. currency to two decimal places, showing dollar at the start)
- contents or source of restricted list (combo box, pull-down list, option groups)
- validation required (e.g. must be between 21 and 65, or combined validation with another field or another file)
- source of the item or the calculation that creates the item (e.g. total for a line on an invoice).

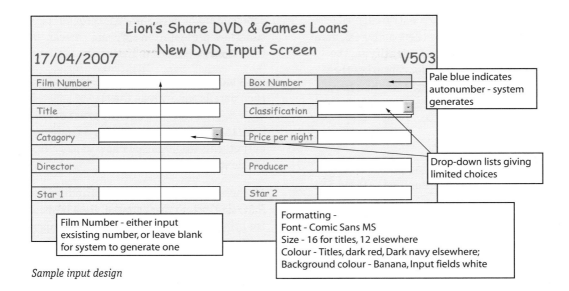

Sample input design

Form callout labels:

- Pale blue indicates autonumber - system generates
- Drop-down lists giving limited choices
- Film Number - either input exissting number, or leave blank for system to generate one
- Formatting -
  Font - Comic Sans MS
  Size - 16 for titles, 12 elsewhere
  Colour - Titles, dark red, Dark navy elsewhere;
  Background colour - Banana, Input fields white

For the whole form, the overall visual format must be specified, the purpose of the form, how the data will be captured (manual or electronic methods are both acceptable), the destination of the data entered, and how the data entered will be **verified**. The data will automatically be **validated**.

Verification

This is the term given to the double-checking of data being entered and processed in a computerised system to help ensure accuracy. At the point of manual data entry, there are two ways of doing this.

The first is to visually check that the data on screen matches the data on the physical data capture form. In this age of details being taken over the phone, this is often done by the data inputter double-checking with the caller before sending the data off to be stored.

The second way is to enter the data twice – either by two people entering the same data and the two versions being automatically compared, or by the same inputter double-entering – an example of this is when a form asks for a new password to be entered twice.

If the data is being entered into a system automatically from a remote source or another internal system, then there may have to be a retroactive form of verification – perhaps sending out the stored details to the subject or owner of those details and getting them to verify their accuracy. One way to automatically verify electronic input is to check some details with data already held that is known to be accurate - for example stock items and prices entered from a remote source could be verified by checking them against your own stock file.

Validation

This is the automatic or computerised checking of the validity of the data entering a system. It can detect unreasonable or incomplete data, but cannot check its accuracy. For instance, a date of birth may be input as 10/10/1985 which would pass the validation check for a correct and reasonable date; however, only verifying that this is the actual date of birth of the subject will ensure it is accurate. Validation checks include range check, presence check, check digit check, type check, format check, length check, list or lookup check, cross-field check and, on batch systems, control totals and batch totals checks.

Validation checks

For each of the validation checks mentioned above, create a table to give a description of each check and an example of where it would be used.

If using an electronic method of data entry, such as capturing images and downloading them onto a PC, data entry specifications are still required, identifying the source of the data, the mechanisms for capturing the data, the method of entering that data into the system and where it is stored and used.

Designing outputs

The analysis stage produced a list of output reports and screens required for the system. Designing these outputs is again an exercise in producing accurate and precise visual forms, with plenty of annotation and explanation that would enable someone else to produce them using the software you have specified.

For instance, it might be that the required output is a slideshow, or a series of slideshows of groupings of pictures from a wedding or a holiday. This is the point where the decision is made about which bits of software will be used, maybe a photo manipulator to add captions to the photographs, an animation package to add fun linking items, a sound recorder and editor to add commentary or music as a background, plus the actual slideshow presentation software choices. Details such as transitions, animation, timings and so on must be added.

For a more conventional output, such as a printed report, then details will include the size of paper, headings, footers, page numbers and the exact number of detail lines to be printed per page. For a multi-page screen output, this would include how to move from one page to the next.

All these items of detail are required, as well as the usual font, size, colour, background, item positioning and so on. For printed reports, the nature of the paper (GSM, shiny/matt, colour, A3/A4/A5, 2-part/3-part, continuous/cut-sheet, pre-printed etc.), the type of printing, frequency, timing and so on could be added. The intended recipient should also be mentioned.

Each item must have details of where it comes from – is it straight from a file or is it a calculated field? Any groupings must be specified – if, for instance, all loans for a person are shown without repeating the person's details on every line.

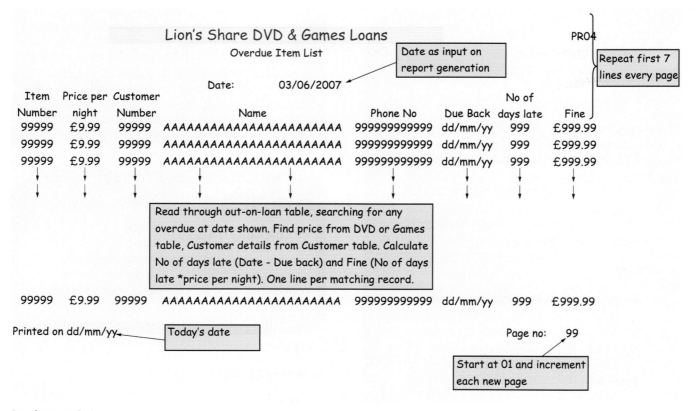

Sample report design

Designing processes

Once the data entry and output designs are completed, it is time to make sure that all the required processes are specified so that someone else could take the entire set of designs and produce exactly the desired system.

For each function of the system, there needs to be a process specification. Some may be quite simple, involving the use of one input screen and the storing of all the data.

Sequence
A series of steps, one following another from start to finish.

Selection
Steps that will only be taken if some condition is true.

Iteration
Steps that are repeated a fixed number of times or until some condition becomes true.

The process specifications need to state which input and output designs, files, tables, and data items are being used and must then list all the steps necessary to complete the process. These steps will use a combination of **sequence**, **selection** and **iteration**.

Below is an example of structured English – a mixture of technical accuracy (file and data field names) and logical narrative. It will include any calculations and data or file manipulations that may be required. It will not necessarily include all variable declarations that may be needed when actually implementing the solution.

For example, if a spreadsheet solution is to be used, the structured English specification might be:

Calculate VAT = Net total * Current VAT rate

The output design specification should have identified the cell references in which these fields can be found.

Structured English is just one way of documenting a process specification – flowcharts are equally valid, as are decision tables, although these should be used with caution and only where they are best suited (where there are complex combinations of decisions to be made, which would look very complicated in structured English or on a flowchart).

Example process

Process: Store New DVD Details

Input screen: VS03

Datafile: DVD details (all fields)

    System file (LastBoxNumber, LastFilmNumber)

    DVD-Box file (dFilmNumber, dBoxNumber)

Start process

Open DVD-Box file, System file, DVD file

On entry

    Search in DVD file for match on film number

    If found,

    Fill screen fields with data held

    Otherwise

    Read system file

dFilmNumber = LastFilmNumber + 1

System file (LastFilmNumber = dFilmNumber)

Append record to DVD file

Move DVD details (dFilmNumber, dTitle, dClassification, dCategory, dPricePN,

dDirector, dProducer, dStar1, dStar2) to record area

Write record

Append record to DVD-Box file

dBoxNumber = LastBoxNumber + 1

Move (dFilmNumber, dBoxNumber)

Write record

LastBoxNumber = dBoxNumber

Re-write system file

Exit process

Storing DVD details:

1 Re-write as a flowchart the above process specification for storing new DVD details.

2 Identify any flaws in the design by trying to add three copies of a new DVD:

Ocean's 14, 12, Adventure, 3.99, Steven Sonderburgh, Jerry Weintrub, George Clooney, Brad Pitt.

Tip: When dry running, create a table that shows all fields in use and fill or change them as each step tells you to.

The final action in design, after specifying all the input, output and processes, plus compiling a test strategy and plan (discussed on pages 51–54); is to refine the action plan. Now it is known how many screens need to be developed, how many reports need creating, how many simple, average and complex processes there are, a more accurate work breakdown structure can be attempted. The example below shows that estimating is now done in hours.

With experience, the plan made at this stage can become very accurate by comparing how long certain things took with how long had been estimated for them.

Stage/Task	No of Hours effort	03-Feb	10-Feb	17-Feb	24-Feb	02-Mar	09-Mar	16-Mar	23-Mar	30-Mar	06-Apr
Implementation & Testing		▓	▓	▓	▓						
Create database structures	4	▓									
Input form 1 - build & test	4	▓									
Input form 2 - build & test	4		▓								
Input form 3 - build & test	4		▓								
Report 1 - build & test	2			▓							
Report 2 - build & test	2			▓							
Report 3 - build & test	3				▓						
Query 1 - build & test	3				▓						
Query 2 - build & test	2						▓				
Query 3 - build & test	4						▓				
Menu system	2						▓				
System test	12							▓			
User test	5								▓		
Rework/retest	8								▓		
User signoff	1									▓	
User Guide					▓	▓	▓				
Installation procedures	2					▓					
Intro	2					▓					
Navigation	2					▓					
Instructions for each function	15						▓				
End of day/month/year	3							▓			
Backup procedures	3							▓			
Pull together Guide	2								▓		
Evaluation									▓		
Evaluate solution	5								▓		
Evaluate own performance	5								▓		
Report										▓	
Finish off	4									▓	
Bind	1									▓	

Updated Gantt chart

1.5 Selection and use of input devices and input media

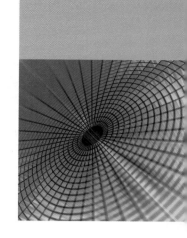

All data, including sounds, images, animation, text, numbers and film footage, can be transferred to a computer system in order to edit, rearrange, alter or enhance the original. The desire to work with data in a digital format means that those using it can make such radical improvements that the alterations can often be used to improve business performance or assist in generating new ideas for products or services. For example, sports coaches use data collected from athletes in order to personalise training programmes.

Market research data, often collected over the telephone or by filling in questionnaires, cannot be easily analysed by working through reams of paper. By placing the collected data into appropriate software it can be manipulated to display patterns, or used to run 'what if' scenarios. By digitising data, it becomes possible to add extra detail, such as an extra sentence to an important speech or another room to the design of a house. Digitised data is also easier to share using electronic communication, which means that after one person has used the data for their specific need it can be passed on to someone else who may use it in a completely different way.

Input devices

There is a range of ways that data comes into a computer. Each method is concerned with sending instructions or information into the computer so that it can be used to carry out a task or wait to be adapted for another purpose. Input devices are concerned with passing in electronic signals, which are then translated into a form that can be understood and recognised by humans. Wireless and Bluetooth technology means that many input devices no longer need to be wired or plugged directly into a computer.

Keyboard

The keyboard is probably the most commonly referred to input device and the one which computer users will interface with every day. Keyboards enable us to add text to documents and numbers to spreadsheets and they make operating software simple. There are many designs of keyboard available, but most standard keyboards will include numbers, every letter in the alphabet, a method to make the letters uppercase, function keys which perform pre-set tasks in software, and navigation keys. There are also Braille keyboards, which have raised dots on the keys as an aid for blind users. Many keyboards now include hotkeys which open email packages, the web or control music or movie playback. Without a keyboard it is still possible to interact with a computer system, but for the everyday user a keyboard is the obvious and convenient method for the transfer of text and numbers into a computer. Writing letters, reports, adding text to websites and naming files are all made possible by using a keyboard.

The concept keyboard is different to the QWERTY keyboard in that it has images, words or symbols instead of letters. A flexible membrane is laid over a QWERTY keyboard;

A concept keyboard

appropriate software allows the computer system to recognise the key pushes relating to the symbols on the membrane. Alternatively, specialist keyboards can be made without the membrane. Concept keyboards are used in places like restaurants, bars and as learning aids for young children. They reduce the need to enter full phrases and so reduce input errors. The retail market makes use of concept tills, which function in a similar way to concept keyboards but can be touch-sensitive screens rather than keyboards.

Touch screen

Touch screen technology is popular mainly because it removes the need for users to input lengthy instructions. Quite often an image or single expression can be pressed to instruct the system what the user wants to do or what information they would like. Touch screen technology can be found in travel agents, where customers can touch the part of the world they would like to visit, then touch the number relating to how many people are going on the tour, then select the dates from the screen along with many other options. This saves a lot of time in the booking process and is often suitable for those who do not have the confidence or expertise to use alternative methods. Teaching children via interactive touch screen technology is popular, as young children can explore fun software without having to worry about spellings or finding the right key on the keyboard. Touch screen technology also means that only the options currently on the screen can be selected, which is good for

Keyboards and touch screens

Find an example of a concept keyboard or touch screen technology in use and produce a short presentation to answer the following questions.

- Where is the technology and what is the nature of the business?
- What features does the keyboard or touch screen include?
- What is the keyboard or touch screen used for?
- What did the keyboard or touch screen replace?
- Does the system produce any useful information at any stage? If so, what?

Touch screen kiosk

'The touch screen kiosk is an ideal way of providing additional support and access to information for parents looking for childcare, training, jobs, and financial assistance towards childcare,' says Maureen Brown, Information Officer for the children's centre and extended school services at Robert Blair Primary School in Islington, London. 'It offers parents coming to the centre the opportunity to search for information quickly and easily, whilst we may be dealing with other enquiries.' The touch screen kiosk has only been in situ at the centre for a few weeks, but is already receiving interest from parents. Foluke Olorunfemi, a mum of four who has used the kiosk, is one such example. 'The kiosk is really very good. It's quick and easy to use and was especially handy when I was searching for childcare. There's a surprisingly huge range of useful information, which is great! I'll definitely be using the kiosk again!' The Robert Blair Primary School kiosk is the first of many to be delivered across Islington on behalf of the London Borough. Each order is for a free-standing touch screen kiosk, inclusive of full service and maintenance. The kiosk comes fully installed with access to a portal home page, allowing users to quickly identify websites of interest, such as Parentline Plus, Jobcentre plus, and ChildcareLink.

As well as providing vital support to families in the local area on a range of issues, such as looking for childcare or returning to work, the kiosk also provides information on things to do with young children, working with children, special needs, housing, health services and much more.

Sarah Sabur, Children's Centre Services Manager, is delighted to have the kiosk in the centre and believes that it acts 'as a point of information where parents can take ownership and help themselves learn about the great resources in Islington'.

A link to this website is available at www.heinemann.co.uk/ hotlinks (express code 2349P)

reducing input errors. In some circumstances a light pen is used on the touch screen, although this technology is being replaced by human touch.

Mouse

The mouse often sits next to the keyboard and helps the computer user to operate the system and other software. By clicking the buttons on the mouse it is possible to open software, highlight areas of a page for editing and select text and icons. Most modern software includes menus and icons, which the mouse is especially designed to select. The design of the mouse has changed over the years to make it more flexible and robust. The first home computer mouse came with only two buttons and was connected to the system by a wire. There are now versions of the mouse that are wireless and have additional buttons that perform further functions. Optical mice, which use light signals to detect movement, are becoming more popular than the original style of mouse which came with a roller ball. This often collected dirt and dust, was difficult to clean and deteriorated the efficiency of the mouse.

Glide/touch pad

The touch or glide pad is the laptop version of a mouse. A glide pad can be difficult to use at first, but familiarity soon grows and it becomes as easy to use as a normal mouse. Not everyone is keen on these devices, and some may use the available ports on a laptop to plug in a mouse. The glide pad usually has two slim buttons underneath it representing the buttons of a mouse, but the mouse button functions can also be activated by a quick tap or double tap on the pad.

Digital camera

Digital cameras have revolutionised the way many people in the publishing industry work. Prior to digital cameras, if someone wanted to convert an image into digital format they would have to use a manual camera, shoot the picture, take the film to be developed (when the roll was full) then place the developed hardcopy of the image into a scanner. Digital cameras are portable and some have capabilities that allow the captured images to be edited, cropped, deleted or emailed to a waiting user, perhaps in a publishing studio on the other side of the planet. Alternatively, digital cameras can be plugged directly into a computer system, the flash card that stores the images can be plugged into a computer, or Bluetooth technology can be used to transfer the pictures from the camera. The methods available will depend on the make and age of the camera. The newer models are more likely to use wireless technology and to include advanced features to manipulate the data before it reaches the system.

Touch pad on a laptop

Scanner

A scanner is used to convert hardcopy to digital form. The hardcopy can be a hand drawing, a glossy photograph or a picture found in a magazine or book. Optical character recognition (OCR) is the process of converting scans to text. OCR technology is used to read postcodes on envelopes to assist in sorting the post. The use of scanners to transfer photographs is being superseded by digital cameras, but can still be useful for digitising photographs taken before digital cameras appeared.

Other types of scanner can capture images from three-dimensional sources. A very neat example of this is the ultrasound equipment used to scan pregnant women to show how an unborn child is developing. Even more advanced scanners are used to create maps which can be used by people on expeditions in difficult terrain so that they can properly prepare for what lays ahead before they leave. The health industry also uses advanced scanning technology to perform brain scans to look for signs of damage or tumours.

Optical Mark Readers (OMR) are scanners which read the series of dots placed in pre-defined areas on paper. Lottery tickets and multiple-choice exam papers are read this way. This reduces the time spent marking the exam paper as the technology can, in a matter of seconds, automatically read the responses and return a grade very accurately, provided the marks are added to the paper as instructed. Magnetic ink character recognition (MICR) involves scanners that read ink containing magnetic ink particles. Such ink is found on cheques, and banks use this technology as a fraud prevention tactic and to process many cheques in a short space of time. The magnetic ink is read followed by the value of the cheque before the relevant accounts are updated.

Web camera

Web cameras (or web-cams) are used by those who want to be seen by other people using the Internet. They are usually placed in front of the computer operator and the camera relays their image, in real time, to the person given access to the view. Web cameras are used in conjunction with software, such as Skype, that provides a digital method for communicating verbally over the Internet infrastructure.

Microphone

Microphones, sometimes mounted on a headset or built into a computer, are used to transfer verbal data or other sounds into digital form. The online community uses such technology for Internet telephone conversations. The headset allows speech to be translated into a form the computer understands, then the messages are transferred around the Internet and converted by the receiver's software into speech again.

Microphones are also used for voice recognition. Users are able to speak instructions, which are carried out to varying degrees of success depending on how much training the user has given the software. For those who have problems spelling or typing, voice recognition is a faster alternative and is improving all the time. The drawback to using it constantly is that if everybody used it in a busy office, the microphone would pick up sound contamination and distort the text that appeared on the screen or the instructions the computer was supposed to carry out.

Global communication

You have a friend who is moving to the other side of the world. You have agreed to stay in touch using the Internet to communicate with one another. Carry out research to find the most suitable equipment you will both need. You must give specific details about what you intend to purchase and reasons why you have made your decisions. At this point in time you don't even have a computer! Present your findings, with images, as a single-paged A4 poster.

Graphics tablet

Joystick

Joysticks are traditionally associated with games. There is a whole spectrum of sizes and shapes but they all perform the same task, which is to send instructions to the software or game to perform a task. Beyond gaming, joysticks are used in flight simulators to emulate flying in as real a situation as can be achieved using technology. The mechanical industry uses joysticks to control robots and heavy machinery. Skilled surgeons have even been known to use joysticks to control medical proceedings and even to operate on patients who are overseas.

Graphics tablet

A graphics tablet can be used to put original hand drawings, as they are being created, directly into the computer. Graphics tablets can be plugged in via the standard USB port or they can be wireless. A stylus is used, instead of a pen, on the flat surface of the graphics tablet, with the resulting image appearing on a monitor.

A similar version of this technology is used on personal digital assistants (PDAs) to translate the words and shapes, which are hand drawn on to the smaller screen, into actual text or sharper images. The stylus can also be used to select icons and navigate through the software installed on a PDA.

Graphics tablets are most likely to be used for technical drawing and computer-aided design work. There is a growing number of people now using graphics tablets instead of a mouse, claiming they are having fewer problems then before with repetitive strain injury. In this instance the graphics tablet is emulating the role of a glide pad on a laptop.

MIDI

To convert music sounds, pitches and notes into a digital form, there is a system called MIDI, which stands for Musical Instrument Digital Recognition. By attaching an instrument to a computer and using the correct software, the musician or sound artist can directly transfer the sounds they are playing in real time into the system. The advantage of this is that notes can later be added or removed to enhance the original track.

Digital Drawing Competition

The second Hong Kong Primary Schools' Digital Drawing Competition came to a successful close Saturday, January 21, 2006. The competition was held by the Hong Kong Catholic Diocesan Schools' Council, together with the Hong Kong Education and Manpower Bureau. By promoting the 'combination of art and technology, for innovation anywhere, anytime' through this event, the Council hoped to strengthen interest in the arts and creative abilities among students.

Participating students had to complete within 2 hours on the morning of the competition a landscape painting based on the surrounding scenery and according to a theme selected by the sponsors. Participants had to scan any images that they wanted to use on-site, and they were not allowed to use or incorporate any past works, photographic images, copies, or any other stored images. Teachers were naturally forbidden from helping them in the creative process.

Because this was a digital drawing contest, traditional art tools such as pencil and paper were replaced by computers and graphic tablets. The Wacom Graphire4 4x5 pressure sensitive graphics tablet was designated as the official drawing tool for this competition.

A link to this website is available at www.heinemann.co.uk/hotlinks (express code 2349P)

Barcode readers

Some of the places barcode readers are used include supermarkets, airport baggage departments and libraries. They read the barcode found on products or labelling tags which are used to identify the product or item they are attached to, and record details such as the time of a sale, where a bag is heading or who is borrowing a certain book. Barcodes are made of straight black and white lines which make scanning them with the barcode reader very fast. The process of paying for shopping rapidly improved when shops installed barcode readers. Barcode readers provide fast, accurate information to computer systems which are often linked to powerful stock control systems or databases that log each transaction.

1.6 Selection and use of storage requirements, media and devices

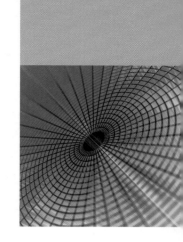

Within the last 10 years, technology has developed at a phenomenal rate and shows no sign of slowing down. As people become more creative and develop new digital products, it becomes necessary to ensure that the data held, played, viewed or heard on them can be accessed with ease at any time, anywhere. The amount of data circulating the digital world has increased so dramatically that data storage – for later use, as evidence in case of legal disputes, or as a way to show it to someone – has become a major industry.

Data comes in the forms of text, numbers, sounds and moving and still images. Almost every idea, old or new, is likely to be recorded digitally somewhere, which means it can be transferred across the global network and shared with other like-minded people who may be working towards similar aims. Sales reports, play scripts, jokes, holiday pictures, share prices, home designs, knitting patterns, recipes and stock figures for major supermarket chains are all made up of data. They are all kept to be looked at again for various reasons. Therefore, in most instances, it is absolutely crucial that they are stored safely and can be viewed when necessary.

Methods of data storage

Before it was possible to store data digitally, the only major option was paper. Ream after ream of invoices and sales documents were stored in 'cities' of filing cabinets. In the event that a certain document needed to be reproduced, someone would have to search the filing cabinets, locate the desired article, photocopy it and return the original for safe keeping. Transferring such data to offices across the world would involve a very slow manual process, such as the postal system. This is all now done electronically in a fraction of the time.

Technology has caused, and is still causing, a massive amount of data to be generated and stored. The desire to locate previous and current information, in order to learn from, manipulate, update, transfer and improve it, will always be necessary in a modern society which is now catering for what has been called the 'knowledge economy'. Data has become such a precious commodity that those who are using it effectively can respond accurately to market needs, which leads to huge profits, new cutting-edge products and more efficient methods of production.

| 52 week | | | | Last week | | Mkt cap | | |
High	Low	Close		Chg	%	(£m)	P/E	Yld
386	93	BAE Systems	127	14	12.4	3,859	–	7.2
1210	898	Cobham	1029.5	13.5	1.3	1,108	18.4	2.2
360	143	GKN	170.5	–0.5	–0.3	1,249	9.1	6.6
878	602	Inchcape	740	–35	–4.5	573	9.7	3.8
236	153	Meggitt	175	3.5	2	503	16.1	3
205	64	Rolls-Royce	80.5	5.5	7.3	1,301	4.8	10.2
895	553	Smiths	676	16	2.4	3,755	15.5	3.5
303	164	VT Group	206.5	0.5	0.2	351	18	3.9

Share prices are an example of data

RAM

Random access memory (RAM) is found inside the computer, working alongside the processor. Adding more RAM to a computer system increases its performance and means more programs can be loaded at the same time. RAM is the type of memory used to hold program code and data during computation. For example, a word processor, spreadsheet and online radio station may all be running at the same time. For this to happen smoothly there needs to be adequate RAM within the system. Commonly used software has so many complex instructions embedded within it that many computer users are forced to increase the amount and type of RAM they have in order to run newly released software. If RAM is limited in capacity it will have problems trying to fit or run all of the requested instructions, which can cause the computer to slow down or crash. RAM can be removed and replaced when it becomes too small for current purposes. As processors get faster, new generations of memory, such as DDR and RDRAM, are required to get better performance.

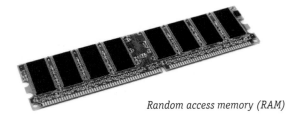

Random access memory (RAM)

RAM is volatile memory, which means that when the computer is switched off all data held in RAM is lost. To avoid data stored in RAM (primary storage) being lost when the system is shut down, secondary storage is required.

ROM

Read-only memory (ROM) cannot be written to. Its main use is for the distribution of software which the suppliers do not want people to alter (by writing to it). ROM stores the instructions used to boot up the computer, which is why it always loads up the same way. ROM is non-volatile, which means that it does not clear when the system is shut down.

Internal hard drive

The hard drive is also referred to as an HDD (hard disk drive) or HD (hard drive). This is the component that stores all the program details as well as the work produced by the user. The hard drive is non-volatile, which means that the data held on it is not lost when the machine is shut down. Hard drives are also found in a variety of other electronic devices, such as MP3 players, PDAs, mobile phones and digital cameras.

Hard drives require protection against contamination from dust, fingerprints and condensation, so they are housed in sealed enclosures. A contaminated hard drive is not likely to store data efficiently, which could result in the loss of important information.

Typical workstations have a hard drive that is between 160GB and 750GB and are able to transfer data around the system at a rate of 80MB/s. There are even faster and larger ones used in industry to store massive amounts of data. Laptops have slightly slower and smaller hard drives but these tend to be quite robust and ideal for transportation. Most hard drives are around 3.5" (3.5 inches wide) or 2.5" but recent developments have seen them produced at 0.85" for use in mobile telephones, with a storage capacity of 4GB. This is astonishing considering the first wholesale machines in the 1980s with hard drives had a 5MB capacity; the equivalent of two short music tracks in digital form.

External hard drive

The external hard drive has very similar characteristics to the internal hard drive in that it is designed to store vast amounts of data. Personal digital music collections, digitised home video, digital photographs, TV programmes recorded from digital television and graphics-based documents are usually among the list of files stored externally by home users. External hard drives are used to back up or store files which are still required but no longer fit on the internal hard drive supplied with the computer system.

External hard drives are also used by industry for similar reasons as those mentioned for the home user. Although the data may vary in content and quality, it is its value and integrity that is protected. The option of external storage means the information is portable and can be kept securely away from the business and restored in case of disaster. In 2007 a 400GB external hard drive cost around £100, which means that almost 400 movies could be stored for £1 each.

Magnetic tape

This type of storage media has to be read sequentially, which means that all the data on the tape, before the part you need, must be read before you can access the required data. Magnetic tape was originally used in 1951 to record computer data with a transfer rate of around 7,200 characters per second. The cost per gigabyte stored on magnetic tape has traditionally been better value for money then alternatives like the external hard drive, which gave it prominence in the storage marketplace. In recent years, improvements of disk storage in terms of capacity and price have forced a reduction in market share for magnetic tape suppliers. Although they are able to hold up to 1TB (terabyte) of data, previous features such as portability and cost have been matched by disk and virtual options. This has made the viability of magnetic tape less than it has ever been. The need for devices to read tape-stored data is likely to linger on for some time due to its former, popular use as a long-term storage facility for archiving data.

Memory/flash card

Memory or flash cards are leading the revolution of storage devices. They started life slightly smaller than credit cards and have gradually reduced in size and increased in storage capacity up to the point they now fit snugly into mobile phones. They can also be found storing digital images in cameras, handheld and portable laptops, MP3 players and video game consoles. Their explosion in popularity is largely due to their unobtrusive size and robustness, and they look set to replace the humble floppy disk. They are portable and can be swapped between the gadgets mentioned and inserted into computers, loaded with extra songs, software or images, and returned. The nature of the devices they coexist with means that they are used frequently to capture and store data but only for a limited period of time before the data is overwritten by something else. The data captured on them can be transferred to a computer and edited before being stored on a more permanent data storage device. One of the biggest issues with memory cards is the range of formats available. This has lead to computer system developers having to provide a variety of extra slots in their machines to read the cards. Alternatively, adapters can be purchased which fit most flash cards and can be plugged into the most common ports found on the computer.

Floppy disk

The floppy disk is a 3.5" portable magnetic storage device which can hold around 1.44MB of data. The actual storage disk is a flimsy material protected by a hard plastic outer case. The case is used to protect the disk from dust and other contaminants that would corrupt the data. The casing also consists of a metal sliding trap that is pushed aside when the disk is inserted into the drive. This sliding trap often bends, causing the disk to get stuck in the drive; much to the annoyance of the user.

This type of storage device was very popular in the 1980s and 1990s when they were used on home computers and to distribute software, back up small files and transfer data between machines, but have become less popular in this age of multimedia files and formats. At the height of their popularity they were used to store whole software applications and even operating systems. The A: drive is usually designated when saving or reading files to or from a floppy disk. In the late 1990s and early 2000s, the coding used in operating systems and all other software grew in complexity and size, meaning that the floppy disk could no longer provide the capacity required to hold them. Today there are more compact, robust and higher-capacity options available, which mean that computer manufacturers now rarely sell systems with floppy drives in them. CD-ROM became the choice for software distributors to introduce their new products and the development of USB ports and flash drives superseded the need for floppy drives and disks. The legend of the floppy lives on and can be seen in many software products representing the image of the icon used to save work.

Zip disk

Zip disks are like large floppy disks that can store up to 750MB of data. They need their own drive. As with floppy disks, they are not used as frequently as they once were.

CD-ROM

CD-ROMs are similar in size and appearance to audio CDs, which were originally designed to hold music but were later adapted to hold digital data and to be read on computers. Once data has been written it cannot be altered. CD-ROMs usually have a storage capacity of 700MB, which is the equivalent of the content of around 1000 average-sized novels. CD-ROMs have been a very popular method for distributing software due to their capacity and general ease of packaging. The data is stored as a series of microscopic pits burnt into the surface, which are read by a laser that scans the reflection of the disk.

Nearly all modern computer systems can read CD-ROMs as well as audio CDs and DVDs. This has been one reason why the copyright laws are under constant review and why the music industry has tried to alter the format of audio CDs so that they cannot be read by CD-ROM drives (which makes them easy to copy). The same moves to try to prevent illegal copying have been attempted by computer games developers and the movie industry.

CD-R and CD-RW

A CD writer is used to transfer data onto a CD-R or CD-RW. In the case of the CD-R, data can only be written to it once, after which the data can only be read. The actual writing process can happen in two different ways, both of which require a CD writer. The first is known as 'Disc At Once'. This is when all the data is written in one session with no gaps. At the end of the session the disk is closed and no further data can be added. The other method is called 'Track at Once'. This allows for multiple writing sessions to take place with significant time gaps between recording. At the end of each session the disk is left open and can be returned to for further recording until its storage capacity is full, which is usually 650MB or around 74 minutes of audio.

Storage space

Carry out a short investigation to discover how much storage space each member of your class uses. Find out what it is used for, what storage devices they use and what changes in storage they have made in the last two years. Present your findings in a report to the teacher.

Extension

Perform the same task as above with three identified groups of people – for example, teachers, accountants and shop owners or students, teachers and parents. Compare the results from each group. What conclusions can you draw?

CD-RWs are very similar but have the capability to have data written to them time and time again. Therefore, data that is no longer required can be replaced or overwritten by new material. The main attraction is the CD-RW's capacity combined with its versatility in adding and removing data. Under the right conditions the CD-RW should be able to be written to up to 1000 times or have a life expectancy of 25 years. The CD-R and CD-RW are both designed to be compatible with audio CD players and CD-ROM drives on computers.

DVD

DVD stands for Digital Versatile Disk. It has the same look and feel as a CD but offers much more storage (4.7GB), mainly due to the smaller pits burnt into the DVD. Most modern computers are equipped to play DVDs in the same drive used to play CDs. A lot of drives come with two different kinds of regional playback (RPC-1 and RPC-2). This is a measure used by publishers to restrict the regions of the world where a certain disk can be played. DVDs are traditionally used to transfer and view movie footage. However, there are currently several formats available.

DVD Audio is used for storing high-fidelity audio content. The claim is that the playback of audio on this format is superior to audio CDs. A further advantage is that the DVD can hold much more audio, therefore increasing its attraction as a portable storage option.

DVD Video is the standard format used for viewing and storing video footage. As a result of its appealing size, ability to move through the scenes with ease, lack of the need to rewind and superior quality, the DVD has superseded the VHS video option. Many video editing programs have a built-in feature that allows captured video footage to be written directly to a DVD. The DVD format has recently undergone changes to accommodate the high-definition market.

DVD-R and DVD+R are competing formats in the writeable DVD market. Both can only be written to once and the DVD-R has a 5-year lead on the DVD+R. The DVD-RW, DVD+RW and DVD-RAM disks can be written to multiple times. Drives labelled DVD±R are able to play most formats, which means that the market dominance the DVD-R originally had because of its earlier introduction has slowly been evened.

There is another format of DVD that is known as 'dual layer'. This holds even more data; up to 8.5GB.

Memory stick

Memory sticks or **USB** storage devices have exploded in popularity over recent years. They are small, neat devices which can easily fit into the pocket, hang on string around a user's neck or even fold into a credit-card-style base to be transported around in a wallet. Originally, like all new technology, the price of the memory stick was quite high, although the attraction remained strong. Within a few years the price dropped significantly and the storage capacity increased dramatically. Many average users find that they are now able to carry almost all of their crucial documents around with them and load them up with ease on alternative machines. This is largely due to plug and play technology, which means operating systems instantly recognise and install the required program code in order to facilitate easy use of the devices. Most modern computer systems have more than one USB port, which means they can accept, read and write to USB storage devices. While the memory stick is a relative newcomer to the storage market, it has the potential to supersede many of the previous options for data storage.

USB
Universal Serial Bus – a standard interface for connecting peripherals to a PC.

Conclusion

In order to select the most appropriate device for data storage, it is important to know how much data needs to

A user's backup reminder

be stored. This will ensure that what is purchased can actually hold what it is supposed to, and is likely to save money as storage costs rise with the number of bytes stored. Backup frequency, personnel and procedures for storing data should also be established to ensure that a good copy is always available if something goes wrong. When data is stored, the location of the backup must be clear. Keeping it next to the home computer on a CD-RW may be fine for personal files, but large companies will want the peace of mind that comes with knowing that the data is safely stored away from the business premises and is easy enough to access if and when required.

Virtual storage

In order to continue to preserve data beyond physical, off-site storage, the option to virtually store company files, software applications and databases was introduced. This is when data is uploaded to a storage facility in another location; it can even be on the other side of the world. Software has been developed to automatically perform the

case study

DVD security measures

The group behind security measures for next-generation DVDs said it has fixed a leak that allowed hackers to discover the keys for unlocking movies on HD DVD and Blu-ray discs.

Makers of software for playing the discs on computers will offer patches containing new keys and closing the hole that allowed observant hackers to discover ways to strip high-def DVDs of their protection.

Digital rights management protection, or DRM, is intended to prevent copying of the movies. Hackers working late last year and early this year were able to observe computer code found on the PC-based DVD players and discover keys that unlock protections on all high-def discs, so copies could be made.

The group that developed the Advanced Access Content System said it had worked with device makers to deactivate those keys and refresh them with a new set.

Companies such as Corel Corp., which owns InterVideo, makers of a popular PC-based playback software, will also distribute more secure versions, said Michael Ayers, chairman of the AACS License Administrator.

'The device keys associated with the InterVideo player are being deactivated and InterVideo has updated its player,' Ayers said. 'They are taking steps that block off access to the inner workings of the application.'

New high-def DVDs will include updated keys and instructions for older versions of the PC-playback software not to play discs until the software patch has been installed.

Stand-alone DVD players, such as the Toshiba HD DVD player and the Sony Blu-ray player, are not affected by the announcement. So far, no problems have been found with their security.

Ayers said future assaults by hackers can be similarly fixed by replacing compromised keys with new ones.

A link to this website is available at www.heinemann.co.uk/hotlinks (express code 2349P)

remote backup according to the instructions given by the user. These instructions can specify what files to back up and how many generations of backups to keep.

Remote backup replaces the need to employ someone to oversee a more physical type of backup system which used to include digital tapes. Automating the process means that data storage procedures are not subject to disruption through an individual's lack of knowledge, carelessness or absence.

When the data is transferred to the online storage facility it is often compressed to reduce its transmission time and encrypted to ensure that, if it falls into the wrong hands, it cannot be read or used. The organisations that offer the virtual storage service are likely to duplicate the data for added protection and have a system that automatically generates an email, to the customers, confirming safe arrival. This is a typical modern business-to-business (B2B) service and, like many technological transactions, there is usually an associated cost. The host company (the

Storage devices

Produce a graphical illustration of the evolution of storage devices. It should include details relating to the storage medium, capacity development over time and related costs.

firm offering the virtual storage service) may charge per gigabyte stored and offer reduced rates per gigabyte as the amount stored increases. Alternatively, they may charge a flat rate and limit the amount of data they will store.

The attraction of this method of storage is that the whole process is maintained by experts, the data is located somewhere other than the company headquarters and lengthy backup procedures are automated.

Storage virtualisation

Storage virtualisation is recognised as one of the best ways for IT managers to streamline routine tasks like backup, archiving and recovery, but in terms of delivering benefits to the business, these advances are just the tip of the much larger iceberg.

Pooling network storage can deliver an array of benefits to your enterprise, including improvements to database performance, capacity utilization and application availability.

'Storage virtualization has been around for a very long time,' says Garry Barker, chairman of the Australian Storage Networking Industry Association (SNIA). 'The marketplace is slowly adopting these rather than jumping in,' Barker continued to say. 'The main reason for gradual growth is because it is difficult for consumers to understand the benefits. But they are actually clear and huge.'

'The great thing about storage virtualization is it knows the true nature of the underlying storage, where the applications couldn't give a damn,' Sargeant says. 'The net effect is to make what appears to be complex, less complex – and simple as far as the applications and users are concerned.'

Graham Penn, an IDC storage analyst, describes storage virtualization as a way to 'better use the capacity you have.' He points out that storage virtualization is also a good way to save on capital costs. 'You get better use of what you've already got because it is all together, and you can manage it from a single point with the same tools, which helps reduce operational costs and manpower.'

'What we generally find is that, for most companies, their initial significant savings are in data migration – taking data from where it is to somewhere else in the pool. Once you have done that you can start to manage the excess capacity,' Penn says.

A link to this website is available at www.heinemann.co.uk/hotlinks (express code 2349P)

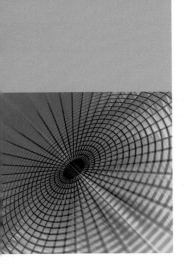

1.7 Selection and use of output methods, media and devices

Humans rely on several senses to understand the world. It is possible to hear spoken words and other sounds with our ears and see life in front of us with our eyes. Output devices are designed to appeal to these senses and ensure that what has been digitised can be seen and heard as expected.

Such devices come in a range of shapes and sizes. They can be attached to our heads, wired or wireless, several metres across or only a few centimetres wide. Their main purpose does not change: to display, project or announce versions of data in the most suitable form.

Aural output devices

Speakers

Speakers play sound and come in many shapes and sizes. This could be music, sound effects or the human voice. Many computer systems are sold with audio recording software installed. The type of speakers purchased will vary depending on what the user requires. For presentations to hundreds of people in a conference centre it may be necessary to use a setup which includes many wall-mounted speakers, all connected to one central location. For personal use, a single set of two speakers is often enough. The ability to attach speakers to computers could lead to a reduction in the popularity of the home music system. Computers are able to play stored music from libraries at similar quality to CD players. Speakers allow visually impaired users to hear what is on the screen and voice recognition technology enables them to interact with the computer. Speakers can be used to broadcast sounds from Internet phone conversations to groups of people while video conferencing, because it is important that each person involved can hear one another.

Headphones

Headphones perform the same function as speakers but on a much more personal level. There is a multitude of different options available, varying in size and shape. The iPod headphones have their own simple but distinct appearance, whereas some other headphones cover the whole ear.

Headphones with microphones are popular for those who use the Internet to make phone calls. These headsets are also used in call centres, which represent the section of a business that makes direct contact with potential customers. The emergency services also use a headset to accept calls prior to dispatching the appropriate service. Some headsets are designed to be worn while jogging; others have wireless capabilities, which mean the wearer is not constrained to listening to whatever is being played in one restricted location. The wireless headset will have a broadcast range, and sound quality is likely to deteriorate as the user moves further away from the transmitter. There is even a headset built into a beanie hat for snowboarders!

Visual output devices

The most common form of output is the computer monitor, which is also known as a Visual Display Unit (VDU). Monitors have evolved from heavy desk-based objects, which were difficult to move, to slim, lightweight items. The newer versions are a great improvement on the design of the original home machine monitor. The amount of space taken up by a computer system is known as the 'footprint'. The footprint of most systems over time has gradually reduced. When using a simple standard machine consisting of a keyboard, mouse and monitor the desire for more desk space meant that the monitor size had to be reduced. Designers managed to achieve this by reducing the back of the monitor, which held the heavy components, but still managed to provide a screen that had a good sized visual output.

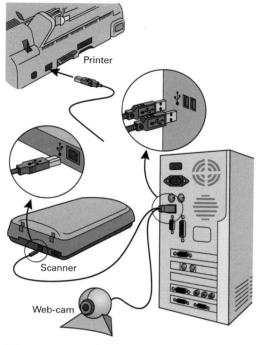

USB port and connector

Thin-Film Transistor (TFT) is the name of the technology that enables monitors to be light and still broadcast good-quality images. TFT monitors come in sizes ranging from 12 to 30 inches and can be in a variety of colours with various function buttons found under the display area. Previous monitors were a technician's nightmare as they struggled around with heavy old units that had broken down. TFT monitors sometimes come with a handle on the back to aid portability as an added design feature. The smaller footprint available from new systems gives those working with computers more space to lay out paperwork, stationery and other technology they might use, such as mobile phones, docking stations for PDAs and digital cameras. There are monitors that have USB ports that allow peripherals to be plugged in and flexible designs allow the screen to be viewed from a variety of angles without moving the base.

The major selling point is the image quality that can be provided based on the resolution available and the size of the actual screen. The reason for choosing one screen size over another is usually dependent on the needs of the user and how much graphic work they do. Architects and game designers need to see crisp, clear images; novelists, who may only work with text, are likely to invest in different monitors. The technology that has improved data viewing is so good that it has been used by television manufacturers, who also pursue image-viewing perfection. Monitors are used mainly by individuals who are working on personal assignments or projects, which means that they may require other forms of output if they are to display their work to a larger audience.

Projector

Projectors are devices that are connected to computers to produce the image from the screen on a larger scale, often on a white screen or wall. Projectors are used to make presentations to audiences larger than the few people who could comfortably sit around a standard monitor. The projector displays a clear image that can be seen, cinema style, across large conference rooms. Common mistakes made by projector users include placing the projector too close to the screen, which limits the size of the image, or failing to set it up properly so that the image is high enough to be viewed or fits on the screen.

The cost of projectors, like that of all desirable technology, has dropped over time. There are projectors which cost a lot less than some modern televisions which means that a user could attach a laptop with TV capabilities and, with the correct setup of wires and software, watch TV on a big screen for a fraction of the cost of a state-of-the-art TV. Clearly this is desirable provided the user has enough wall space for viewing and the know-how to ensure that the setup does not cause conflict with other uses of the technology.

Projectors can be ceiling-mounted or wall-mounted. The decision to mount a projector will depend on how much it will be used in a single place or whether it would be better not to mount the unit so that it could remain portable and be used in a variety of locations. Classrooms and function rooms may be areas where projectors are permanent fixtures, whereas small meeting rooms are more likely to rely on a portable setup.

Miniaturisation

Cameras, MP3 players and memory chips are growing smaller by the day. The next challenge is to shrink the projector, a device used day in day out in lecture halls and for video presentations.

However, all attempts at miniaturisation have so far come up against certain physical boundaries: the core piece of the classic projector is a micromirror array comprising a million mirrors. These can be tilted in one plane and are evenly illuminated. By turning towards or away from the light source, they produce light or dark pixels that together form the projected image. But not only do the arrays preclude miniaturization, their unaffordable prices also make it difficult for projectors to enter the consumer goods market.

Researchers at the Fraunhofer Institute for Photonic Microsystems IPMS in Dresden and the Fraunhofer Institute for Applied Optics and Precision Engineering IOF in Jena have now come up with an alternative to the previous micromirror arrays. The result is a projector the size of a sugar cube. 'We use just one single mirror,' reveals Andreas Bräuer, director of the Microoptic Systems division at IOF. 'This mirror can be tilted around two axes.'

The next obstacle in the miniaturisation process is the light source. The customary high-pressure lamp will have to give way to small diode lasers if the projector is to shrink to the size of a sugar cube. While red and blue diode lasers are already small enough, green lasers are still too bulky.

Today's technology allows RGB projectors with a side length of ten by seven by three centimetres to be produced. Although this is still distinctly larger than a sugar cube, it is only a quarter the size of a standard projector. Researchers around the globe are attempting to scale down the green light source. Together with the blue and red diode lasers, it will ideally form the new red-green-blue source. 'If green diode lasers are successfully reduced to the size of red ones, then RGB projectors the size of sugar cubes will become a reality,' states Bräuer.

Such would prove useful in many areas. The automotive industry, for example, requires small, cost-effective laser arrays to act as distance sensors that measure the gap between the car and the nearest object when parking. Sensors of this type are also used in robotics and installation technology. Yet another area of usage for the mini-lasers are digital projectors, which can be integrated in mobile devices such as laptops or PDAs.

A link to this website is available at www.heinemann.co.uk/hotlinks (express code 2349P)

Some projectors have zoom capabilities, which give the operator the option to highlight selected areas and place special emphasis on what they are talking about. This may be useful when looking at detailed designs or even CCTV footage when a crime is being investigated to get a better look at the suspect.

Projectors

Imagine projectors in a mobile phone or PDA. In pairs, produce a list of as many uses as you can for this technology. For example, how could the police use it? Who else could use the technology and how?

Printer

A printer's primary function is to produce a hardcopy of what is being displayed on a monitor. The output will need to be printed on certain material, depending on what it is intended to be used for. Paper, plastic and transparencies are familiar options. Hardcopies can then be taken away and read, drawn over, amended and recycled when no longer required. As long as there is a digital copy, the ability to produce a hardcopy should always exist. There is a wide range of printers on the market. Some of the older models, like the dot matrix printer, are not so common today mainly because they are slow, the quality of print is not always suitable and the machine is noisy. Replacements can be faster and quieter. Buying a standard home colour ink-jet printer can be fairly cheap, although the refill ink cartridges may not be, and again the quality is not always as desired. The features offered by a laser printer usually include high-quality output, very little sound and good speed. Laser printers can be networked, and provide the option of producing **duplex** copies automatically.

Some laser and ink-jet printers can only produce black and white copy, whereas others can produce colour. The price of colour laser printers has dropped considerably, which gives home users the option to buy one for personal use without spending a small fortune.

Duplex

Duplex (double sided printing) means that both sides of a page can be printed without interference whereas ink-jet printers would need the user to reverse the page and feed it back into the printer to achieve the same result.

Case study

Printer security

The multifunction printers found in many offices are not dumb devices, but are computers that can be hacked, a security expert has warned.

In a presentation at the Black Hat security conference, Brendan O'Connor, a security expert at an unnamed U.S. financial company, showed how he could gain control over a Xerox device and wreak all kinds of havoc.

'Stop treating them as printers. Treat them as servers, as workstations,' O'Connor said in his presentation on Thursday. Printers should be part of a company's patch program and be carefully managed, not forgotten by IT and handled by the most junior person on staff, he said.

In the case of the Xerox system, O'Connor said the multifunction device was, in essence, a Linux server. He was able to exploit a weakness in the security of the device and gain full control of the machine. O'Connor noted that he also looked at devices from other manufacturers and found similar security faults, but did not list any names.

Once a printer was under his control, O'Connor said he would be able to use it to map an organisation's internal network; a situation that could help stage further attacks. The breach gave him access to any of the information printed, copied or faxed from

the device. He could also change the internal job counter, which can reduce, or increase, a company's bill if the device is leased, he said.

The printer break-in also enables a number of practical jokes, such as sending print and scan jobs to arbitrary workers' desktops, O'Connor said. Also, devices could be programmed to include, for example, an image of a paper clip on every print, fax or copy, ultimately driving office staffers to take the machine apart looking for the paper clip.

One of the weaknesses in the Xerox system is an unsecured boot loader, the technology that loads the basic software on the device, O'Connor said. Other flaws lie in the device's Web interface and in the availability of services such as the Simple Network Management Protocol and Telnet, he said.

O'Connor informed Xerox of the problems in January. The company did issue a fix for its WorkCentre 200 series, it said in a statement. 'Thanks to Brendan's efforts, we were able to post a patch for our customers in mid-January which fixes the issues,' a Xerox representative said in an e-mailed statement.

However, O'Connor believes the fix is inadequate, and therefore he decided to make the presentation at Black Hat. The threat is real, even though printers are mostly on internal networks, he said. 'There is always the insider threat,' O'Connor said.

A link to this website is available at www.heinemann.co.uk/hotlinks (express code 2349P)

Many modern printers have plug and play capabilities, which means the owner can attach the printer in seconds via a USB port and start printing with very little technical knowledge.

Printers can serve many more purposes than simply printing. Some have fax machines, scanners and photocopying capabilities. For a reasonable price such machines can be purchased for home use. These types of machine are often quite slow and the scan size is limited to A4 but, as ever, technological drive and market demands are likely to make the product even more desirable in the future.

Flash card technology has seen developments within printers that now have loading slots and display screens. The printer will allow the user to insert their card, search for certain pictures and images, perform some editing tasks and produce a quality printout on proper photographic paper. At an industrial level this process is too slow but some personal users find it attractive.

The type of printer required will depend on the task it is intended to perform. Publishers and producers of glossy magazines would use a high-quality printer, which represents images in great detail. A student producing an essay may only need a simple black and white printer. The graphics industry and those working with images and computer aided design (CAD) will want printers that can produce images in high quality and to a perfect level of accuracy on varying sizes of paper. Circuit boards and plans for mechanical devices fall into this category and a plotter would be the most suitable option. Plotters involve the use of a pen that physically draws the required image over the print area.

Carvalho Dance School

Carvalho Dance School has recently opened in your area. The school uses a small community centre and teaches a range of dance classes to varying age groups. What IT equipment would you recommend it buys and why? Give specific details relating to the output devices, including the price, and compelling reasons for your decisions.

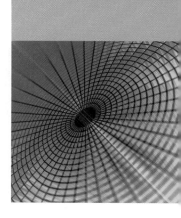

1.8 Selection and use of appropriate software

Software is the word used to describe the lines of programming code that make the computer perform tasks. Software enables computer users to interact with hardware. Without software a computer is simply a collection of wires, plastic and super-fast processors. Every day, millions of people switch on their computer, listen to it rumble and have no appreciation of how many millions of complex calculations are being run simply to show a welcome screen.

Software engineers and developers are constantly pushing the boundaries, producing programs that can perform tasks that the standard computer user can hardly comprehend. Software allows us to organise our finances, design spacecraft, communicate across the globe, play online games and purchase products from shops on the other side of the world. Software has been developed to examine cell particles, date fossils, evaluate dangerous environments, control artificial intelligence, and power robots.

Robots are run by software that tells them how to behave

The Holy Grail in terms of software development is to create the Killer Application. This is software which changes the way a certain job or task is done forever. Examples include the word processor and the web browser; both revolutionised how information can be viewed, presented and shared.

The primary role of software is to allow computer users to perform tasks that would otherwise take a very long time to achieve. Software is often developed in order to satisfy a particular market need. For example, large supermarket chains use software on a second-by-second basis for recording sales of stock, logging purchase trends of individuals and producing reports advising suppliers of what deliveries are required and by what date.

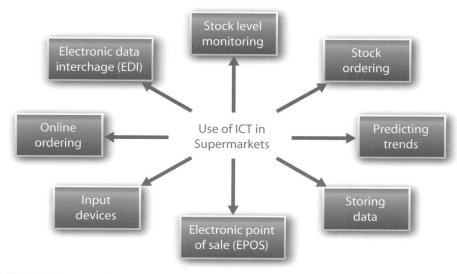

Use of ICT in supermarkets

Voice-activated search services

The world's largest Internet players are jockeying for position in voice-activated search services as they strive to extend their reach beyond computers to mobile phones. With mobile advertising revenues forecast to grow eightfold in the next four years, to $11.5 billion (£5.8 billion) and the market for directory enquiries worth $8 billion a year in the US alone, Google, Yahoo! and Microsoft, the leaders in web search, are all targeting the sector. Competition hit a new pitch after Google unveiled a telephone-based service that allows users to dial a number and vocally request details for local businesses in American cities. Google Voice Local Search uses voice-recognition technology to process queries and delivers answers using Google Maps. The move comes only weeks after Microsoft agreed to acquire Tellme Networks, a privately owned specialist in voice-recognition technology, for an estimated $800 million.

Tellme already has deals to supply voice-activated information such as stock quotes and weather updates to groups including AT&T and Verizon Wireless, the joint venture between Verizon Communications and Vodafone. The world's largest software group has already demonstrated its commitment to voice technology at its 'home of the future' site based at its headquarters in Redmond. The model house, designed to showcase technologies that Microsoft believes will be viable within a decade, is activated by Grace, a listening, speaking interface.

Yahoo! is also staking its claim to the mobile market through its oneSearch product, which is tailored to handheld devices and will be rolled out in Europe this month. Yahoo!, which has been berated for falling behind Google in traditional search services, is also thought to be working on a mobile-based social-networking service, which would seek to replicate the success of sites such as Facebook and Bebo.

A Google spokesman said that Google Voice Local Search 'really is totally experimental at this stage', adding that the company has no plans to offer it outside the US. However, the company has recently focused on broadening its mobile footprint, most recently by signing a deal to pre-install its software in LG mobile phones. Google is also thought to be working on its own operating system for mobile phones, and possibly its own branded handset. Google Voice Local Search does not charge users for the information but they will be charged by telephone companies for making a phone call or receiving a text message of results. Users can then search by saying a business name or a category of service – for example, 'Giovanni's Pizzeria' or 'pizza San Francisco'. Users can say 'text message' to receive details by SMS if using a mobile phone.

Meanwhile, Internet groups have rushed to have their software pre-installed on mobile handsets as they seek to capture market share. Microsoft has signed up LG Electronics, Toshiba and Hewlett-Packard to build handsets that would run on its Windows Mobile operating system. Yahoo! already has deals with Nokia, Motorola, RIM, LG and Samsung, the handset manufacturers, to have its software shipped on certain handsets. It also has a partnership with HTC, a Taiwan-based company that has been named as a possible partner to Google in its mobile plans.

A link to this website is available at www.heinemann.co.uk/hotlinks (express code 2349P)

Software is also used for its level of precision. Advanced calculations can be returned within seconds to whatever degree of accuracy is required, while measurements can be taken to perfection and used to simulate how a product or mechanism will look or work. Software enables businesses to produce models to help forecast what might happen in the future if certain decisions are made.

3D animation

'My lifelong dream was to win a Stanley Cup,' says Kevin Tureski of Alias/Wavefront holding his Oscar statuette. 'An Oscar is like a Stanley Cup.' The Academy has awarded the Scientific and Technical Award to (the) Toronto software giant responsible for Maya, computer software used in cutting edge animation technology. From *The Lord of the Rings* to *Star Wars* to *Spiderman*, it's nearly impossible to find a film that doesn't use the Maya technology.

The Oscar confirms Canada's status as a leader in the field of 3D animation, something that designer Bill Buxton finds ironic. If anyone had suggested there would be an industry around this technology back in the late 70s and early 80s, says Buxton, they would have been laughed out of the room.

A link to this website is available at www.heinemann.co.uk/hotlinks (express code 2349P)

Animation software or special effects

Identify three films you have seen recently which included the use of animation software or special effects. Word-process a description of the scenes in the movie where technology was used and explain why?

Software is also used to monitor and control certain pre-set environments. Robots working in high-tech factories are run by software that tells them how to behave; usually depending on when another process is completed. Only when the instructions are given incorrectly will a robot or similar machine not function properly.

The entertainment industry has become increasingly popular and powerful and has embraced the potential of software in order to enhance game-play experience and the moviegoers' enjoyment at the cinema. There have been some stunning visual effects created by world-class animators, using extremely powerful software at the request of ambitious movie directors. *The Lord of the Rings*, *Shrek* and *The Matrix Trilogy* were among the first films to really push the potential of technology to new heights.

The music industry also uses software to create new sounds. It is even possible to combine a number of artists on one track even if one of the singers died 20 years previously. A Radio 2 advert in 2006 combined a range of famous musicians on one stage; they were each introduced by Elvis Presley despite the fact some of the artists weren't even born before he died.

Software can be used to record virtual diaries, store years' worth of family photos, train concert pianists, emulate the style of Renaissance painters and produce fitness programmes for future Olympians.

The limitations are firmly at the door of the humans who generate the code and create the ideas to power further development. For this reason many firms employ teams of staff to review current software, look for emerging market needs and suggest ideas for the types of function the next level of software could support.

System software, function and purpose

Most commonly used system software incorporates windows, icons, menus and a pointing device (WIMP). The windows display several open applications, or the contents of folders that store files, on the screen at once. The icons are used to perform various tasks at the click of the mouse button. The pointing device (typically a mouse) is used to navigate the screen, to select text or images and to activate the icons. The menus hold further functions that allow a user to customise the way the software looks and acts. The WIMP setup is intuitive and forms the basis of most successful commercial software.

Operating system software is referred to as the platform. This integral piece of software shows the welcome message when the machine is switched on and, more importantly, provides the gateway to operating the computer system. The operating system acts like a stage for the software to perform upon. Operating system software has a range of main functions, including process management, memory management, networking, security and providing the graphical user interface which allows users to interact with the software.

The Microsoft Windows operating system dominates the software market; together with the Apple platforms, it can be found on most machines on the planet. Another platform is Unix, which is recognised in industry as being incredibly secure and the free Linux version is popular with hobbyist programmers. The range of potential software available on the Unix platform has grown with its credibility as a real alternative to Windows and Apple OS.

Most modern operating systems are viewed via a graphical user interface. This increases user friendliness and means that the a wealth of clever syntax and programmers' jargon are not required to make it all work. This opened up the personal computer world to millions of users.

There is a range of gadgets and peripherals that can be plugged into a modern computer, all of which require software drivers in order to make them work properly with the system. In the past, each new device would be accompanied by a CD-ROM which held the instructions

that would make it compatible with whatever platform it was to run on. Today, system software has been cleverly developed which negates the need for the CD-ROM and makes the process of installing new hardware – such as printers, digital cameras, MP3 players and scanners – far simpler. This is known as plug and play technology.

The operating system performs the complex task of process management. Each time a mouse button is clicked, a key pushed, a request for printing made, or a calculation needs to be performed, the operating system is in charge of the order of events – it is communicating with the central processing unit and providing it with the order in which it should perform each task.

Plug and play technology

Attach a new input or output device to a PC and observe plug and play technology in action. Use the device and check that it works.

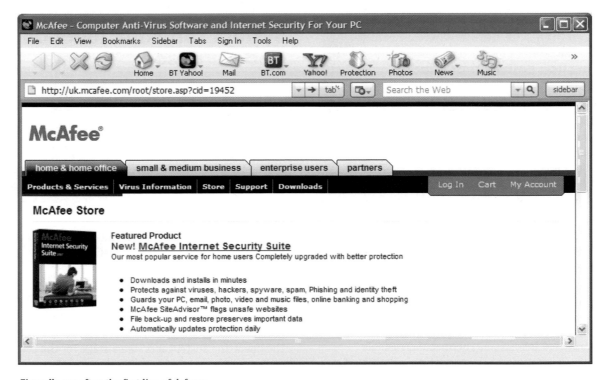

Firewalls are often the first line of defence

Memory management is another vital function of the operating system. This is when the operating system ensures that there is enough memory available to the user to perform whatever task they are currently working on. When a user is multi-tasking between a word processor and spreadsheet, while listening to an online radio station, it is the task of the operating system to make sure that memory is allocated correctly.

With so many computers linked via digital networks, the software industry had no option but to produce operating systems that could work comfortably with other computers. Networking facilities built into most modern operating systems mean many computers can share resources over short, medium and long distances using wired or wireless connections. Printers, scanners and files are just a few examples of the resources that can be shared.

The security of data within a network will be a concern. By attaching a computer to the Internet, users are connecting to the biggest network in the world. A machine 9,000 miles away can access another within seconds and strip it of all its files without the victim knowing much about it until it is too late. Operating systems can be configured so that only those with pre-set access levels on a specified network can share the files and data stored on them.

Firewalls are often the first line of defence to prevent access to a system from those who are not welcome to view the data. Passwords and usernames are other forms of protection an operating system can deploy to prevent access to a system. Systems with a high level of security are provided which contain auditing facilities. These allow the owners of networks to monitor what has actually happened on their network.

Application software, function and purpose

Unlike the operating system, application software is not always given away with the purchase of a machine. The most popular and commonly found range of software comes from Microsoft who developed a brand called Microsoft Office. There are other options in the market such as Apple and smaller specialist firms as well as the free option called Open Office, which can be downloaded from the Internet for no charge.

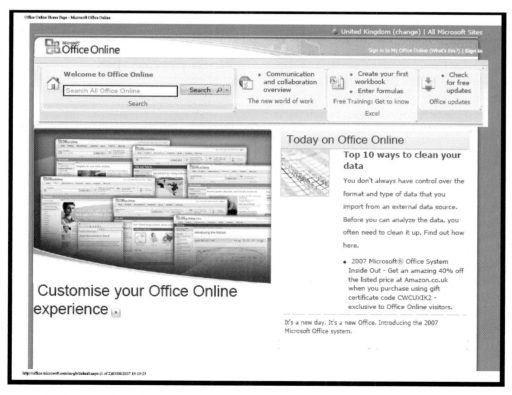

Microsoft Office is widely used

The most common forms of application software are word-processors, spreadsheets, databases, web editors, graphic design and presentation packages, also known as **generic software** as opposed to **bespoke software**.

Generic software

Generic software is an application package that can be used by many people for many purposes.

Bespoke software

Bespoke software is made to perform a particular specified task like producing invoices for an international shipping company or keeping a register of parts for NASA. As NASA and a shipping company will have slightly different operating needs from their competitors they are likely to require software specifically designed to perform tasks that match their business aims.

These applications are often found sold as a bundle called a software suite, and have a consistent look and feel about how they are viewed and used. The save, print and bold options, for example, are usually in the same location of each piece within the bundle. Other forms of application package include accounting software, music players and web browsers.

When deciding on what software to use, it is vital that the most appropriate package with the most suitable features is selected. A common mistake is to use software that has some but not all the facilities required, which means users find they have to switch to another package in order to complete the initial task.

A spreadsheet is ideal for calculating financial data but would not be the best option for creating a report to the managing director detailing future spending proposals. In situations like this a better decision can be made when a user knows what the software can and cannot do and whether it can be used alongside another package. Using a spreadsheet to accurately calculate the financial data, which can then be imported into a word processor where the report can be generated, would probably best perform the task.

Software choices

1. Get a sheet of blank A4 paper. Write in the middle 'Software used today'. Draw a spider diagram detailing all the software you have used or will use today and give brief details about why it was used.

2. Find a partner and discuss your initial work from Task 1, then make additions or amendments to your spider diagram.

Extension

3. Convert the spider diagram into an animated digital display using the most appropriate software.

Word processors

Word processors are typically used to handle text that can form reports, letters, essays and most other written projects. This kind of software is probably among the first type of package used by most computer users. The facilities which make it attractive include spell checking, a vast array of different font style and size options, and the ability to centre, **bold** and underline text to give impact to a document. It is often possible to draw and include images, but not always to the degree of accuracy that graphic designers require. Most computers have a simple word processor pre-installed but this is likely to lack the functionality of those sold and used commercially.

Presentation software

Presentation software is used to give details to an audience and is usually projected on to a large screen. The software is set to display information in a logical order running through various details displayed on a number of pages. The presentation can be automated to change page at set intervals. Presentations can include audio commentaries, video clips and animations. Using presentation software is often not too difficult, but problems can occur when it is overused or the pages are crammed full of text. Presentations should be used in conjunction with other presentation methods, such as a knowledgeable and interesting speaker and tangible items that can be passed round, otherwise viewers tend to stop concentrating after a short period of time. Presentation software allows the pages from the presentation to be printed in a variety of formats so that if someone is absent they can be sent a copy of the key notes.

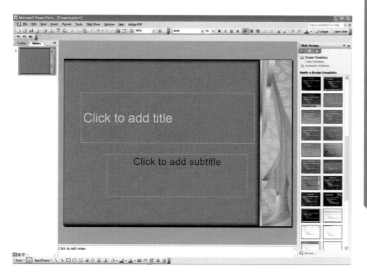

Microsoft PowerPoint is presentation software

activity

Bains Management Training Company

You are the Sales Manager at Bains Management Training Company, which specialises in outdoor management team-building projects. Your role is to visit companies to sell them time at your residential camp. You need to produce a presentation that you will use to generate bookings from interested companies.

1 Produce a word-processed plan saying what software you will use, the facilities it can offer and why they are appropriate. Your plan should also include what equipment is required to view the presentation and what other material you might require. You will also need to clearly make recommendations for delivering a good electronic and verbal presentation.

2 Make the presentation (no longer than eight slides) and present it to your class.

3 Review the presentations. This might include producing a form to fill out while you watch other presentations. You need to be able to provide feedback to your peers about their presentations. The feedback should be word-processed and include comments that identify the following:

- What was good?
- The quality of the information provided
- The length of the presentation
- The quality of the images used
- What was not so good?
- Use of the package's facilities to convey the message.

4 Make improvements to your presentation based on the feedback.

Desktop publishing software

Desktop publishing (DTP) software is similar to word processors in that it can handle text and images. The key difference is that DTP software is specifically designed to assist in the production of publications such as books, newspapers, magazines, menus, leaflets and brochures. The more advanced versions offer many templates, which can be used to help style a document with a pre-set layout. The features mentioned for word processing are usually included in DTP packages.

Spreadsheet software

Spreadsheets are used to handle numerical data and accommodate text, usually in the form of labels, to describe what the figures represent. Another important aspect of a spreadsheet is its ability to transfer tables of data into graphs and charts. More advanced users make use of macros which are programs created by the user recording the actions they take to carry out a task that is likely to be repeated. When the recording of the process is complete, the macro is saved and can be assigned to a button, which executes the task previously recorded. There are many mathematical formulas and functions built into spreadsheets, which make them the most appropriate type of software to carry out any statistical or financial analysis.

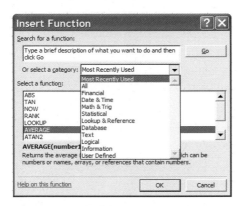

Many functions are built in

Databases

Databases are files that hold vast amounts of data, which can be searched and sorted as the user desires. The ability to search through masses of data is needed by businesses that interrogate systems in order to spot current or seasonal trends or to locate archived data such as the address of an ex-employee. Databases are hugely important to businesses; companies often tailor them to hold most of their important day-to-day data. Databases are especially useful for extracting the exact information that a user needs at a certain time, meaning the process of manually searching through millions of records is reduced to mere seconds.

Graphics software

Graphics software has several uses. It can be used to improve the quality of images such as those shown in glossy magazines. Quite often the subject of the photograph has been digitally enhanced using a technique known as airbrushing. Another use of graphics software is to create original images. Every new company will need an identifying symbol known as a logo, which can be produced in graphics software. Graphics applications vary in the tools they provide and the level of accuracy and precision available. Basic drawings of stick men to detailed designs of a hotel can all be achieved, but it is often a good idea to explore the market to ensure that the package proposed can cope with the demands a user has in mind.

Web editors

Web editors provide individuals and businesses with the opportunity to produce their own websites. Web editors make it easy to incorporate pictures, text, animations, sounds and movies into a website that can be uploaded onto the World Wide Web for everyone to see. These applications have been developing rapidly as more and more people want to make more functional and attractive commercial sites in order to persuade consumers to buy their products online. Web shoppers expect to be able to order and pay for products all within the space of a couple of minutes. This level of web production is beyond the ability of most users but newer software often builds in the features demanded by the users, therefore the tools to make a website a commercial success will soon to be at the fingertips of anyone with a relatively new web editor.

Most of the above packages allow data to be transferred between them, which gives users the ability to use the strengths of each application before combining data into one complete master file which could include graphs, original graphics, text and photographs.

Web browsers

Web browsers make the Internet come alive. They require very little interference from users although, like most software, they can be customised to suit a certain viewing preference. The browser interprets the programming code found within the pages produced in a web editor and displays the pages as the producer would hope them to be seen. There are fewer web browser package options compared to other types of applications software, mainly because most users are only concerned with surfing the Internet for information and are not concerned with how it is achieved.

Music players

Music players have become more popular, largely due to the expansion of the digital music industry. In order to capture a share of the market, some companies provide music players free of charge via download with intelligent links to online music stores where people can download tracks to transfer to their MP3 players. Apple and Microsoft both supply music players, free of charge, which can organise an entire collection and even allow people to burn their library of music onto their own personalised compilation CDs.

Communication software

Email packages allow you to send electronic messages to anyone who has an email address. Prior to email, individuals and companies had to rely on the manual postal system to send letters and messages. The postal system is still used, thanks largely to the increasing number of deliveries resulting from online purchases. Email gives users the opportunity to send short or long messages very quickly to the other side of the world if required. Emails can be used informally, to friends and to make contact with like-minded people, or formally within a business, where drafts of documents can be sent for review, orders sent to suppliers, orders received from customers and so on.

Pandora: online music streaming service

Pandora is an online music streaming service designed to help find and enjoy music that one will love. It is powered by the Music Genome Project, which is a comprehensive analysis of music. The inspiration for the company came from the experiences of the founder as being a musician. The company was founded to help musicians find their audiences and to make a living out of their craft.

The Music Genome Project started in January 2000 by a group of 35 trained musicians with the idea to create the most comprehensive analysis of music ever. They set out to capture the essence of music at the most fundamental level. They ended up assembling literally hundreds of musical attributes or 'genes' into a very large Music Genome. Taken together, these genes capture the unique and magical musical identity of a song, which can be compared to DNA. That includes everything from melody, harmony and rhythm, to instrumentation, orchestration, arrangement, lyrics, and the rich world of singing and vocal harmony. It is not about what a band looks like, or what genre they supposedly belong to, or about who buys their records; it is about what each individual song sounds like. Over the past six years, they have carefully listened to the songs of over 20,000 different artists, ranging from popular to obscure, and analyzed the musical qualities of each song one attribute at a time.

Since November 2005, Pandora started with the service they now provide to everybody. More than three million people have signed up since. On Pandora, all is based on the actual quality of the song. That does not take into account whether a group of people think of one particular band fitting into one genre, or if a radio station plays one particular song because the record label wants them to play it, it is all about what the actual musical qualities are. It is really unique in that respect.

A link to this website is available at www.heinemann.co.uk/hotlinks (express code 2349P)

Multiple emails can be sent to several people all at once by including more than one email address in the 'To:' section of the message. Messages can be sent with attachments, such as documents, pictures and audio files.

There are many commercial services that provide email storage space and spam filtering with added security for a monthly fee, and also free services, which tend to have more limited features and to be more restrictive in storage capacity.

Conclusion

Probably the most significant advancement in software development is the user-friendly and intuitive graphical user interfaces that mean many novice users can operate basic software with very little tuition.

The main limitation to using any software is often the person using it or the company that has it installed. There are often many features stored within the software that gather virtual dust from not being explored or used. As a result, many people still use application software inefficiently because they have never been trained to use all the features available.

1.9 Implementation of ICT-related solutions

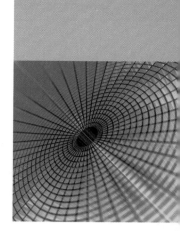

Having designed the solution properly, with detailed and accurate input, process and output specifications, plus a data dictionary with a list of all files and data items required for the system, and having chosen all hardware and software required for the implementation, you can proceed to implement it.

The first step is to review the plan and to make sure that all hardware and software is set up, installed and ready to go.

The next step is to gather the data for capturing, if that is a step on the way – for instance, taking photographs, shooting video and so on. Remember to use the correct filenames and folders for storing any data you capture. There may be templates to set up, so that input forms all look and behave in the same way. There may be a database structure to set up and the data to populate it may have to be imported and checked.

The tasks involved in implementing a system depend on the system, the hardware and software being used and the detailed plan that should have tasks set out in a logical sequence.

If you are using the system as part of your evidence to be taken into the section examination, then remember to capture any tests that you may do along the way, in case you need them for evidence. Remember to capture any problems that occur and record the solutions. Keep a diary of events so that, if necessary, you can refer back to it when writing the evaluations.

Do not keep copious screenshots of how a particular function in a particular piece of software was used. It is not necessary – the examiners do not need to be taught how to use the software, they are only interested in how it was used or applied for this system.

The examination questions are testing your understanding of the processes of system development, not the actual doing of it. This means that many, much smaller, pieces of work using many variations on 'computer', 'data input or output device' and 'storage device' can be used. It is suggested that all types of data are the subjects of systems, so cover text, numbers, images and sounds.

Communication technologies are changing all the time, so different technologies should be explored in relation to system developments – how image and music files are transmitted between different types of microprocessor, for instance, changes almost weekly.

Bluetooth

Bluetooth technology is how mobile phones, computers, and personal digital assistants (PDAs), not to mention a broad selection of other devices, can be easily interconnected using a short-range wireless connection. Using this technology, users can have all mobile and fixed computer devices totally coordinated.

A link to this website is available at www.heinemann.co.uk/hotlinks (express code 2349P)

A bluetooth earpiece

Third Generation technology (3G)

What are third generation (3G) wireless communications?

Second generation (2G) cellular data networks in Japan deliver data rates up to 9.6 kbps for upload and up to 29.8 kbps for download. PHS networks in Japan deliver data rates up to 128 kbps for terminals which are not moving at high speeds (e.g. PHS does not connect well in high-speed trains). Third generation (3G) wireless networks in Japan deliver datarates from 64 kbps for upload and on the order of 200 kbps for download. Increasingly 3G networks in Japan are up-graded to deliver data connection rates on the order of 2 to 10 Mbps. These higher speeds allow the trans-mission of video and two-way video telephony, rapid download of movie sketches, music and JAVA applica-tions. Other data connections, e.g. download of infor-mation or JAVA applets, are also several times faster on 3G networks than on older 2G networks. In Japan there are three parallel, independent and competing 3G networks. Costs to the carrier are lower, so that compe-tition drives prices down.

What is the 'killer application' for 3G? Is there one at all?

If there is a 'killer application' for 3G, it's mobile music! Chaku-Uta downloads on KDDI-AU mobile phones have similar download numbers as iTunes in the US with a very much smaller potential user pool. One can therefore safely say that mobile music downloads seem to be substantially more attractive for paying users than conventional fixed line internet music downloads.

A link to this website is available at www.heinemann.co.uk/ hotlinks (express code 2349P)

Fourth Generation (4G) wireless communications

What is fourth generation (4G) mobile?

At present the download speed for mobile internet connections in Japan are between 9.6 kbit/s for 2G cellular, up to 128 kbit/s for PHS, typically 200 kbit/s (nominally 384 kbps) for DoCoMo and Vodafone 3G cellular, and 2.4 Mbps for KDDI/AU CDMA2000-1x-WIN service. However, in actual use the data rates are usually slower, especially in crowded areas, or when the network is 'congested'. 4G mobile data transmission rates are planned to be up to 20 megabits per second.

What type of services will 4G allow?

Of course it is impossible to predict technology developments and the evolution of culture and customer needs. 4G in principle will allow high-quality smooth video transmission.

Is video really a killer application for 3G and 4G?

Usage data in Japan do not show that video telephony is a real killer application for 3G. However, this may change if quality and market penetration improves or different marketing models are found. We believe however that music is a killer application – compare for example the success of iPod. At the moment (3G) only very short music clips can be downloaded. 4G is likely to enable the download of full length songs or music pieces which may change the market response dramatically. Music rights management will be a major issue to solve.

A link to this website is available at www.heinemann.co.uk/ hotlinks (express code 2349P)

The principles of system development are the same for all types of ICT system, even if the implementations could be quite different. The primary aim is to produce a working solution that meets the client's requirements. This is done by following through from the analysis into the design, then from the design into the implementation, testing what is produced against the requirements at every level of the system, then letting the system run for a period before evaluating it and seeing if it needs improvements. This is called the Software Development Life Cycle.

1.10 Testing of ICT-related solutions

Testing is a very important aspect of system development. After implementing a solution it is absolutely crucial that a range of pre-determined tests are carried out to ensure the system does what it is supposed to according to the original specification. When a system is due for release on the market it will have been pushed through a whole range of vigorous tests to make sure that it does not break down when it carries out complex tasks and to see if it is secure. In this respect the developers will use the feedback from the testing phase to make alterations and improvements. Those involved with testing are particularly trying to find weaknesses and even break the system. If they are able to disturb the normal functions of the system, the chances are that the client will also find limitations.

The initial stage of testing is to produce a test plan according to a strategy. Effective test plans will feature several sub-sections that investigate how the system will react to certain types of data. The types of data used within a test plan are called 'normal', 'extreme' and 'erroneous' (see over). The plan may also include a section called System Testing where the testing of basic functions, such as navigation, and expected features, such as printing, takes place.

Another important aspect of testing is to include the end user's specification. The end user is the person who will use the system and who provided details relating to what the system must do in order to be a success. The plan must be written carefully to ensure that the data used throughout pushes the system to its limits and produces the desired outputs.

case study

US missile defense system

A minor software glitch led to a... test failure of the US missile defense system in Alaska and the Pacific [in December 2005].

The test of the Ground-based Midcourse system failed when the interceptor rocket carrying a non-exploding warhead did not take off as planned. An analysis of computer data from the failed test showed that the acceptable rate of information flow from the flight control computer to the thrust vector controllers on the rocket – mechanisms that control the pitch and yaw – were set too high...

The agency will repeat the failed test in February. The software code will be fixed by the rocket's maker, Orbital Sciences Corp. Similar fixes will be carried out to the rockets already in silos through their 'umbilical' systems.

The December test, called IFT 13C, was the first to use a realistic booster rocket, similar to the ones that have been placed in silos. Earlier tests used Minuteman III rockets, which are considered slower than the rockets that will be used by the missile defense system. The December test was expected to prove that the Exoatmospheric Kill Vehicle – the nonexploding warhead that sits on top of the rocket – can perform as designed with the new rockets.

A link to this website is available at www.heinemann.co.uk/hotlinks (express code 2349P)

Test data

Normal data, when entered into a system, should be accepted as the end user requested. This could be numbers set to a predefined range or words at a certain length or a date within a certain time frame. For example, the system may include a space where a person's age is to be entered. If the system is set to only accept ages between 18 and 30 years of age, normal data will be any number within that range; nothing else.

Extreme testing attempts to test the limits of a system regarding the data that can be entered. The maximum and minimum requirements of the system need to be tested and this can usually be done using small, detailed tests. If the example above is tested to see that only extreme values are accepted, the data to use would be 18 or 30 only. This will make two tests. One test is the minimum age the system should accept and the other is the maximum.

Erroneous testing is used to ensure that data the system is not expecting is rejected. Quite often it would be appropriate to display an error message informing the user that what they have attempted to enter is not allowed. To test the same example above for age we could use 31. 31 is outside the range expected and should be rejected. Alternatively any word like 'Twenty' or 'Hair' should also return an error. If erroneous data is accepted into a system it is likely to output incorrect or inaccurate results.

The test plan

A test plan must be detailed and provide sufficient evidence to demonstrate that the system works. A plan should include a reference for each test. Therefore when a plan is completed, any future discussion about a certain test can be instantly referred to and explained. Each test must also have a description. This allows the person carrying out the testing to place data in the correct place. Data to use is another important part of testing that must be given for each test, otherwise the plan will be fairly useless. Details of the expected outcomes should be provided.

When a test is carried out, the tester should know what will happen when certain data is entered. This can be worked out even before the system is built as it helps to focus on how the system should be developed. Poorly constructed systems usually show little understanding of what their

Test number	Test description	Data to use	Expected outcome	Actual outcome	Corrective action
1N	Enter age for client 1	21	Data is accepted	Data was accepted	See figure 1.1N

Normal testing

Test number	Test description	Data to use	Expected outcome	Actual outcome	Corrective action
1Ex	Enter age for client 1	18	Data is accepted	Data was accepted	See figure 1.1Ex
2EX	Enter age for client 1	30	Data is accepted	Data was accepted	See figure 1.2Ex

Extreme testing

Test number	Test description	Data to use	Expected outcome	Actual outcome	Corrective action
1Er	Enter age for client 1	31	Data is not accepted and an error messages is displayed. The user cannot proceed until an age within range is entered.	Data was not accepted and error message was displayed	See figure 1.1Er
2Er	Enter age for client 1	Twenty	Data is not accepted and an error messages is displayed. The user cannot proceed until an age within range is entered.	Data was not accepted and error message was displayed	See figure 1.2Er

Erroneous testing

purpose is and what the end user requires. A test plan will indicate what formula, validations and features a system must incorporate to pass the tests in the plan.

The actual outcome of each test must be recorded as evidence to prove it works. If a test is a success and has been correctly documented, the tester will move on to the next test. If the test does not go according to plan, corrective action needs to take place, and this will also need documenting. After corrective action has been carried out, the same test should be run again until it can be documented as successful.

The tests on ages between 18 and 30 could be represented in a plan similar to the one above.

The layout on the previous page is only a suggestion, but it illustrates the kind of detail required for it to be useful and assist in clear documentation. A similar plan can also be produced for the end user. End users may perform tests that the developers did not consider, which might yield useful results and expose weaknesses in the system.

Validity and accuracy of data

Despite the best efforts of those involved with testing systems, there is still the potential for things to go wrong. For a system to provide accurate outputs, the quality of the data entered has to be assured. Computer systems can be set up to accept various data formats, lengths, ranges and types, yet it is still possible for unintended data to make its way to the processing phase and influence the outputs. For example, a system could be designed to accept prices between £1.00 and £2.00 using validation built into the software. The data entry clerk may wish to enter the figure £1.30. Instead, they enter £1.03 and continue entering other data. The system has accepted the data because it is valid – it falls within the validation limits of £1.00 and £2.00 – but it is not accurate. The consequences will not be known until later when the figure is processed and an output obtained. The process may involve multiplying the figure by 2000 and putting it towards a company purchase plan. The effect of such a small error could mean over- or under-ordering on key stock and adversely affecting future sales. It is crucial that the test plan takes into account the potential for invalid data entering the system by testing validation and verification methods.

Accuracy of output

In industry and commerce, the outputs gained from any system are used to aid further decision-making. Managers will want the outputs to be accurate and delivered at specified times. Should the outputs lack detail or include misleading figures the consequences could be very serious. For example, the wrong postcode entered into a satellite navigation system by an ambulance crew might delay their arrival at a serious incident. The wrong date entered into a ticket ordering system could mean a business delegate arriving one day late for an important conference.

Presentation of output

When the system has accepted data and produced an output, there needs to be scope to test the usefulness and quality of information presented. Tests should be drafted to ensure that the outputs provide the details required of them. The audience for the system should be asked to give comments relating to the printouts gained and the on-screen view. They should provide feedback on how easily they located what they wanted and how they found the system to operate. Should key data be difficult to find on a complex and cluttered printout, or the screen layout cause confusion and stress, the system designers will have to do go back to the drawing board and produce alternative output layouts.

The navigation and security of the system can also be documented, but is not so simple to document with images. Useful comments should be provided as evidence.

Cornforth and Co.

Cornforth and Co. are a firm of solicitors. They have just provided a detailed requirements specification for a custom database to store details of their clients. Produce a short test plan that will test to see that the system accepts client data. You will first need to consider what client details Cornforth and Co. would hold before making the test plan.

You should be prepared to discuss your plan with peers to help you make refinements.

Alpha and beta testing

Alpha testing is performed by a person or company that produced a system, before letting the system be given to the users. This is usually the first stage of testing and is carried out within an organisation by those who did not produce the original system. It is sometimes known as system testing and, in a traditional development team, would be carried out by a team under the supervision of the systems analyst using data provided by the analyst. During this phase, feedback is provided to the developers and updates to the code and system are made.

Another phase of testing is called beta testing. This is usually carried out by a real end user who will agree a timescale for use then report back to the developers. Again the software/system can be modified from the results. It is usually after the alpha and beta testing stages that a system will be adopted and used as intended.

1.11 Evaluation of ICT-related solutions

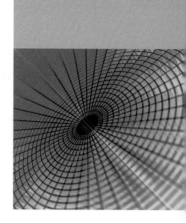

The evaluation is an assessment of the effectiveness of the solution in meeting the client's requirements. It allows you to show an understanding of what makes an ICT solution effective.

Step 1: Does it do what it is supposed to do?

Here, the evaluation criteria that were written in the analysis stage come into their own. Each one is examined and the solution as currently implemented is critically reviewed to see if it has met the criteria. Testing evidence should be cited to provide backup for any simple statement – a sentence that says 'yes, my system does x' without evidential proof, is not a sufficient answer.

Quantitative criteria can be addressed by proving that a function takes x seconds to load and store, or that the logo is on the top right-hand side of every page. Test evidence, or (in the case of some multimedia applications, say using sound or moving image) a witness statement from a teacher or the client, would be evidence enough of testing.

Some criteria can only be met by qualitative judgements. The developer is not sufficiently qualified to make qualitative decisions – the client or perhaps a selection of the eventual system users are the only ones who can say 'yes, the colour is OK, not too intrusive' or 'yes, it's easy to navigate if you're a novice user'. There are two ways of doing this – getting a client to try out the system and make signed comments or using a short questionnaire for some users. In either case, you will need to summarise the results of the opinions.

For the examination, it is not necessary to include all 10 completed questionnaires, for instance; just one and a statement saying how many were completed would be fine.

Step 2: Does it do it *how* it was supposed to?

Sometimes, although a solution produces the right results, it is by a combination of tortuous routes rather than in a straightforward manner.

For instance, some online shopping systems let you choose your items, fill in your personal details, then tell you if the item is in stock or whether you can get the delivery time you want. If the item is not in stock or the delivery slot is not available, the system sends you back to a blank form, or it has cleared out the choices you have made about delivery or collection. If all circumstances are then correct later, if you can be bothered, you have to fill in some details all over again.

Other problems may be when the design of the data entry is not logical for the data inputter. With most input form painters it is possible to stipulate the order of the fields if the Tab key is pressed. Most modern forms have a series of input fields for data, sometimes as a long vertical list and sometimes as fields in more than one column, or dotted about the screen. For instance, there may be four or five entry fields for different lines of address – do they follow on from each other if the Tab key is used, or does the Tab key jump out to a telephone number or date of birth field between town and county?

If there is a natural order of functions, then does the system follow that natural path? Are the functions easy to find from different menus? Do logically grouped functions appear together on the same menu?

Step 3: Is the solution an effective one?

Have you answered the previous questions with a 'yes'? What are the strengths of this solution? Where can best practice be identified? For example, consistency of the human–computer interface, use of sensible naming standards, technical documentation that would enable someone to maintain the system with ease, and a comprehensive User Guide (if appropriate) that is suitable for the target audience.

If answers to steps 1 and 2 have been 'no' or 'maybe', then the weaknesses need to be identified.

For each weakness, the evaluation needs to be brutally honest, discussing reasons why it happened, what the causes were (and lack of time is rarely an honest reason), and what could be done to improve the identified weakness, immediately or in the future, so as to remedy the problem and make the solution more effective.

Evaluation of own performance

Although not a major part of the AS requirements, it is worth mentioning here that, in all walks of life, an element of self-awareness is normally required as to the quality of your own performance through a period of time, whether in the form of an annual review, perhaps linked to a salary upgrade, or a self or peer review at the end of any major piece of work.

It is worth noting the following, for each piece of work undertaken during the study of this section:

- What skills have been learnt or improved?
- What went well – in the solution and in terms of time management?
- What problems arose? And how did I cope with or solve it?
- For each stage:
  - Was the analysis good or bad – what could have been improved?
  - Was the design good enough to implement or were there more questions or design decisions to be made?
  - How did the implementation go? Was everything in place? Does it all work? Thoroughly?
  - Was the test plan adequate to test every function and every path?
  - How many errors occurred? Why?
- Is the documentation produced at the right level of detail and language for the intended recipient?
- Is it all produced professionally (e.g. title page, contents page, each page with header, footer and page numbers, bibliography)?
- Is spelling and grammar all correct?
- Has the documentation been verified?

1.12 Practical exercises

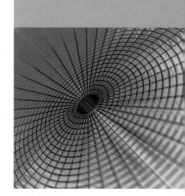

Sports day

Shane O'Brien, the Director of Sport at Boatlake School has been organising the school sports day for several years. He has used a manual system to record pupils' finishing positions and then works out how many points each place is worth.

The school has five year groups – 9 to 13 – which are divided equally into five teams called Red, Blue, Yellow, Orange and Brown.

The school has 300 pupils with 60 in each year group and everybody is supposed to do every event where they can earn points.

- 10 points are awarded to the top 10% for each event.
- 7 points are awarded to the next best 20%.
- 4 points are awarded for all those in the next 20%.
- 2 points are awarded to those who are placed in the bottom 50%.

The events that take place are:

- 100m
- 200m
- 400m
- 1500m
- shot putt
- long jump
- high jump.

Shane needs a system that will work out and display:

- the top 10% for each event with their team name
- those who fall between the best 70–89% and their team name
- those who fall between the best 50–69% and their team name
- those who are placed in the bottom 49% and their team name
- the best three performers in each event and their team name
- the best five performers for each year group and their team name
- the best team in each year group based on total points scored from all the events
- the best overall team based on total points scored from all the events.

10 points are awarded to the top 10% for each event

Task 1

What data will you need to make this system?

What processes will happen to the data?

What outputs are required?

Task 2

Design how the screen will look which will hold the collected results. What other sections need adding and why? Include these on the design.

The identified outputs need to be displayed. Design a layout that will show the desired outputs.

Task 3

Produce a test plan that will demonstrate that the system works as requested. Remember to include normal, extreme and erroneous test data.

Produce test data just for year 10 and the 200m and long jump events, with expected results.

Task 4

Decide what hardware and software are required to create this system – list these.

Create a system according to the designs made in Task 2. Allow for all year groups and all events.

Task 5

Test the system using the plan designed in Task 3.

Document the results of the testing phase and make comments.

Task 6

Evaluate your system. Comment on how successful the system was at fulfilling the requirements identified.

Extension task

Add Year 8, also with 60 pupils and the 10,000m event.

Document the success or difficulties faced while amending the system.

Carry out further testing – did the results go as planned? Were there any major problems to deal with?

Driving school

Stuart Fleming has been running his own driving school for seven years. He gives lessons to people within the Bradford area and enters them for tests when he feels that they are ready. The tests he enters them for are the theory test followed by the practical driving test. Only when his clients pass both tests does he no longer need to take them for lessons.

He likes his clients to have at least one lesson a week, which costs £17.50. His clients vary in age and gender. He currently records all of his clients' details and driving appointments by hand in a diary and also makes notes about whether they have passed either of the two tests or how many attempts they have had. In the summer last year Stuart lost his diary, which caused chaos for his clients and meant he lost details of bookings as well as how many lessons and tests each client had had.

Stuart needs a system that will:

- store all his clients' contact details
- allow him to enter new lesson bookings
- show how many lessons each client has had and when they were
- produce a list of lessons he is due to take each day and with whom
- calculate how much he will earn from driving lessons each week based on the number of lessons taken
- show how many of each test a client has had, and how successful they were
- show which clients have completed both tests.

Stuart runs his own driving school

Task 1

What data will you need to make this system?

What processes will happen to the data?

What outputs are required?

Task 2

Design how the screen will look that will be used to enter the data. Are there any other features that can be added to the screen?

The identified outputs need to be displayed. Design a layout that will show the desired outputs.

Task 3

Produce a test plan that will demonstrate that the system works as requested. Remember to include normal, extreme and erroneous test data.

Produce test data for three clients and their lesson and test details.

Task 4

Decide what hardware and software are required to create this system – list these.

Create the system according to the designs made in Task 2.

Task 5

Test the system using the plan designed in Task 3.

Document the results of the testing phase and make comments.

Task 6

Evaluate your system. Comment on how successful the system was at fulfilling the requirements identified.

Extension task

When people have passed their tests and no longer need lessons, Stuart would like to archive their details. Add an archive facility to the system.

Document the success or difficulties faced whilst amending the system.

Carry out further testing – did the results go as planned? Were there any major problems to deal with?

Fan website

You are the secretary of a fan club (music, football club, famous movie star, etc.) and have decided to set up a website for other fans. The purpose is to be up-to-date and informative about the object of your obsession and to enable other fans to make contact.

Your website should hold some of these items:

- a home page that welcomes people to the page
- a page counter to show how many visitors have seen the site
- a page with the history of the band/person/club
- a page showing forthcoming related events, with links to booking agencies
- a page with latest news
- photos, videos and sound, some of which should be original
- a fans' page, for them to add pictures, comments, etc.

Task 1

Decide who the client is for the website.

Decide who the website is for (the audience).

Make a list of requirements for the website.

Research other, similar websites for ideas.

Task 2

Design the structure of the website.

Design a basic 'look' that will be used.

Make a list of elements that will be required and where they will come from.

Make a list of hardware and software that could be used.

Task 3

Design all the pages, showing where each element will go and how the pages link.

For each element, make a list of hardware and software that will be used while developing it.

Write a statement covering health and safety, data protection, security and copyright issues.

Task 4

Write instructions for uploading the site onto the Internet.

Identify the keywords that would be used to help the site get recognised by a search engine.

Write a test strategy that will show how you intend to test the site.

Produce a test plan that shows how you will test the site.

Task 5

Create the website to your specification.

Task 6

Test the website using your test plan.

(Extension: Upload the website and test the uploaded version, using different search engines and different browsers.)

Document the results of the testing phase and make comments.

Task 7

Evaluate your site – get others to make comments, too. See if the site fulfils the requirements set in Task 1.

Extension work

Add a database to hold details of fans who wish to be kept updated on forthcoming events and news – just name, email address, and an assigned membership number. Attach this to the fans' page.

Add a method of contacting the fan club to ask a question.

Make a digital recording and edit it before adding it to the site.

Create a cartoon persona to guide visitors through the site (with animation, voice and sound).

Ensure you document and test these extra features.

1.13 Practice exam questions

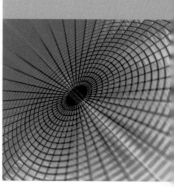

1. A clerk working in the accounts department of a large company spends all day entering employee timesheet data into the company's payroll system. The clerk uses a terminal linked to the company's main computer. To ensure the health and safety of the clerk, state, with reasons:
   (a) two work practice procedures that the company could introduce (4 marks)
   (b) two design features that the workstation the clerk uses should have (4 marks)
   (c) two design features that the software the clerk uses should have. (4 marks)
   (AQA June 2005)

2. All spreadsheet packages allow users to format the contents of cells. State **four** formats that can be applied to the contents of cells. (4 marks)
   (AQA January 2006)

3. State **three** formatting facilities that are offered by word processing software. (3 marks)
   (AQA June 2005)

4. What type of software would normally be used for the following tasks?
   (a) creating a directory, or folder, on a computer (1 mark)
   (b) writing a report (1 mark)
   (c) viewing a website (1 mark)
   (d) creating an electronic mark book. (1 mark)
   (AQA January 2006)

5. A student at a college is using the Internet to carry out research for an essay that she is writing.
   (a) Describe how she can access a website when:
      (i) she knows the Uniform Resource Locator (URL) or address (2 marks)
      (ii) she does not know the URL or address. (2 marks)
   (b) Describe two concerns that the student might have about the information that she obtains from the Internet. (4 marks)
   (c) The student has been told that she must provide the details of all the websites that she has used when writing her essay. State one detail about each website she has used that she should provide, and explain why it is necessary. (2 marks)
   (AQA June 2005)

6. A student loan calculator program has just been released for sale. The program calculates repayments on loans between £1000 and £15,000.
   (a) Explain why it is important that this piece of software is thoroughly tested. (2 marks)
   (b) State, giving an example of each, **three** types of test data that should have been used during testing. (6 marks)
   (AQA January 2006)

7. A school has decided that the four printers on its Local Area Network need replacing.
   (a) For one type of printer that the school might consider purchasing:
       (i)   name the type of printer (1 mark)
       (ii) give **one** capability of the named type of printer (1 mark)
       (iii) give **one** limitation of the named type of printer. (1 mark)
   (b) For another type of printer that the school might consider purchasing:
       (i)   name the type of printer (1 mark)
       (ii) give **one** capability of the named type of printer (1 mark)
       (iii) give **one** limitation of the named type of printer. (1 mark)
   (c) Should the school purchase four new printers of the same type, or should it purchase two
       different types of printer? What would your recommendation be and why? (2 marks)
   (AQA January 2006)

8. A system contains several flat files that are to be replaced by a relational database.
   (a) Describe **two** problems that can occur when data is stored in flat files. (4 marks)
   (b) Give **three** features that would be available when using relational database management software
       for the updating and retrieval of data. (3 marks)
   (AQA June 2005)

9. A new scanner is supplied with a set of drivers. These drivers are provided on a CD-ROM, together with
   Optical Character Recognition (OCR) software for use with the scanner.
   (a) State **three** functions of a scanner driver. (3 marks)
   (b) Give **one** reason why the drivers are not provided on a floppy disk. (1 mark)
   (c) Give **one** other method of providing the scanner drivers. (1 mark)
   (d) Describe **one** advantage of using OCR software. (2 marks)
   (AQA June 2005)

10. A small company is purchasing new computer hardware and software.
    (a) Name and describe **three** items of software that the company will need to buy, explaining
        why each item is required. (9 marks)
    (b) State **two** types of printer that the company could purchase and give one advantage of each type. (4 marks)
    (AQA June 2005)

11. Poorly designed computer workstations can lead to health problems. State **three** features of a well-designed
    workstation, and for **each one** state the health risk that could be reduced. (6 marks)
    (AQA January 2005)

1.14 Section 1 topic round-up

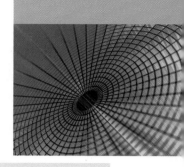

Health and safety

Health and Safety at Work Act 1974

- Employer's responsibilities
- Employee's responsibilities

Addendums 1992

- Provision of H&S reviews/risk assessments
- Provision of training
- Appointment of person responsible for H&S
- Definition of computer user
- Workstation regulations
- Regular breaks/changes of activity
- Eye care/screening

Health problems and design

- Eye strain – font type/size/colour and background colour/contrast
- RSI – unnecessary input (have auto-filled, default fields)
- Migraine/fits – flashing parts/bright colours
- Colour blindness – colour choices
- Stress/frustration – unnecessary steps/instructions/ illogical designs/inconsistency of designs/not intuitive

Analysis

Problem Identification

Client-User-Audience

Requirements analysis

Investigation techniques

Inputs

Processes

Outputs

Design

Design techniques and tools

Planning

Data capture form design

Verification

Validation

Process design

Output screens/reports design

Third-party implementation

Selection of input, output and storage devices

Characteristics of methods of input and output

Appropriate situations for each method

Devices and media for each method

Limitations of devices and media

Why data is stored for future use

Location of stored data

Characteristics of storage devices

Appropriate contexts for each media type

Devices needed for reading or writing data to the storage media

Limitations of current devices and media

Selection of software

Concept of software

Function of software

Systems software – role and functions

Application software – role and function

Appropriate used of currently available application software

Implementation and testing of ICT-related solutions

Steps in producing a solution

Technical documentation

User documentation

Test planning

- strategy
- item testing
- functional testing
- user testing
- normal, erroneous and extreme (boundary) data
- expected results

Test execution

Test reporting

Error-handling/re-testing

Test reviewing

Evaluating solutions

Re-visiting user requirements/evaluation criteria

- Does the solution produce what is required?
- Does it work how it was supposed to?
- Is the solution effective?
- What improvements could be made?

ExamCafé

Relax, refresh, result!

Relax and prepare

What other students wish they had known before the exam...

Hot tips

Jamie

"I didn't know not to use brand names at first and perhaps I could have done more reading."

Shaheen

"I prepared really well and did all the reading but made the silly mistake of not reading the questions properly in the exam. I could have easily got more marks otherwise. I'll be careful not to miss simple marks in the future."

Lizzie

"I was ill when they did the advanced features of word processors and although my teacher gave me the exercises to do to catch up, I didn't bother. I should have gone over all my basic skills first when I started revising."

How can you learn from Jamie's, Shaheen's and Lizzie's comments as you prepare for your AS exam? What do you need to do differently?

Getting started...

What's so different about AS?

It is harder than GCSE: You might find yourself tempted to put in minimal effort, particularly if you did OK in your GCSEs without revising.

It is not a memory test: Whilst you will need to remember a lot of information, the exams are testing whether you can apply the relevant information in answering the question.

It requires longer answers: The questions are of an essay style and, although you could give quite brief answers to some of them, you will not fully answer the question (and hence get good marks) unless you give an extended, detailed response.

Refresh your memory

Revision checklist

Use the following checklist and refer back to pages 63–65 to remind yourself of the sections within the following main topics; check them off when you've refreshed your memory on them. Use the Exam Café CD-ROM for a bigger checklist.

- [ ] Health and safety
- [ ] Analysis
- [ ] Design
- [ ] Selection of input, output and storage devices
- [ ] Selection of software
- [ ] Implementation and testing of ICT-related solutions
- [ ] Evaluating solutions

Common mistakes

▷ If the question asks anything about a 'difference' make sure you state both sides of any point made. For example, if talking about volume, explain the difference between choosing a floppy disk, which has a small volume that might take one large text file or a few small text files, and a CD-ROM, which has a larger volume that will take large multimedia files or a photo album with at least a hundred images.

▷ The terms 'Give', 'State' and 'Name' normally require a few words or a short phrase to get the mark, but watch out for the question asking for 'a use of' or 'a reason for' which means more marks are available. Make sure your answer addresses what is asked for, rathe than merely saying what it means.

Get the result!

Here, the students have each attempted an exam question, and the examiner has marked them.

Model answers

Exam question

Explain a function in a word-processing package that you would use to carry out the following tasks:

a) Writing a personalised letter to be sent to all customers of a travel firm confirming their holiday dates. (2 marks)
b) Putting together a holiday itinerary for a customer embarking on a round the world trip, showing dates, flight numbers, airports, arrival and departure times. (2 marks)
c) Making sure that a draft contract cannot be copied and used for illegal purposes. (2 marks)

Examiner says:

a) It doesn't look as though Lizzie has actually used many of the functions and facilities in a word-processing package. She hasn't heard of the mail merge function.

b) Using columns is one way of setting up a tabular list like this, but the whole page would have to be set up in these columns, which might be awkward if the itinerary does not take up a whole page and there is further information that needs to be written on it. However, columns are a function, so she might gain the 2 points for this answer.

c) This is not a good answer, as it is easy to delete the word Draft with correction fluid. Making some details wrong would make it difficult for the recipient to check the details.

Student answer (Lizzie)

a) You could write the first letter and use overtype of each separate part that is different for the remaining ones.

b) You could use 6 different columns on a page, the first for date, the second for flight numbers and so on. You can put lines between the columns.

c) You could put a big title that says Draft and make sure that not all the details are right.

Examiner's tips

Make sure your sample work is clearly laid out, so you will not have to read through every page to find where your answer is. The recommendation is that there are no more than about 20 pages of work in the sample work, just enough evidence to show that you have covered the required items, which are:

- a problem identification with a list of requirements for that problem, interpretation of those requirements as input, processing and output

- a test plan and clearly annotated samples of testing evidence cross-referenced to the plan.

Student answer (Enzo)

a) Mail merge could be used – the name, address, booking details could be set up in a database and merged into a letter that has merge fields embedded. The travel company may already have a database system set up with these details in it, although it can be done in a spreadsheet package or even in the word-processing package itself. This way all the outstanding letters can be merged and printed in one go. You can even make up envelope labels using the same database.

b) A table is the easiest way to set up tabular data for the itinerary. This way, each column in the table has similar data in it and each row is for one step on their journey. The first row should contain titles for each column, and by choosing to repeat the heading row, if the itinerary goes over a page, the heading rows will appear again.

c) One way to make sure that it is hard to copy or use a draft document is to put a watermark on the document. You do this by adding something, e.g. a picture or word art text, into the header, and it will then show on every page in the document. In this case, the word DRAFT could be made up in word art and stretched to fill the page corner to corner. Sometimes you have to adjust the colour so it does not drown out the words on top.

Examiner says:

Enzo has shown that he fully understands different capabilities of functions in word-processing. He has made sensible suggestions for all 3 tasks and explained them clearly. He has scored the maximum 6 marks.

Examiner's tips

There is one section of this exam paper that requires you to use the sample work that you have done during your studying of the section. If you haven't done it before, please number every page from front to back. The questions ask for page references to highlight specific points and you also have to write on the sample work at that page stating which question and part number it is demonstrating.

AS Section 2

Living in the Digital World

This is essentially a theory section that is assessed by a one-and-a-half-hour examination. Living in the digital world affects everyone, and this fact is frequently taken for granted. There are numerous issues arising from the use of ICT for individuals, society and organisations. The issues change rapidly and, as ICT use becomes more and more widespread, these often involve environmental and ethical aspects.

The section is designed to help you to understand the basic terms and concepts involved in the study of ICT, and to give a wider picture of the use of ICT. By the end of this section, you should be able to discuss and comment on issues from a position of knowledge. You should be able to query whether using ICT in a particular instance is necessary or appropriate, what the implications are now and in the future, and how it affects society.

The use of ICT topic areas cover the differing uses of ICT in many diverse areas and situations; there is ample opportunity to investigate and experience practically a wide range of examples of the uses of ICT.

Having already studied Section 1, you should be aware of a wide range of hardware, software and communications technology. Using imaginative teaching and learning, an appreciation of the practical applications of living in the digital world with ICT can be gained. Ideally this could be achieved by actually visiting and observing different examples of ICT use by businesses, commercial organisations and individuals. If it is not possible to plan actual visits, then by using the case studies included, arranging visiting speakers, and employing directed research, the required fundamental understanding can be gained.

The section covers:

- base knowledge about ICT and ICT systems
- the people involved with ICT
- transferring data across networks
- the safety and security of data in ICT systems and legislation involved in holding and processing data
- backing up and recovering data after loss
- using ICT in:
  - Education
  - Banking
  - Retail
  - Health Care
  - Industry
  - Publishing
- what ICT can provide.

There are practice exam questions after each section. The second Exam Café again has teacher and examiner advice, and some example exam questions and answers, with comments as to the standard of the answers given.

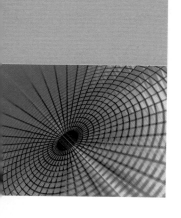

2.1 An ICT system and its components

What is ICT?

ICT is the use of technology for the **input**, **storage**, **processing** and **output** of information.

Input

Input is any method of entering data into a system. Input methods can be manual or automatic. Manual methods include the use of a keyboard, a scanning device, a mouse-click, a touch-screen and a microphone. Automatic methods include electronic file exchange and downloading from other sources, for instance a digital camera.

Storage

Storage is any method of holding data either temporarily or permanently; for instance, random access memory (RAM) is temporary storage, whereas a hard drive, DVD-ROM or pen drive is permanent storage. Permanent storage holds the data when the computer is switched off.

Processing

Processing is the element of ICT that turns the input data (whether directly input or from storage) into the output information by performing some calculation or manipulation.

Output

Output is when the processed data is formed into meaningful information. It can be produced in many ways, including hardcopy (printed), softcopy (on an electronic device) or through speakers.

The same data can be processed in many different ways, using different output formats to produce information that is meaningful to different recipients. For instance, a shelf stacker in a supermarket may have a printed list showing them exactly what products, and how many, need to be put on a particular shelf. A warehouse manager would need to see how many of a particular product needs reordering, but this information may come up on-screen before being converted into an electronic file to send direct to a supplier.

What is a system?

A system consists of input, processing and output. Data is input and then manipulated and organised to produce information, which is output.

System flowchart

A system does not have to be ICT-based to be categorised as a system. A system is defined by the output required by the user of the system.

For instance, suppose a cake is the required output.

The inputs to the cake-producing process are the raw ingredients – flour, eggs, butter and sugar.

The process is the mixing of these ingredients together and then baking the resultant mix in the oven for a known time. Filling and icing may be added.

The output is a ready-to-eat cake.

What is an ICT system?

An ICT system works on the same theoretical principles as any non-ICT system, the only difference being that it makes use of technology and that the output from an ICT system goes directly to either a human being or another ICT system.

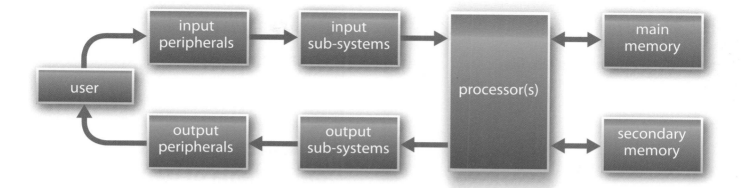

An ICT system with human input

ICT systems are all around us and are used constantly in our everyday life, from the diary and organiser functions on a mobile phone, to the systems that register attendance at school, to the banking systems involved when taking out money from an account, to the passport and driving licence application systems.

ICT system

An ICT system is defined as a complete set of components – hardware, software, peripherals, power supplies and communication links – that makes up a computer installation, with the addition of the data that is input, the information that is output, the procedures that it uses to process and the people that are involved.

Management of curriculum options at GCSE and A level

Organisation Name: Skinners' Secondary School

Size of Organisation: 501 to 1,000

Budget: £101 to £500

Brief description of the project

This secondary school is moving gradually to make greater use of ICT in gathering and handling pupil data. As a further step it wishes to capture the choices of pupils at GCSE and A level electronically as part of a review of its current process for managing curriculum options. This should also allow the data to be used electronically for timetabling, assessment and examination entries.

The school is employing a copy typist for 60 hours as a one-off exercise to enter all the pupils' options, forms and set lists into an appropriate database.

Data can then be manipulated electronically to assist timetabling, assessment and examinations administration. In future years the task will be undertaken by existing administrative staff within the school.

Outcomes of the project

The new approach will relieve the deputy head teacher of a significant burden and make the data more readily available to teachers and administrative staff involved in other activities. It will also reduce the amount of time used in re-entering data for assessment, timetabling and examinations purposes.

Much of the input to this process falls either prior to, or in, the first half-term of the school year. The deputy head has estimated that his own input in constructing timetabling 'option blocks' will reduce from 15–20 hours to one hour per year. Introduction of the database will cut the administrative input from 15–20 hours to 5–6 hours per year.

A link to this website is available at www.heinemann.co.uk/hotlinks (express code 2349P)

ICT systems in daily life

Make a list of 3–5 ICT systems with which you come into contact on a daily basis. For each system, identify:

- one item of data that is input, and who is involved
- one process that happens to the data
- one piece of information that is output, and who receives it.

CAF ICT systems

Make a list of how people are involved with the CAF ICT systems in the case study below and what elements of the system are particularly relevant to the staff of the organisation.

Components of an ICT system

People are the most important part of an ICT system. Without them there would be no point in having a system. ICT systems are used for people and by people.

Contact a Family

What does 'Contact a Family' do?

Contact a Family is a UK-wide charity whose primary aim is to reach the parents of all disabled children – no matter what their child's health condition. They provide general advice, information and support and also enable parents to get in contact with other families, both on a local and national basis, either through their helpline or a new secure web-based service (http://www.makingcontact.org).

How does 'Contact a Family' use ICT?

Contact a Family allocated £50,000 to update and develop the organisation's ICT systems. The main aims were to:

- ensure the computers at Contact a Family had productivity software, email, web-browsing and facilities to share internal information related to CAF

- introduce a new version of their database which would give staff access to accurate information for dealing with external enquiries. This would include information relating to services, support groups, other organisations and medical conditions, which were to be included in a hierarchical structure to ensure statistical and contact information was properly structured. Statistical information about enquiries to the charity also needed to be stored and managed

- improve the organisation's intranet to fulfil requirements such as displaying in/out status of staff, room booking and a diary sheet showing free/busy status in advance, but not the exact contents of people's office schedules.

An integration of the internal information sharing requirements, via an intranet, with the medical conditions database was proposed. To make this as effective as possible, a web-enabled solution was discussed as this had a number of advantages which included:

- minimal learning curve for users as people were generally familiar with a browser and website forms, rather than learning a new interface

- single login for the intranet and database, to make it accessible remotely without the need for a Virtual Private Network (VPN).

What difference has ICT made?

At Contact a Family ICT is now seen to be reliable, and has been central in the expansion of Contact a Family's services and methods of delivery.

A link to this website is available at www.heinemann.co.uk/hotlinks (express code 2349P)

People specify what is required, and use the information output from a system. People are involved in creating or collecting and, in some cases, entering the data that is input. They are involved in developing the software, building the hardware that makes up a system, and in testing and interacting with it.

Data is collected from various sources, or is created using a procedure and is then coded and structured for subsequent processing by an ICT system.

The **procedures** make up an important part of the ICT system. Procedures are used in the collection and input of data, control of the organisation, manipulation and distribution of the output information, and are specified and used by the people involved in the ICT system.

Software is required to interface between the **hardware** and the humans that use the ICT system. An ICT system is not complete without this interaction. There is **systems software** to operate the hardware at the functional level, **communications software** to enable use of external links and **applications software** to perform specific ICT tasks (see Section 1 for more details).

Software
Software is all the programs that make up an ICT system and the data held within it.

Systems software
Systems software can include the operating system, which controls how the ICT system's hardware components work together, software to protect the system from outside attack, for example, firewall and anti-virus software, peripheral driver software to enable the various hardware components to 'talk' to the processor and software to organise and control file usage.

Communications software
Communications software can include electronic mail, network connection software, browser software and search engine software.

Applications software
Applications software can include general packages for text, number, image and sound manipulation, as well as software that is written for a specific purpose, such as accounting software or stock control.

Hardware
Hardware is all the physical components that make up the computer system that the ICT system is based upon. It consists of the processors that perform the manipulations and obey control instructions from the software, storage devices and input and output peripherals, including communications devices and communication media (see Section 1 for more details).

CPU
The processor, or central processing unit (CPU), is an integrated circuit which consists of an instruction set, a control unit that manages the execution of instructions and a set of registers which are used whilst processing instructions, either for controlling the order of instructions or for holding results of calculations.

USAID Famine Early Warning System Project

USAID's Famine Early Warning System (FEWS) is an electronic information system designed to help decision makers prevent famine in Sub-Saharan Africa. FEWS specialists in the US and Africa assess remotely sensed data and ground-based meteorological, crop, and range of conditions for early indications of potential famine areas. Other factors affecting local food availability and access are also carefully evaluated to identify vulnerable population groups requiring assistance. These assessments are continuously updated and electronically disseminated to provide decision makers with the most timely and accurate information available.

A link to this website is available at www.heinemann.co.uk/hotlinks (express code 2349P)

Early warning systems
In a group, discuss the implications of not having a system such as FEWS in place, in terms of timely availability of the information required. Think about how other ICT systems might help in trans-world projects such as this one.

Storage devices include both internal and external devices. **Main memory**, held alongside the **CPU**, is used for holding programs currently being run and data currently being used in the ICT system, and is termed volatile – i.e. the programs and data will be wiped if the power supply is switched off. **Auxiliary memory** is for long-term storage and data will remain until it is deleted and overwritten by other data. Hard drive capacities are now measured in gigabytes on personal computer systems. There are many external storage devices for storing and transporting data, from those that hold a megabyte of data to those that can hold many gigabytes.

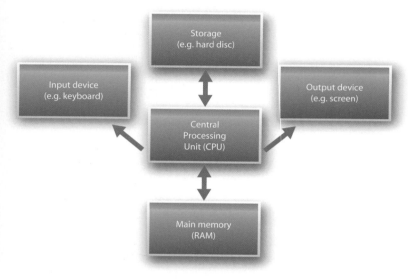

A PC system

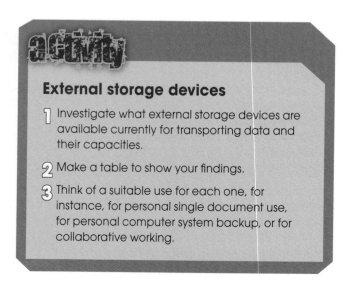

External storage devices

1. Investigate what external storage devices are available currently for transporting data and their capacities.

2. Make a table to show your findings.

3. Think of a suitable use for each one, for instance, for personal single document use, for personal computer system backup, or for collaborative working.

Input, output and communications devices, also known as **peripheral devices**, are those items of hardware that enable data and information to enter and exit the ICT system, and are the methods that provide the human–computer dialogue.

External storage devices

Information is the output from an ICT system. This can take many forms and formats and will be distributed to various recipients using a variety of methods. Information distributed to a human recipient from an ICT system can be visual or aural.

Data and information

Raw facts and figures are the data that is entered into a computer system. Data items, such as Name, Address, Date of Birth and so on are collected from a **data source**.

Related data items will be collected in a **data file** or **data store**.

Data files can consist of text data, numeric data, a mixture of text and numeric data (known as alphanumeric data), sound data or image (still or moving) data. In reality, all that is held is a series of 0s and 1s, which is what a digital computer recognises; however, the format of the data file will be known to the computer system, as the file will be encoded as one of these formats of data.

To the ICT system user, some data file types can be recognised by their file extension.

Type or format	File contents	Example extensions
Alphanumeric	Numbers, letters and other keyboard characters	.txt, .doc, .htm
Numeric	Binary, integer, currency and date	There are no numeric-only file extensions
Audio	Sounds and noises	.mp3, .wav
Image	Graphics, photos and other images	.jpg, .gif, .bmp
Video	Moving pictures, graphics and images, often combined with sound	.avi, .wmv, .pps

File formats

Some extensions indicate that files could be of mixed data types, such as .pdf, .xls and .mdb.

Data files can be processed through a computer program and, without the data items being changed in any way, can be presented as information. For instance, a list of member details for a club of any kind might not change any of the data as it is held, but it may be presented in alphabetical order of surname. Thus, each individual item has not been changed or manipulated, but the data file has – it has been sorted so that the output report is in the sequence required.

Sorting data in a spreadsheet

Another way of using such input data to produce information is to perform calculations using one or more of the data items. For instance, the same member report may need, instead of the date of birth of each member, their age at a particular date to be output. The process would take the 'date of birth' field, subtract it from the required date and calculate the age of the member. This result would then be included on the output report.

Data is derived from different sources, both within (or directly for) the organisation, or outside (or indirectly for) the organisation.

For instance, at the point of sale in a shop, direct data input includes the barcode reader used to scan the barcode into the system, and the card reader through which customer's credit or debit card is swiped. Any automatic data entry, such as at an Automatic Teller Machine (ATM) to get cash, a system for handling cheques or a multiple-choice exam paper, is also classed as a direct data source.

Indirect data is derived from other places, for instance, from a questionnaire filled in by market researchers, being transferred from a form by a keyboard operator entering the data onto a system. Phone orders into mail-order firms, where a customer service operator listens to details and types them into an on-screen application are indirect.

Either way, data needs to be encoded in the correct format on input, so that the ICT system knows what the data file contains. To ensure that the data has been correctly input, various techniques, such as verification and validation, must be employed. These are described in Section 1.

Some data merely represents the data item. This is termed the coding of data. This is often employed when categorising answers on a questionnaire, for instance. Ages may be put into bands, where it is assumed that all people in an age group, say 30–49, are comparable; qualitative answers to questions that are based on subjective opinion may be coded 1–5 (for strongly disagree to strongly agree) and so on. This approach to recording of data is not wholly accurate as, for instance, the opinions that are in between the numbers are not represented.

In order for useful information to be derived from the data that is held in an ICT system, various processes must be performed.

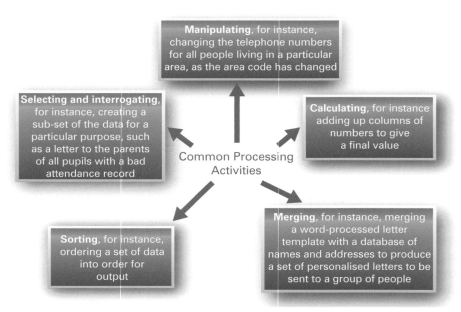

Manipulating, for instance, changing the telephone numbers for all people living in a particular area, as the area code has changed

Selecting and interrogating, for instance, creating a sub-set of the data for a particular purpose, such as a letter to the parents of all pupils with a bad attendance record

Common Processing Activities

Calculating, for instance adding up columns of numbers to give a final value

Sorting, for instance, ordering a set of data into order for output

Merging, for instance, merging a word-processed letter template with a database of names and addresses to produce a set of personalised letters to be sent to a group of people

Common processing activities

After processing, the data might require further refinements in order to become useful to the recipient.

Conversion may be required to change a code back to a narrative form on an output screen or report, so that rather than reporting the age as Band 2 or 3, the output would read 21–29 or 30–49. Numeric data may need converting into graphical format for inclusion in a formal report. An image file may need converting to a different file type to reduce its size, so that it can be used in a newsletter where there is a file size limit.

Editing the data may be another necessary refinement. Images may need to be changed or cropped, or the colour amended. Sounds may need another track adding. Images are sometimes airbrushed. It may be decided that only the initial letter of a forename will be printed on a report, rather than the whole field, for space reasons.

Information, therefore, is processed, converted, edited data. Information has a purpose and it is important that that purpose has been well defined so that it is the right data that has been included to make the information presented useful to the recipient.

Information can be presented visually, written on paper (hardcopy) or on-screen, from an automated presentation to a live web-chat; aurally, using speakers (music or multi-media style presentation), or using a communication system such as Skype; or using sensory outputs, such as applications designed for disabled users.

Information can be categorised in terms of its purpose and use. For example, it could be general information, common to a number of people, users or systems, or it could be specialist information, unique to particular people, users or systems.

To be useful, information has to have particular qualities to serve its purpose. It needs to be:

- complete – everything that needs to be included, has been
- up-to-date – for example, if looking at the sales figures for the first quarter, then all figures from January, February and March must be present
- accurate – if dealing with numerical data, then the figures given are accurate to within a particular tolerance (for a bank this may be to a fraction of a

penny; for a manufacturing organisation producing screws, this may be to the nearest thousand – it all depends on the situation exactly what 'accurate' means)

- relevant – the information presented must all be useful to the overall purpose
- reliable – it must have come from a verified source, either from another internal system or by a verified route into the organisation
- in the right format for use by the intended recipient, whether that is listed, prose, presented, visual or aural
- delivered at the right time – by arrangement or procedure, there will be a set time for a particular output to arrive with the intended recipient. If this is met, then the organisation will continue to run smoothly with all required detail to hand
- delivered to the right person – for instance, suppose the chief accountant needs records of all sales and receipts, promptly at the end of each month, or the head receptionist needs the daily menu from the chef by 7.45 each morning so she can print it and display it on her desk by 8.00 every day.

activity

Prevention of good quality characteristics

1 In groups of two, list things that might occur to prevent each of the above list of good quality characteristics. Try to think of more than one for each quality.

2 Compare your list with that of another group. See if you can think of anything else that is important for information.

3 As a class, review your lists.

Practice exam questions

1. Every ICT task involves the input of data, which is processed and then information is output.
   Using an example of an ICT task with which you are familiar:
   (a) state what the task is (1)
   (b) give **one** example of data that is input, stating how it is input (2)
   (c) describe **one** process needed to fulfil the task (2)
   (d) give **one** example of information that is output, stating how it is output. (2)
   AQA June 2006

2. Name, and give an example of, **three** characteristics of information that give it value and importance. (6)
   AQA Jan 2006

3. Explain, using examples, what is meant by each of the following terms:
   (a) data (2)
   (b) information. (2)
   AQA Jan 2006

4. An accountant calculates an organisation's profit and loss based upon financial information from many sources.
   Name **three** characteristics that this information must have to be described as good information for the accountant and, for each characteristic, state why it is necessary. (6)
   AQA June 2006

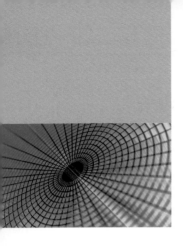

2.2 People and ICT systems

An organisation that neglects to adequately fund IT provisions may find itself using inappropriate software on obsolete hardware on a poorly maintained network prone to attack from hackers and viruses. Not every company will be able to purchase the latest and most exciting IT equipment and software, but those who understand the potential of IT within their business are able to safely utilise the equipment they can afford.

The benefits derived from astute planning and careful use of IT resources may result in better productivity, fewer expenses and less waste, which could provide the opportunity to upgrade IT provisions.

Systems that do not have full support and appreciation from senior management are those most likely to become less efficient. It is senior management's responsibility to allocate funding and personnel to ensure that the current IT system supports the daily and long term objectives of the business.

The components of a computer system must be carefully designed and forged together to ensure that they are operable by humans. Computer systems consist of hardware, software and data that is input, processed, then output or stored. If any element is not carefully considered before, during and after implementation, the system may throw up deficiencies and not be fit for purpose.

Small firms with limited financial resources may opt to develop their own systems to save money. This can be achieved if the requirements are simple and they have enough in-house skill. Larger firms with complex business dealings and a range of departments require specialists to develop and run the whole corporate IT infrastructure. The initial system installed and approved is only the beginning as constant performance demands are made and improvements sought to give a competitive edge over rivals.

Companies may desire a system that can reduce its lead production time of a major commercial product whilst others may want a system that enhances the presentation of its documents. There will be companies who want to improve data exchange between international offices and to improve direct communications.

Characteristics of users

Simple input devices attached to some form of visual and hardcopy output operate most ICT systems. Cashiers' tills use barcode readers, a screen displays the products purchased and a printed receipt is generated. Details of the entire purchase and payment are stored and linked to other systems, which allows for future data interrogation and stock control.

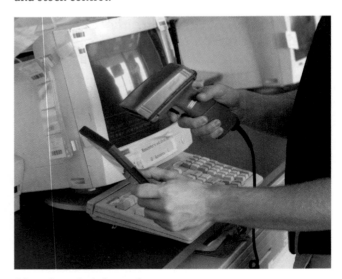

A barcode reader being used

Often organisations who may not have their own specific system development department may commission an outside firm or software house to develop software to suit their particular needs.

The type of business and its operational goals will determine the type of system they require and who their users will be. An international accountancy firm will have different requirements to those requested by a warehouse that specialises in construction material. Budget and time-scale for development will also be considered before decisions are made.

There will be a range of organisational users. Managers may use a system to supply statistics and managerial and operational information from within the organisation and from external sources, enabling effective decision-making. Tactical staff will use the information from ICT systems for planning and control purposes. 'Everyday' users will also use the ICT system as part of their job, either in an operational sense or a tactical way.

Teleworking

Teleworking is becoming more and more common. It involves employees using IT to work from home or away from the actual physical workplace. Technology allows documented work to be emailed direct to an office. Video conferencing means that staff across the world can hold meetings from their homes and achieve the same level of productivity as if they are all in the same room. Teleworking gives the workforce greater flexibility, enabling them to plan their work routines around family commitments. In addition, they do not have to make expensive commutes to the office and they can customise their working environment to suit their needs.

Teleworking

Discuss the advantages and disadvantages to individuals, organisations and society of an increase in teleworking. This work should be presented as an essay of up to 1000 words. Include a front cover, relevant sub-headings and reference all sources.

There is no template to describe the type of user found in the ICT industry, largely due to the scope of tasks that are undertaken. There will be basic users who check their email on a regular basis and use application software in a general way to support administrative tasks. Others will use the capabilities of the Internet to assist with research, while many use technology for buying and selling things. Some people will need equipment which provides mobile functionality so that they can perform tasks away from a central base. There will be those who are tasked with simple data entry, and those who bring together a range of data and information for presentations. Most of these activities are supported by the programmers, who have further differing needs.

Video conferencing from home

Ace Beverage

'We tried to get all our orders in by 6 p.m. each night, and the trucks started rolling out of the warehouse about 5 a.m. the next morning,' explained Mike Krohn, vice president of finance and administration at Ace Beverage, a major Anheuser-Busch distributor. 'That gave us 11 hours to dispatch and load the trucks. If it's a heavy night and you have hiccups, you end up incurring overtime in the warehouse. If it's a bad hiccup, your drivers get started late and you start incurring overtime with the drivers as well. It has a snowball effect…'

The first step was to provide its pre-sales force with new tools to reduce the time it took to send orders from the field to the warehouse and load delivery trucks, as well as to maintain searchable electronic records.

MiT Systems' EzSales, a field-force automation and customer relationship management (CRM) software solution, was chosen. MiT recommended Intermec Technologies' Windows-based mobile pen tablets as the hardware of choice, AT&T VPN (virtual private network) and Sierra Wireless Air Card to build a wireless data system that could communicate real-time throughout the day.

Ace Beverage chose to equip its 11 chain store pre-sales reps with Intermec mobile pen tablets. 'Now, basically every hour or so the pre-sales rep can tap the upload key on the Intermec mobile computer screen and we start getting data,' Krohn said. 'We ask our reps to start sending in data by 10 a.m. and finish sending by 4 p.m.

'With the wireless system, when orders are in house by 2 p.m., we can start building loads by stops and we have a tremendous jump on our loading process,' Krohn said. 'We can start preparing loads early by picking the products from the warehouse inventory and staging them without loading them on to the trucks.

'For us, one of the major benefits it's accomplished is that we're not running into overtime,' he said. 'This system eliminates the problem before it happens. Right now, we estimate the mobile computers, wireless system and software are saving us 15 to 20 hours in driver and loading overtime each week. Additionally, we are expecting a cost saving of approximately $50,000 for warehouse equipment we didn't have to buy.'

At this point, the rep can send the order from his mobile computer wirelessly over the wide area network to the sales order server in seconds. It is quick, because the mobile computer is sending only a condensed file, not an entire set of database records.

'With the computer, you key in data once and the office never has to re-key the order,' Krohn said. 'It saves a lot of time on the administrative side as well. From the sales rep's point of view, it saves him time because it's a lot faster to put data into the computer once. Plus you have much more information on the mobile computer. It is unlimited as to how far back the reps can go for sales and inventory information.'

A link to this website is available at www.heinemann.co.uk/hotlinks (express code 2349P)

How users interact with ICT systems

New hardware and software is introduced to the market every day. Carelessly buying what looks appealing is not the best way to introduce an ICT system. When making additions to a system, you must consider how the changes or upgrades will affect the people that are to interact with it. When asked to use a new system the users will want it to be intuitive. They will want to be able to work out how to operate hardware and software. Turning the machine on and loading the correct software may sound straightforward, but if the users' needs have not been considered, the designers and producers of a system may have missed simple and important details. How to print, save, transfer data, draw a box, spell check, change the screen resolution or turn up the volume may all be necessary requirements and it may frustrate a user if such facilities are hard to find.

A system must be user friendly. People who work with the front end of software do not want to be hindered by having to learn and use complex programming language. They will want to be able to click or press recognisable icons. They will be keen to complete repetitive tasks without having to

The Wii console

The price includes one wireless Wii Remote controller, one Nunchuk™ controller and the groundbreaking collection of five different Wii Sports games on one disc, which anyone can play using simple movements, experienced or not.

Every Wii console includes another distinctive feature: a series of on-screen 'channels' that make up the Wii Channel Menu, which makes the console approachable and customisable for everyone, from the most avid gamer to people who have never played before. The Wii Channel Menu is the starting point for all of the console's functions. The 'channels' offer a gateway to a rich variety of entertainment options. When connected to a TV, the Wii Channel Menu offers a simple interface, letting users pick games to play, get news or weather, view and send photos or even create playable caricatures of themselves to use in actual games. Additional

functions allow users to redeem Wii Points and download classic games to Wii's Virtual Console™. The variety of options available through the Wii Channel Menu motivates both gamers and non-gamers to turn on Wii's power every day.

Wii is creating worldwide excitement with its unique control system, an inventive, first-of-its-kind controller whose position can be detected in a 3-D space. The new controller allows users to pinpoint targets in games or move through the Wii Channel Menu with precision and ease. This intuitive control system will be understood immediately by everyone, regardless of their previous experience with video games. With this one small controller, Wii makes games both easier and more intense than anything previously experienced. For example, in the Wii Sports tennis game, players swing the Wii Remote like a racket to hit the ball, as in real life. They can add topspin or slice the ball just by angling their hands and wrist like they would in a real match.

A link to this website is available at www.heinemann.co.uk/hotlinks (express code 2349P)

---

ask for help or falling into a state of confusion. The screen layout should be logical and familiar. People become anxious in unfamiliar environments and this may be true when they are presented with a new working environment such as a strange-looking desktop or hardware with slots and wires that have no obvious purpose. The ability to customise the system to suit the user can be important. Having the ability to alter the look and layout of software is desirable to some users and helps them to personalise their work area.

Help and support are key attributes of a system. The amount of investment could reach several millions of pounds – this will have been fruitlessly spent if the full capabilities of the system are not explored and utilised. Frustration tends to build when users feel lost within a system and a good support system, be it online or over the telephone, is crucial for ironing out teething problems. Meaningful error messages, a 'frequently asked questions' (FAQ) resource and appropriate human support are key features to integrating a successful system.

Users of any system will want it to perform tasks that are specifically related to what they do. By highlighting the exact requirements of a system, a company is more likely to find a product that suits and supports all the needs of the workforce. Trying to make additions to a system after it has been installed could be costly and may even render the original solution useless. The users of a system will expect it to be robust. In some cases it should be able to handle several open applications at once, allow for mass data transfer, automatic backup, VoIP and the use of multimedia tools all at the same time. Extras built into systems might represent unnecessary added cost and can be avoided by thoroughly investigating what is required. The extra cost of producing a complex system could prove worthwhile if productivity and profit figures rise. The method of interaction will also need to be considered.

How data is input into the system is a consideration as the fastest and most accurate method will be desirable. Optical character recognition (OCR) and barcode readers may appeal to some companies who have data that can

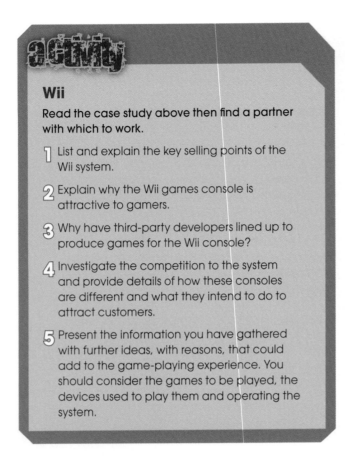

activity

Wii

Read the case study above then find a partner with which to work.

1 List and explain the key selling points of the Wii system.

2 Explain why the Wii games console is attractive to gamers.

3 Why have third-party developers lined up to produce games for the Wii console?

4 Investigate the competition to the system and provide details of how these consoles are different and what they intend to do to attract customers.

5 Present the information you have gathered with further ideas, with reasons, that could add to the game-playing experience. You should consider the games to be played, the devices used to play them and operating the system.

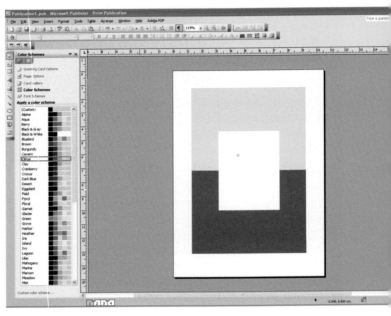

Graphical user interface

be read this way, whilst others may need to use voice recognition technology or simply a keyboard. Some systems are operated by joystick or concept keyboards, depending on the environment.

For example, chemical plants may require workers to wear large gloves, which means a keyboard is not an appropriate option. Other companies may find they rely on their customers to upload data, which shifts the emphasis towards having a simple process to help reduce errors.

User interfaces

To communicate with systems there are several interface options. The command-driven interface relies on the user inputting predefined instructions which carry out specific tasks. The more experienced user is likely to be at ease with such a system as it can be flexible and more logical to use.

Menu-driven interfaces provide users with a set of options to choose from. An example of this can be found in ATMs (cash machines). After you enter your debit card, the screen provides limited options next to buttons.

There is no need to enter any text-based commands or to navigate around the screen to select specific features. Designs of such systems have to ensure that the majority of popular requests are included and that they are presented in a logical and uncluttered fashion.

The **graphical user interface** is the most popular. This is made up of labelled icons, images and folders. It relies on the brain's capacity to interpret images rather than having to learn complex syntax. The Microsoft Windows and Apple Mac operating systems take full advantage of the graphical user interface. Pull-down menus are incorporated to avoid clutter on the screen and simple shortcut keys can be used. Novice users and those who are comfortable using a mouse to navigate would expect their system to be graphical.

A **natural language interface** is similar to those found in search engines, which try to find matches to the key words or phrases that the user has entered. The appeal of a natural language interface is the ability to communicate with a computer system using the same language that is used every day. However, a lot of our language is ambiguous, which means the system might misinterpret requests and so produce unreliable answers. To overcome these limitations, the natural language interpreter's knowledge would have to be vast in order to match the expectations of its users. An exciting development for the natural language enthusiast is the opportunity to control the system by voice rather than keyboard entry. Improvements in voice recognition technology have made this a real possibility.

Investigating user needs and experience

1. Select an adult who you know works with or uses a computer as part of their occupation – provide their name, where they work and a description of their job.

2. What data and information do they use to perform their job? Give some non-confidential examples, such as customer names, share prices, or car dealer addresses.

3. How do they obtain their data? Where does it come from? What source? Do they buy it from somewhere? Do they generate it themselves, and if so how?

4. How do they know their information is accurate? What do they do to ensure its integrity?

5. Provide details of any software they use. Do they use specialist packages or common products like those found at school? If so, what for?

6. What benefits have they found from using a computer to perform their job?

7. What problems would they have performing their job if they didn't have a computer for a week?

8. Is there anything they would want the computer or software to do which it currently does not? Do they know why this limitation exists?

9. Do they use ICT to communicate overseas? If so, what advantages has this given, if any?

10. What other technology do they use to perform their task and what do they use it for? (For example, PDA, mobile phone, fax or teleconferencing.)

11. What skills do they think they have or need to work productively with ICT?

12. Present your findings to your class using a suitable method.

The needs and experience of the users must be investigated. The system will have to be flexible to accommodate a wide range of skills and uses. Technical staff, clerical workers, senior management and shop-floor workers will have different needs and will all need the system to support their daily and long-term plans. A system that is too complex may limit novice users, whilst a simple system may be frustrating for advanced users. Individual jobs and tasks should be audited to help formulate a system that suits the majority and can be developed and adapted in the future.

Working in ICT

There are many qualities required to work successfully within the IT industry. The range and variety of positions have steadily grown to fill the void left by the decline in the manufacturing sector. Jobs that require competent users of specialist software and jobs that require people to develop software all fall under this umbrella.

There is a distinct difference between those who understand and deploy code to make functioning software and those who use it in their everyday work. Those who are engaged with software development, network maintenance and technical aspects are said to represent the **skills-driven** computer sector. The **task-driven** element of ICT represents those who use IT systems on a daily basis because it is a requirement of their job and assists them in achieving the aims of the company. These people tend to know less about how software is constructed but have a fine appreciation of the capabilities of a particular system or set of systems that they use in order to complete their jobs successfully.

Although task-driven and skills-driven personnel appear to be poles apart, there are certain characteristics desirable from both types of worker.

At varying levels, the ability to communicate verbally and on paper with clarity is a must. There is a lot of technical jargon used by IT people, who tend to abbreviate job titles, application processes and project names. Uncovering exactly what people are talking about requires great patience and skill.

Someone working on a help desk needs to be wary of using technical vocabulary to someone who has no idea what any of it means. This situation is likely to result in further calls for help rather than a successful first-time assist with a problem.

Verbal communication skills are also important in a project team. For instance, project information may be passed verbally from the system's commissioner to the team and then committed to paper if it is to form a contract. Timescales, budgets and the expectations of each team member have to be carefully and clearly explained to make sure that the project is completed on time and to the expected level of satisfaction. Speaking too fast, with a mixture of technical words and abbreviations, whilst referring to past projects, may cause confusion and hinder progress and does not constitute good communication skills!

Clear documentation will also be required for new support processes or new software. If such documentation is incomprehensible to the intended audience, it will be worthless. Project plans, evaluations and progress reports will also need to be clear and logical.

Being able to train colleagues is important to prospective employers. Technological changes and new system requirements place demands on a workforce that require them to have constantly changing and developing skills. The ability to transfer new information and skill within a firm helps to maintain a competitive knowledge base and ensure that as many staff as possible are comfortable with new initiatives and processes. Having access to staff who can competently train others can save on costs because the need to use an external training source is eradicated.

Due to the competitive nature of the IT industry, there is often a need to target staff who have relevant levels of experience in a particular discipline or hold specific qualifications directly related to certain posts. There are many IT-based courses and qualifications aimed at people working in industry. The probability of one single IT qualification encompassing all the requirements to work in the IT sector is slim.

However, there is such a wide range of tasks and opportunities that specific courses and certificates have been introduced to match the skills required for particular elements. It is possible to gain network management, project management, system development, software maintenance and software security qualifications.

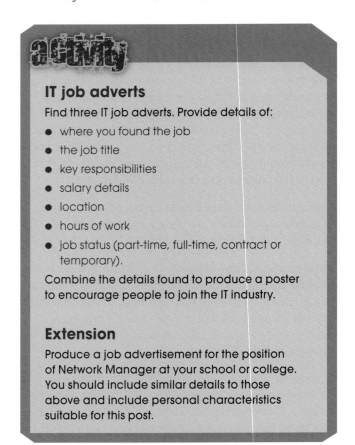

IT job adverts

Find three IT job adverts. Provide details of:

- where you found the job
- the job title
- key responsibilities
- salary details
- location
- hours of work
- job status (part-time, full-time, contract or temporary).

Combine the details found to produce a poster to encourage people to join the IT industry.

Extension

Produce a job advertisement for the position of Network Manager at your school or college. You should include similar details to those above and include personal characteristics suitable for this post.

IT qualification certificates

Potential employers often request qualifications because they provide evidence of an individual's ability and competence within a certain discipline at a specified level.

IT staff should be able to work with a variety of other people. When projects are broken down into teams, the group dynamic has to be productive and cooperative otherwise the project could struggle to meet the deadline, which will affect the budget. When people work in teams it is because they often have specific skills that will help move the project forward. Technical skills are important, and having the right balance of experience should also be considered when constructing a team.

More general traits that IT workers should have include pragmatism, common sense and the ability to take the initiative and solve problems on their own. Dynamic, creative individuals often find ways to solve problems that have not been thought of, or get more out of a current system and people than was originally expected. On the other hand, in certain circumstances, it is important for a team member to have the ability to accurately follow instructions or standards that they may feel are rigid or onerous, for the long-term good of the project.

Those who welcome change and prepare themselves by continually upgrading their skills are those more likely to succeed. By keeping abreast of latest developments and industrial innovations, an individual can transform themselves into a valuable asset and resource. Such value may be rewarded financially, with greater responsibility, or both.

Those in management positions will have to demonstrate experience and leadership. This can take time to accrue but by working on smaller projects over time, experience will be gathered. When someone's career develops, they are able to witness first-hand those who manage well and make good decisions and those who struggle.

The careful observer will be able to draw on their positive experiences and apply good practice when they are given the opportunity. They will need to be able draw up logical plans, assemble teams with a range of skills to cover each aspect of a project, and encourage each team member to perform to their potential.

Teams will be made up of different personalities that may clash. It is the manager's job to ensure such clashes do not interrupt the project and that adequate support is in place to deal with any potential difficulties. The manager

What employers want from graduates

Employers want graduates who have a firm grip on the 'world of work' – according to this year's annual Association of Graduate Recruiters/ Financial Times survey of Britain's top employers.

The results point clearly to the fact that employers' priorities centre on work experience and key skills training such as IT.

Competition for jobs means that employers increasingly looked at CVs for clues to people who were interesting, well-rounded and with experience of leadership and teamwork in the real world.

Maxine Packer, at Logica, the software and computer services company, believes graduates need to exhibit some understanding of how businesses really work, both internally and in the way in which they interface with clients.

'They need an insight into the way businesses actually work – for example, they need to be more pro-active in finding things out and not expect to be spoon-fed,' she said.

Many employers echoed the idea that applicants need to show that they know how the world of work actually operates. Student life alone does not prepare students for dealing with conflict – for example – in teams, or for seeking out information in a hierarchy.

Several employers warn that it is wrong to assume that all work experience is good work experience – especially if the aim is to gain basic life skills. 'They should have an understanding of the transferable skills that are learnt through work experience. You could work for a very good company and learn nothing in terms of transferable skills,' said one.

And then of course there is getting a good grade in your final exams. Despite all this talk about fitting applications to the needs of employers there are still many careers where the first stumbling block is the quality of your degree.

A link to this website is available at www.heinemann.co.uk/hotlinks (express code 2349P)

must control a budget and keep senior personnel informed of the progress their team is making. They will have to do this verbally in the form of a presentation to justify or explain their progress and in report form to maintain accurate records.

Some IT professionals will have access to vast amount of company data, which may include personal details about colleagues. For this reason, IT workers are expected to act ethically. This means they do not abuse the information they have at their disposal and should respect the rights of individuals to not have their personal details made public beyond what is acceptable.

Acceptability of how data should be handled will be detailed in a company's code of conduct or ethical conduct statement. This kind of document clearly states what network and IT users can and cannot do with the information available to them. A breach of the code of conduct or ethical statement may result in the termination of employment or, in extreme cases, legal action.

Practice exam questions

1. Why would the timescale of a project affect the budget?   (2)

2. Professional progression within the IT industry requires more than just technical skills. Give **three** other necessary qualities and explain why they are important.   (6)

3. Professionals involved with ICT systems often have to work with people who have little, or no, understanding of the ICT systems that they are using. Describe **two** personal qualities that IT professionals should have to enable them to help such people effectively, and give an example of when each quality would be needed.   (4)

4. Using a different example for each of the following personal skills, describe why they are important for an IT professional:
    *   written communication skills
    *   listening skills
    *   problem solving skills.   (6)

2.3 Transfer of data in ICT systems

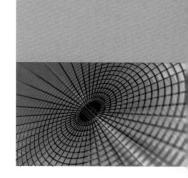

Current and emerging technologies

A local area network (LAN) is a group of computers and associated devices that share a common communications line or wireless link. Typically, connected devices share the resources of a single processor or server within a small geographic area (for example, within an office building). Usually, the server has applications and data storage that are shared in common by multiple computer users. A LAN may serve as few as two or three users (for example, in a home network) or as many as thousands of users (for example, in an multi-campus college or university).

Communication technologies

'Ethernet typically uses coaxial cable, or a special grade of twisted pair wires, and is also available as a wireless network. Most commonly called 10BASE-T, Ethernet provides transmission speeds of up to 10 Mbps (Megabits per second). Fast Ethernet systems are called 100BASE-T and can provide up to 100Mbps transfer speeds. Gigabit and 10Gigabit systems are also emerging, providing fast 'backbone' support to large and traffic-heavy LANs. Collision (of data) sensing and preventing is in-built.

Token Ring networks are where computers are connected in a ring or star topology and a bit- or token-passing scheme is used in order to prevent the collision of data between two computers that want to send messages at the same time. The IEEE 802.5 Token Ring technology provides for data transfer rates of either 4 or 16 megabits per second.

FDDI (Fiber Distributed Data Interface) is a set of standards for data transmission on fiber optic lines in a LAN that can extend in range up to 200 km (124 miles). The FDDI protocol is based on the Token Ring protocol. In addition to being large geographically, an FDDI local area network can support thousands of users. FDDI is frequently used on the backbone for a wide area network (WAN).'

A link to this website is available at www.heinemann.co.uk/hotlinks (express code 2349P)

The main communication technologies associated with LANs are **Ethernet**, **Token Ring** and **FDDI**.

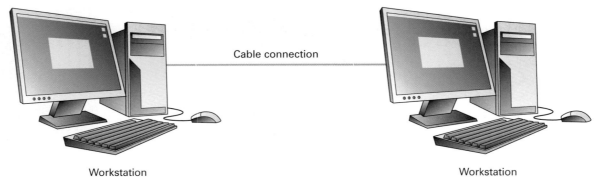

Workstation   Workstation

A simple LAN connection

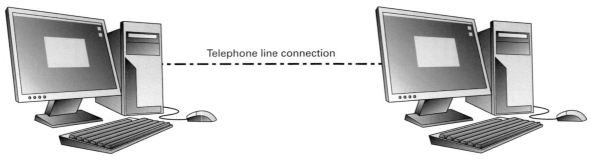

Workstation in London   Workstation in Birmingham

A simple WAN connection

Where LANs are essentially confined geographically to one organisation and, generally, to one site of one organisation, WANs can cover wide geographical distances. An organisation can have its own private WAN, allowing access to its own staff and privileged customers or suppliers; or an organisation, or any individual, can make use of a public WAN. The Internet is such a public network.

To connect to the Internet, and to allow for successful and speedy data transmission, various advances have been made. In the 1980s, it was first widely possible to link remotely to a mainframe using a dedicated telephone line, or a dial-up line, through modems. The technologies emerged to increase speeds from 56Kbps to the installation of digital telephone exchanges in the 1990s and the introduction of ISDN (Integrated Services Digital Network) offering 128Kbps. Cable modems enable the computers, typically fitted with 10BASE-T Ethernet cards, to be hooked up to the TV cable system and offer speeds of up to 1.5Mbps; Digital Subscriber Lines (DSL) and further versions (ADSL, HDSL and RADSL) offer speeds of up to 6.1Mbps, although that depends on the traffic on the system.

Broadband is the term used to describe some of the above technologies, where the bandwidth of the transmission is wider, thus allowing for more data to be passed at a time. However, it is frequently used in a more technical sense to refer to data transmission where multiple pieces of data are sent simultaneously to increase the effective rate of transmission, regardless of the actual data rate. High transmission speeds are required for the new types of data transfer that many modern organisations want to be able to do, for example, video streaming.

Wireless networking refers to any type of network that does not use wires. They are generally implemented with some type of information transmission system that uses electromagnetic waves, such as radio waves. A wireless LAN uses radio waves for data transmission. The Global System for Mobile Communication (GSM) enables cellular (mobile) phones to communicate and send and receive data, and to connect to other networks (typically the Internet). Wi-Fi is the term used when connecting to the Internet or other Wi-Fi enabled devices.

Voice-over Internet Protocol (VoIP) has emerged more recently as a technology that routes voice transmissions over the Internet or other IP-enabled network. This effectively means that an organisation which uses VoIP instead of traditional telephone wires will no longer have an extra phone bill, but will be using capacity on the network connections that they are already using for traditional data transfer.

Network topologies

A network topology is the name given to the ways in which the networks are physically organised in terms of how they are wired together. The descriptions indicate how the devices on the network, the computers, printers, servers and so on are connected to each other.

Bus network

A **bus network** has each of the devices connected directly to a main communications line, called a bus, along which signals are sent. The bus will frequently be a twin cable of some kind, e.g. coaxial cable. There is a terminator at each

New and improved technologies

Every year, new and improved technologies are developed and marketed.

1 Find out more information about **two** of the above technologies.

2 Research the latest communication technologies.

3 Write up a fact file for each.

4 Draw a comparison table showing speeds, uses and availability.

5 Recommend **two** new technologies that you think would benefit your school or college, with reasons.

end of the cable. One or more of the stations on the network acts as a file server and controls the hard disks that are used for all the common resources and the users' files.

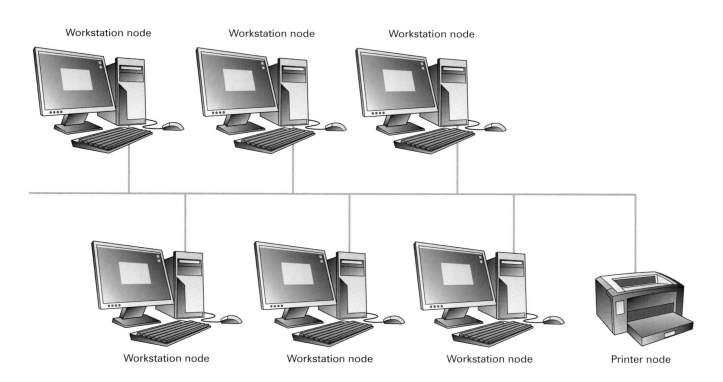

A bus network

The bus network is cheap to operate, for large numbers of computers, as less cable is used. As a result, this topology is popular with business and educational establishments. The attachment of devices is straightforward and the cable can be extended, if necessary, to add additional segments.

Bus networks are not the most reliable of networks. If there is a fault in the network cable then all the machines will be unable to use the network. However, if the fault is with a particular workstation then it simply stops communicating, but the rest of the network can carry on as usual.

Ring network

A **ring network** (peer-to-peer) has each of the devices on the network connected to a ring communications line around which signals are sent. The information is sent around the ring as variable-sized packets of data. In addition to the data, a packet will contain the address of the sender and the destination address. The packet is passed continually around the ring until the receiving node signals that it is ready to accept it. Acceptance of the packet is determined by the destination address, which is examined by each node it passes. If the address matches the node's own address, the node takes the packet; otherwise, the node repeater regenerates the signal to be passed to the next node in the ring.

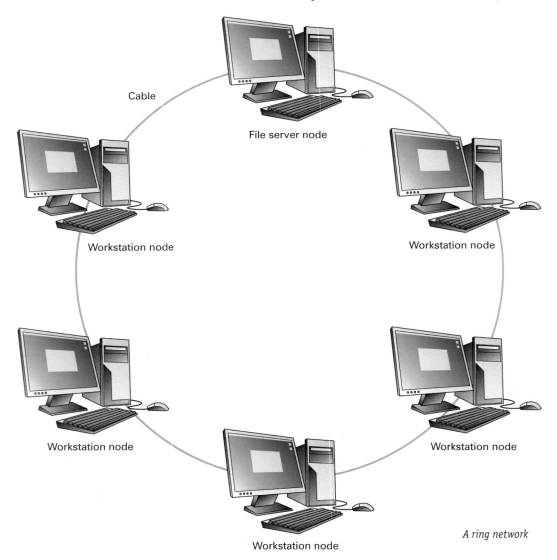

Cable

File server node

Workstation node

Workstation node

Workstation node

Workstation node

Workstation node

A ring network

The main advantages of a ring network are as follows.

- There is no dependence on a central computer as data transmission around the network is supported by all the devices in the ring.
- Very high transmission rates are possible.
- Routing between devices is relatively simple because messages normally travel in one direction only around the ring.
- The transmission facility is shared equally amongst the users.

The main disadvantages are as follows.

- The system depends on the reliability of the whole ring and the repeaters – if one node breaks down, transmission between any of the devices in the ring is disrupted, although it can be designed to bypass any failed node.
- It may be difficult to extend the length of the ring because the physical installation of any new cable must ensure that the ring topology is preserved.

Star network

A **star network** (server-based or client-server) has the central resources for the network located at the centre (hub) of the star. Each workstation, or node, is connected to the central computer or file server by means of its own unique link.

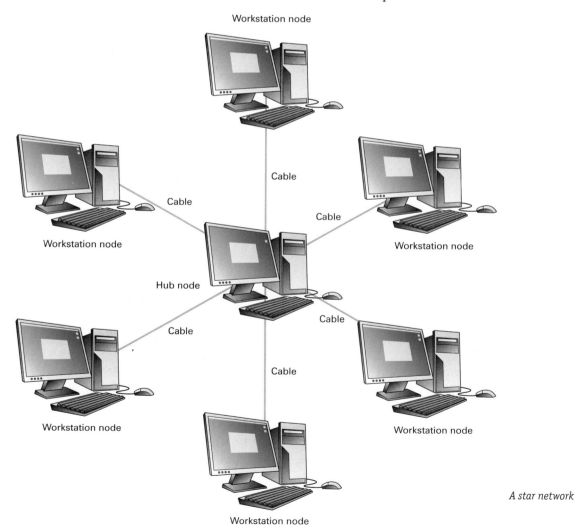

A star network

The star network is by far the most popular for WANs, because most large organisations start with a central computer at head office, from which branch computer facilities are provided through the telephone network. The main aim is to provide computer communication between the branches through head office. Most other networks aim to provide communication between all the devices on the network. Star networks can also be used for LANs.

The advantages of a star network are as follows.

- Security is higher as no workstation can interact with any other without going through the central computer. Actions on many workstations can be monitored from the central server.
- Each spoke in the star is independent of the rest and a fault in a link will not affect other stations.
- It is easy to add new stations, including peripherals that can be shared, without disrupting the network.
- The data transmission speeds used can vary from one link to another. This is important if some links transmit using high-speed devices, such as disk drives, whilst others transmit from low speed devices, such as keyboards.
- Backup of data/information can be done centrally, rather than having to back up data on each station.
- Software (system or application) can be stored on the file server, simplifying installation and upgrading procedures.
- There is consistent performance even when the network is being heavily used.
- It is suitable for WANs where organisations rely on a central computer for the bulk of processing tasks, perhaps limiting the nodes to their local processing needs and the validation of data, prior to transmission to the central computer.

The main disadvantages are as follows.

- The network is vulnerable to hub failures, which affect all users.
- For a LAN, the network may be costly to install because of the length of cable needed, plus a file server has to be purchased.
- For a WAN, the control of communications in the network requires expensive technology at the hub. Complex operating and communications software is needed to control the network.

Comparison between network topologies

Create a table listing the advantages and disadvantages of the three types of network topology:

- bus network
- ring network (peer-to-peer)
- star network (server based).

Communication devices

The original telephone link – the Public Switched Telephone Network (PSTN) – was designed for voice (analogue) transmission and operated at fairly low speeds. Computers work with digital signals, and need a **modem** to 'modulate' and 'demodulate' the signal.

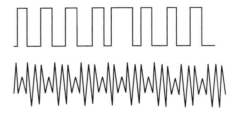

Digital and analogue signals

Modem

A modem (**modulator–demodulator**) is an electronic device used to convert digital output from a computer system into an analogue signal, suitable for transmission over a non-digital public telephone system. It also converts the analogue signals from the telephone into digital input into a computer system.

More recently, high-speed networks, called Public Data Networks (PDNs), which are specifically for digital data transmission, have been built. Integrated Services Digital Network (ISDN) carries voice, data, images and video through a single digital line. With PDN and ISDN systems, it is no longer necessary to convert the signal into analogue form for transmission (no modem is needed).

Broadband technologies have taken this even further, with the digital signal travelling along cables directly into homes and offices.

Backbone

The term **backbone** refers to the physical layout and type of cable used (see below).

Typical cabling includes the following.

- Ethernet – based on thick or thin coaxial, but has rapidly moved to twisted pair and fibre. Supports 10Mbps.
- Token Ring – based on twisted pair and operated at 16Mbps.
- Token Bus – based on coaxial cable and normally found in manufacturing environments. (Coaxial consists of a solid copper core, a layer of plastic insulation, then a second copper mesh – they have the same 'axis'.)
- Fibre Optic – optical cabling – very expensive, used mainly to join networks via a bridge, or for very long connections (little degradation in signal).

Repeater

In a LAN, a signal generated by one station clearly has a maximum distance it can travel before it degenerates in quality to such an extent that it is no longer recognisable. The maximum distance for a signal to travel is well established. If we want signals to travel further than these distances then we need a relay device to boost or regenerate the signal. Such a device is called a repeater.

Hub

A hub is used to allow sharing of a line or resource in a LAN. It acts as a convergence point allowing the transfer of data packets. In its simplest form a hub works by duplicating the data packets received via one **port** and making it available to all ports, therefore allowing data sharing between all devices connected to the hub.

Port
A port is a real (hardware) or virtual (software) connection point between two computers.

Bridge

A company may wish to join two separate LANs, or decide that one LAN has become so big that it would be more efficient to split it into two – people mainly working in their own section. Occasionally, people in each LAN may wish to communicate with the other LAN. Such a link is called a **bridge**. (Imagine two parts of a primary school, on either side of a busy road – the children need a bridge to travel safely.)

Switch

A switch is used in place of a hub or bridge, but it does not simply repeat the signal onwards. Instead, a switch actually examines each packet of data as it arrives and decides where its intended destination is. If the destination and the source are in the same network segment, it 'filters' the packet and stops it going on to another segment. Otherwise it forwards the packet on to its destination segment.

Because a switch examines the contents of the packets, it has the opportunity to identify bad packets and reject them, so saving unnecessary network traffic. Switches are easy to install, and most are self-learning. They determine the Ethernet addresses in use on each segment, building a table as packets are passed through the switch. This 'plug and play' element makes switches an attractive alternative to hubs and bridges.

Router

Routers used to be knows as gateways. Routers may be used to connect two or more Internet Protocol (IP) networks, or an IP network to an Internet connection. A router consists of a computer with at least two network interface cards supporting the IP protocol. The router receives packets from each interface via an input network interface and forwards the received packets to an appropriate output network interface.

Networking software

Network software is the information, data or programming used to make it possible for computers to communicate or connect to one another. It has many functions over and above the software used to operate a stand-alone computer.

Network management software

Network management software controls the usage of the network. Network management software:

- configures the network topology by controlling the addresses of the network elements (e.g. the name, location and IP address)
- manages faults by partitioning off a suspect collision domain whilst the fault is rectified
- monitors the network performance by accessing the managed elements and displaying current statistics in a graphical format to evaluate the behaviour and effectiveness of the network
- restricts unauthorised users' access to the network resources by application of intrusion control procedures.

Network accounting software

Network accounting software may be separate from the network management software or it may be a part of it. It is concerned with the reporting of network usage. It gathers details about user activity including the number of logons and resources used (disk accesses and space used, CPU time, etc.). This data can then be used to make decisions about network expansion, to charge different users or groups of users for the resources that they have used, or to identify unusual patterns of network usage that might be suspicious.

File transfer software

File transfer might simply mean sending a file somewhere – usually to the printer, or to a colleague on the network. Special software (FTP – File Transfer Protocol) allows fast transfer of files to and from the Internet and checks for and corrects any error occurring during the transfer. Sometimes the transfer is made automatically without the user even being aware it has happened.

Firewall

A firewall is a hardware or software device configured to allow or deny data through a computer network that has different levels of trust. Typically this forms the interface between the Internet, a zone of no trust, with an internal network, a zone of high trust.

Data transfer media

Data can be transmitted over a combination of several different types of media.

- **Twisted-pair cable** is mostly used for phone lines and is usually considered to be unable to transmit data at a fast enough rate to be used on all but the smallest of LANs.
- **Coaxial cable** is the commonest type of cable that is used for LANs. It is very high-quality cable that is well insulated to prevent external interference from other electrical devices. It is commonly referred to as 'Ethernet' cable and can be used for much faster data transmission than twisted pair cable.

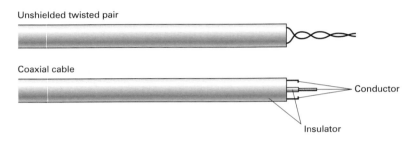

Twisted pair and coaxial cabling

- **Optical fibre cable** is not made of copper but instead it is made of a long, extremely thin strand of glass. It is made of very high-quality materials, which makes it an excellent medium for very high-speed data transmission. It works by shining flashes of light along its length from a transmitter to a receiver; each flash of light represents a data bit.

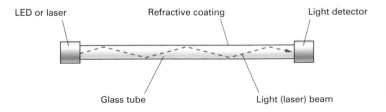

Optical fibre cabling

- **Microwaves** are similar to radio waves and can carry data at ultra-high speed. Such wireless transmission is used nowadays by more than just mobile phones.

- **Communication satellites** are used to transmit data around the earth. Data is transmitted to them by radio waves and it is bounced back to a receiver that is thousands of miles away. There are hundreds of communication satellites in the skies above the earth and any one of them or a combination of them can be used to transmit data to any part of the world instantaneously.

Communication satellite

The role of communication satellites

Characteristics of networks

An individual or organisation can connect to the **Internet** via various devices and, normally, through an Internet Service Provider (ISP), which allows connections to take place and filters messages in and out of the individual connection. Email is one service normally provided by an ISP.

To access content on the **World Wide Web** (WWW), web-browsing software is required. Search engines are also needed for finding resources by keyword, if the Internet address of the resource is not known.

Internet and World Wide Web

The Internet is not the same as the World Wide Web. It is a series of interconnected networks that communicate with each other. The World Wide Web is the content and services that are available by using the Internet connections.

activity

Web servers and email servers

1 Investigate the uses of web servers and email servers.

2 Write a paragraph (about 75–100 words) on each, outlining these uses.

Websites are held on a machine somewhere on the network. Each machine has an IP address that typically looks like this:

196.168.0.X

The series of four numbers is called an octet, and is split into two parts, the net section and the host section. The net section identifies the network that a computer belongs to; the host identifies the actual computer.

As IP addresses are hard to recall, most websites also have a URL, or Uniform Resource Locator. A typical one looks like this:

www.payne-gallway.co.uk

The address normally gives clues as to the name or type of organisation and its originating country.

- The www signifies this is a website on the World Wide Web.
- Payne-Gallway is the name of this organisation.
- The co indicates it is a company.
- The uk indicates the country.

Web addresses

Research web addresses – make a list of 10 addresses with different styles of name and try and find at least six different country suffixes. What other clues are there in the URLs you found?

An **intranet** is a service making use of the technologies of the Internet to distribute information within a single organisation over its internal network. It usually makes use of HTML (Hypertext mark-up Language, used for creating web pages) over HTTP. The aim is to move information around that organisation. Before the advent of the term intranet, similar services existed as bulletin boards or information repositories that were accessible only from an internal connection. They are used for disseminating information to employees, and for collaborative working where staff can be spread over a wide geographical area. Using Internet technologies and web browsers makes access very simple as most machines can have easy access using existing software. Generally internal logins and passwords allow access to the organisation's intranet.

An **extranet** is an extension of the intranet that allows company-specific information to be available to selected other companies and individuals. Each is given a user identity and password that allows access to the information. Post-sales customer support or early product reviews may be disseminated on an extranet.

With an intranet, there does not necessarily have to be any access to the Internet. For an extranet, where Internet access is required, use of gateways and firewalls will be necessary to safeguard the organisation's network.

Most organisations will also have their own website on the World Wide Web, which would be freely available to anyone browsing.

Uses of communication technologies

There are few organisations that do not have some form of computer network. However, there are occasions when having independent (stand-alone) machines may be prudent. For instance, if the data they hold is super-sensitive, then stand-alone machines would solve the problem of data being stolen whilst being transmitted along communication lines. If the task that the computer has to perform involves high processor activity and is time-sensitive, then the interruptions from data packets may cause problems.

The question is whether an organisation needs to have an intranet, an extranet or a website. It depends on the size of the organisation, the type of the organisation, its aims and objectives and what information it needs to disseminate.

It is true that by having a network within an organisation, there are many advantages – shared resources, easier collaborative working, more control over security and backup (if set up correctly), and wider and faster access to organisational resources when staff and connected organisations are remote from the information they need.

Benefits of intranets and extranets

Here's how an extranet for clients freed up time and improved customer service.

Noiseworks is a specialist IT public relations company providing media relations, training and research to technology businesses. Founded in 1990 and based in Maidenhead, the business employs 21 people. Account Manager Tom Cheesewright explains how an extranet has increased client satisfaction and boosted overall efficiency.

What I did

Pinpoint objectives

'All our clients had different reporting requirements and we found we were spending large amounts of time compiling and presenting information in different ways. By introducing an extranet we hoped to cut that time, and instead use it to deliver results.

'We also had a desire to become more open and effective in our communications with clients, and wanted to offer them 24-hour access to information in a self-service format. The system also needed to make it easier for us to work with overseas partners.'

Select a solution

'We chose an extranet system that various members of our team had either seen or used before. It's basically an online information store, with user-friendly screens that can be accessed from anywhere with an Internet connection.

'As well as being easy to use, the solution you pick should also reflect the amount of information you want to store and exchange and the level of access you and your clients require. If you don't have IT skills in-house, consider a reputable IT service provider who can help with set-up, hosting and on-going support.'

Monitor and review

'After a few months, we undertook a formal review to see how much time the system had saved us. The results showed an overall 25 per cent saving in our time, which freed people to work on client projects and business development activity. In addition, the extranet has delivered the benefits of flexible working, thus enabling our staff to work from home.

'Client feedback has been excellent. They found that the extranet reduces their own workloads, speeds up their document approval processes and gives them instant access to information, such as press releases and photography.

'The system has also proved useful during new business pitches. Potential clients recognise the benefits and it sets us apart from competitors.'

What I'd do differently

Know when to call it quits

'The majority of clients love the extranet, but there are some whose internal processes aren't suited to it. In the early days, we wasted time trying to force it to fit everyone. These days we review a client's extranet usage after six months. If they're not getting value out of it, we explore alternative methods.'

Don't put everything in

'When you start, it's tempting to throw in every bit of information you've got. This is a mistake because it makes it difficult for users to find what they really want. It took us a while to instigate regular housekeeping sessions, where unnecessary content is deleted.'

A link to this website is available at www.heinemann.co.uk/hotlinks (express code 2349P)

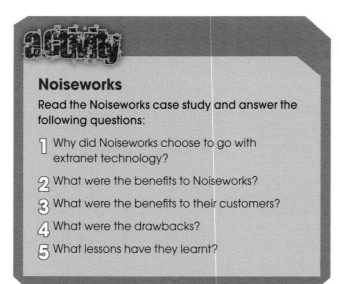

Noiseworks

Read the Noiseworks case study and answer the following questions:

1. Why did Noiseworks choose to go with extranet technology?
2. What were the benefits to Noiseworks?
3. What were the benefits to their customers?
4. What were the drawbacks?
5. What lessons have they learnt?

Data transfer standards

Standards are not only required for data transmission, but for the transfer of data across applications.

For the following standards, find out what the letters represent and give examples of when these standards would be used and why.

1. ODBC
2. DDE
3. RTF
4. PDF

Standards

Whichever transmission method is selected it is vital that all devices on the network are using the same method and settings. Strict sets of rules, called **protocols**, have been established to ensure that all devices can communicate effectively. These protocols specify device connections, type of cable, transmission mode and speed, data format and error detection and correction method. Because these protocols are strictly set out, any devices that use the same protocol can be linked together and have effective communication between them.

If two or more devices cannot use the same protocol, it is still possible to connect them using a special conversion device called a **protocol converter**. This device would be useful for connecting devices such as a PC and a mainframe that use completely different protocols. This overcomes compatibility problems between devices such as:

- different types of transmission – the PC may use asynchronous transmission, and the mainframe synchronous transmission
- different character representations – PCs commonly use ASCII to represent characters, whereas many mainframes use EBCDIC and other devices use Unicode or other systems
- different error detection and correction, such as extra check bits that are calculated and added to each block of data, to be checked on receipt.

OSI 7-layer model

1. Investigate the OSI 7-layer model.
2. Write a short description:
   - explaining what it is and why it came about
   - stating what each layer is and what it is used for
   - discussing how relevant it is in today's networking.

Transfer of data across the Internet

The Internet protocol **TCP/IP** (Transmission Control Protocol/Internet Protocol) came about from the 1970s use of networking. These two protocols were the first that were defined. The original IP had four layers, but has evolved into five layers for data transmission.

- The **Application layer** allows other protocols, such as HTTP (Hyper-Text Transfer Protocol), TELNET and FTP (File Transfer Protocol) to communicate without trouble.

- The **transfer layer** is where other protocols such as TCP work, where they verify the correct delivery of data from client to the server.
- The **Internet layer** covers IP (now on version 6) and other protocols. IP moves the packet of data from node to node, forwarding each packet based on its address.
- The **data link layer** covers the logic of linking, using, for example, FDDI or Ethernet.
- The **physical layer** is where ISDN lines, Ethernet physical layer and modems lie.

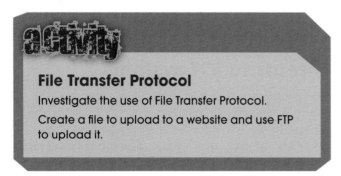

File Transfer Protocol

Investigate the use of File Transfer Protocol.

Create a file to upload to a website and use FTP to upload it.

Practice exam questions

1. There are 10 employees in a local estate agent's office. Each employee uses a networked PC on a Local Area Network (LAN).
   (a) Give **four** benefits to the office of using a network, rather than stand-alone PCs. (4)
   (b) The office is part of a national chain that is connected together over a Wide Area Network (WAN).
   (c) Explain the difference between a LAN and a WAN. (4)
   (d) Give **two** benefits to the estate agent's office of using the WAN. (2)
   (June 2006)

2. The World Wide Web is supported by a network infrastructure. This consists of a number of components.
   (a) Describe the role of a router. (2)
   (b) Describe the role of a web server. (2)
   (June 2006)

3. College staff can obtain the A Level specifications for their subjects from the AQA website. These are provided as Portable Document Format (PDF) files.
   (a) Give **three** possible reasons why PDF has been selected as the format in which to provide these files. (3)
   (b) The AQA website has an Internet Protocol (IP) address, which has the form:
   nnn.nnn.nnn.nnn.
   Explain the role of IP addresses in the functioning of the Internet. (2)
   (c) College staff do not need to know the IP address of the AQA website, as they can use the Uniform Resource Locator (URL) instead:
   http://www.aqa.org.uk
   Explain **two** benefits to the college staff of using the URL. (4)
   (June 2006)

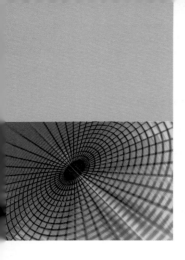

2.4 Safety and security of data in ICT systems

The need to protect data

The arrival of global technology, and the ability to transfer data while on the move, has seen the evolution of crimes that are keeping the legal system busy writing new laws. One of the difficulties encountered is that criminals could be helping themselves to the funds in electronic accounts that are held by people thousands of miles of away. The laws in one country may provide some form of recompense for the victim, but the country harboring the criminal may have no such laws, which ultimately creates a legal void between nations. Closing this void is proving to be a challenge across the globe.

Without the technology found in most homes in the developed world, a lot of crimes would simply not exist. Identity theft, bogus web traders, hackers and virus planters are all supported by the type of technology available from most electrical retailers. Technology has also helped to increase other areas that fall foul of the law. For example bank robbers, fraudsters and paedophiles have all utilised technology. As the criminals become more technically astute, they become harder to catch and bring to justice.

If a school pupil accesses a friend's school account and deletes the latest essay the outcome could be a detention, a less than favourable comment on a report or simply having to hand the work in again. Large organisations are frequently under attack from those whose intention it is to steal, alter or delete data. The outcomes in this situation become incredibly serious.

The consequences of a large telecommunications PLC having customers' bills reduced by 50% or a large insurance company losing all of its clients' details to a competitor would be commercially disastrous. This kind of action is known as **industrial espionage**. Each client's address, monthly premium, type of cover (car, building, land or business) being lost, stolen or corrupted could spell ruin for the company concerned and for their clients if they need to make a claim.

Threats to ICT systems

Most people recognise that physically stealing and damaging property are crimes that are punishable by the law. By using a computer, theft can be committed discretely and effectively without a shotgun and get-away driver. Data has become such a valuable commodity over recent years that modern day criminals target servers and company networks in the hope of lifting account numbers and other financial data.

case study

Confidential financial information

During a fraud investigation, in the USA, something bothered the investigating officer about the furniture in one of the bedrooms. It seemed oddly oversized. His attention focused on an expansive canopy over the bed. When he pushed at the draping, he found that it was weighed down with files. They contained reams of confidential financial information about hundreds of individuals whose identities had been pilfered in an intricate scheme that illicitly netted more than $50 million and affected at least 30,000 people nationwide. The suspect had been involved in the lifting of financial personas to secure bank loans, credit cards and mortgages.

A link to this website is available at www.heinemann.co.uk/hotlinks (express code 2349P)

Online crime

All that is required to commit online fraud like **phishing** is a connection to the World Wide Web, determination and some technical knowledge. Crimes can even be committed at work, using the facilities provided by an innocent employer. This is why it is important to acknowledge that digital equipment has taken crime to new levels.

Phishing
Phishing schemes use email messages to lure unwitting consumers to websites by masquerading as home pages of trusted banks and credit card issuers. Online visitors are induced to reveal passwords as well as bank account, social security and credit card numbers.

In the twentieth century, issues surrounding technology and crime revolved around virus planting and hackers. However, since criminals first started to use technology to infiltrate systems and destroy or steal data, the variety of illegal activity undertaken has grown to worrying proportions. The number of people cautioned or charged over Internet child pornography offences quadrupled between 2001 and 2003 to a record 2,234 cases. In 2004, card fraud over the Internet cost the UK £117m and 77% of medium to large businesses reported virus attacks costing £27.8 million, while 17% suffered financial fraud costing £121 million.

Malicious attacks on data

Cyber-crimes, committed by cyber-terrorists using state-of-the-art technology and tailor-made systems, occur all over the world. Examples of cyber-terrorist activity include the use of information technology to organise and carry out attacks, the support of the group's activities and perception-management campaigns. Experts agree that many terrorist groups have adopted information technology as a means to conduct operations without being detected by counter terrorist officials.

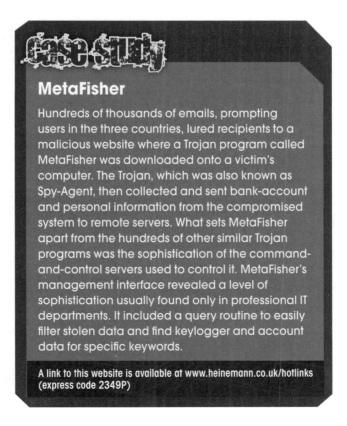

case study

MetaFisher

Hundreds of thousands of emails, prompting users in the three countries, lured recipients to a malicious website where a Trojan program called MetaFisher was downloaded onto a victim's computer. The Trojan, which was also known as Spy-Agent, then collected and sent bank-account and personal information from the compromised system to remote servers. What sets MetaFisher apart from the hundreds of other similar Trojan programs was the sophistication of the command-and-control servers used to control it. MetaFisher's management interface revealed a level of sophistication usually found only in professional IT departments. It included a query routine to easily filter stolen data and find keylogger and account data for specific keywords.

A link to this website is available at www.heinemann.co.uk/hotlinks (express code 2349P)

Cyber-terrorism is a deliberate, motivated attack on data or systems, committed across networks and intended to create a danger to life or health. Terrorist groups all over the world may plan to use the Internet as a weapon. Attacks against the computer systems of the world's largest companies could cause economic crisis. Attacks against control systems are extremely dangerous as they could result in the failure of communications, transport, data transfer and financial payment systems.

Malpractice

Another element that can threaten the integrity and security of data is malpractice. This is when an individual or group of individuals are responsible for the loss of data, interruptions to normal, daily processing or other disruptions related to working with or using information technology. This is caused by employees not following company procedures properly, not testing software adequately or failing to design a system to perform as it was expected to perform. The ensuing disastrous results may not be deliberate, but usually come about through professional incompetence. For example, failing to log off before going home could result in an office worker leaving important, confidential documentation free for unauthorised staff to look through and potentially use for non-authorised purposes.

Internal and external threats

Not all **external threats** are technology-based; some come in the form of natural disasters such as lightning strikes, tsunamis, earthquakes, fires, floods or volcano eruptions.

When Mount Vesuvius in Naples erupts again it is likely to take out a massive part of the coast, including all the local

Case study

Theft of classified information

A naval officer had his laptop stolen in the latest computer mishap for the armed forces and security services. The officer, reported to be an intelligence expert, lost the computer and his personal luggage after boarding a train at Paddington station in west London. The Ministry of Defence (MoD) has insisted the computer did not contain any classified information. However, according to The Sunday Times, it held specifications for the next generation of fighter aircraft and details of how they can be controlled from the ground. The paper claimed the thief sold the computer on to a dealer who then tried to sell the contents of the laptop for £15,000 to a newspaper. The MoD spokesman said: 'The laptop did not contain any classified information and MoD police have been informed. An MI6 officer left one in a taxi after a night's drinking in a tapas bar in south London and another was snatched when an MI5 officer put it down to buy a ticket from a station.'

A link to this website is available at www.heinemann.co.uk/hotlinks (express code 2349P)

businesses, thousands of families and all the ICT systems in the region. The cost to human life can be avoided by moving the population away, which is a proposal the Italian government have suggested to the population, together with a cash incentive, and the same can happen

External threats
External threats to an ICT system come from people who do not work for the company and who want to infiltrate the system for financial gain or simply to destroy the data.

Activity

System and data threats
Many firms are ignorant of the dangers that face their systems and data.

Produce a poster that could be displayed in an office to warn about the threats to systems and data.

with the data, provided each organisation has made the appropriate provisions. Without a good contingency plan and planning for the future, many lives and much data are likely to be lost.

Internal threats can be as simple as the computer freezing before work is saved, or the main server being infected by a virus and crashing. Failure of hardware is frustrating and costly, which is why specialist technicians are often employed to run, maintain and protect systems. Data could even be at risk when there is a change in procedures. For example, a wholesale upgrade of an old server to a new system could see data accidentally being deleted, or old backups overwriting current data. If an essay started weeks ago was to suddenly replace the finished article, it would be annoying!

Internal threats
Internal threats are threats to data which originate within the organisation itself.

Many firms have had to write internal policies for dismissing employees from an office environment. This is because when people are fired they may be upset, log onto their machine, slip their USB storage device into the machine and take a lot of data home or to their next employer. They may plant a virus to destroy the system if they are given enough time. In some cases they may delete as much data as possible or phone customers up and sell

products at a massive discount. The key factor here is that they need time to cause mayhem.

A policy would typically include notifying the network administrator as soon as it is known that an employee is leaving. The date and time on which to terminate the employee's access to computer and telephone systems will need to be clear and the process must be executed with efficiency. Exiting employees should then turn in all company books and materials, keys, ID badges, computers, mobile phones and any other company-owned items. They may be accompanied to their desk, helped to clear up and escorted from the building. Having their access to the network blocked and entry to the building denied removes the opportunity, in the first instance, to cause too much damage. Giving someone a week's notice after serious disciplinary action is asking for trouble!

Protecting ICT systems

The range of threats cannot be covered by one simple protect-all system. To protect data there are various methods available to commercial and personal users.

Password management is amongst the simplest forms of protection. Despite its simplicity, many users still leave the door wide open for unauthorised access. Good passwords should be a combination of letters and numbers and not written down and left near the workstation. The password should be memorable by the user but not obvious to those who might want to guess what it could be. Using the names of partners, pets, parents or children is not wise, nor are 12345 and QWERTY as these are often amongst the first passwords tried by hackers. Changing the password regularly is recommended, although some people forget they have changed it and lock themselves out of systems that only allow a certain number of attempts. You should not tell anyone your password. Remember not to walk away from the computer without logging off; if you don't log off, a good password is useless.

The first line of defence against digital threats is to use anti-virus software. This software is designed to destroy malicious code that may have entered your system. There are many good options in the market but even the most expensive and complex virus software will become ineffective if it is not constantly updated. This is because new viruses are released every day. For this reason, virus-protection companies have to constantly add to or amend their own software so that it will continue to wipe out such threats. It is normal that a fee is charged when the original software is purchased. This fee may also cover downloads over a certain period of time before a new payment is requested. This period of time may be a month, a year or even longer. There are some free anti-virus products to be found online but these often have limitations and are not suitable for company networks. Needless to say, regardless of where the software comes from, it is a good idea to run it on a regular basis otherwise viruses could creep in and start to corrupt data.

A firewall is used to stop unauthorised access to networked machines. If a computer is connected to the Internet, it is connected to the biggest network in the world. Anyone can access another system provided they have permission or the know-how. A firewall is set up to prevent hackers from entering a system and accessing data they have no right to see.

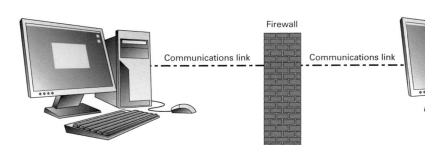

Communication through a firewall

Another way to ensure that data is kept intact is to train staff how to use the equipment properly. This will help them avoid saving incorrectly or accidentally accessing and corrupting data. How to run and use utility software like firewalls and anti-virus software may also form part of the training process. When people are made aware of the threats and value of data, they may take more care with its preservation.

Network managers can enforce access levels that restrict access to certain data groups. This ensures that users only view, handle and work with data that is relevant to their jobs. This reduces the quantity of data that an individual can disrupt, erase or steal. The level of access granted to employees varies from post to post but is likely to become more extensive with seniority and strategic importance within an organisation.

There are measures that can be taken whilst data is being digitally transported. Encryption is when the data is scrambled and can only be read by the intended receiver, who should have software capable of unscrambling the data. Whilst it is still possible to extract data whilst it is being transferred it has very little meaning or use in an encrypted state. Data that is stored in a physical location on media can also be encrypted, which protects the sensitivity of data should it be stolen in this form.

As well having measures in place to protect data, backups should be taken; these can be referred to or restored if the original is somehow lost.

Physical protection can be used to protect the hardware where the data is stored. Locking doors to the server and computer room is a logical start. Guards can be used to protect the premises; windows should be locked to 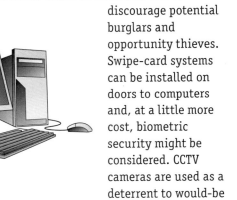 discourage potential burglars and opportunity thieves. Swipe-card systems can be installed on doors to computers and, at a little more cost, biometric security might be considered. CCTV cameras are used as a deterrent to would-be criminals who might be thinking about raiding the building. However, the cameras can only film the equipment being stolen, not physically stop the theft.

Legislation

There is legislation designed to protect computer users and the data with which they work. Such legislation covers the use of computer hardware and specifies what can and cannot be done with personal data. Legislation also covers inappropriate use of hardware and software, and safeguards intellectual property rights. These laws give the opportunity to individuals and organisations to apply legal restrictions and sanctions to those who may have caused them harm in some way or have made gains from the ideas of others.

The Data Protection Act 1998

This Act is made up of eight principles which govern the rights of companies who hold personal data about individuals as well as the rights of the individuals concerned. The Act is aimed at preventing organisations from using or disclosing personal data in a manner that may be inappropriate, against the wishes of the data subject or likely to cause offence or harm. Organisations that hold personal details about individuals must register with the Data Commissioner.

Personal data is defined under the act as data which relates to a living individual who can be identified: (a) from those data, or (b) from those data and other information which is in the possession of, or likely to come into the possession of, the data controller, and includes any expression of opinion about the individual, and any indication of the intentions of the data controller or any other person in respect of the individual.

There is also personal sensitive data that includes details like political opinion, religious beliefs, trade union status, physical or mental condition, sexual life and proceedings for any offence committed or alleged to have been committed and subsequent sentence or court proceedings. Inappropriate disclosure of details such as these could influence the treatment received by the data subject or the opportunities they may be seeking.

The principles state that data must be:

1. processed fairly and lawfully

This means that the organisations should explain to individuals what the information will be used for and that it will not be used to break any laws. When a company collects personal information they must tell the data subject that they have done so.

2. processed for one or more specified and lawful purposes, and not further processed in any way that is incompatible with the original purpose

Should the company holding the data start to use the collected data in any way other than that which has been stated, they are in breach of the Act.

3. adequate, relevant and not excessive

Companies should only collect data that they intend to use.

4. accurate and, where necessary, kept up to date

Information about individuals can become out of date. For example, someone may move house prompting a change of address, or they alter their surname, perhaps by getting married. Companies holding personal data are obliged to check that the data they hold is accurate and up-to-date. They can achieve this by asking the data subject to check the details held about them and amending any that are not correct.

5. kept for no longer than is necessary for the purpose for which it is being used

When an organisation has no legitimate reason for holding personal data, it must be deleted. Likewise, when it has served its purpose it should no longer be kept.

6. processed in line with the rights of individuals

The data subject has the right to prevent direct marketing by making a request in writing. They have the right to obtain the information held about them and have it corrected if it is incorrect or misleading. Data subjects have the right to compensation should they have suffered as a result of a breach of the Act; such matters and rewards are determined by the courts.

7. kept secure with appropriate technical and organisational measures taken to protect the information

Holders of personal data must ensure that it is as safe as possible from sabotage or theft by using appropriate preventative and security measures.

8. not transferred outside the European Economic Area (the European Union member states plus Norway, Iceland and Liechtenstein) unless there is adequate protection for the personal information being transferred

This complements the principle above to maintain some legal form of protection over the data on behalf of the data subject.

Exemptions

Despite the principles outlined above, there are still certain exceptions to the Act. Organisations are exempt from the Act if the data they hold is required for the purpose of safeguarding national security. Organisations are also exempt if the data they hold is used for the prevention or detection of crime, the apprehension or prosecution of offenders or the assessment or collection of any tax or duty or of any imposition of a similar nature.

activity

The Data Protection Act

Find an example of where the Data Protection Act has been mentioned in news. Produce a short presentation that details your findings.

The Computer Misuse Act 1990

The Computer Misuse Act came into force as a countermeasure to make hacking and the introduction of viruses criminal offences. Both offences have the potential to be carried out on company machines as well as personal equipment. Companies aggrieved enough with the employee who has planted a virus or used company resources to hack other networks can resort to the law or apply their own disciplinary procedures.

The Act identifies three specific offences.

1. Unauthorised access to computer material (that is, a program or data)

This would involve using another person's ID and password to gain access to a network and their files without the other person's permission or knowledge. Such action could give access to sensitive data, such as exam papers or bank account details. When access is gained, the ability to copy or obtain a hardcopy of the data of interest is not difficult.

2. Unauthorised access to a computer system with intent to commit or facilitate the commission of a serious crime

The issue here is similar to the above but difficulties arise when trying to apply the law or seal a conviction due to the inability to show that there was intent to commission a serious crime.

3. Unauthorised modification of computer material

This includes modifying files, deleting files, introducing a virus or any other action which would result in a change to the original material. Altering exam results, increasing a bank balance or changing the prices of stock all fall under this category.

A fine or prison sentence may be served, but the severity of the sentence will depend on the damage caused by the perpetrator.

Criminals can now steal from a distance

Wireless hijacking under scrutiny

A recent court case, which saw a West London man fined £500 and sentenced to 12 months' conditional discharge for hijacking a wireless broadband connection, has repercussions for almost every user of wi-fi networks.

It is believed to be the first case of its kind in the UK, but with an estimated one million wi-fi users around the country, it is unlikely to be the last.

'There are a lot of implications and this could open the floodgates to many more such cases,' said Phil Cracknell, chief technology officer of security firm NetSurity.

Details in this particular case are sketchy, although it is known that a Gregory Straszkiewicz had 'piggybacked' on a wireless broadband network of a local Ealing resident, using a laptop while sitting in his car.

He had been seen in the area on several previous occasions over the past three months and is believed to have been reported to police by a neighbour concerned that he was acting suspiciously.

The case is some way away from that of Brian Salcedo, who was sentenced to nine years in a US jail last year for the far more serious crime of siphoning credit card numbers over the wireless network of hardware store Lowes.

Unauthorised access

The criminal aspect of the case of Salcedo is obvious and is clearly reflected in the sentence dished out.

But the crime committed in the case of Straszkiewicz, where he appears simply to have used the network, is perhaps less obvious.

Not to Simon Janes, a former head of the Computer Crime Section and now operations manager for computer forensics firm Ibas.

'Gaining unauthorised access to someone else's network is an offence and people have to take responsibility for their actions. Some people might argue that taking a joy-ride in someone else's car is not an offence either,' he said.

Gaining unauthorised access to a computer is an offence covered by the Computer Misuse Act. In Straszkiewicz's case, he was prosecuted under the Communications Act and found guilty of dishonestly obtaining an electronic communications service.

'I guess, and it is a guess, that they couldn't prove he accessed the actual computer and that is why they used another legal avenue,' said Mr Janes.

But whatever route the case took, the outcome proves that borrowing someone else's network is not as harmless as the hobbyist wi-fi user might think.

It is not just those people driving around in search of a 'free' network who have to worry.

The perception among domestic users is that providing security is difficult and it does depend on the competence of the user.

People with criminal intentions have, in the past, attempted to use the openness of their own wireless networks to cover their tracks online.

'There have been incidences where paedophiles deliberately leave their wireless networks open so that, if caught, they can say that is wasn't them that used the network for illegal purposes,' said NetSurity's Mr Cracknell.

Such a defence would hold little water as the person installing the network, be they a home user or a business, has ultimate responsibility for any criminal activity that takes place on that network, whether it be launching a hack attack or downloading illegal pornography.

Despite this, businesses and residential users continue to fail to take that responsibility seriously by securing their networks, said Mr Cracknell.

A joint survey by RSA Security and NetSurity, conducted in March of this year, found that more than a third of wireless networks in London and Frankfurt had the basic security features turned off.

Many had failed to turn on the encryption that scrambles the data traffic between users and the access point…

With wi-fi operating at speeds of up to 20 times faster than broadband it is unlikely to slow the system down

Continued

noticeably unless the borrower is downloading huge files and, unless the owner of the network has intrusion detection software, he or she is unlikely to notice the squatters.

The fact that Straszkiewicz narrowly escaped a harsher sentence, had to pay a £500 fine and had his laptop and wireless card confiscated indicates such squatting might not be worthwhile.

Detective Constable Stephone Rothwell from Ealing CID was involved in the case and said future cases would be treated in the same way.

A link to this website is available at www.heinemann.co.uk/hotlinks (express code 2349P)

The Copyright, Designs and Patents Act 1988

This law is designed to protect intellectual property rights concerning works such as song lyrics, manuscripts, manuals, computer programs, commercial documents, leaflets, newsletters and articles. Many of the literary works mentioned can easily be duplicated using computer technology. The law gives the creator of the material the rights to control the ways in which their material is used.

As soon as intellectual property is created, it is automatically covered under the Copyright, Designs and Patents Act. Most modern software leaves a digital footprint in that the date, time and author are recorded at the time of creation; this makes proving ownership slightly easier than when literary work was paper based. For the law to take full effect, the work must be deemed original and exhibit a degree of labour, skill or judgement. The expression of an idea is covered, although the actual idea is not. For example, a story about a wizard boy going to wizard school is a neat idea, but the idea cannot be copyrighted. However, the development and expression of the idea as a seven-part novel charting the boy's school days is covered. Likewise the idea to present a computer system with a graphical user interface is an idea; the development of software to execute the idea is covered as it takes time to program original code. This is why Apple Macs and PCs have similar GUIs but operate in different ways.

The law aims to stop people taking someone else's work, like computer software that has cost the company a lot in development, and attempting to gain advantage from it. Such advantages might include gaining a good essay mark by handing in someone else's work, or a financial reward for an article or song lyrics. The original creator is likely to be aggrieved at being out of pocket and receiving limited recognition for their efforts. The law restricts copying, renting, lending, performing, broadcasting or showing the work in public without the author's consent, which may come at a fee. There are a few incidences not covered by the law, including using the work to assist with private and research study purposes; performance, copies or lending for educational purposes; and criticism and news reporting. In each case it is wise to acknowledge the source in a reference section of the resulting work.

Activity

Legislation and regulations

Split into groups and do one of the following activities. Write a presentation on your findings to present to the class and use as a basis for discussion. A class discussion will help you cover both topics.

Group 1

1 Investigate other computer-related legislation. Anything that covers data and information will be relevant (there could be more than one recent piece of relevant legislation, ask your teacher for advice/ guidance).

2 Identify if it is legislation that is restricted to certain types of organisation, for example, the finance industry has many rules associated with it.

3 Identify the geographical reach of the legislation and who has the power to enforce it and how.

Group 2

1 Investigate current regulations that apply to users of the Internet.

Normally the individual or group who produced the work will exclusively own the work. However, if a work is produced as part of employment then it will normally belong to the person or company who hired or commissioned the individual.

Backup and recovery

To back up data is to ensure that there is a copy securely kept elsewhere, which can be used if the original is lost. Full and complete backups are hard to make because of the frequency with which some companies add to their data. However, there must be some provision built into a company's IT policy which states the procedures for backing up operational data and systems. The policy must also state how the backed-up data will be streamed back into the daily system. It is all well and good having lots of backed-up data, but if no one has considered how it will be fed back into the system then the procedures are likely to be flawed.

Data is probably the most important commodity used by businesses and individuals. All data is kept for a specific purpose. Digital photos are stored on home machines and viewed to bring pleasure. Details of bank transactions are kept within massive systems and databases to be used by information systems to track customer accounts and transactions.

Despite the varying nature of data or information held, there will be a need to back it up. The consequences of losing data could prove fatal for some small traders, embarrassing for others and devastating to those to whom the data relates. Should a bank, plumber, guitar teacher or insurance company be unfortunate enough to lose all their client details, their financial trading details, their company records and business plan, the following days, months or years are likely to prove very costly and their reputation could be severely damaged.

Those who appreciate the value and vulnerability of what they have take the sensible measure of backing up data and systems. Senior management must drive support, funding and appreciation of the need to back up. They generate profit and investments from the use of data and must take responsibility for ensuring its ready presence if it is ever under threat.

The sooner a firm realises how important its data is and how quickly it can be corrupted the better. They can then

Protection of information

Schools, colleges and universities are targeted by people who would want to remove, copy or delete data and information kept in files.

1 Produce a list of data that might be of interest to thieves – see if you can get to 20.

2 Select five from your list and say why is it important that the data and information identified is protected.

3 Select a different five from your list and explain the consequences of an unauthorised user having access to the data or information.

4 Produce a plan of recommendations that details how best to protect all the data and information you have identified.

start to consider investing in a suitable backup strategy built around sensible policies and schedules. More home users are investing in different types of media to preserve personal data, while businesses form departments to oversee this important process.

There are particular key elements which need to be established if the backup and recovery routines are to be successful. A backup and recovery plan is termed successful if hardly any data is lost, if daily business processes are minimally interrupted and the whole system is back to normal within a given time frame. Any backup plan that does not cater for providing a copy of a company's most precious data and interrupts operational efficiency will need to be reconsidered. Any recovery plan that takes days rather than minutes to implement will also need to be re-evaluated.

A good backup strategy will identify the data that will need to be backed up. This will be the data that is used to assist the business in its daily trading and operations. To establish what this data is, staff must be surveyed to ascertain what part of the system they cannot function without. This will vary from one company to the next but must be specified and targeted for backing up.

Backup systems vital in post-9/11 world

At Akamai Technologies Inc., a framed photo of a smiling young brown-haired man serves as a daily reminder of terrorism's toll, and the importance of preparing for the unexpected – a growing need at a company responsible for shepherding as much as one-fifth of the world's Internet traffic.

Next to an American flag at the front desk of Akamai's headquarters hangs a portrait of Danny Lewin. In the late 1990s, the graduate student at nearby MIT helped develop mathematical algorithms to ease Web traffic congestion – work that made up the core of Akamai's business when the company he co-founded began offering Web content-delivery services in 1999. But the married father's life was cut short at age 31. Lewin was on a business trip Sept. 11, 2001, when his American Airlines jet was hijacked and crashed into one of the World Trade Center towers.

Lewin's death, Sagan said in a recent interview, 'is clearly a reminder that companies have to be prepared for the unthinkable.'

The Internet is a much bigger and busier place today than it was five years ago, when Akamai and other firms that route Web traffic helped keep links running smoothly despite spiking online activity and days-long phone outages near the attack sites. Meanwhile, corporate America depends more than ever on instant data retrieval and suppression of computer viruses and worms to maintain an uninterrupted flow of goods and services.

That's made disaster planning far more expensive and complex than in the 1990s. Back then, many companies large and small did little more than stock closets with emergency supplies and draw up contingency plans with a goal of returning to normal operations within a few days of a calamity.

Now, many firms are spreading data centers to far-flung parts of the globe and beefing up back-up systems to ensure they can avoid disruptions should any single piece of their operations fail.

'We've come a long way in seven or eight years,' said Donna Scott, a disaster planning expert at the technology research firm Gartner Inc. 'Until 2000, the scenario planning was based only on fires, floods and natural disasters.' Today, Scott says, 'disaster recovery times are getting shorter, and businesses want their products and services to be available all the time.'

Although disaster preparations in the late 1990s for the Y2K computer bug are a distant memory, the terrorism threat looms large.

There's been no shortage of recent disasters, from Hurricane Katrina to the Northeast blackout of 2003. And some new threats have emerged – for example, the Washington-based Disaster Recovery Institute now offers a course for businesses to prepare for a possible bird flu pandemic...

Some of corporate America's post-Sept. 11 steps have been small. For example, at Akamai, Lewin's death inspired a rule allowing no more than two senior executives to fly on the same plane.

But companies intent on preventing a single knockout blow from terrorism or other disasters also are spreading offices and employees to multiple geographic locations, and expanding backup systems to keep computers and phones operating and shuffle employees among work sites.

In its eight-year history, Akamai has branched out to the point that the company believes it can maintain operations without interruption from any one of four sites: an operations centre at the Cambridge headquarters; two newer operations centres in San Mateo, Calif., and Bangalore, India; and an emergency backup office five miles away from headquarters.

In the event that all three operations centres are simultaneously knocked out, Akamai's Cambridge staff could use the emergency backup office, or manage the server network by using laptops and logging onto a secure internal computer system.

'Whenever you decentralize, you spread your risk, and when you centralize your information technology, you reduce costs,' Scott said. 'But if you centralize and something bad happens, it has a much bigger impact.'

A link to this website is available at www.heinemann.co.uk/hotlinks (express code 2349P)

The frequency with which the backup is to take place must be established. This could take place on a second-by-second basis using sophisticated technology that streams a copy of every data change to another location off-site. Or a backup could be taken once a day, once a week or once a month depending on the nature of the business and the data.

The type of backup must be clear. A full backup is a backup of every file and change made to the system. Therefore, if anything is lost, a copy of it should be on the media holding the full backup. A full backup is likely to take up the most media and longest time to perform but will provide the quickest restore time.

Incremental backups are backups made only to files that have changed since the last full or incremental backup. Therefore any files which have not been altered will only be preserved on the full backup media. Incremental backups are the fastest to apply but take the longest to restore.

Differential backup is similar to incremental backup, but backs up every file that has changed since the last full backup. This tends to be the middle ground between full and incremental backup.

When a backup is taken, it is important to consider its location. Leaving the backup on a floppy disk next to the machine it was taken from is not wise. A more logical approach would be to locate the backup away from the original source so that it does not get destroyed with the original if a disaster should strike. Off-site, fire-proof safes or underground storage facilities may be the location of choice for some, whilst smaller firms may share copies of the backup between the employees who may simply take them home for safekeeping.

Someone should be designated to be responsible for ensuring the backing up of data takes place and for getting the data back online should the need arise. In large companies this may be a team who monitor automated systems which take the backup. A small partnership may employ a company to make daily visits to the premises and take the backup at a pre-arranged time. There will be variations of the 'who' factor but it needs to be clear what role personnel have in the backup process.

It is important to decide what media the backups are to reside on. The chosen media must be able to accommodate all the data destined for it and be robust enough to preserve the data. A whole range of options, at varying costs, can be considered. In such instances the selection of the most suitable media will need to be taken by someone who understands the potential of each option and its suitability.

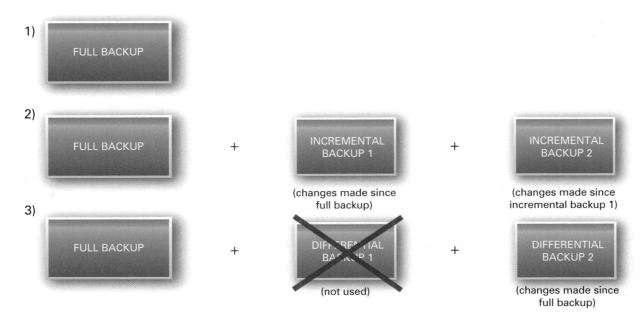

Three different approaches to backup

When budget constraints are in place it will be up to the person responsible for the backup and recovery procedures to clearly explain what they are able to do with the funds they are given and what limitations they face. Some organisations cannot afford to implement the latest automatic backup technology and will have to rely on cheaper methods. However, provided the strategy is worked out in advance, is tested and understood, there is no reason why it cannot succeed.

If several people take it upon themselves to take random backups, confusion will reign. It is imperative that backups are kept in a logical order, are recorded and can be tracked to the most recent and fullest copy. Several copies taken at different times may not agree on what was backed up or when it was done.

The actual process of backing up and recovering data will be different in every organisation and possibly even between systems in the same organisation. Timings, personnel, media, volume and location will all be unique to each situation, but the key foundation of the strategy should not. Constant reviewing, evaluating and testing of the backup system are recommended to ensure that the increase or variation of data within a system can remain

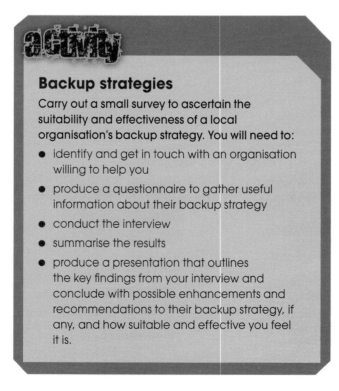

ID number:	001	System objective:	**Upgrade computers in the Finance and IT departments**	
Name:	Daniel Browne	Department: Networking	Job title:	IT Support Administrator

Tasks undertaken each day:
- Remove backup disks and take them off-site
- Set up new users on the system
- Set up security on the file system
- Produce system documentation and procedures manuals
- First line support - help desk
- Assist with installations and upgrades

Communicates with: Network manager, other IT support staff in the department, users at all levels, software and hardware manufacturers

Documents used:
- new user set-up forms
- Internet access forms
- backup schedules
- support call log

Constraints and problems:
1 Too much documentation
2 Users sometimes have to make multiple requests for passwords because there is no tracking system of who applied when, and sometimes the set-up forms are mislaid

User solutions:
Make the support call log automated, using a database
Better storage system and introduce a tracking system

Please tick the following if you agree:
Problems exist with the followiing

Network ☐   Operating system ☐   Other software ☐   Inexperienced users ☐

Please identify how the above have contributed to problems with the IT system:

Any other information:
User complaints about the time it takes to attend a call-out. Network keeps crashing especially between 8:00 and 9:00 in the morning.

Sample questionnaire

accommodated in a backup system designed to support data from the previous day, hour or minute.

The RAID system

RAID stands for Redundant Array of Inexpensive Drives. This is a very common and popular method used to back up systems and data. It involves several hard disks that divide or replicate data automatically. Therefore multiple copies of data are automatically created at the same time as the original. Provided a log is kept, several copies should be available in different locations if required.

activity

Backup strategies

Carry out a small survey to ascertain the suitability and effectiveness of a local organisation's backup strategy. You will need to:

- identify and get in touch with an organisation willing to help you
- produce a questionnaire to gather useful information about their backup strategy
- conduct the interview
- summarise the results
- produce a presentation that outlines the key findings from your interview and conclude with possible enhancements and recommendations to their backup strategy, if any, and how suitable and effective you feel it is.

Practice exam questions

1. Explain, using examples, **four** different ways in which the Internet is being used to support illegal activities. (8)

2. Information Systems need to be protected from both internal and external threats.
   (a) Explain, using examples, the differences between an internal and an external threat to an Information System. (4)
   (b) Describe **one** measure that a company can take to protect its Information System from:
   (i) internal threats (2)
   (ii) external threats. (2)

3. What technical innovations have made the infringement of copyright laws easier? (3)

4. State and explain **three** different threats to commercial data. (6)

5. An A-level schoolboy hacks into the Pentagon and removes several files relating to the latest missile technology and details about Pentagon staff. He then sells the plans and staff details a to country who are trying to develop similar technology.
   (a) Has the schoolboy broken any law? Explain your answer. (6)
   (b) Explain what consequences, if any, the schoolboy might face. (3)

6. A publishing company administers its business by using a database system running on a network of PCs. The main uses are to process customer orders and to log payments.
   (a) Give **two** reasons why it is essential that this company has a backup strategy. (2)
   (b) State **five** factors that should be considered in a backup strategy, illustrating each factor with an example. (10)

7. The owner of a small newsagent uses a computer to manage her orders and deliveries. Every week she copies the files onto a number of floppy disks and puts the disks into a drawer next to the computer.
   (a) State **three** problems that may be caused by this method of backup. (3)
   (b) Describe a more appropriate backup procedure. (6)

8. Passwords are often used as a method of protecting data against malicious access. Give **three** rules that should be followed in relation to using passwords. (3)

9. A company has procedures to back up the data files held on its computer system on a regular basis. Explain why recovery procedures should also be in place. (3)

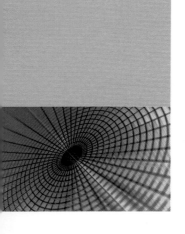

2.5 ICT in society

What ICT can provide

Organisations such as banks, mail order companies and utility companies have millions of customers and have thousands of transactions occurring every hour. Before computing power made this possible, orders and invoices were dealt with manually and a backlog was inevitable. Computing and ICT data-processing systems have made it possible for these organisations to expand exponentially and to keep up with the processing required, by giving them the ability to offer fast repetitive processing.

Retail sales data warehouse

Project description

Amadeus Software was approached to design and develop a data warehouse for a major UK retail organisation's daily sales and ancillary data utilising the existing SAS technology. The data is polled daily through the Electronic Point of Sale (EPOS) system and stored on a UNIX computer. The SAS system is used to access this information and present it through a series of OLAP++ tools to users for a range of business solutions.

Data warehouse design

The data warehouse was designed with expansion in mind, as the final stage of this project was to incorporate atomic-level detail data. The data warehouse houses a large volume of data and the SAS/MDDB™ Server was used to provide fast and efficient access to the information. The data storage was optimised by using a mixture of SAS datasets and MDDB files. SAS MDDB files are stored on a local client and all reports and viewers use and access the MDDB.

Data warehouse reporting

One of the main features of this data warehouse is the ability to create a wide variety of standard and ad-hoc reports quickly and easily. Amadeus Software developed a 'Dimension Reporter' that allows fast specification of 'down', 'across' and 'group' variables, as well as selection of analysis variables. This Dimension Reporter accesses the dimensions in the data warehouse and allows users to select any of the variables that make up the dimensions. All reporting options allow instant export of the data to Excel and other spreadsheets. The reporting aspect of the data warehouse is a high priority for the users of the sales information and the comparison of target and actual sales information reveals a level of detail that was not previously available.

Fast access times

By using a combination of SAS MDDB files and SAS datasets, and providing a graphical user interface with the extensive reporting screens constructed through SAS/AF® and SAS/EIS® software, Amadeus has created a data warehouse that combines speed with flexibility and functionality. Access times for 3 years' worth of data in a standard report are now below 1 minute compared to 15 minutes in the previous software and in many cases below the 10 second mark for a comprehensive drill-down screen.

A link to this website is available at www.heinemann.co.uk/hotlinks (express code 2349P)

The amount of storage now required has been met by advances in storage media with ever-increasing capacities. Where once a storage device was measured in terms of kilobytes, megabytes and gigabytes, it is now measured in terabytes (a thousand gigabytes) and petabytes (a thousand terabytes).

As systems and the data stored in them get larger, so do their data storage requirements. **Data warehousing** is now the norm in big companies where data has to be stored for years, and be available to be searched and filtered to provide information that takes the business forward.

Data warehousing
Data warehousing is the storage of large amounts of historical data in a structured way.

Data warehousing
Read the case study about the retail data warehouse, then answer the following questions:

1 Find out what the following abbreviations stand for, and write a short sentence describing each.
- SAS
- MDDB
- OLAP++

2 Describe what factors influenced how the data warehouse was designed.

3 What facilities did the data warehouse provide for the client?

4 What are the benefits to the client of using this way of storing their data?

5 Give **four** reasons for choosing to use a data warehouse for organisational data.

Appropriate use of ICT

It is easy to assume that ICT is the answer to all society's problems and that organisational use of ICT for all their activities is a given. Of course, this is not the case; it is not always appropriate to rely on ICT to provide the solutions.

A computer is still a logical, programmed machine that does what it is told to do. The advent of sensor-activated decision-making by some ICT systems may give the impression that the machines can 'think', but in reality they are responding in a pre-programmed way. Research laboratories around the world strive to discover a method for producing truly intelligent machines, but experiments are still in their infancy.

Turing test
1 Research the Turing test and write a short description in your own words.

2 Discuss the implications with the rest of the class.

Advances in technology have meant that ICT is used to improve life for many, for example in the field of cybernetics where programmable devices make life easier for many disabled people. ICT can remove much of business drudgery, enabling more speed, more volume of work and more creativity from employees.

ICT as a tool to improve life
Research an application of ICT that has helped an individual to live life more easily – this could be in the field of sight, hearing, movement or speech. Create a short presentation and present it to the class.

The information that an ICT system produces can only be as good as the data that was entered into it and the processing that took place to provide the information. Characteristics of good information were mentioned in an earlier section, but those of completeness, accuracy, relevance and up-to-datedness are most important for the pertinence and use of the information.

Dissemination of information

ICT can be used to present data and information in many ways. Different types of information are suited to different ways of presentation – for example, numerical information is probably best shown in tables or represented as graphs, whereas sound information would be presented using speakers or headphones.

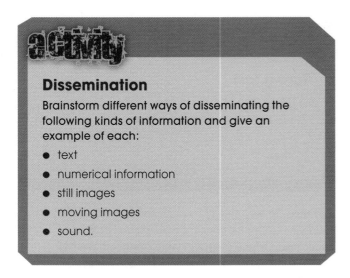

Dissemination

Brainstorm different ways of disseminating the following kinds of information and give an example of each:

- text
- numerical information
- still images
- moving images
- sound.

How information is presented can be almost as important as what it is. Numerous different ways include:

- on computer printouts (or hardcopy)
- using the principle of exception reporting for brevity and clarity; i.e. print only the information that is required
- on a display monitor
- as a report or a 'slide show' produced using a presentation graphics package
- in desktop-published form, incorporating company logo, graphs, diagrams, photographs etc.
- orally

- 'over the grapevine', by telephone or in formal presentations
- using videoconferencing to enable several people at separate locations to participate in meetings and information exchange
- over a company-wide intranet
- on an internal network to which all employees have access.

The way that information is presented will depend to a large extent on who it is intended to reach.

Information on products and sales may be intended for three different groups of people:

Information aimed at customers might be presented through video

Item	Item	Size	Item	Qty
Self-help book 'Impairment to Empowerment' written by Bunty Levene and Val Tait.	M14		£14.99 (plus p&p)	
Hearing Concern Magazine Hearing Concern's quarterly magazine for individuals, professionas and organisations. One copy free.	M15		£2.75	
White t-shirt with HC logo in red Fruit of the Loom white cotton t-shirt with the HC logo over printed on red.	CL01	M L XL	£6.50 £6.50 £6.50	
White polo shirt with HC logo in red Fruit of the Loom polo shirt in white with an embroidered HC logo.	CL08	M L XL	£13.50 £13.50 £13.50	
Ash grey polo shirt with HC logo in red Friut of the Loom polo shirt in marl/ash greay with an embroidered HC logo.	CL09	M L XL	£13.50 £13.50 £13.50	
Sky blue sweatshirt with HC logo in red Fruit of the Loom sweatshirt in sky blue with an embroidered HC logo.	CL05	M L XL	£13.50 £13.50 £13.50	
Ash grey sweatshirt with HC logo in red Friut of the Loom sweatshirt in marl/ash greay with an embroidered HC logo.	CL06	M L XL	£13.50 £13.50 £13.50	
Coin keyring Handy keyring with a £1 coin size pendant that can be used for shopping trolleys and gym lockers.	K02		£2.00	
Pen Frosted white pen with the HC logo along the barrel.	M08		90p	
HC label badge – Silver and white badge with the HC logo.	B09	24mm²	£2.00	

Information for wholesalers might be presented in a table

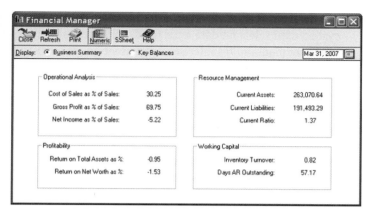

Information for company accountants might be provided in a database

Every time you withdraw cash from an ATM you are performing a transaction that has to be recorded at some point in time and must update the balance in your account. If this is not done until late at night along with everybody else's transactions, this is known as a **batch** system.

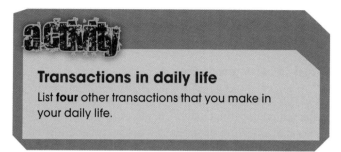

Transactions in daily life

List **four** other transactions that you make in your daily life.

Master files and transaction files

A master file is a collection of records holding information about an entity such as a person or a product. For example, a payroll master file will contain information about each employee, such as first name, surname, address, date of birth, department, date joined, rate of pay, tax code, National Insurance number and bank account details. These are fields which will not change often. In addition, there are also fields which do change regularly, such as gross pay to date, tax paid to date and National Insurance contributions.

A transaction file holds information about events occurring in the company. In the case of a payroll file there will be basically two kinds of transaction.

1. A weekly or fortnightly file containing information about hours worked, which will be used to calculate wages.

2. Every so often there will be other transactions to process – additions, deletions and changes to the file, such as change of address.

Batch processing

Batch processing occurs when the data can be gathered over a period of time then processed at once, particularly if the output is not required immediately. A typical example is payroll. This has both features: output is not required immediately and the data is gathered and processed once a month.

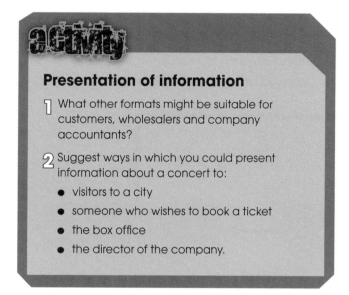

Presentation of information

1 What other formats might be suitable for customers, wholesalers and company accountants?

2 Suggest ways in which you could present information about a concert to:

- visitors to a city
- someone who wishes to book a ticket
- the box office
- the director of the company.

Types of processing

How quickly the output is required from a system depends on the type of processing. There are several different ways in which data can be processed, the main distinction being made between **batch processing**, **interactive processing** and **transaction processing**. All these involve some kind of transaction.

Transactions

Transactions are events that need to be recorded in connection with the production, sale and distribution of services and goods.

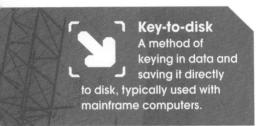

Key-to-disk
A method of keying in data and saving it directly to disk, typically used with mainframe computers.

The data can be prepared off-line, away from the main computer system, using **key-to-disk** methods.

Another good example of a system that uses batch processing is a mail-order business.

Stages in batch processing

In a typical large-scale batch system where data is collected on paper documents (such as applications for renewal of a driving licence or TV licence) the following stages are gone through.

1. The paper documents are collected into batches of, say, 50 and checked. Control totals and hash totals are calculated and written on the batch header document.

2. The data is keyed in off-line (i.e. a separate computer system used solely for data entry) and validated by a computer program. It is stored in a transaction file.

3. The data is verified by being keyed in a second time by a different keypunch operator. Any discrepancies are followed up and corrected.

4. The transaction file is transferred to the main computer. This may be done electronically or by carrying a magnetic tape from one room to another.

5. Processing begins at a scheduled time, maybe overnight when the computer is not busy dealing with online users. All further processing steps can now continue without operator intervention.

6. The transaction file may be sorted into the same sequence as the master file (using a utility program) to speed up the processing of data.

7. The master file is updated.

8. Any required reports are produced.

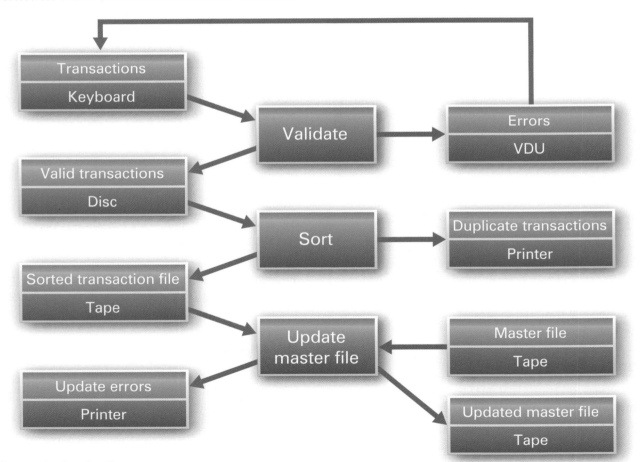

Batch processing data flow diagram

Interactive processing

Interactive processing means you are interacting with the computer but it does not necessarily mean that the processing is done immediately.

With some systems you may interact with the computer in such a way that your transaction is recorded but is only carried out later in a batch update run. For example, some stores with their own debit cards use this system, as it is more cost-effective to connect to head office once a day than to have an expensive line open all day. Other examples are point-of-sales terminals that can access a stock file to look up the description and price of an article when the bar code label is scanned, but will only alter the quantity in stock later in batch mode.

Cash point machines allow you to query your balance and withdraw cash, but do not update the balance until late at night.

Transaction processing

Transaction processing deals with each set of data from a user as it is submitted. This is normally used in commercial systems. A transaction may be a booking, an order or an invoice. Each transaction is completed before the next is begun.

The processing is done as quickly as possible, where not to do so can cause problems. For example, in an airline seat reservation system, if processing was not done immediately, you could end up with double bookings.

Criteria for choice of processing mode

The choice of whether to use a batch processing system or a transaction processing system depends on several factors.

1. Whether the information needs to be up-to-date at all times.
2. The scale of the operation. Batch systems are well suited to huge volumes of data when it becomes economical to have an off-line, key-to-disk system for data entry.
3. Cost. A real-time system is generally more expensive because of the more complex backup and recovery procedures required to cope with power failures or breakdown in hardware.

4. Computer usage. The advantage of a batch system is that it can make use of spare computer capacity overnight or at times when the computer would otherwise be idle. Batch processing is often carried out on mainframe computers.

Many organisations (and even applications) use a combination of batch and interactive processing.

	TXU Energy	Palace Theatre	Air2000
Batch processing	Printing electricity bills	Setting up seating plan for new season	Setting up flight schedules
Interactive processing	Outstanding bill enquiry system	Seat enquiry system	Flight enquiry system
Transaction processing	Engineer visit booking	Theatre seat booking	Plane seat booking

Examples of processing types

Processing

1. Think about the ICT systems in use at your school or college. Examples may include:
    * the application process
    * examinations system, entries and results
    * attendance and progress tracking
    * timetabling and scheduling.
2. Find out about one of these systems and identify what type or types of processing may be suitable for two or more identified functions within the system.
3. Share your findings with the rest of your class.

Factors affecting the use of ICT

This section is just an overview of the types of factor that could influence the use of ICT in society. Current issues must be investigated at the time of studying, as they change all the time.

Cultural factors

Cultural factors include issues relating to age, gender, ethnicity and corporate ethos. History has a large part to play in cultural issues, and acceptance or resistance to change. The changes that can be brought about by the use of ICT can figure greatly when discussing cultural factors.

Cultural issues in ICT

1 Hold a class discussion on what cultural issues you think are currently important pertaining to the use of ICT.

2 Summarise this discussion in no more than 10 bullet points.

Economic factors

Economic factors include the local and global economy of the time. Interest rates and current inflation may influence whether or not ICT is the chosen solution for a problem. Economic factors may also influence how an organisation procures its ICT systems, both hardware and software.

ICT and the economy

Discuss in groups what effect the current economic position might be having on the research and development of ICT – read trade papers and financial papers and see if the high-tech organisations are showing activity.

Environmental factors

Environmental factors include choices for organisations and individuals about where to build new premises, what are the most environmentally friendly ICT systems, what is the safest forms of transmission and so on.

ICT procurement

Information and communication technologies (ICTs) are at the heart of economic growth in the modern world. They enable us to process and exchange information in increasingly greater quantities, at higher speeds, with more detail and provide easier and wider access to information. There is a mass of analysis on how the benefits of ICTs can be captured for economic gain via e-business and e-commerce, and increasing attention to the social and economic impacts of the use of the technology. There has been less attention by users to the environmental impacts of the hardware they're using, particularly in its manufacture and disposal. They have accordingly not exercised any significant influence on manufacturers, and progress has tended to come from manufacturers' voluntary initiatives and through some regulatory and NGO pressure.

A link to this website is available at www.heinemann.co.uk/hotlinks (express code 2349P)

ICT and environmental factors

Investigate the environmental issues further and draw up some guidelines for ensuring that use of ICT considers environmental factors.

Legal factors

Legal factors cover storage, processing, dissemination and transmission of data and information, legal use of ICT, and software copyright.

ICT-related legislation

1 Research ICT-related legislation.

2 Make sure you are familiar with the main points of each type of legislation – discuss the ways in which having to abide by legislation has an affect on how ICT is used in an organisation.

Ethical factors

Ethical factors include:

- personal and corporate ethical issues
- intellectual property rights
- privacy and confidentiality
- ICT misuse
- ambiguity regarding ICT status, use and capability
- transparency of actions and decisions related to ICT
- adherence to relevant laws
- standards in, for example, development, documentation and training
- relevant professional codes.

Ethical factors

Discuss ethical factors in a small group. Produce a single slide that can spark a whole group discussion.

Social factors

Social factors include where and how ICT is used in everyday situations, what is acceptable use and what is not. Consider how ICT is used in the home, in leisure activities, in education and in the commercial world.

Uses of ICT

1 Choose a situation and, in small groups, brainstorm the uses of ICT. Split these into categories to suggest everyday use, occasional use, acceptable use, unacceptable use and so on. Come up with some different categories if necessary.

2 Present your results to the whole class.

Guidelines for presentations

A presentation could take either of the following forms.

- A talk accompanied by overhead projector transparencies or slides.
- A slide show prepared in a presentation graphics package.

Either way, the information on each screen or slide should be:

- **simple** – no more than five or six clearly legible lines, in clear English
- **brief** – bullet points are a good communication tool
- **visually appealing** – don't use too many different fonts, or all uppercase letters; graphs and charts are useful where numeric information has to be imparted.

Be careful with colour. Red-green or blue-brown combinations can cause problems for anyone who is colour-blind. Garish or neon colours might put some people off and detract from the message.

Be careful with images. Images should enhance the message rather than take attention away from it. They can be used with very good effect.

The background is also important. Check it looks okay with the chosen font in the situation it will be presented in – what looks good on a small screen may not look so good blown up and projected.

Transitions, animations and sounds need to be chosen with care – too much, or too slow or too irritating will lead to audience boredom, irritation and fidgeting.

Presentations

1 Take a presentation that you have already produced (or produce one with no more than ten slides) and critically evaluate it.

2 Could you have produced this to equal effectiveness in another format? If yes, what could you add to the presentation that would make it only appropriate to be shown through a data projector? If no, then describe the features that make that the case.

3 What else could be added that could improve your presentation?

4 List some benefits to the presenter of using presentation graphics software.

5 List some benefits to the audience of using presentation graphics software.

6 List some drawbacks of using presentation graphics software.

Practice exam questions

1. Name **one** mode of processing that would be suitable for each of the following ICT systems.
   (a) Airline ticket booking   (1)
   (b) Production of electricity bills   (1)
   (c) Internet banking   (1)
   (d) Controlling a nuclear power station.   (1)
   (June 2006)

2. A theatre booking system uses interactive transaction processing.
   Explain what is meant by the terms **interactive processing** and **transaction processing**.   (4)
   (January 2006)

3. Examination boards publish past examination papers and mark schemes on the Internet.
   (a) State **two** benefits to an examination board of doing this.   (2)
   (b) State **two** benefits to a teacher of making use of this facility.   (2)
   (June 2006)

4. For each of the following areas, state **one** benefit and **one** limitation of the use of ICT. Your benefits and limitations must be different in each case.
   (a) Education   (2)
   (b) Leisure in the home   (2)
   (c) Manufacturing   (2)
   (d) Medicine   (2)
   (e) An office.   (2)
   (June 2006)

2.6 ICT in context

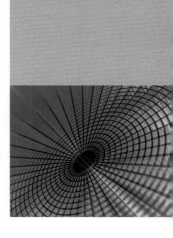

This section contains descriptions, case studies and activities for seven different contexts of the use of ICT in today's society.

The content does not derive exactly from the specification, but the requirement to gain knowledge and understanding of the uses of ICT in the digital world in which we live, and to be able to apply it, mean that some overview of a wide range of contexts beyond the home, the school and the part-time job, may be required.

The sections can be read on their own, and the activities within them used to engender an appreciation of the widespread use of ICT in the digital world, or they can be used simultaneously with studying the other sections, to give a context on which to apply learning of the other topics in Section 2.

The more contexts you are exposed to, the better your basic understanding will become. An ability to apply knowledge learnt at AS will mean that an unfamiliar context presented as an exam question will not come as too much of a surprise and will form a sound basis for carrying on the study of ICT to A2 level.

While the AS content is more generally aimed at applications of ICT as used at a personal level, there are areas where a wider understanding is required. The areas of education, retail, health care and leisure should all be familiar to the average AS level student; however, the areas of banking, industry and publishing may not.

ICT in education

Since the printing press was invented over 300 years ago, pupils in schools across the world have had access to more and more information from a variety of different sources. Now, thanks to the advances in information and communications technology, there is an unprecedented amount of information at our fingertips. It is possible to find out the names of shop owners in Finland, the uses of every element in the periodic table and how far it is to the nearest petrol station at the click of a mouse button or at the touch of a screen.

Just as the amount of information available continues to grow, so too does the range of devices that allow data to be accessed. With such grand resources becoming ever more common within schools across the UK, it becomes clear that the way learning takes place now and in the future will be radically different to anything seen before.

The stereotype model of the teacher who is stressed, wears elbow patches on his jacket, carries around stacks of disorganised paper and folders and often hands back work with wine stains on it is becoming a thing of the past.

A modest question to ask is 'are teachers really still required?' Students can pre-record lessons, project them onto large screens, pause, rewind and zoom in on any content, play them on iPods and download extension tasks from resource banks from anywhere in the world. Is it conceivable that pupils will not have to rely on adults to direct them from the front of the class, provide content and mark work? The simple answer is, 'yes, it is conceivable, but hardly desirable'. Someone has to control the class, lead discussions, look after pupil welfare, create a safe learning environment and direct learning.

Technology in the classroom (1)

The following activity gives you the opportunity to look at the technology available and suggest ways it can be used within the classroom.

In groups of no more than three, produce a simple digital learning resource for primary school children to encourage them to read. You should consider:

- the needs of the audience
- the content of the resource
- how the resource will look
- the features it will include
- the most appropriate software to use

Extension

Produce a system that can be used by teachers to track and record progress of a group of pupils who are required to produce four essays all scored out of 60. It should show the percentage for each essay, an average percentage of all four essays for each pupil, and should automatically produce a grade based on the average relating to the following table.

A 80%+	B 70%+	C 60%+
D 50%+	E 40%+	F 30%+

What are the needs of the audience?

The technology on show in schools often includes the school computer suite with its printer and scanner. Following this are electronic whiteboards and projectors. Some schools make use of digital and DVD cameras, as well as sound-recording equipment. Even satellite navigation is used by teachers taking pupils on trips or to away fixtures. Pupils also add to the list with mobile phones, MP3 players, laptops, USB devices, digital cameras and PDAs.

Without software, the technology mentioned is fairly useless. The software provides us with web browsers and an attractive, intuitive graphical user interface which mean that pupils of virtually any age can open and start most software with minimal tuition.

This throws open the opportunity for pupils to learn more practically than ever before. Pupils are able to enter simulations which show how machinery works, listen to a commentary and actually see what happens if they attempt to alter how the machine functions. Learning becomes safer as pupils can mix any chemicals they like together and see what happens without having their goggles melt onto their face or burning down the science lab!

Pupils no longer need to burn down the science lab!

Such interactive learning packages have been given away on cereal boxes, which means that 10-year-olds have already had the chance to mix the latest tracks downloaded from the Internet to produce their own compilation albums, that then get transferred to friends via email or downloaded on to their MP3 players. All this is happening while older relatives remember how carefully they had to place vinyl onto the record player, taking more care not to scratch it before it finished playing. If pupils use so much technology beyond the classroom to be creative and expand their knowledge base then it is evolutionary sense for the majority of learning undertaken to follow suit.

At present, teachers make use of DVD footage selected at just the point they want the class to see it. Prior to this, time was spent lining up the video, making sure the TV was tuned in, and getting the class to gather around the screen to comprehend the muffled sound.

Pupils as young as six work with animation software to make simple characters that move. Digital photography is used to capture data for use in thousands of publications, from websites to fixture cards and project work. These are manipulated in specialist software to suit the publications being worked on, or simply deleted and replaced by something better with minimal fuss. The

capture of primary research data can happen with digital dictaphones or cameras, which can be used during interviews. Voice recognition technology means those who have problems with spelling or typing speed can get on with expressing their idea without having to worry about how long it will take them or how poor it might look.

During the development phase of any work, pupils can easily contact industrial experts or academics to gain the latest view on the area of study they are currently involved with. It is feasible that a pupil could send a design idea as an email attachment to a large manufacturer who might take the idea further into production.

activity

Technology in the classroom (2)

This activity will help you identify just how much your teacher is using technology within his or her role as an educator.

With your teacher, list all the tasks performed throughout the day then describe the technological alternative, if there is one.

Example:

Task	Teacher takes register
Is technology used?	No, teacher uses a mark book
If yes, how?	Not used
If no, how could technology be used?	Pupils enter room with swipe card, which is read by card reader in door and sends information to a central database that pupil has entered the room; database records that the person is present

Extension

Undertake research in your school or college to investigate what technology is used in various departments and offices and what it is used for. Present your findings as a presentation to promote your school to potential new pupils and parents.

Pupils now have access to past exam papers, mark schemes and reports which give them the opportunity to understand exactly what examiners are looking for and what difficulties previous students had with certain questions. Model answers and feedback are all provided on exam board websites; if not, there are independent sites that can supply such detail.

Language labs are popping up in schools. In these labs, pupils put on a headset, load up software and start learning a language. The software is smart enough to track progress, provide feedback, structure learning to suit the pupil's ability, repeat difficult tasks and even provide certificates as certain levels are conquered. This provides pupils with the opportunity to learn at their own pace, select content they find interesting, interact with native speakers and have the pitch of their pronunciation

recorded and played back with recommendations on how best to improve. Teachers can use the same software to track how a whole class is coping and compare progress with other groups. Individual pupil records can be extracted and used to assist report writing. The teacher can turn this technology off and use the traditional one-to-one method to really see how effective the software and learning has been.

case study

SKYPE in Education

World Class Schools Director Michael Cunningham announced this week that their organisation is testing a new project that will revolutionize the face of education. Cunningham: 'Education depends on cutting edge technology and with proper application of this new Skype technology a school can turn a computer room into a language lab.

World Class Schools, a collection of forty high schools and organizations all across the world, is introducing several innovative projects for 2005. One of their most ambitious and innovative projects is the Skype Foreign Language Lab Project. This project uses technology from the Skype Company and applies it to the classroom.

Cunningham explains that Skype technology allows a person sitting at one computer to call a person at another computer and then talk to that person for free. He adds that this allows for projects like their Skype Foreign Language Project to turn a classroom of computers into a language lab by allowing students in a language class the opportunity to call and talk with native speakers on a daily basis for free.

A link to this website is available at www.heinemann.co.uk/hotlinks (express code 2349P)

activity

ICT to enhance learning

This activity gives you the opportunity to both investigate how you use ICT to enhance your learning and help to decorate the classroom.

Produce a page from your digital diary that details how you have used ICT over a single day to help you with your learning; remember to include details beyond school as well. The finished product should include:

- appropriate images
- text which is not too detailed but is adequate enough to get the message across
- other design ideas which give your page visual impact.

Extension

Produce a detailed email to your overseas friend describing your day at school/college in the year 2025.

Schools produce reams and reams of information that can be easily accessed by any pupil logged on to the school intranet. Details about school trips, dinnertime staff rotas, sports fixtures, clubs, societies and new staff are just a few items which may appear on the homepage of a school intranet. The technology may also make it possible for parents to access school records.

Parents can use the web to access a school's management information system to check their child has arrived at school, what they will be having for dinner, what homework they have been set, if they have a football match and where it is and to look at their latest report. With such information to hand, parents will be in a better position to support their children with academic study and to assist them in keeping up-to-date. Parents may even have the opportunity to use the system to offer any expertise they might like to add to the resources already on offer.

Many schools use the Internet to broadcast a site that promotes their school. Often pictures, news articles and upcoming events are placed on such sites and provide potential parents with an initial resource to view prior to visiting (they can even download directions).

Pupils have access to search engines, which can find thousands of links to any query within a second of the request being made. MySpace, Facebook, YouTube and other social networking sites are further resources that some schools exploit as a learning tool because they know these are sites that pupils frequently visit and where they

case study

The School Network and ICT Resources

The use and application of ICT for staff, students and the community throughout Parrs Wood has been evolving at a phenomenal rate. Parrs Wood can offer access to its network through both wireless technologies and a hard wired infrastructure.

Our aim is to continually provide both staff and students with the best ICT service and support in order to help raise achievement.

Evidence suggests that ICT is a contributor of learning and teaching and is a tool for whole school improvement. Since March 2000 the school has been incorporating ICT into many of its frameworks to ensure that ICT and associated new technologies play a vital part in the development of these frameworks.

At Parrs Wood all teaching staff are issued with a laptop and the development of all staff's ICT skills are supported by an in-house training programme in the effective use of ICT.

Staff are encouraged to use ICT within the classroom as an everyday piece of equipment and not to think of it as an additional teaching aid that is separate from their own subject specialism.

Through ICT our students can access learning 24 hours a day, seven days a week, at any time and from anywhere!

- Complete access to the network across the entire campus via wireless technology.
- All rooms throughout the school have a minimum of four network points.

- Every teaching room has at least one computer.
- Seven dedicated ICT teaching rooms (two in the 6th Form).
- Six class sets of laptops in rechargeable trolleys with wireless access.
- Data projectors distributed across faculty areas (many ceiling mounted).
- Interactive whiteboards distributed across faculty areas.
- A plethora of peripheral devices e.g., scanners, digital cameras (still and video), data logging equipment etc.

To ensure that our network operates 24 hours a day, 365 days a year we have full time dedicated ICT support staff.

Their roles are vital within the school. They have specialisms in:

- Network Management
- Database Management
- Systems Analysis

With their support we can ensure that the staff and students are provided with the best and most appropriate ICT facilities that are available to our school.

Staff utilise the skills and knowledge provided by our support staff to develop new ideas that are related to ICT within their subject area to develop new resources.

A link to this website is available at www.heinemann.co.uk/hotlinks (express code 2349P)

ICT in the classroom: Mobile phones welcome here

Most art galleries ban mobile phones. At The Study in Poole, Dorset, they're positively encouraged. So keen is education officer Sandy Wilderspin to see them being used that she has a stockpile of Nokia 3G handsets that she loans to school parties. With them, children are able to compile their own digital scrapbooks which are automatically downloaded to their own personal websites.

Along with The D Day Museum in Portsmouth and Urbis in Manchester, The Study is piloting a Culture Online initiative to reinvent the traditional school visit to a gallery or museum. Called OOKL (an anagram of 'look' –geddit?) it's a name silly enough to give it credibility in the digital world, and cleverly emphasises how it can change the way that children respond to exhibits. They don't just look, they ookl.

First the bad news for any visiting school party: the mobile phones are not linked to any commercial network so they can't be used to phone mates stuck in school to tell them what a great time you're having. And the good news: as pupils from Haymoor Middle School in Poole quickly discovered, there are other ways to make the most of a Nokia.

They were soon in text mode and thumbing in notes on the modern paintings and sculptures that they found rlly v v intrstng. The Study is devoted exclusively to modern art but kids don't seem in the least intimidated by the abstraction, finding their own narratives in the swirls of colour. The gallery catalogue might describe Jeffrey Steele's Toccata as asymmetric inter-related rectangles but Hollie conveys so much more when she notes that it's 'like when you are so busy that your mind is muddled.'

The mobile can also be used as a dictaphone so Lucy with all the professional aplomb of a talking head on The Culture Show, interviewed Rebecca about a painting that had taken her fancy. There's nothing like knowing that a recorder is running to get interviewees to do some serious thinking about a picture and try to distil their thoughts into a coherent soundbite.

The phone's in-built camera offers pupils further opportunities to chronicle their visit. They photograph whole works or home-in on a detail than interests them. Better still, they can snap their chums standing alongside a painting or contorting their bodies in the abstract geometry of a modern sculpture.

'Instead of just walking around, the phones encourage the children to interact with the art. And that process is what's important not the photographs and text they end up with,' says Sandy Wilderspin. Once pupils have raced around seeing what's on offer, she insists that they restrict their collections to the 15 objects they most like. 'It makes them have to think about what they like and why they like it. I want them to see themselves as curators having to make decisions about what they'd like to collect for their own galleries.'

And using OOKL they really do collect art works. Most of the exhibits are labelled with a two digit code. When a pupil keys the code into the mobile, a digitised image of the exhibit is automatically added to their scrapbook. They are simultaneously sent a text message containing background information about the object and the names of other pupils who have chosen it. This enables classmates to meet up for impromptu chats about their mutual choice – like a couple of the Haymoor lads – to exchange congratulatory high-fives.

The second phase of the work begins back at school. Pupils can access their online scrapbooks where they'll find the downloaded images, text messages, photos and sound files. They are now free to edit them, to add new text or even import multimedia material from other applications.

They can also disregard the 'only 15' rule and delve into The Study's database of other images that they might have overlooked during the visit. Better still, they can take a peek into their classmates' galleries and borrow any images that take their fancy . . .

A password system ensures that these school galleries are for private view only. But a teacher can choose to publish the best of them on the OOKL website. It's still in its infancy, but over the years this compendium of other visitors' impressions could grow into a fascinating and useful educational resource.

A link to this website is available at www.heinemann.co.uk/hotlinks (express code 2349P)

access information. Even after pupils leave school they can still relive the glory days via Friends Reunited and other reminiscing sites.

Many teachers are using Virtual Learning Environments (VLEs). These provide pupils and staff with a place on the web to share resources, and to set up chat rooms so that whole classes can meet in the evenings and chat over the latest developments within the subject with the teacher keeping track of what is being said and written. VLEs are also places where work can be set for pupils to download, which can later be uploaded for marking by a given deadline. Such sites can easily link to other learning communities, which potentially means that the best teachers in the world are able to share and exploit the best resources in the world, which is undoubtedly great news for pupils. This also means that pupils can form multi-continental links and gain a more realistic appreciation of a culture from a primary source.

The world's learning resources are opening up not only to pupils but also to teachers. They are able to contact like-minded colleagues, exchange ideas, attend online courses and collect resources within a very short space of time. The best lesson plans can be downloaded within seconds and implemented to an information hungry class who can become accustomed to quality practice because the teachers have access to quality material and the best training.

In 2006, Google announced an initiative to digitise the world's literature. Therefore it could be possible that, within a few years, pupils will be carrying one device which plays music, stores files and projects, takes pictures, searches the Internet and contains a selection of novels and reference books; oh, and makes phone calls!

case study

How £50m went to waste on a whiteboard

Hi-tech electronic whiteboards are now in half of all classrooms in England.

Replacing school blackboards with hi-tech interactive whiteboards has been a waste of £50 million, say academics.

Ministers wanted the whiteboards to help personalise teaching to meet the needs of individual pupils and help children learn at their own pace. But a Government-funded evaluation has found they have had no impact on performance. Pupils were reduced to spectators as teachers produced faster and more complicated electronic displays.

The large, touch-sensitive boards are connected to a computer and projector which can use video, animation, graphics and sound. They are now in half of all classrooms in England. The report from London's Institute of Education said: Although the newness of the technology was initially welcomed by pupils any boost in motivation seems short-lived.

Statistical analysis showed no impact on pupil performance in the first year departments were fully equipped. Sometimes teachers focused more on the new technology than on what pupils should be learning, the report suggested.

For instance, the focus on interactivity as a technical process can lead to some relatively mundane activities being over-valued. 'Such an emphasis on interactivity was particularly prevalent in classes with lower-ability students,' the report said. 'In lower-ability groups it could actually slow the pace of whole class learning as individual pupils took turns at the board.'

Schools Minister Jim Knight said the report reflected the early days 'before electronic whiteboards had settled into classrooms'. He said he believes passionately that such technology 'can be an excellent tool in helping teaching and learning'. But he added that it would never be a substitute for good teaching. 'Only when teachers have the skills to use it properly can we expect them to use the technology to support and transform traditional teaching methods.'

A link to this website is available at www.heinemann.co.uk/hotlinks (express code 2349P)

It is only a matter time before the facilities available are deployed much more effectively within education to the benefit of every pupil, in every subject, provided they have a connection to the Internet, wherever they are.

ICT in education

In this activity you are expected to be able to clearly argue a case for or against using ICT in education.

Based on the previous case study and your own further research, investigate whether ICT is really useful within education. Present your findings and conclusion to your class in the form of short bullet-pointed notes and a verbal presentation displaying your findings. You might like to comment on:

● the use and advantage of freeware

● the barriers to using ICT

● the problems with using ICT

● what new opportunities ICT can provide for education.

Questions

1. State **two** advantages and **two** disadvantages of the use of ICT in Education. (4)

2. A teacher needs to prepare a lesson about global warming. Explain how IT can assist with this task. (5)

3. Describe how IT can make lessons interactive. (4)

4. Many schools use a database to store information about their pupils.
   (i) List **four** items of data a school would hold about each pupil, not including name and home contact details. (4)
   (ii) For each of the items listed in (i) give a reason why the school would have this information. (4)

5. Schools have many ways of keeping in touch with parents.
   (i) Describe **two** technology-based methods schools can use to do this. (4)
   (ii) What kind of information might schools send home? (2)

ICT in banking

A bank is usually an institution found on the high street in every city, town or village in the country. They are places where business and personal accounts can be opened and money deposited or withdrawn. Prior to the technological boom, cash or cheques were the most common method for making deposits and these were often done in person at a branch over a counter. When a deposit or withdrawal was made, a manual update of the holder's account was made and the transaction concluded.

Today, things are very different. Anyone with the required technology and the financial means can open an account from home using the Internet. When a request to open an account online is made, banks have had to ensure that the account is lawful and is genuinely in the name of the person making the request. To achieve this, the bank will not activate the account until written confirmation, usually a signature on a contract, is returned to the bank. A customer is also required to set up security online before viewing the account. Most banks have several layers of security including a user number, PIN and secret password. Any attempt by someone who is not authorised to view the account will be refused if any of the security details are incorrectly entered.

Once an account is active and security has been organised, the customer can access their details anywhere they have an Internet connection. The kinds of services banks offer online will be the same as those offered within the branch. These include the ability to view the account details and to see what has been paid in (credits) and what has been paid out (debits).

By electronically accessing the account, customers can make payments for household utility, credit or store card bills, even mobile phone bills, without having to write a cheque and post it. The advantage of online bill payment is that it can normally be done a day or two after a cheque would have to be posted.

Account-holders may request an overdraft online. An overdraft allows the account-holder to withdraw more money than they actually have in the account. The whole application process can be done electronically and a decision provided, by email, in a very short space of time. Loans too can be sought. Before approving a loan, the bank will check the applicant's credit history – they will be able to access these credit details online and see a digital record of a person's financial history. It will show what loans they have taken out in the past and what direct debits they currently pay, as well as other financial details that will help the bank decide whether to authorise the loan or not. The ability to use such electronic services to check credit ratings and account details means that banks can make more decisions, with more accuracy, in less time, which allows them to offer more services.

Banks make their profit from selling loans and issuing overdraft payments by charging interest. The rate of interest is usually very similar amongst all banks who follow the advice of the Bank of England, which sets a recommended interest rate. Banks and building societies are the main lenders of mortgages. These are loans used to help finance the purchase of a house.

There are several banks that only operate online. They do not have the expensive overheads of those found on the high street. Banks that only operate online do not incur costs such as staff, lighting, heating and the cost of maintenance, rent or of purchasing a site. The savings made by reducing overheads are often passed on to customers, who are offered better rates on their savings. For example, a high street bank may offer 5% a year on a savings account whereas an online bank may be able to afford to offer 7%. Conversely, online banks should also be able to offer better rates on loans so the borrower would not have to pay back as much interest as they would if they used a high street bank.

Mongan and Waldron Financial Advisors

Mongan and Waldron Financial Advisors have asked you to investigate the online banking market. They have specifically asked that you carry out research into online accounts for new university students. Your task is to find **three** alternative accounts for students, provide details of each account and conclude with a recommendation, with reasons, which account Mongan and Waldron should promote to their customers. The work should be presented as a business report with appropriate headings and a company logo.

Online banking allows customers to transfer money from their account to someone else's. This is known as a standing order and can happen as a one-off payment or arranged to happen on the same date each month until it is stopped. Customers can request and pay for foreign currency. By using quote providers on the bank's website, customers can check the best possible exchange rate for their money and literally buy another country's currency. This often takes place before going on holiday. However, a shrewd route to take would be to shop around on the Internet and compare exchange rates, as some banks may offer a better rate than others. Just like a retailer, banks are selling a product and nowadays they are at the mercy of customers who are better informed than ever before. This means that they have to offer good rates, in line with their competition, to secure sales.

Further services include using the website facilities to obtain quotes for house or car insurance and applying for credit cards or savings accounts. All the details required for the customer to make an informed decision should be provided on the bank's website, as well as information about the charges likely to be enforced.

Debit cards are increasingly used to make purchases. These allow clients to authorise retailers to access their account and deduct the amount owing to conclude a sale. This system is known as Bankers Automated Clearing Services (BACS). BACS takes three working days to process. On day one the details of the transaction are entered into the system, on day two it is processed and on day three the transaction is cleared. The BACS system has come under pressure because of lead time between the start and end of transactions. In Scandinavia, a system called ELLE (Early Late/Late Early) is used, which sees funds arrive in accounts on the same day as the sale or transaction took place. Consumer groups, backed by the Office of Fair Trading, have requested that such a system be in place in the UK by 2008, reducing lead times from 3 days to 3 hours.

To access the customer's account the retailer will swipe the debit card and ask the shopper to enter their **PIN** into a device which checks that the account has sufficient funds and transfers money from one account (the buyer's) to another (the retailer's). The 'chip and PIN' system was introduced as a measure to combat card fraud. Without a PIN it is not possible to use the debit card. Therefore if a card is lost or stolen, the finder or thief can do very little with it. The chip is built into the card and contains

How ATM fraud nearly brought down British banking

Phantoms and rogue banks

This is the story of how the UK banking system could have collapsed in the early 1990s, but for the forbearance of a junior barrister who also happened to be an expert in computer law – and who discovered that at that time the computing department of one of the banks issuing ATM cards had 'gone rogue', cracking PINs and taking money from customers' accounts with abandon.

In February 1992 Kelman got a call from Sheila MacKenzie, head of the Consumers' Association (which publishes Which? magazine), who said that members were complaining by the dozen about phantom withdrawals, and was he interested? Kelman was, and met MacKenzie, with two of the association's members, Mr and Mrs McConville from Liverpool, who had had a number of phantom withdrawals from their Barclays account. They already had a solicitor, but needed someone with computer expertise in the law to make their case. Kelman at this time was able to charge £1,750 per hour – each hour being broken into six-minute chunks. Oh, and don't forget VAT too. That's £206.62 per six minutes.

He showed his value pretty quickly, pointing out that banks must have a legal mandate to debit someone's account. If they take it away from a customer without a mandate, they must refund it. So the legal point of phantom withdrawals hinged on the question: if a PIN is typed into an ATM with a card that matches an account number, is that a mandate by the customer for the bank to debit their account?

As long as you didn't breach the terms of the contract by leaving your card lying around (which would give implicit authority for use), then you, as the customer, could simply say that the withdrawal was not mandated, and demand your cash back.

How could the banks respond? They'd have to give all the phantom withdrawal money back where they could not show that the customer had typed in the PIN – unless, that is, they claimed that their systems were infallible. Yes, only by going where no computer system had ever gone before could the banks deny that phantom withdrawals were (1) taking place and (2) their responsibility to refund.

Kelman took the case on legal aid and decided to bundle up more than 2,000 people's cases into a single class action against all the high street banks taking part in the ATM network. He trawled newsgroups for information on how crackers might decode ATM cards.

He also met two key people in the course of his research. The first, early on, was Andrew Stone, an ex-con who had been done for fraud, who claimed to had (sic) taken £750,000 from ATMs by combining techniques such as shoulder-surfing and grabbing receipts from ATMs (which in those days often had the full account number on them). Stone – who was soon back in prison – was proof in himself that criminals could make 'phantom' withdrawals.

Professor Ross Anderson, a cryptography and security expert who was an expert consultant to Kelman on the case, explains: 'Stone had been working with building

Continued

access systems using cards with magnetic strips, and one day he thought he'd see what it could read of his ATM card. Then he tried it with his wife's.' Stone figured that the stream of digits was probably an encrypted PIN.

'Then, because you can change the content of the magnetic strip, he wondered what would happen if he changed the number on his card to match his wife's. He found he could get money out using his old PIN.' The high street bank Stone used had not used the account number to encrypt the PIN on the card – meaning that any card for that bank could be changed and used to make withdrawals on any other account in it, providing you knew the right details (such as branch sort code and account number. The name of the card holder of course was unimportant, because it was not on the stripe.)

'After that,' says Professor Anderson, 'it was just a question for Stone of collecting as many account numbers as he could.' Until the police caught up with him, at least.

In September 1992 Kelman met a woman he called the 'Lotus Lady', because she worked for Lotus at a time when he was considering buying some groupware to organise the rapidly-growing class action; he had already put the names and other details of all the litigants into a relational database to search for patterns in victims and withdrawals. The Lotus Lady was interesting because her ATM card didn't debit her account. It gave her money, but heaven knew where from.

Kelman thought for a moment and realised that there must be thousands of such cards – and after a little more thought, how it had happened.

How could there be thousands of such cards? Because the chances of any two random people meeting in the UK population at that time were 25 million to 1. For one of them to have the only card in existence that debited other peoples' accounts was absurd. He'd been on the case for six months, met – say – 3,000 people through it – and one of them had such a card. The odds only work if thousands of people are walking around with cards like that, or potentially could be. They had the wrong magnetic strip on the card: the front was embossed with the holder's details, but the account and PIN encrypted on the strip pointed somewhere else. How wouldn't that be spotted?

Simple: dummy accounts. To do their testing in an environment where the bank systems had to work all the time, the computing teams set up a parallel universe of dummy banks, dummy branches and dummy accounts. But they generated real ATM cards for them, and could take out real money – authorised by the banks. Some people were getting dummy cards.

But equally, Kelman saw, it would be possible for a 'rogue' computing department to start tweaking the cards to take money from innocent customers.

A link to this website is available at www.heinemann.co.uk/hotlinks (express code 2349P)

PIN

PIN stands for Personal Identification Number, typically a 4-digit number. Most cards allow users to change the PIN to something more memorable than the random PIN initially assigned to the card.

the account holder's details, which are read electronically. Chip and PIN helps to keep payments secure during a physical purchase but does not protect so well when online purchases are made and the PIN is not required.

Debit cards allow the holder to withdraw cash from machines found attached to the outside of banks. These are known as Automatic Teller Machines (ATMs) or, informally, as 'the hole in the wall'. ATMs have a slot where the user enters their card, which is read by the machine. The details of the customer's account are accessed after they have typed in their PIN correctly. The services available from the ATM will depend on the type of account the user has. The most common uses of the ATM are withdrawing cash and checking the account balance. It is also possible to order chequebooks and to change the PIN.

Customers can access their cash even when the bank is closed. ATMs mean that bank staff do not have their time taken up dealing with requests that the machine can do just as quickly and efficiently. The main high street banks and some supermarkets who offer ATM services do not charge; however, some cash machines have been cunningly placed in bars and casinos, which give people access to their money in a place where they are likely to spend it, and these machines often have a charge. There are literally billions of pounds moving around a virtual economy. Money is transferred from one account to another, from one country to another and from one business to another. The more valuable a transaction is, the more attractive it will become to those who would use technology to interfere in the process. This is an area of concern for banks, who employ specialists to look at improving the security of their customers' funds. Very few people will pay their mortgage by cash, which means a sizeable electronic payment is being made each month to the bank. If many of these payments are being made at the start of each month, it is crucial that the bank has adequate security in place to prevent unauthorised access and loss of funds.

Banks make use of computer systems for standard operations, such as storing and interrogating customer account details. This allows them to specifically focus products, such as loans or specific accounts, on those most likely to need or want them. They are able to search customer account histories to identify trends in expenditure and income.

ATM machine design

In a small group, using what you know about how people interact with computer systems, produce a new design for an ATM machine. Consider what features are included now and how they can be improved, how the users will interact with the system and what security precautions would be in place. The design and supporting ideas should be presented as a sales pitch to Gillespie's Bank PLC, who are keen to hit the high street with a new and innovative design.

Questions

1. Why is it important for banks to make accurate decisions when considering loan applications? (3)

2. Describe **three** benefits of online banking to customers. (6)

3. Describe **three** benefits of online banking to banks. (6)

4. Describe **three** factors that informed bank customers should consider before opening an online bank account with a specific company. (6)

5. What security measures do banks use to protect
   (i) their online system (3)
   (ii) customer funds? (2)

ICT in retail

Retail is the act of selling goods or merchandise to customers. In this section, retail is concerned with the purchase of physical products (such as those that can be worn, eaten or driven) and less-tangible products (such as insurance and investment opportunities).

The whole production chain of most products is concluded, as far as a business is concerned, when the product is sold. New technology and innovative marketing have radically changed the face of the retail industry, opening up markets to consumers whose options were previously more limited.

Before retailers embraced the Internet to encourage sales, individuals, families and businesses had to physically find the shop that sold what they wanted. Pot luck would often be relied upon to find the best supplier at a good price. When the best or most appropriate supplier was found, the buyer would then move around the supermarket, hardware store, pet shop or fashion outlet hoping to locate whatever it was they came to buy. The selected products would then be taken to a checkout where they would be paid for using cash, cheque or maybe a debit or credit card, before being taken away and used.

This long-standing method of getting products from the supplier to the buyer held for many years purely because there was no alternative. Those who originally constructed and provided the Internet as a source of sharing ideas, looking after military interests and exchanging research notes probably never envisaged that the web's infrastructure would go on to support the shopping habits of millions.

What can ICT provide?

The introduction of online shopping is only one of the innovations employed by the retail industry to drive sales.

Sophisticated ordering and stock control systems linked over company intranets are regularly installed, updated and enhanced by most businesses who understand and appreciate the need to deliver what the customer wants exactly when they want it.

The retail industry is incredibly competitive and consumers have become less loyal to single traders and more careful when it comes to making a purchase. In the past, it was not unusual for shoppers to be known faces in local stores and for them to know the name of the shopkeeper. The very nature of shopping for weekly groceries may well have been a matter of grabbing the shopping basket, walking down the high street and visiting several specialist outlets to buy such things as meat, bread or vegetables. If the store had run out of a particular product, going elsewhere may not have been a viable option and probably meant that a return later in the week was required to complete the weekly shop.

When retail stores started to use computers, the way they did business changed forever. On a simple level they could produce lists of products they had or could have for sale, print them in quantity and distribute them to potential clients.

National companies that produce glossy catalogues, which are sent specifically to the customers who are most likely to make a purchase, have furthered this simple process. By constructing massive databases of individual customer purchasing habits, retailers are able to specifically design, produce and target products exactly to the audience that is most likely to add to their sales figures. This is known as direct marketing; also categorised as junk mail by some, or seen as opportunities by others.

Online shoppers look for the 'S' in secure

Internet shoppers are becoming more security savvy, according to a new poll conducted by web usability consultancy Webcredible. The poll, which questioned internet users on what makes them trust a website, found that 40 per cent of respondents look for the 'S' after http in the URL before committing to an online purchase. Https indicates that the internet connection is secure and information such as credit card details will be encrypted.

However, the poll also reveals that a number of Internet users are putting their trust in the wrong place. For example, 28 per cent of respondents stated that dealing with the website of a reputable brand provided the most reassurance when buying online, while 16 per cent confirmed that they judge a website's security primarily on its professional look and feel.

Trenton Moss, director, Webcredible said: 'It's surprising, but very encouraging, to see that so many online shoppers understand the importance of essential security measures like https. However, it is frightening to see that some internet users will naively put their trust in a website based solely on the way that it looks. Online security is of paramount importance and shoppers need to be clued up on what to look for when visiting ecommerce websites to be sure that their card details and personal information will be safe when they make their purchase.'

A link to this website is available at www.heinemann.co.uk/hotlinks (express code 2349P)

Consumers still physically visit shops and it is seen by some as a leisure activity. Window-shopping is the term given to the act of roaming shops looking at what is on offer, usually with the intention of returning one day to buy.

Jackson and Barklem

Jackson and Barklem is a small printing firm that sells advertising space in A5 brochures to high street traders. The brochures are distributed to 4,000 local homes. An online trader that would like to advertise in the brochure has recently contacted them. Jackson and Barklem sees this as an opportunity to sell more advertising space to new online businesses. The partners have asked you to investigate the market for them. You need to:

- use the Internet to find at least **10** local businesses that trade online
- provide details of what they sell, make or supply
- provide contact details and other useful information
- produce an 8-page A5 sample brochure to show to the partners of Jackson and Barklem.

It is now possible to log on to a computer, use a search engine to locate the item that is of interest and read the details about the product. With this tool the advantage the shopper has is hugely increased over their weary, high-street-searching predecessor. Online window-shopping means potential customers can use the power of the net to find the same product on the sites of many different retailers, all of which may offer different prices or deals. With the customer being able to access such information in a relatively short space of time, in the comfort of their home and with hardly any physical effort, the retail industry has had to acknowledge the Internet as one of the first places to create an impression to the buyer.

There are very few specialists around who are likely to be the only supplier of a particular product. Therefore, retailers have to ensure that not only is the price appealing but the quality and after-sales service match the expectations of a more demanding shopper.

In modern retailing it is not acceptable for shelves to be empty. This annoys customers and they will go elsewhere. Having a virtual shop does not mean that shelves can run dry either. If a buyer is making use of technology to make a purchase, they will not expect to wait longer than it takes to send something by first class post before they should receive their item. Having to wait can cause frustration and again could mean the loss of a sale, or more if the buyer decides to tell other people about their poor experience.

A stock control system networked to EPOS (electronic point of sale) tills means that when the bar code of a product is read, information is added to a database. This database is likely to hold details about the sale. Even if the sale is for a simple tin of beans, the database will add information, such as when and where it was bought, at what price and, if a loyalty card has been used, by whom. This information is fed into sophisticated software that will recognise that a sale has been made, will understand that the shelf has one less of this item and will know how many should be on display on the shop floor. With this data the system can instruct shelf-fillers what shelves to fill and will contact the supplier's system to ask them to deliver more.

Marks and Spencer was among the first of the high street giants to use such technology. It was quickly followed by its competitors, who saw not only the potential in using a clever stock control system but the potential of recording sales in a database. With many millions of transactions taking place every day through the web or within the stores it is the supermarkets that have pushed the technological boundaries to new levels in order to satisfy the customers' desire to buy.

Of course, not all purchases are bought as a 'want item'. Supermarkets primarily provided the daily essentials of toiletries and food. Their ability to use records of previous sales stored in an ever-growing database gave the opportunity to interrogate the data being collected on a daily, weekly and annual basis. This meant the likes of Tesco, Sainsbury and Asda could, fairly accurately, predict what would sell at certain times of the year and, more importantly, what wouldn't. There is likely to be nothing more frustrating and embarrassing for a supermarket manager than having to explain why he purchased so many bananas at a time when they are most likely to go off and stink out the store rooms!

Supermarkets used to use much of their floor space as storage, which restricted how much room they could use for active sales. The advanced stock ordering system, which logs sales and automatically informs the warehouses what they need, attempts to be as up-to-date as possible and ensure that only stock that is very likely to sell is delivered at the time it is expected. For very large stores this quite often means several deliveries a day from massive warehouses, while smaller stores are still going to expect at least one delivery a day to replenish stock.

Staples, inc

Fujitsu worked closely in partnership with Staples to implement a state of the art PoS system in Germany and Portugal that could later be extended to the retailer's European store network in the UK and Netherlands

With 2005 sales of $16.1 billion, Staples serves consumers and businesses ranging from home-based businesses to Fortune 500 companies in 21 countries throughout North and South America, Europe and Asia. Stores are located on the outskirts of shopping centres and in busy high-street locations.

In 2005, Staples undertook a review of its legacy EPoS software, identifying that this no longer met the requirements of its business and would not support ambitious targets of 20% year-on-year growth. An independent consultancy was appointed to evaluate alternative solutions on the market.

The new system would need to be robust and flexible and provide Staples with the necessary functionality to manage its global stores estate. Specific requirements for the system were that it could handle multiple currencies and be adapted to take account of differing VAT levels and regulations, as well as the different payment methods available in each of the country markets in which the retailer operates. The system would also need to be flexible to enable configuration to the languages spoken in the retailer's stores worldwide.

Staples selected GlobalSTORE, a complete retail software solution from Fujitsu Services. The solution was chosen based upon the significant operational performance enhancements it could offer the retailer, as well as the extra functionality it would provide. In addition, the system would provide a flexible platform to support the development of the Staples business.

Benefits to our Customer

A number of business benefits from the rollout of GlobalSTORE have already been realised by Staples:

- **Lower total cost of ownership** – the retailer will operate one EPoS system across its European network, delivering lower total cost of ownership through economies of scale.

- **Robust and stable platform** – offers a future-proof foundation for future development.

- **User-friendly PoS** – minimises staff training requirements and has led to a significant reduction in the number of support calls recorded.

- **Flexible architecture** – that has been tailored to meet the bespoke requirements of Staples and offers in-built flexibility allowing for adjustments to be made to the system by Staples to optimise revenue opportunities through in-store promotions and CRM.

- **Speedier transaction processing** – has increased the time available for store staff to interact with customers by 25%.

- **Real time reporting** – through the introduction of trickle-feed polling has enhanced visibility in the supply chain.

- **Store support** – provided at country level ensures a rapid response to issues encountered with the system.

Our Approach

Fujitsu worked closely with Staples to implement a state of the art PoS system in Germany and Portugal that could later be extended to the retailer's European store network in the UK and the Netherlands.

The need to standardise the software across the European stores estate and introduce best practice needed to be balanced with the need for some country-specific marketing customisation, particularly with regard to EFT and language.

The speed of the rollout also needed to be managed in order to minimise disruption to the stores, whilst minimising the potential impact of a PoS failure on the business.

Integration testing was undertaken to ensure compatibility with the Central systems deployed in each country and a pilot phase was implemented to include training of store staff, site surveys, installation and support. Finally, a phased rollout was planned, beginning with the 56 Staples stores in Germany operating as Staples Büro-Megamärkte.

A link to this website is available at www.heinemann.co.uk/hotlinks (express code 2349P)

Loyalty card

A loyalty card is issued to a customer, who presents it at the till when they are paying for goods. The more the customer spends the more rewards they receive. The rewards can come in the form of discount vouchers, which can be used to reduce the monthly shopping bill or put towards larger purchases. In return for the reward, the outlet is making a record of everything that the customer has bought from their first purchase to the current day of trading.

Loyalty cards capture consumer shopping habits

activity

The EPOS system

In small groups, design an information poster which displays the EPOS system in action. It should include:

- customers
- warehouses
- stock
- the checkouts
- payments
- delivery methods
- the EPOS system
- any other information and images that will give it impact.

The data captured by retailers is priceless if they are to function at the cutting edge of competitiveness. One of the most important methods deployed to captures consumer shopping habits is the **loyalty card**.

Retailers are able to combine the sales information into specialist management-information systems which can be interrogated to identify purchasing patterns. When a loyalty card is issued, the consumer usually fills out a simple form which collects their personal details such as name, address and date of birth. The retailer can combine this small amount of information with your purchase details and keep a record of when you made a purchase, what it was and how much it cost. They are able to identify which age group buys the most of a certain product and use such details to forecast future sales. They can identify who their best customers are based on total sales. This means that they know who to promote new ranges and discounts to, thus avoiding an expensive marketing campaign aimed at a population of consumers who will have no interest in the products at all.

ICT gives information and power to the buying population as well as to the retailers. People can leave feedback about certain traders on specialist consumer websites. They can even email details of shoddy service to TV programs that are happy to take up issues on behalf of consumers and to physically address, to the nation, the shortcomings of the trader, with the trader, to an audience of millions. This kind of mass-media treatment can be fatal for moderate-sized retailers, while the massive supermarket chains are often able to flex their retail muscle, apologise and promise to improve service.

Before a retailer can sell to the general population, they too must first make the initial purchases, which means they can stock their shelves and advertise their wares to attract sales.

Retailers are able to use technology to find alternative suppliers of products. This is a sample of business-to-business trading (B2B). Just like normal consumers, retailers are always looking for the best deal. Large retailers are able to build megastores that sell everything you could sensibly need; they also need a huge range of suppliers to provide such products for sale.

Positions such as Buying Manager and Purchasing Agent are crucial within retail. Some retailers will market themselves on quality of products, while others will focus more on cheaper prices. Whatever their strategy in terms of attracting customers, the purchasing personnel will always be looking for the best deal for the store. This means that the smaller suppliers have to work harder and become more efficient in their production process to keep their cost down so that they can sell to the larger retailer. Without the popular outlets, many businesses find it hard to sell what they make.

Many types of retailer use application software. They often use databases to help locate products they have or to provide further details to potential customers.

A database is very good for storing a company's stock list. Some organisations find it very useful to know where all their stock is and how long it would take to send it to the customer from the warehouse. Businesses can also store information about their suppliers, which gives them the opportunity to keep records of who provides what and at what price.

Smaller retailers may simply use spreadsheet software for keeping track of sales figures and perhaps calculating staff wages. Larger organisations are more likely to commission outside firms to produce custom software to undertake some of the more complex tasks that their business might perform.

A lot of modern retailing takes place over the Internet. One of the biggest e-commerce success stories is the auction website eBay (other auction sites exist, but eBay is the largest and most well-known). Although not specifically what would be classified as a retailer, eBay does provide a service which links people selling products to people who might want to make a purchase. The way that eBay operates means that now, probably more than any other time in trading history, anyone can become a retailer. By having access to a computer and opening an eBay account, anyone who has something to sell can advertise it. If more than one person is interested in the item for sale, they bid against each other, which ultimately pushes the price up.

Many established retailers use eBay as an extension of their physical store, as it gives them exposure to a larger market than just running a small unit on a high street. Consumers are able to leave feedback when the transaction is complete, rating how good the product is and the quality of the service they received. Quite often those who pay little attention to supplying what they promised or who fail to provide

anything at all will be left poor feedback, which may put off potential customers in future.

There is very little doubt that online trading has revolutionised the way retailers and customers interact and exchange transactions. Customers can browse online stores, found through search engines, for products. They can compare prices between different suppliers, contact traders for further details and request the product be delivered on a certain date at a certain time.

Quite often the online trader is able to offer competitive prices because of their low overheads. If they are trading online, they do not need to pay for a store with furniture, staff, light and heat. The savings mean prices can be reduced, which will appeal to buyers. The location of the store does not become an issue either, because products can be ordered from anywhere there is a computer and posted from the store stockroom or warehouse, which could be thousands of miles away.

There are so many traders online that those who can afford it advertise on other people's websites. The more visitors a site has, the more appealing it becomes to traders looking to buy advertising space.

In an attempt to reduce queuing time, supermarkets have been trying to develop a system that will automatically detect what is in a shopper's trolley, total up the purchases and deduct payment without having to swipe cards. The most appropriate method for this appears to reside in **RFID tags**. The potential for a customer's card and products to be read and acted on without human intervention is some years away, as the technology is still quite expensive and not yet a viable option for replacing barcodes.

RFID tag

RFID tags are radio-frequency identification chips that store data identifying whatever they have been built into. They are incredibly small and can be placed into almost any product. They could also be built into payment cards. The information on the RFID tag is read by radio wave technology.

eBay

Mike Benson, a St. Louis lawyer, is looking for a rare baseball card of Stan Musial. In seconds, he finds 84 different Stan Musial cards up for auction on eBay, including one for the very card he wants. To bid, he simply enters the highest amount he's willing to spend. In this case, it's $50. He eventually lost the card to a higher bid of $63.

Every time there's a sale, eBay takes a cut of the action. As a result, eBay's market value is now worth more than Bloomingdale's, Macy's, Sears, and Toys 'R Us combined.

'It was an entirely new idea that took advantage of the Net,' says Whitman. 'There's no land-based analog for eBay. We hold no inventory, we ship no product.'

This is a marketplace where a Madonna fan can buy an outfit from the singer's world tour, and a prospective homeowner can spend $2,100,100 for a country house in New York State with its own missile silo.

Sixteen million items are up for sale every day. And eBay users aren't just buying and selling – they're also talking online in chat rooms.

'We spend more time together on the boards than I do with my family,' says Judy, an eBay user.

Four years ago, Laurie Liss began selling discounted designer clothes and shoes that she picked up on sale at department stores. Now, the entire family is part of the action. Laurie models an outfit, her sister snaps the picture, her brother-in-law puts it on eBay. As the bids start coming in, her mother monitors the auction.

The shipping department is in the kitchen, where mom and dad are packing boxes to send around the globe. They keep their inventory – their Prada shoes, their Guccis, and their Chanels – in the garage. They ran out of room in their original home, so they just bought three new houses all in a row with their eBay profits…

And it's a good family business. They've become so established on eBay that they no longer have to go looking for bargains. Now, the deals come to them.

'The day the manager tells the salesman, 'Hey, this stuff is going to get marked down 50 percent tomorrow,' our phone rings,' she says. 'They call us, so

we tell them to pull everything. They pull it all and just ship it to us.'

It doesn't take long before it's sold on eBay and shipped to the buyer. 'I had a Prada shoe,' Liss says. 'I got home with it, took a picture, listed it and, I think, 17 minutes later it was purchased. I had it going to Germany in less than an hour. It was already on its way…'

And that's how eBay got really hot. About a year ago, eBay started something they call 'Buy It Now.' Sellers no longer had to set up an auction – they could sell retail directly to the customer, just as Liss did with her Prada shoes. That's when the heavy hitters arrived…

'Big companies do sell on eBay,' says Whitman. 'And they find it to be a very cost-effective distribution channel. But they sell on the same terms as you, an individual, would sell.'

There is no advertising and no promotion: 'We think it's important to have this level playing field,' adds Whitman. 'So your neighbor next door has an equal chance of success as a large corporation.'

That democratic idea, the core principle of the company, comes from Pierre Omidyar who started eBay as a hobby and is now worth about $4.5 billion.

'I sat down, frankly, over Labor Day weekend 1995, after having kind of thought about these issues for a couple of months, and I just whipped up some code,' says Omidyar. 'By Monday afternoon, Labor Day, I had the site up.'

He sees its potential as limitless and has even developed a feedback system, rating customer satisfaction. The reputation of a seller is critical; too many negative comments and you're banned as an eBay seller forever.

eBay investigates fraud claims, but relies mainly on buyers and sellers to police themselves. Omidyar estimates that only 30 sellers out of a million fail to deliver on their promises.

'Our business model is to connect buyers and sellers,' she says. 'And so ultimately our buyers and sellers may do more economic activity than a Walmart. But it is not one group of people deciding what to buy. It is the power of many sellers.'

A link to this website is available at www.heinemann.co.uk/hotlinks (express code 2349P)

A magnified RFID tag

Technology is employed around stores to protect the products. Many stores attach tags which trigger alarms if they are not removed before a shopper leaves the store. Automatic recording on CCTV often takes place, which involves recording continuously everything that happens within a store day and night, even when there are no shoppers. Technology can be used to store, categorise and interrogate hours of footage. This can help to identify criminals wanted by the police and can provide evidence to help seal convictions. Security guards often use technology with simple headsets, which allow them to stay in contact with each other and help to coordinate patrols if they are watching a suspected shoplifter.

Despite the advantages and ease of use offered by online shopping, there are still some good reasons why consumers may still wish to go to stores. It is not always possible to judge quality, size, fit and feel when shopping online. This is particularly important for the purchase of clothes, or of electrical devices which may need explaining. Many people still want to leave the house, meet other people, talk to sales staff and try things on. This cannot be achieved online. Some consumers are sceptical about paying electronically over a website, especially if it is a site they are not familiar with. Large high-street traders attempt to advertise that payment online is secure, but not everyone is convinced and many still prefer to use the traditional payment method of cash.

Questions

1. Describe **three** reasons why some people do not use online shopping. (4)
2. What advantages does EPOS bring to high street traders? (4)
3. What advantages do retailers gain from having an online presence? (6)
4. What advantages do customers gain from shopping online? (4)
5. What technological methods do high-street stores use to ensure stock and payment safety? (6)

ICT in health care

Millions of pounds have been spent integrating IT systems into the health care system in the UK to help improve services. Advanced technology has revolutionised the way doctors and nurses work, with the general aim of making more people better and improving health and well-being for all. Software has been developed which speeds up the analysis and diagnosis of problems, which in the past might have resulted in the GP having to consult books or colleagues before recommending a course of treatment or surgery. Technology has made decision-making more accurate, which has prolonged the life-expectancy of many people. There are very few places left in the human body where technology cannot intevene, test or improve. Exciting opportunities to make worthwhile enhancements attract investment and encourage the generation and support of new technologies and ideas.

The following is a small sample of how technology is used within health care and the benefits it provides to patients and doctors.

Patient records and appointments

When someone feels ill, they contact the surgery by phone and make an appointment to see the doctor. This process can be automated and bookings can be done through surgery websites. At some surgeries there is a welcoming touch-screen device where patients register their arrival by touching specific responses on the screen and navigating their way through simple menus to confirm who they are and which doctor they are seeing. The software is able to suggest how long the patient will have to wait before they are seen.

Each patient has a unique identifier which the doctor will enter into a computer system to access the patient's records. The doctor is able to look at the medical history prior to the patient entering the room. They are able to question the patient and compare previous treatments before recommending a new prescription. The software installed on the doctor's machine may even be extensive enough to help diagnose the problem. By entering symptoms described by the patient, the doctor can rely on the diagnosis drawn from experts who contributed to the construction of the software. This is known as an **expert system** because of the nature of the data in the system and how it was collected. Prior to the introduction of such technology, humans were relied upon. They were required to book in appointments, organise thousands of files and make correct diagnoses based on their immediate knowledge, medical journals, books, colleagues and previous experience; all these tasks can be quite time-consuming and may lack the accuracy that technology can provide.

> **Expert system**
>
> An expert system is a computer program about a specific subject, set up by experts in that subject to provide answers to questions about it. Simple expert systems use a sequence of yes/no questions to guide the user to an answer to their question, although more advanced techniques can be used.

How many legs does it have?

4 legs — less than 4 legs

What noise does it make?

Barks — Miaows

It is a: Dog — It is a: Cat

Simple questions guide the user to the answer

Donating blood

Details of blood donors are stored in a database that automatically sorts and organises the data. Usually, after a donation, the donor is supposed to wait a set number of weeks before making their next donation. The database used to store the details has been designed to automatically send letters, as a reminder, to registered donors 2 weeks before they are next due to give blood. The database is able to track how often people donate, how many times they have donated and can even send rewards when landmarks are reached, such as 50 donations. When the blood has been taken away, technology is used to test the blood to ensure that it is safe to for transfusions.

Calling 999

When a 999 emergency call is placed, it is routed through an advanced telephone network to an operator. When the call is answered, the operator asks for the location of the emergency. A postcode or street name can immediately be input into a navigation system, which guides the drivers to the emergency using the quickest or clearest route. By arriving quickly, the ambulance crew has more chance of saving lives. While the ambulance is travelling to the emergency, the operator keeps the caller on the line to gather more information about the nature of the emergency. With this information they are able to consult files which provide details of immediate assistance; again this information

The ambulance crew can save more lives by arriving quicker

may be life saving. There is technology in some ambulances that transmits the heart rates of patients in transit to the hospital for analysis by waiting doctors. This is used on people who have cardiac-related chest pains and gives the doctors vital information to act upon before the patient even arrives.

Body scanners

By using the latest magnetic resonance imaging (MRI) technology, radiologists can take images throughout a patient's body. This type of technology can quickly and comfortably examine and detect a range of conditions before they become life-threatening. Heart anomalies, cancer and vascular disease can all be detected using the MRI scan. Radio waves are sent through the body, which lies inside a large cylindrical magnet. The radio waves cause reactions in the body that are picked up by the scanner and translated into images by a computer system.

An MRI scan creates digital images of parts of the body surrounded by bone tissue, and is the best technique used to examine the brain and spinal cord. It is particularly good at identifying benign or abnormal growths and assessing whether existing tumours have spread.

Up until recently, whenever an X-ray was taken, the patient would have to wait for the image to be developed, wait for a specialist to look at it and wait for a diagnosis. New procedures have been introduced which automatically transfer the X-rayed image to a specialist, who could be in another building or even in another county. The specialist will view the images on high-definition screens and electronically return a diagnosis. This reduces the time spent moving and sorting images around buildings and, because they are instantly digitised, they can be uploaded into a vast database for storage and future referral.

Dentist

Dentists have turned to technology in the pursuit of the perfect smile. As well as all the record-keeping and patient-tracking systems, dentists have innovations to help improve the work they do inside the mouth. They have tools that make examining the patient less intrusive and painful, and give clearer pictures. Images taken with tiny cameras, which greatly magnify the view inside the mouth, show decay in crevices and cracks that the naked eye cannot see. Detected problems can be shown to the patient on a monitor and discussed. Early intervention may help to avoid potentially painful treatment and discomfort in the future. Dentists can use digital imaging to offer a preview of how a patient might look if they had teeth-straightening, whitening or cosmetic dental procedures. This kind of technology may promote future work for the dentist who can furnish his clients with images of what they could look like after treatment.

Computers used to aid sight and hearing

1 Investigate how computers are used in the field of either sight or hearing. What options are there for diagnosis of sight or hearing problems and how has the digital world benefited those who need it?

2 What are the options for the person requiring to buy glasses, lenses or hearing aids?

3 Present your findings to the rest of the class as a point for discussion.

NHS Direct

The National Health Service (NHS) has produced a comprehensive website for patients to access from home. The NHS Direct system allows people to consult a virtual health encyclopedia that provides details, advice and information about many health issues. To cater for those who do not speak English, there are other versions in other languages. The encyclopedia is image-driven to make it easy for novice users to intuitively navigate and understand.

There is an online enquiry service where questions can be emailed to experts and feedback forms are returned. This option is probably not suitable for extreme emergencies, but it can be helpful for gaining informed information about the care treatment of someone who is sick. To complement this there is a help guide which determines if symptoms experienced can be managed at home or whether an ambulance is required. The website provides an online magazine which gives regular features about physical well-being, as well as the latest health news. There is a facility which can locate the nearest health service for a given post code. A further search facility is included, where a keyword can be added which takes the user to the most relevant part of the website. Such an online resource could be used by those confident enough to diagnose simple aliments while doctors get on with the business of dealing with more serious concerns.

NHS Direct provides a virtual health encyclopedia

Online medical resources

1. Using the Internet, investigate the features and facilities offered by three online doctors or medical resources. You could pretend that you have various symptoms to test the usefulness of the sites.

2. Compare your findings with two of your peers and, in your small group, produce a short presentation. Provide details and recommendations based on the facilities you found useful and interesting.

Lucy Andrews

Lucy Andrews runs a private plastic surgery specialising in facial work. She works from a prestigious house in a smart part of London. Business is slow at the moment and Lucy has asked you to produce advertising for her that can be displayed in her window to be viewed on screen by passers by. She would like the advertisement to include the following:

- before and after images
- a brief history of her surgery
- some details about how she uses technology
- the range of treatments she can offer
- opening times
- how to book a consultation
- contact details.

Plastic surgery

The skills and ingenuity of plastic surgeons were tested to their limits during World War II. Modern society has seen a huge upsurge in personal requests for plastic surgery to enhance, correct or improve the performance of different body parts. Plastic surgeons are able to use technology to assist with every stage of the process, including using digital imaging to show a patient how they would look after treatment.

Magic Million finds new monitoring equipment

The intensive care facilities at the hospital were located in severely over-crowded conditions. In addition, the equipment in the unit was very out-of-date. The authorities had a vision to transform a little used part of the hospital into a first-class facility for the sickest children, including babies born at the neighbouring hospital, The Queen Mother's Maternity Hospital. NHS Greater Glasgow contributed £5 million towards the total re-build and the remaining sum of £1 million raised by the general public was put towards re-equipping the unit with monitoring equipment. The new Intensive Care and High Dependency Unit was opened by HRH Prince Edward and brought together two separate areas within the hospital to form a modern, bright, purpose-built department with fourteen PICU beds and ten HDU beds. The new monitoring system installed in the department enables care teams to cope with the massive amounts of clinical data generated for every patient, enabling them to form a coherent picture of clinical patient status at the bedside and beyond. The new department has given a major boost to paediatric critical care in the West of Scotland and beyond due to the department's involved in national services.

The Trust when re-equipping the unit obviously looked at all the options for monitoring equipment and invited all the major vendors to submit specifications, from which they compiled a short list. The Trust had various criteria on which they would base their decision including functionality, ease-of-use, ergonomics and integration with workflow; flexibility, reliability and support; education and implementation, as well as central monitoring. Philips Medical Systems was able to tick all the boxes and scored well above other suppliers in all categories. Dr. John Sinclair, Consultant Paediatric Intensivist at GHSCH says, 'Philips offered the most flexible answer for our needs; the user-friendliness of the equipment and strong maintenance backup were particularly important factors in our decision to go with Philips.' The solution provided by Philips Medical Systems

consisted of IntelliVue monitors including a server. Dr. Sinclair continues, 'We found the monitors exactly matched the specific requirements of our paediatric and neonatal intensive care units.

The new monitoring system has made a dramatic improvement to the patient care within the unit. The previous monitors being over fifteen years old had minimum functionality and were a definite handicap for staff. Benefits from the new system include increased measurement capacity and considerably more detailed information. Charge Nurse Chris Lamb says, 'We now find that we can spend more time on direct patient care. In addition, as much of the equipment is carried on a ceiling mounted pendant system, we have been (able) to improve the use of the space we have available, and we find we have greater manoeuvrability of our medical equipment.'

Clinical benefits of the equipment

Chris Lamb continues, 'The new monitors have helped us respond to an increase in workload. In fact, they have transformed the way we work. For instance, we are able to hold a case conference in a meeting room and share the information from the bed-side in real-time.'

The key to this important facility is the IntelliVue Information Center, which at the heart of the monitoring network combines the real-time monitoring surveillance of a central station, with sophisticated clinical analysis tools.

Philips' clinical decision support tools are designed to assist in the processing of vast amounts of data by presenting data in forms designed to reflect clinically thought processes. Dr. John Sinclair comments, 'In a noisy and stressful environment, the presentation of the data in a clear graphical format relieves some of the strain created by information overload.' Just such a tool is Philips' unique patented ST Map. The ST segment is the portion of the electrocardiographic tracing that can indicate less-than-normal blood flow to the heart. Standard tabular displays of the data can be difficult for clinicians to interpret.

A link to this website is available at www.heinemann.co.uk/hotlinks (express code 2349P)

Computer imaging systems

'This is such a powerful tool and is so very valuable to the patient and to me,' said Dr. W. Russell Ries, associate professor of Otolaryngology. 'I show patients what desired changes on their faces will look like. It's not a guarantee, but it's a very realistic approach. No matter what, it must be something that I can achieve in the operating room.

'And it's very beneficial, I think, to show changes on their own faces. We can always show pictures (of) other patients who have undergone similar procedures, but it's so much more beneficial to show them the changes on their own face.'

Ries uses the computer imaging system to preview rhinoplasty, blephroplasty, face-lifts, chin implants, cheek implants, and even scar revision.

Sitting at a computer keyboard, Ries can measure angles for the tilt of the end of a nose, can enlarge cheekbones, minimize fat on the chin, or can even tighten skin around the eyes, all with the flick of a mouse button and a touch of the keyboard.

He can even 'morph' the computer image, going from the 'before' picture to the doctored 'after' image.

The computer-imaging system can also demonstrate laser resurfacing by manually blending away the fine lines and wrinkles on the patient's computer image.

'It's not a dramatic change, it is not supposed to be. It will give me a good representation of what can be done with CO_2 laser resurfacing,' Ries said.

There are also special modules on the computer system for teaching about specific surgical procedures and for preparing presentations to fellow physicians...

Ries says sometimes patients even decide against surgery after seeing the computer image.

'I will make changes that I think are reasonable and feasible to accomplish, and a patient will say, "No, no, no. I want it more narrow." If I don't think I can do that or I doubt the desired outcome can be achieved, then I have to tell them that. That is a good thing for both patient and doctor to understand before surgery.'

A link to this website is available at www.heinemann.co.uk/hotlinks (express code 2349P)

Training

Technology is used to simulate real scenarios to prepare doctors and surgeons to perform operations and give expert advice. There are online training manuals available for download. Information about the latest developments in research and medicine is conveyed via email to interested groups, and there are online forums where experts can share experiences and advice. Simulation software allows student doctors to practise a variety of operations, sharpen their skills and gain feedback, allowing them to make mistakes in a safe environment. Such simulations take vocational training to new levels – damaged ligaments or broken bones can be examined and treated by clicking a mouse in various patterns replicating the moves a real surgeon would make. This removes the need for an expensive live environment and personnel working on a living subject. It is important to

point out that such technology is vigorously tested and results have proved positive.

Despite the great technology on offer to doctors and patients, it will be some time before the general public are totally convinced that some of the uses are sustainable or trustworthy. Some patients may not be able to access the online resources, whilst others may not trust advice given by a website. Some may doubt the suitability and reliability of simulators for training and others may be wary that the medical industry is using technology to commercialise health and to provide medical wants rather than medical needs. Many people still feel the need for human interaction and reassurance that a real doctor can give on a personal level, as they may not be comfortable pouring out their symptoms to a machine that gives cold, calculated responses. However, it is important to acknowledge that this is a care industry and many

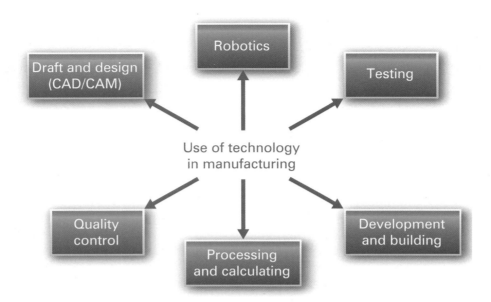

How technology is used in manufacturing

advances have improved the care and welfare that is provided, a trend that is likely to continue. The question that causes most concern is 'at what cost?'

Questions

1. Describe the characteristics of medical expert systems and the benefits they can bring to patients and doctors. (8)

2. What are the benefits to patients of accessing NHS Direct? (4)

3. What are the benefits to the NHS of patients using the NHS Direct system? (4)

4. Why might some people wish to consult a doctor rather than use technology to investigate their aliment? (4)

5. On a global scale, what advantages can improved communication technology and the Internet bring to medical treatment in areas of poverty and under-development? (6)

ICT in industry

Gone are the days when the economy relied upon the manufacturing talents of the workforce. There is still a manufacturing industry in the UK but the processes of production have been radically overhauled by implementing computer systems that are automated

to perform tasks, monitor output and improve quality. Computer systems have revolutionised the performance and shape of industry, and those who have embraced technology are reaping the benefits. Improvements in communications have meant that many organisations, connected to the same supply chain, can be in touch with each other with greater efficiency at each stage of the manufacturing process. Raw material suppliers can contact manufacturers when the materials are ready for delivery. Manufacturers can manage their workforce according to the delivery date of the materials. Sales and distribution outlets can be contacted when the raw materials have been converted into products for the shops. The shops and customers will drive the process by making requests for goods to sell or buy.

With established communication links at each stage, all elements can operate productively with minimal waste and lead-time. Email, video conferencing, fax, text messaging, mobile communication and websites have all enhanced the way businesses interact with one another. Such advances also make each part of the chain vulnerable because they can be swapped or replaced by another company that can provide a better service or price.

A key part of the manufacturing process is locating the raw materials. Obvious material, such as wood, is not difficult to find. However, raw materials below ground, such as oil, can be much more difficult to find. Oil has

The oil industry

The oil industry is one of the most powerful and wealthy on the planet. In a small group, carry out research to identify how the oil industry uses technology. Possible options to investigate include:

- locating oil
- extracting oil
- converting oil for use
- detecting leaks in the pipelines
- selling oil.

Produce a presentation of your findings, with illustrations, and present it to the rest of your class.

The oil industry is one of the most powerful and wealthy on the planet

many uses in the commercial sector and those who supply it are attracted by the potential profits.

Some manufacturers need lots of floor space in which to conduct their business. This might involve constructing cars, printers, televisions or fridge freezers. Most will not want space taken up with components that are never or rarely used or are out of date. Components might include screws, metal panels, or springs – any of the ingredients that make up a finished product.

A good business will use modelling software that can break down a product into every component and calculate how many of each is required to complete a set number. The software will also be able to calculate the overall cost for each finished unit based on the component costs, and recommend a supplier based on previous business dealings.

By using such a system, the manufacturer is able to order the exact stock of components at the exact time they are needed. This means that, as deliveries of parts arrive, they do not take up valuable storage and floor space but are added straight into the production process. By ordering only what is needed and employing efficient production processes, companies have been able to cut the cost of wastage and storage considerably.

This is a fraction of the 'just-in-time' model, which, when linked with computer systems, provides accuracy for ordering and ensures that only whatever is required to be used is ordered, reducing the need for a warehouse full of parts gathering dust. There is also no frustration of waiting for parts because the system will have calculated and ordered the correct amount of components required just in time for physical use.

JIT – background and history

JIT is a Japanese management philosophy which has been applied in practice since the early 1970s in many Japanese manufacturing organisations. It was first developed and perfected within the Toyota manufacturing plants by Taiichi Ohno as a means of meeting consumer demands with minimum delays. Taiichi Ohno is frequently referred to as the father of JIT.

Toyota was able to meet the increasing challenges for survival through an approach that focused on people, plants and systems. Toyota realised that JIT would only be successful if every individual within the organisation was involved and committed to it, if the plant and processes were arranged for maximum output and efficiency, and if quality and production programs were scheduled to meet demands exactly.

JIT manufacturing has the capacity, when properly adapted to the organisation, to strengthen the organisation's competitiveness in the marketplace substantially by reducing wastes and improving product quality and efficiency of production.

There are strong cultural aspects associated with the emergence of JIT in Japan. The Japanese work ethic involves the following concepts.

Workers are highly motivated to seek constant improvement upon that which already exists. Although high standards are currently being met, there exist even higher standards to achieve.

Companies focus on group effort which involves the combining of talents and sharing knowledge, problem-solving skills, ideas and the achievement of a common goal.

Work itself takes precedence over leisure. It is not unusual for a Japanese employee to work 14-hour days.

Employees tend to remain with one company throughout the course of their career span. This allows the opportunity for them to hone their skills and abilities at a constant rate while offering numerous benefits to the company.

These benefits manifest themselves in employee loyalty, low turnover costs and fulfilment of company goals.

A link to this website is available at www.heinemann.co.uk/hotlinks (express code 2349P)

Products and components

1. Select a product commonly found in the home.

2. List the components/materials required to produce the product.

3. Find the best supplier and price for each component.

4. Produce a total price of the materials to produce one product.

5. You need to produce 100 units of the same product. Does the cost of materials change at all? Can you explain? What effect will this have on the sale price?

Being able to automate the production process has given manufacturers the opportunity to produce more variations of the same product and to change colours or displays, with very little human intervention. Large-scale machinery can be programmed to drill holes in different places depending on what is required at the time, or dip products into different coloured dye pots for each batch. Having to realign machinery or reposition pots of dye can take some time but an automated process simply requires that the components are in the right place for a machine to locate, pick up and mould. By pre-programming what machinery should do and how many of the intended tasks it needs to perform, it is possible to use the skills of humans in less mundane activities.

When a product is ready for the shop shelves, advanced delivery systems are used. Companies specialise in collecting and transporting products all over the country.

Logistics
Logistics is the process of controlling the movement of resources in a supply chain.

They do this as economically as possible by using **logistics** software that plans routes and drop-offs in the most efficient way. The fruitless task of picking up from one supplier and taking it to one trader has been surpassed by systems that construct a detailed plan for multiple deliveries and pick-up services in one outing. This helps to reduce fuel costs and wear on the vehicles, and gets the products to where they are supposed to be when they are expected.

Manufacturers spend millions of pounds on new product development. Before releasing a new range or product, intensive research, design, testing and marketing takes place. Companies use software to collect data. This data can be processed and analysed to inform decisions relating to new products.

For example, car designers are responding to feedback from customers relating to running their cars economically. The reaction to these concerns is hybrid cars that run on a combination of electricity and lead-free petrol. The road tax for such cars is lower then for big gas-guzzlers, and daily running costs are halved. By reacting to what the consumers want, companies stand more chance of producing products that will sell.

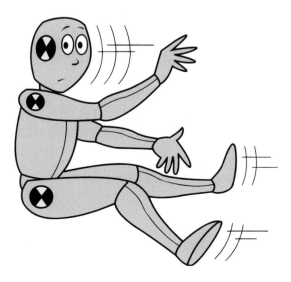

Car manufacturers use crash test dummies to simulate car crashes

Data can be collected using online forms, which are linked to websites likely to be visited by potential customers. Data is analysed by powerful software, patterns tracked, trends identified and forecasts modelled. When the necessary decisions relating to new products are made, prototypes are created and tested.

Car manufacturers, in particular, have stringent safety guidelines to reach before they can sell their cars. They use crash test dummies to simulate a variety of crashes. Sensors and high-definition cameras record the impact, and software is used to analyse the data. This data helps car designers make the vehicles safer, which saves lives.

The actual design of any new product can take place using computer-aided design (CAD) software. Product dimensions, colour, weight and features can all be manipulated until satisfaction is agreed and the designs are approved for production. Various views can be seen by rotating three-dimensional images and sent to potential customers to gather further opinion.

While the designs are in digital form, they can be transferred across the world to experts who may make further additions as part of their job before passing them on to the next person. By producing detailed designs on computer, manufacturers are able to gain a good perspective of the final product without having wasted any materials in the process.

Some products can even be tested in a virtual environment, although physical tests will always follow on most products. The material and components of the products can be determined on a computer system, which can also link to other software that calculates the production cost for each unit, can recommend a timescale and may even suggest the best supplier for each component.

Technology has been used to improve relations between customers and manufacturers. Communication between the two has become stronger largely due to the number of ways customers can interact with those who produce goods.

Despite the growth in use of technology, there still remain a lot of cottage industries. Many traders and customers still like the authentic or traditional methods of production and often regard the hand-made approach as more valuable than an automated process. Some people prefer the taste of food produced using old machinery and methods, while hand-made clothes and cars still command

Crash Test Dummies Deliver Loads of Intelligent Data

Even the most careful drivers can sometimes be the victims of circumstance and end up in an accident. Thanks to some 'smart dummies' employed by Ford, however, these unfortunate occurrences may carry less dire consequences.

Ford uses approximately 18 different advanced crash-test dummies to conduct the myriad crash tests required by the federal government as well as many Ford-specific in-house tests.

Each of the dummies mimics the human shape, size and weight and is tailored for a specific test. Adult frontal-crash dummies include a small female (103 to 105 pounds), mid-size male referred to as the 50th percentile male (175 pounds) and a large male dummy that equates to a 6-foot, 3-inch man who weighs about 225 pounds. Child dummies include 6-, 12- and 18-month-olds, and three-year-old, six-year-old and 10-year-old siblings.

The SIDs family (side impact dummies) consists of one small adult female and three mid-size adult males. BIORID, a mid-size adult male, is used for rear impact 'whiplash' tests.

'Data is gathered from head to toe,' says Risa Scherer, supervisor of Ford's Anthropomorphic Test Devices Laboratory. 'The typical body regions monitored are the head, neck, chest, pelvis and legs. For side impact, we also monitor the abdomen and shoulders.'

Depending on the dummy size up to 212 channels of data are sent to the computer during the crash sequence. The data is used to determine if changes need to be made to the restraint systems or vehicle designs. The data also helps to support computer modeling, allowing engineers to build more precise virtual models.

'Once the models are validated with the data gathered from the dummies,' says Scherer, 'then the virtual dummies can be used in computer crash simulations.'

Scherer says the technology has advanced significantly over the past ten years. Instrumentation and data collection systems have gotten smaller. More transducers can now be packaged into a smaller area yielding even more data.

'Data collection systems are incorporated into the dummy so we don't need to carry any extra weight on the vehicle,' says Scherer. 'Their small size also reduces their influence on the performance of the dummies.'

The Virtual Crash Test Dummy

The future automotive crash test dummy is currently being developed inside a computer. Ford safety engineers are working on the Human Body Model, a Finite Element Analysis (FAE), or computer tool that will help engineers better understand what happens to the human body during a crash.

Ford began building the human body model in 1993, creating the regions of the body such as the head, neck, ribcage, abdomen, thoracic and lumbar spine, internal organs of the chest and abdomen, pelvis, and the upper and lower extremities. These regions were brought together in 2004 to create the full body model.

The human body model represents an average adult male and is constructed using technologies like data gathered from MRI scans and topographies from human body anatomical texts. Validation of the computer model is done through cadaver and volunteer human testing.

The model features such things as a highly detailed spine with all the vertebrae segments and cartilage attached, and a very comprehensive brain model that has been used to determine the extent of injuries that can occur during a crash.

Saeed Barbat, manager, Passive Safety Research and Advanced Engineering, Ford Motor Company says that in the future, virtually-pressurized 'blood vessels' may be developed to help determine how internal organs react during specific types of crashes.

The data collected using both actual and virtual crash test dummies will help Ford develop and bring to market innovative safety technologies faster than ever and in advance of possible future government regulations.

A link to this website is available at www.heinemann.co.uk/hotlinks (express code 2349P)

premium prices. The balance between the new and the old is down to personal preference, although the trend for each generation is slowly tilting more in favour of the computer-driven industry.

Questions

1. List and describe **three** benefits information technology can bring to modern manufacturing. (9)
2. State and describe **two** examples where software models are used by manufacturing. (6)
3. State **three** methods of communication used in the manufacturing supply chain and give examples of how each would be used. (9)

ICT in service and leisure industries

The service and leisure industries have to always consider the needs and wants of consumers. Often their products are not taken away, driven, eaten or worn, but have a different nature. The leisure industry is all about keeping people entertained or providing a space where they can relax or keep fit. There is a huge range of information technology to support these needs.

Personal trainers use software that constructs personal fitness programmes. These are generated after various bodily readings, such as blood pressure and lung capacity, have been taken and fed into the system. The desired type of body improvement is taken into account as another variable before a final regime is delivered. By using accurate, purposeful data, the fitness programmes produced are more appropriate to the users' needs and help them achieve the results they want faster.

Cinema tickets can be booked and paid for online via websites which show what films are available, their rating, price and time of show. In some instances it is possible to select a seat location. Prior to the start of the film, on arrival, the customer can collect their ticket from a machine, which delivers their ticket after validating their payment method. Alternatively, a ticket can be purchased on the day of the film from a similar fast-track machine, which removes the need for queuing.

Similar systems are in place for purchasing flight tickets, tickets to sports events and train tickets; basically any type of ticket for any type of event can be purchased and paid for online. It is even possible to check who the lead actors are at a West End show before booking.

Bars, clubs and restaurants allow customers to book tables online. They are able to specify what courses they want before arriving, which speeds up service time on the actual day.

Children's entertainers, hog roasts, bouncy castles, spray tans and river cruises can all be investigated online. A good web presence is common practice for many involved in the leisure industry. Such services have grown in recent years because the potential of the Internet has opened up audiences to most types of leisure activities.

Online groups and societies can be formed where details of current events can be shared and exchanged.

The travel and tourism industry has seen a decline in high street sales, whilst online sales have grown rapidly. This indicates that consumers are taking advantage of technology to explore their options and to cash in on the number of incentives found by purchasing online.

'The Main Event'

C & J Main Sports, promoters of 'The Main Event', have asked you to investigate the range of big sporting events due to happen over the next three months. They want you to use your research skills to locate the best sites and deals on behalf of clients who want to go to the events.

Your research should generate a small brochure giving dates, times, events, prices, deals and discounts available for at least **six** different events which C & J Main can use as a resource when clients contact them.

Digital television has revolutionised how time at home is spent. Not so long ago, UK citizens had access to only four channels. By installing a digital receiver, a satellite dish and paying a monthly fee, households are able to tune into hundreds more channels. Channels about lifestyle, buying homes, history, holidays, DIY, cars and bikes, gambling and sport are all ready to be accessed any time of the day.

Sky Plus, amongst others, gives TV viewers the option of recording onto hard drive, and pausing live programmes. Sports channels have interactive options, which give multiple views of a match, statistics, highlights and alternative commentaries. People are able to gamble straight through their television set with some channels or enter interactive competitions and games.

Furthermore, if someone misses their favourite show they may be able to log on to the channel's website and watch it online. This type of home-based facility gives the user flexibility to view what they want when they want – 'on-demand TV'.

Questions

1. State and describe **three** benefits the Internet has brought to businesses in the leisure industry.   (6)

2. A travel company has decided to offer online holiday and flight booking to its customers.
   (a) Give **two** benefits to the company of selling its services online.   (2)
   (b) Describe **two** benefits to a customer of the company deciding to sell its services online.   (4)

Digital television has revolutionised how time at home is spent

ICT in publishing

Publishing is the preparation and distribution of information and literature to the public. Books, magazines, newspapers, posters and brochures all fall into this category. Technology has added software and websites to the list of publications. Websites can hold digital books, collate information from groups who share an interest in a specific subject and reproduce the content of any journal.

The Internet

The publishing process involves a variety of different stages. Technology is able to enhance each stage and link others together to provide opportunities to those who may have never had them before. Literally anyone with a connection to the Internet and the right software can produce their own website.

Most websites have a theme that will attract like-minded viewers. Business websites aim to sell a product, service or ideas. They will employ skilful graphic designers to make a site that looks good and is easy to navigate. The designer can use software to prepare and manipulate images prior to uploading. He or she is quickly able to try a range of graphics with different colour properties without having to go through a lengthy re-drawing phase each time. In a couple of mouse clicks an image can be flipped, rotated and recoloured. Major organisations take the look, feel and content of their websites very seriously, as websites can quite often be the first contact they have with potential customers. Organisations need to provide an accurate and clear interface that can be navigated effortlessly so that customers can find the information they require without having to work too hard.

In order to produce a good, appealing website, the first phase in the publishing process needs to be carefully considered. Before presenting any literary work, there needs to be a development phase. During development, text, graphics, buttons and additional features like search boxes or a shopping trolley all need to be established. The chosen content must be consistent and deliver the intended message.

Developers and designers are then charged with combining all the elements to showcase the information and attract viewers. Many personal sites do not consider the audience and produce very dull websites with limited content; often a reflection of the software skill level of the website's creator. Other sites can go too far and use clashing colour schemes, large images, incomprehensible text and poor layouts. Most businesses are conscious of the pitfalls associated with poor design, which is why they invest so heavily in employing experts to design their websites.

Prior to any type of publication, the work produced must be sampled. This allows for the editing out of mistakes and addition of content that may have been omitted. By using technology, it is possible to digitally transfer several copies of text to several proofreaders in different locations. The combined feedback from a range of sources can often add quality or provide new ideas and perspectives which were originally overlooked. This may well include several different page layouts or themes. Communication technology can also be used to keep everybody in the process informed about what stage they are at. This helps publishers to manage deadlines and to produce plans that allow for the various activities involved in publishing to take place at the right time.

Desktop publishing

Desktop publishing, which allows users to handle text and experiment with different text-based formats, is one of the major advancements in the publishing industry. Font colour, size, style and location can all be altered to test different designs. Templates can be used to establish and maintain a corporate identity. Templates are also ideal for those with limited design ability, as they have preset placeholders for text, graphics and repeating features. DTP software is specifically designed to combined text and images in multiple layouts. Columns, cropping and resizing are just a few of the simple measures used to fit content. Special tools exist for borders and shapes to add impact, with hundreds of different text options available to add greater emphasis and draw the attention of the reader. In a matter of seconds, a page can be transformed from one theme to another and designers can enjoy having artistic licence to experiment with so many tools.

Graphics software is used to complement DTP software. When images are transferred into graphics software the possibilities are endless. The front cover of every fashion magazine shows a glamorous model. Air-brushing techniques are used to trim or shape their waist. Colour is added to the lips to make red lipstick redder. The whites of the eyes are made really white and the skin given a healthy glow. All this is done to make the celebrity look as the magazine readers expect them to look. When these highly attractive images are added to expertly presented pages, the result is a publication fit for the newsagent's shelf.

Case study

Beatles Abbey Road cigarette airbrushed

The Beatles were all heavy smokers in the 1960s. United States poster companies have airbrushed the classic Beatles Abbey Road album cover to remove a cigarette from Paul McCartney's hand. The move was made without the permission of either McCartney or Apple Records, which owns the rights to the image …

'We have never agreed to anything like this,' said an Apple spokesman.

'It seems these poster companies got a little carried away, …

The 1969 image has been a poster classic since it was taken near Abbey Road studios in north London, where the group recorded most of their music.

The Beatles were all heavy smokers

A link to this website is available at www.heinemann.co.uk/hotlinks (express code 2349P)

LePaih Publishing House

A group of 13-year-olds is due to visit The LePaih Publishing House where you work. The manager has asked you to produce a double-sided A4 information leaflet. The leaflet should demonstrate a range of font options with examples and explanations of how they might be used in live publications.

The production phase will vary depending on what is being published. Websites are digitised and will need to be uploaded once to the web and kept up-to-date, while books and magazines need to be produced multiple times. The technology used to mass-produce glossy magazines and novels needs to be vast to meet consumer demand and print in high quality.

Uploading to a website

Investigate the different ways of uploading text and image content to a website. Write a list of at least **five** ways, then choose **two** of those on the list and write a short description of how these work.

After the designers and developers have produced the website, book, magazine or other publication, it will have to be sold or presented to an audience. The theme of the publication will strongly dictate the nature of the marketing activities, which again can be supported by technology.

Target marketing involves using vast amount of data, usually stored in a database, which identifies the most likely group of people who will be interested in the publication. Data is collected from online forms, competition entry coupons, and high-street surveys, or purchased from specialists that supply such information.

Advertising will take place in the areas that the intended readership will visit or view. This could be related websites that support advertisements, billboards, television or other related publications. Giant posters are produced on industrial printers and pasted up on billboards, and leaflets may be dropped through letterboxes.

The retail sector uses graphics and imaging software to create packaging labels. It also uses specialised printers to cover flexible, plastic packaging and boxes. The thought and detail attributed to this sector of commerce is immense. Teams of designers spend hours creating images on packaging that will attract and promote sales of the product stored within.

Distribution of literature on the Internet can be done by just about anyone. There are no limitations to what can be found on websites, which means that the validity and accuracy of some of the data and information is questionable. Some pages will deliberately or unconsciously display false information, whilst others will only represent the view of a minority of people who may be biased.

The retail sector uses graphics and imaging software to create packaging labels

If viewers hope to use information in a balanced and reasoned way, it is imperative that the source is verified, reliable and not swayed by political opinion or bias. Clearly the value and uses of data found online will vary from one person to the next. Trivial information, such as the TV schedule, will not promote mass panic if the soap opera times are printed incorrectly. Share prices and company financial trading data, for a potential investor, is important reading – should such information be misleading and acted upon, the outcome could be very costly and have legal implications.

The future of publishing is open to all. Books are available for download, which means they can be stored and shared with others. This presents new considerations for the law relating to copyright. The cost of mass-producing leaflets is falling, while the price of printers is reducing and output is steadily rising. Anyone with a message of hope, peace or destruction can quickly take it to an audience of millions to influence opinion and cause great damage or joy. The lack of control over what is published in the digital world is a major concern and one that will demand further attention from those who claim to safeguard individual interests.

Broome and Hyde Ltd

Broome and Hyde Ltd presents online holiday reviews sent to it by tourists from around the world. The company has asked that you produce a checklist to be followed by the staff members who upload the reviews. The checklist should consider:

- handling images
- validity and accuracy of text
- layout of the page
- date of the review
- location of the review
- integrity of the reviewer.

The Making of an E-Book

Here's how MBS converts print text into e-books for students:

Publishers provide a digital version of the print text, which MBS converts into Adobe 7.0. MBS creates links from the table of contents to each chapter.

Then MBS sets the digital rights, which is especially important because these rights protect the text's intellectual property. Digital rights control how the e-book can be printed, shared and whether it will include a read-out-loud function.

MBS provides participating bookstores with a card, similar to a gift card, which is associated to a particular book. When the student purchases the e-book, the card is activated from the store's point-of-sale system and is available for download over the internet. Then, the student goes online and enters a series of codes from the card and is given the link to download the e-book.

A link to this website is available at www.heinemann.co.uk/hotlinks (express code 2349P)

Questions

1. Describe the consequences a commercial company can expect if it displays a poor website. (3)

2. State and explain **three** general factors that make a commercial website a success. (6)

3. Describe **four** features of DTP software that are used on magazine front covers. (8)

4. Why should information on the Internet be treated with caution? (3)

5. What methods could be used to verify the authenticity of data found on the Internet? (3)

2.7 Section 2 topic round-up

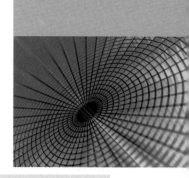

An ICT system and its components

What is an ICT system?

- Input
- Storage
- Processing
- Output
- Communication

What are the components of an ICT system?

- People
- Data
- Procedures
- Software
- Hardware
- Information

Data

- Text
- Numeric
- Still images
- Moving images
- Sound

Information good qualities

- Complete
- Up-to-date
- Reliable
- Relevant
- For the right person
- At the right time
- In the right format

People and ICT systems

Characteristics of users that influence use of and usefulness of ICT

- System commissioners
- Client
- End users
- Experience
- Physical characteristics
- Environment of use
- Tasks to be undertaken
- Age

Human–computer interaction

- Types of interaction (passive, active)
- Types of interface (menu, touch-screen, command-line, graphical, natural language)
- Help and support systems

Working in ICT

- Available job roles
  - Analyst
  - Tester
  - Programmer/developer
  - Website developer
  - Database administrator
  - Help desk/first line support
  - PC engineer
  - Network engineer
- Personal characteristics for each job role
  - Good listening skills
  - Good written communication skills
  - Flexibility

- Problem-solving
- Technical know-how plus knowledge of limitations
- Overarching professionalism (abiding by codes and laws, etc.)
- ICT team desirable characteristics
  - Leadership skills
  - Monitoring plans, progress and budgets
  - Good team communication
  - Allocating right task to right person
  - Having a good balance of the skills that are required
  - Mentoring skills if trainees are part of the team

Transfer of data in ICT systems

Networks

- Communication devices
- Networking software
- Data transfer media
- LANs and WANs
- The Internet and the World Wide Web
- Intranets and extranets

Standards and protocols

- For connecting devices
- For transferring data over a LAN
- For transferring data over the Internet

Safety and security of data

Protection of data

- Privacy of data
- Legislation involved
- Commercial value of data

Threats to ICT systems

- Internal threats
- External threats
- Malpractice
- Crime

Protecting ICT systems

- Hardware measures
- Software measures
- Procedures to protect systems
- Legislation to follow for the protection of systems

Backup and recovery

- Backing up for individuals
- Backing up for groups of users
- Backing up systems
- Needs for backing up
  - Options dependent on what, when, how and storage (media and location)
  - Responsibilities
- Continuity of service

ICT provision

What ICT can provide

- Fast, repetitive processing
- Vast storage capacity
- Ability to search and combine data
- Improved presentation of information
- Improved accessibility to information and services
- Improved security of data and processes

Limitations of ICT use

Limitation in the information provided

Appropriateness of use

Type of processing

- Batch
- Interactive
- Transaction

Factors affecting the use of ICT

- Cultural
- Economic
- Environmental
- Ethical
- Legal
- Social

ExamCafé
Relax, refresh, result!

Relax and prepare

What other students wish they had known before the exam…

Jamie

Sometimes I made the mistake of not checking my work at the end of the exam. If I had done so, I could have picked up marks. The reading and activities I did really paid off, as I was able to give good, relevant answers for the whole of each question.

Hot tips

Shaheen

I repeated myself many times in the exam. I only really mentioned a few things and didn't show off what I knew as best as I could. If I had to do it again, I would read the question properly, set my answer out clearly and think carefully about giving really good responses which demonstrate that I appreciate how ICT is used by the organisations mentioned.

Enzo

By the end of the exam I felt like I was running out of time and concentration. I hadn't revised some areas and my thinking was shot, making it doubly hard. I have never seen videoconferencing so had no personal experience of it. I learn best by doing, so when it comes to studying the A2 topics I will make sure that I give myself as much practical experience as I can of everything that is in the specification.

How can you learn from Jamie's, Shaheen's and Enzo's comments as you prepare for your AS exam? What do you need to do differently?

Getting started. . .

What's so different about AS?

It is harder than GCSE: You might find yourself tempted to put in minimal effort, particularly if you did OK in your GCSEs without revising.

It is not a memory test: Whilst it is true that you will need to remember a lot information, the exams are testing whether you can apply the relevant information in answering the question.

It requires longer answers: The questions are of an essay style and although you could give quite brief answers to some of them, you will not fully answer the question (and hence get good marks) unless you give an extended, detailed response.

Refresh your memory

Revision checklist

Use the following checklist and refer back to pages 161–163 to remind yourself of the sections within the following main topics; check them off when you've refreshed your memory on them. Use the Exam Café CD-ROM for a bigger checklist.

- [ ] An ICT system and its components
- [ ] People and ICT systems
- [ ] Transfer of data in ICT systems
- [ ] Safety and security of data
- [ ] ICT provision

Common mistakes

▷ If the question asks anything about a 'difference' make sure you state both sides of any point made. For example, if talking about networks, then a difference between a LAN and a WAN may be that one is usually confined to a single site and the other could have a wide geographical spread.

▷ The terms Give, State and Name normally require a few words or short phrase to get the mark, but watch out for the question asking for 'a use of' or 'a reason for' which means more marks are available. Make sure your answer addresses what is asked for, rather than merely saying what it means.

Get the result !

Here, the students have each attempted an exam question, and the examiner has marked them.

Model answers

Exam question

A multi-national company uses a videoconferencing system to enable meetings to take place between the London and the Los Angeles offices.

(a) Describe the benefits to the employees, the company and society of providing this facility. (10)

(b) Describe the limitations that the employees may experience when videoconferencing. (6)

Student answer (Lizzie)

(a) For the employees, having a videoconferencing activity means that they can collaborate with other staff the other side of the world with little notice and little inconvenience from their daily tasks. They do not have to be away from home for work purposes, which is especially good for those staff with families. For the company, it saves both the time of travelling which means that their employees can be working all the time not wasting their time waiting for planes, and the expense of air fares and hotels for their staff. Videoconferencing can be as good as a face-to-face meeting as you can see the other person's body language. For society, the fewer people there are travelling by air the better for fuel emissions and so better environmentally for the whole world in the face of global warming.

(b) Sometimes there is a time delay between sending and receiving the images, so that the pictures are jumpy, which can cause communication problems for the two lots of staff. Sometimes the computer gets overloaded with all the images and crashes.

Examiner says:

Lizzie made a good answer to part (a) of the question, gaining all 10 marks. However, her answer to part (b) was a bit thin, but managed to gain 4 of the 6 marks. As she had mentioned face-to-face as being no problem, she didn't think to mention it again as a limitation. However, 14 of a possible 16 is a very good score on this question.

Examiner's tips

Describe and Explain normally carry 2 or 3 marks each, but look at the allocation. Some questions with these words may be worth 6, 8 or even 10 marks. Use the guidelines above to structure your answer to make sure you have made enough valid comments to have a chance of gaining all available marks.

Student answer (Enzo)

(a) Videoconferencing can be a benefit to both company and employee. To the company, it saves the cost of travelling and means that all the employees can be working at their normal jobs, just pop into the meeting room and have a meeting with whoever, as if they were there. For the employee, it means they can get on with their work. It makes no difference to society whether a company has this or not as everybody flies around the world anyway.

(b) The limitation to the employee is that they don't get to visit New York with the company paying and they don't get to meet the American staff and get to know them, go to a baseball game etc.

Examiner says:

Enzo has been quite flippant in his answers and it is obvious that he doesn't really understand the business reasons for using videoconferencing. However, his answers to Part (a) do bring up some valid points: costs and lack of work disruption. It gains 3 of the 10 marks. In Part (b) he has looked at this from a purely personal level and has not made any valid points, so gained nil points.

Examiner's tips

Discuss is another command word that may appear at least once in this paper – again, see how many marks there are for the answer and plan your response sensibly to cover as many discrete points as you can. There's no penalty for saying more than is required. Just beware the urge to waffle!

A2 Section 3

The Use of ICT in the Digital World

This is the theory section for A2. It is assessed by an examination that is 2 hours long and can be taken in January or June each year. Some of the topics studied in this section can be used as a basis for the coursework section 4.

The section looks at the fast-changing subject of ICT, including developments in technology and the capabilities of ICT, in relation to how these are used in organisations of different sizes and in the world as a whole.

The content addresses the issues concerned with the management and use of ICT in organisations. Part of the examination is based upon a pre-released case study that describes an organisation and a situation. This approach is the best way to study this section – looking at a range of organisations, including charities, clubs and societies, medium and large commercial businesses, independent, national and multinational, and both public and private.

The numbers of people involved with ICT in these organisations could range from one or two to many thousands, and it is their needs and requirements for ICT that are studied. Each organisation will have the same ICT-related issues to consider on a scale appropriate to their own needs. External entities will also be involved, and these will be part of the study.

ICT systems are there to support the activities of an organisation and the many topics covered in this section include:

- information and systems
- managing ICT in organisations
- developing ICT solutions
- techniques and tools used for investigating, business process modelling, data modelling and testing
- issues to do with large-scale ICT systems
- training and supporting users
- the external and internal resources required to use ICT in organisations.

Future developments are looked at first. The best way to further study this is by conducting research and investigating any new technology or use for ICT. It is likely that there will be one question on every exam paper that requires you to demonstrate that you have done some recent investigations.

If possible, a period of immersion in a real-world organisation would be of great benefit to every student of this A2. Rather than merely reading some words, you will gain a far greater insight by observing how ICT is used, understanding why data is captured here, reports are generated there, when things are processed and in what manner, who is involved at each stage, who enters the data, what processing is done, and when, then who uses the reports.

Many of the concepts of this section should be studied over a range of organisations; the case studies should give you some ideas for types of organisation to study. However, there is nothing better than real experience.

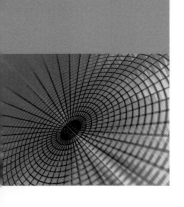

3.1 Future developments

Working with case studies

A pre-release case study will form the basis for the first section of the exam paper for this section. This will be published approximately two months before the examination, which gives plenty of time to study the situation and to discuss the organisation and its probable use of ICT. The case study may be based around a particular ICT system, or it may be more general. The questions using the case study may come from any area of the INFO3 specification (for example, development, management, training and support) or they could come from any part of the AS sections previously studied (for example, networking, data transfer, security and so on).

In groups, tabulate, for five systems (using a particular package as directed, or one of your choice, or as a paper exercise) the following information:

- What is the context/business?
- What is the system called/what does it do (title)?
- What kind of hardware is used for
  - data collection
  - storage
  - processing
  - output?
- Where does the data come from?
- How does it get into the system?
- Who wrote the system/where did it come from?
- What software was used to write the system (generic/specialist)?
- Is it part of a bigger system?
- Where does information get sent? And how?
- Is it part of a network?
- What security is used?
- Who controls the system?
- Who operates the system?

Brainstorm in your group and add as much of the following information as possible:

- Who uses the system?
- Is it a Data Processing System, an Information System or a Management Information System (or combinations)?
- Who uses the output from the system (likely to be many people)?
- What type of output is it? Operational, tactical or strategic?
- What levels of personnel use the system?

Whole-class evaluation

Review the tables from other groups and suggest improvements. Try to group the systems into a set of businesses, so that you are creating a set of case studies that can be used later when applying theoretic knowledge to real situations. Amalgamate the best information and, using some form of presentation or DTP software, make it into a reference for later study. It could even be made up as a website and held online for all to read and reference.

After each topic is studied, this reference work can then be reviewed and improved where necessary. It will form an invaluable revision aid as most A2 exam questions are context-based.

Write down a list of ICT systems that you studied during the AS course:

● everyday systems, such as shop-based, home-based, banking, DVD hire and so on

● any systems that you studied that were slightly less obvious, such as manufacturing, aeroplane control systems, online shopping and so on.

For each of the types of system described, find out what it entails:

● Who is involved as its users?

● What data is entered, and how?

● What information is output, and how?

● What choices do organisations have for procuring this type of system? If there are commercially available packages, find an example.

A range of organisations should be studied and, in an ideal world these would be real organisations. However, given time constraints during the teaching period, it is unlikely that all students would be able to experience a wide enough range to be able fully to appreciate the issues for all types of organisation and all types of system.

Systems in use in most organisations, whatever their size and purpose, include:

• payroll, pensions, application tracking, performance tracking (also known as personal development; part of a personnel tracking system) – if the organisation employs staff

• purchase ordering, stock control, warehouse/stock room organisation – if the organisation holds stock for any reason (it could be stock parts used to make a product)

• order tracking, production, storage, distribution – if they make a product for selling

• vehicle maintenance, vehicle allocation and use – if they own lorries, cars or vans

• accounting systems (purchasing, payments in and payments out)

• building services

• asset management

• a website or extranet.

In the absence of available real organisation experience, use the short organisation descriptions that follow to form the basis of discussions about organisational use of ICT. The notes are brief so, as you are going through the chapters in this section, pause at the end of each topic and make notes for each type of organisation on how that particular organisation might respond to the topic.

● Does it impact on the organisation?

● What does the organisation need to do to take account of the topic/issue?

● Are there external requirements?

Be as specific as possible – these notes will help in your revision for the examination.

Supermarket

- This is a large national chain of stores, with warehouses in four locations, serving a number of stores.

- It employs staff in the thousands, full- and part-time in the stores and warehouses.

- Its head office is in the south-east of England.

- It is floated on the stock market.

- It has its own Information Systems Development department.

- Most systems are written in-house.

- It has its own training department.

- It has a private WAN, an intranet, an extranet and it offers online shopping.

- It uses EDI with its suppliers, using just-in-time techniques.

- It has its own fleet of delivery vehicles.

Suggested systems to look at: Stock Control, POS and/or Ordering.

Bank/building society

- The head office is in the north-east of England.

- It has 200 branches all around the country, each employing 10–30 staff.

- It has its own Information Systems Development department.

- Most of its systems are bespoke, developed in-house.

- The ongoing maintenance and support of some older systems is outsourced to various outsourcing companies.

- Its business is regulated by a central government body.

- Each branch has its own LAN; the whole organisation has a secure WAN/intranet.

- Online banking is available.

Suggested systems to look at: Banking or Financial Product Marketing.

College

- This is a single-site college.

- It has 800 full-time and 3,000 part-time students.

- Most software is bought in as packages for specific tasks.

- It has an Administrative LAN and a separate Academic/Student LAN.

- Funding councils and examination boards are two very important external information providers/recipients.

Suggested systems to look at: Student Tracking or College Budgeting.

Solicitor's practice

- This is a local firm with 20–30 employees.

- Most of its work is done on standard packages.

- It has a small LAN with a dial-up Internet connection.

- There is no ICT expertise in the firm.

- It mostly deals with family matters – wills, divorces, house moves.

Suggested systems to look at: Client Information or House Conveyance Tracking.

Mail order firm

- All administrative operations, including the call-centre, are run from one site in the north-west of England, but there are two warehouses, north and south of England.

- There are about 40–50 staff at each warehouse, plus around 200 at head office.

- It has state-of-the-art call-centre software and equipment, feeding into the mail ordering system that was written in-house 15 years ago.

- Ordering is now available online.

- It has in-house Information System Development and Support teams.

- Its suppliers are worldwide, mainly in the Far East.

Suggested systems to look at: Ordering, Distribution or Purchasing.

Sensors in the home can open the security gates

Emerging technologies

It is probably hard to imagine what technology will bring in the future, but on the horizon are some exciting developments ready to take the digital age into uncharted waters.

Home and transport networking

Digitally customised homes are being developed that include sensors placed all over the home with each given a variety of tasks to perform. An approaching car can be detected by sensors in the home, which turn on the lights on the drive, open the security gates and front door. Similar sensors can be activated to run a bath at the desired temperature, turn on the entertainment system, and adjust the lighting or load up the home computer system on the user's favourite Internet page. This is all possible now. Dishwashers and washing machines are currently being programmed to detect what they are to clean, so they can execute the most appropriate wash

to not only clean the clothes or crockery but to preserve them as well. Wireless technology and increasing data transmission speeds are helping to make networked homes a reality.

Train users who travel through the Channel Tunnel are able to access a broadband connection on their journey, even under the sea. The tunnel has been lined with devices that transmit signals to the trains, which broadcast signals to laptops, enabling the user to surf the web and send emails on the move.

Virus detection

Scientists have developed a microchip that can detect and distinguish between different flu strains. There are 72 flu strains, including bird flu, which it can detect in less than 12 hours. This kind of technology can be used to quickly ascertain and recommend the best course of action for a sufferer before serious problems develop.

Global Positioning System (GPS)

GPS technology is used to help navigate from one location to another. It is used by transport companies to calculate distances and best routes. It can be used by taxi drivers in the form of satellite navigation systems to ensure they never go to the wrong address and they will not need to memorise thousands of street names. GPS is also used

Global Positioning System (GPS)

GPS is a global navigation system using microwave signals sent from an arrangement of satellites. A GPS receiver can use these signals to determine its location and velocity.

by explorers or soldiers on expedition, so that they don't get lost. GPS can be used to track the location of vehicles, people or products. This means stolen cars can be tracked to criminals, freight in transit can be located and reported on and people can be found if kidnapped. The technology is not massively widespread yet, but the potential for the recovery of stolen goods and for finding people in remote or dangerous places is appealing to some organisations.

Case Study

Suppliers for Wal-Mart Stores Inc. may have balked at having to deploy radio-frequency identification, but at Graniterock, in Watsonville, Calif., customers can't deploy the technology fast enough.

Since the construction company deployed RFID at all its locations, customers have benefited from a wealth of information based on the arrivals and departures of trucks through Graniterock's asphalt and quarry operations.

With more than 3 million pounds of granite, sand and other construction materials being loaded onto 600 trucks per day at the A.R. Wilson Quarry, Graniterock's largest, customers are happy to get as much information as possible.

In fact, the company has been able to reduce by half the amount of time it takes to load customer trucks at its quarries.

Graniterock's IT managers decided to take a page from the railroad industry's technology playbook and use RFID tags – the same kind used to identify rail cars – on the company's trucks. The TC IP Ltd. passive tags (which transmit information but don't collect it) are mounted on the driver side of the truck's cab and collect data on inventory and supply movement. The RFID system processes the arrival and departure of trucks through the company's asphalt and quarry loading locations.

The night before a customer's truck is scheduled to make a pickup, the customer calls Graniterock to provide information on the truck, including its RFID tag information, the load that's scheduled for pickup and the job for which the load will be used.

As a truck passes through a loading gate, the RFID tag is scanned, and the GraniteXpress 2 application determines which vehicle has entered the quarry and which company owns that truck. Electronic signs then automatically direct the truck driver to the loading station that has the materials the truck is scheduled to pick up. After the truck pulls into the loading station, the RFID system verifies the correct truck is in place, and then the construction materials are loaded. A checkout station then reads the RFID tag again, weighs the truck and prints a receipt. The data is also used by Graniterock to generate billing invoices.

At the end of each day, Crystal Reports queries the company's Microsoft SQL Server database for information on the pickups that occurred that day and e-mails a report on each truck and its load to the truck's owner.

Customers use the reports to determine how quickly a particular construction job is progressing and how efficient their supply chains are.

'We now have statistics we can provide to our customers on how well each truck is doing,' Snodgrass said. 'Crystal Reports enables us to provide a customer with complete visibility of what's going on in their organisation so that they can compare the performance of different trucks and ask certain drivers why they were late.'

A link to this website is available at www.heinemann.co.uk/hotlinks (express code 2349P)

Radio-Frequency Identification (RFID)

Bermuda has launched a new automated vehicle registration system. Each vehicle will be fitted with an RFID tag and monitored using antenna, readers and a database. The system is designed to generate over $11 million in lost fees from unlicensed and uninsured vehicles. Each car will have a personal identifier that is transmitted by the RFID tag to the antennas and recorded in the central database. The RFID tag is embedded into a sticker placed on the car windshield after it has been registered or inspected. Cars which do not emit a signal will be detected by tripod and hand-held readers. The data from the RFID tag will show if the car is registered, when the registration will expire and will identify prohibited vehicles in certain areas and issue fines.

> **Radio-Frequency Identification (RFID)**
> RFID uses low-power transponders in RFID tags attached to products to send signals identifying those products. RFID tags may be passive (powered by the incoming signal) or active (with an internal power supply).

VoIP

Games consoles have recently been sold which incorporate **VoIP** technology. This enables game players to speak to each other through headsets from different locations while they play against each other. Game developers now have to consider this new element when they design new games. It is not necessary to be playing a game or to have great IT skills to use this technology; it has proved useful in the corporate world, allowing businesses to conduct phone conversations cheaply or for no charge at all. The use of verbal-command-driven applications is growing, as is the need for voice-control security measures.

> **Voice over Internet Protocol (VoIP)**
> VoIP is a technology for encoding speech as data and sending it across a network (typically the Internet) in real time. This technology allows people to speak to one another for free, even if they are in different countries, as long as each is on an Internet-connected computer with a headset and the appropriate software.

ID cards

The Government plans to launch national identification cards, which is set to cost over £5.3 billion. The costs involved relate to the development and production of a system that can produce cards that hold biometric details. This might include a retina scan, fingerprint details and a whole host of personal information all stored on a chip embedded in the card. Identification cards are common in many other countries, but do not hold the kind of detail the UK cards will store. In due course, everybody in the UK will have their own ID card, which could potentially represent a passport, driving licence and national insurance card. It is hoped that ID cards will bring down levels of fraud related to these other cards, because ID cards will be completely unique and hard to replicate without the correct technology.

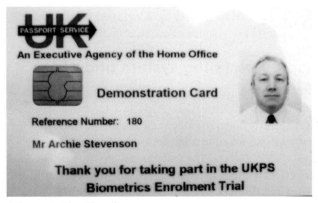

A demonstration ID card

Crime dashboards and flying drones

Police are set to use digital displays to map the location and timings of crimes. This will be available online to all police forces, who will then be able to analyse patterns of specific crimes. For example, the location of burglaries can be displayed, which will clearly identify areas that have been targeted and are most in need of patrolling or extra security. Visual display can help police to identify patterns, allowing them to coordinate activities in areas where they are most required.

Police are also using small remote-controlled drones that can be flown into crimes scenes, riots or other hard-to-reach places. Images are transferred back to a display unit that shows the police exactly what is happening below the drone. Police can use the information to help decide what action to take next. Drones can replace expensive

An example of a drone used by police

helicopters when tracking criminals on foot, and can ascertain the level of danger in certain areas before officers are committed. Over time, the speed and quality of image will improve, and the ability to record what is being filmed will be useful as evidence when cases go to court.

Display planning system and pizza delivery

Confectionery producers are using software that automatically plans the way their products should be displayed, for maximum impact, when they reach the supermarket shelves. The software is used by mobile sales staff to show shop managers various display options to help raise sales and capture customer interest. The shop will suggest how much space it can spare per product and the software does the rest.

Customers can use the Internet to order pizzas with the toppings of their choice to be delivered at a pre-defined time. The system has helped Domino's Pizza to improve its delivery system and to ensure they have the required ingredients to accommodate each day's orders. The system also allows them to plan the best routes for the delivery riders and to recruit the optimum number required each night or day. The ability to pay for the delivery online and order in advance has helped to streamline the whole service and improve customer satisfaction.

Digital paper

Several companies are designing displays that can present the same type of information as a computer monitor, but which can be rolled out or folded away. Internet usage on mobile phones has been slow to grow due to the small

screen. The idea of digital paper is that it can be folded out from a handset and used more practically to display web pages. Other uses might include displaying digital content from novels stored on tiny microchips instead of books. The digital paper could have touch-sensitive buttons to allow pages to be turned. Digital bookmarks could be used too, and the material could store many books, rolled up discreetly and packed away like a few sheets of paper. The reduction in weight would be more attractive than carrying a load of books around and the ability to access a whole range of digitised reading material in one portable system may appeal to students, academics and book lovers all over the world.

The reduction in weight would be more attractive than carrying a load of books around!

The Third World

Certain technology may be commonplace in the developed world, but it is seen as emerging in other parts of the globe. Low-cost receivers are being used in the Third World so that remote communities can access vital information relating to agriculture, health, HIV/AIDS, the climate, technology and general news. People have been trained to use the technology and to disseminate the information they receive. Various languages are translated and broadcast so that as big an audience as possible can benefit from the information.

Satellite technology constantly monitors the climate in order to predict potential drought problems, to recommend early aid requirements and suggestions for harbouring backup supplies. Education programmes are released to bolster formal and informal classrooms that cannot be physically supported by teachers. Technology allows remote communities to share a wide range of materials and to interact with one another to improve community relations and provide a new generation of people that are numerate, literate and can access and benefit from new technology.

Solar power is used to heat water, power laptops that connect to the Internet and charge mobile phones, which allow villages to keep in touch with one another.

Robots

Robots have been a source of fascination for many years and refinements are made to existing models on a daily basis. The robot pet was introduced to homes not so long ago. Sitting, standing, and following a few simple commands were quite good fun but fairly limited in terms of practical use. As ever, the military is at the cutting edge of technology, funding billions of dollars worth of investment to push the boundaries of robotic development. Various armed forces are planning to replace humans with robots in dangerous combat situations and already use them to sweep for roadside bombs. The ultimate aim could be to create an unstoppable machine, which is bomb-proof, fire-proof, a crack shot, an expert at assessing potential threats and has the speed and agility

to crush insurgents quickly and with minimal loss of life. Quite a specification, but, behind closed doors, testing is likely to be taking place. One of the more quirky obstacles is trying to improve the motion of a robot from walking to running. The mechanics of this process have kept hobbyists and specialists busy for a number of years, but it is likely that with persistence and lots of funding this aim will be achieved.

The industrial and commercial business sectors are developing robots to carry out exploratory work in uninhabitable climates. Robots have been designed to detect pockets of fuel, to carry out collection and analysis of materials found on other planets and, less glamorously, to hoover the office floor. Artificial limbs are modified in the hope of giving wearers back the same sensation they lost when they were separated from their real limbs. The potential is to give a user a new arm 10 times stronger than the one they lost. Care robots are being developed to work in hospitals and care homes, which can navigate halls and corridors to deliver medication and messages.

The appeal of using robots to carry out tasks that humans can't or won't do is the driving force in their development. They cost billions to make and maintain, but if they can do the work of 1000 in less time, and to a better degree of accuracy, the investment will be worthwhile. The potential to improve upon current artificial intelligence means that a robot will have the capacity to think and make decisions based on what it sees, hears and senses, just like a human.

Robots have been a source of fascination for many years

After being used to explore Mars, to make cars and to clear bombs, robots are moving into the home, ready to single-mindedly vacuum carpets, mow lawns and act like humans as industry targets the consumer market.

About 1.3 million 'personal or domestic service robots' were in use at the end of 2003 and their number is set to expand by 6.7 million until 2007, the UN's Economic Commission for Europe (UNECE) said in a survey released on October 22 (2004).

Some 607,000 of the current stock are designed to do domestic tasks and 691,000 are entertainment and leisure robots, but the home-help robots are set to outstrip their less useful counterparts.

Colin Angle, chief executive of the iRobot company, said: 'I think it's perfectly reasonable to imagine having a robot in every home, certainly within ten years.'

Sukhan Lee of South Korea's Sungkyunkwan University predicted that developments in information technology would drive robots into the home.

'Ten years ago we also asked whether there would be a personal computer in every home, we weren't certain it would happen. But the Internet pushed it,' he added.

While a South Korean company advertised a two-legged, near life-size 'humanoid battle robot' to bring computer games alive, industry executives at an exhibition organised by the UN emphasised more peaceful and practical applications.

The automatised vacuum cleaner, which can be left to take care of a room while the owner is at work, should account for just under half of the predicted growth in the coming years.

'When you get to things like cooking or taking care of a person, those are much more abstract, it's not a good place to start. We have to build up confidence,' he added, predicting wall-climbing window washers and laundry-folding robots.

Cleaners already on the market carry a battery of electronic sensors that are meant to prevent them dropping off the edge of the stairs, to bypass obstacles like furniture, and size up a room.

As this correspondent was accosted and examined by a long-necked blue surveillance robot, another more amiable service robot – used by a car maker in its customer centre – whirred over to offer some information.

The South Korean company demonstrated a squat 'hobby robot' that can play and dance with children and teach them languages thanks to its computer screen.

Asked by a journalist if there would soon be a robot that could take care of a baby, an executive responded with a flat 'no'.

A link to this website is available at www.heinemann.co.uk/hotlinks (express code 2349P)

1 Produce a list of jobs or tasks that you personally do not like doing.

2 Discuss and make notes with a partner about each item on your list and answer the following questions:

- Is it a suitable task or job for a robot to perform?
- If not, why not? If it is, what makes it appropriate?

- What advantages do you gain by a robot performing the task?
- What tasks or jobs would you not want a robot to perform and why?

3 Present your work to the rest to the class.

Potential future uses of ICT

Technology has permeated the workforce, home and education. It is used by teachers, students, nurses, doctors, the military, farmers, scientists and hairdressers, to name but a few. Our daily news is digitally broadcast from one continent to another, food is mixed by pre-programmed machines, cars are designed and built by robots and young minds are exposed to more information, facts and details than they can ever consume in one lifetime. The future uses of technology would only appear to be limited by human imagination. If an idea is feasible, the chances are the challenge will be taken up and developed for commercial gain, the advancement of human knowledge or well-being.

The future might include robots who undertake all dangerous industrial activities, perform domestic housekeeping and go shopping for the weekly groceries.

If robots are performing all the above tasks, this should give the human race more leisure time. The ability to talk to other gamers using VoIP is available, but how about competing against full-scale holographic representations instead of digital characters in shoot-'em-ups or sports challenges? Virtual reality is already used to train fighter pilots, so the potential to bring this technology into the home already exists, although it is probably too costly at the moment. Projectors, headsets and space to play may be all that is required.

Personal media players that store digital music and films are shrinking in size. It would not be surprising if manufacturers replace the main unit with a more compact ear piece which holds all the audio and video files. Voice commands could drive it; verbally selecting the music you want to hear would save scrolling through thousands of tracks. Perhaps digital paper will provide the screen to view digital films, or tiny gadgets appear that can project the film onto any flat surface, in any size.

With data transmission becoming possible without cables, all electronic devices can be networked. Mobile use of computer systems would not be hindered by wires, and power supplies may have developed to the extent that most systems run on solar power after being placed in an overnight recharging docking station. Increased transmission speed and digital entertainment could see the end of high-street music, video and book shops as consumers choose to download what they want to hear, see and read.

The cost of domestic computers may continue to fall, which will give more people the opportunity to buy PCs and get online. Developing communities could establish business links around the world that might help to improve their economic situation. They can improve their manufacturing processes and use technology in the production of buildings which provide shelter and habitable climates in hot, dry seasons so that crops can grow.

VoIP means that the whole world can talk for free over the Internet, thus encouraging the sharing of new ideas, improving family links and opening remote communities to the attention of the world.

Space exploration and even holidays may be an opportunity within the next decade. Space buildings, like satellites, could be sent into orbit and visited by scientist and tourist alike. Robotic miners may be sent to other planets to find precious minerals and fuels, which could be transported back to Earth and provide alternative power. Telescopes could become more powerful and may even detect the signs of life so many believe to be out there.

More microchips for disease detection could be developed that enter the body, locate viruses and destroy them; a bit like current anti-virus software but on the human body instead. Alternatively, nanotechnology could be used within the body to make it stronger, to improve the capacity to think or to help it to relax. RFID tags could be placed inside the body and our whereabouts tracked at all times. This would have considerable opposition from human rights activists and those who value their freedom, but could see a reduction in crime as alibis become harder to support. Such devices could even have a control system built which could slow people down or inject adrenalin at any given time.

If is difficult to imagine life without the Internet, electricity and mobile phones, but these gadgets are relatively new in terms of the history of the human race. The inventions due to emerge within the next hundred years are within comprehension but beyond our technology at the moment. The way we live is likely to change as planes become bigger and faster, housing becomes more environmentally friendly and our lifestyles and leisure pursuits radically alter as new opportunities are opened up.

Gallagher and Brown Interiors have asked you to produce a specification for the home of the future. The company is keen to see and hear a plan of your ideas about the kind of technology you would incorporate and what facilities you would include. Produce a presentation with images and text to help explain your plan.

Implications of future developments and future uses of ICT

The world could be a wonderful place if all the investment in technology was used to solve the problems of food shortages, child poverty, wars and violent crime. This is not the case. Although there is some good work being done in these areas, there still remains a large commercial drive fully aimed at maximising profits.

The cost factor is one of the first hurdles to overcome when developing new technology. Researchers, programmers, scientists and robotic engineers do not come cheap and neither do the materials they use. Because of this, large and powerful companies are in the best position to drive the technological revolution, while the rest of the world waits to see what they produce next.

The armed forces in the US were largely responsible for the development, funding and staff of the Internet, in its primary years. Supercomputers filled rooms and software programmers worked tirelessly to make a few machines exchange data. Soon hundreds of computers were networked, then the Internet took off and millions hooked up to the online dream.

The military are also among the lead contributors to robotics funding. Robots use cold logic and do not have compassion. They cannot yet read emotions, which excludes them from working in many specialist human fields. A robot can only make decisions based on the programmer's input and it will only learn from experience by adding to its databanks.

If all technology is networked and wireless, there will be huge implications for data security. It is already possible for people to piggyback on home-owners' routers and use their connections to download whatever they wish. The ability to access and remove files, music, films and personal details from business systems becomes an option for everybody if all technology can be networked. This means that better network security must be developed and updated on a regular basis.

Piggybacking on unsecured wireless connections is already possible

The employment market will become flexible as companies take their pick from a pool of specialists spread throughout the world. Technology means that staff will not need to be based in one central location and will be able to speak a variety of languages and regularly update and improve their skills by using a range of online tutorials and courses. Potential employees will be able to market themselves directly to employees via personalised websites and thoroughly research future employers before making an application.

The web provides online communities that are used by teenagers to self-advertise. The problem with social online networking is that the current generation are uploading so much information about themselves and what they have been doing that such data may be used against them in the future. Bebo, MySpace and Facebook are popular sites where young people post images of themselves doing things that potential employers can check before inviting applicants for interview. Some people have already expressed regret at posting images of themselves streaking, smoking drugs or joining controversial groups. The issue of privacy of information and self-promoting while young is set to be debated loudly in the future.

There is very little doubt that the current generation is more technology-savvy than any other before it. The youth of today may be technologically astute, but they still need to be educated about the power of web media and the potential for it to turn on them when they least expect it. Teenagers are probably best poised to develop more intuitive products to suit mass markets because this is part of their natural world. The tools have been developed for them to let their imaginations run wild and make the world a more interesting or dangerous place.

Practice exam questions

1. Give **three** situations and advantages of using a robot to perform a task instead of a human. (6)

2. Would a robot be suitable to work as a babysitter? Explain your answer. (4)

3. Describe **two** potential uses of RFID tags in the domestic appliances industry. (4)

4. Describe **three** advantages to the Third World of having access to the Internet. (3)

5. The military uses technology to detect roadside bombs and to detect night-time movement behind enemy lines. Provide and describe **two** more examples of how the armed forces use new technology. (4)

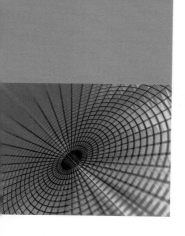

3.2 Information and systems

Information

All organisations need information in order to operate. This information will flow internally and externally on a daily, weekly, monthly and annual basis. Information is produced from the processing of data that comes in from one or many sources.

For example, consider someone employed in a job in the UK that pays by the hour. Each week or month, their work hours are multiplied by their rate of pay, and various additions and allowances are added, then various taxes and insurances are subtracted to give a pay amount. This is normally shown on a payslip, which also has information about pay and tax to date, the department number and so on. At the same time, a report is generated showing the information needed to send to the bank so that the money is transferred from the employer's bank account to each employee's bank account. The employee's annual P60 is an information report that details all money earned, tax and National Insurance contributions paid

in the previous tax year. The company also has an end-of-year information report detailing all monies paid and so on. These end-of-year reports are then used to fill in official government tax and National Insurance returns. The data that started this process off came from many sources – personal details from the employee; tax codes and NI numbers from official government departments; company details, such as place worked, department, grade, hourly rate, from the employing organisation; and hours worked, perhaps from a clocking-in system or a log-book.

Using your school or college as a case study, identify one example of information that might occur

- daily
- weekly
- monthly
- annually

and identify **three** pieces of data, with their sources, that have been collected in order to produce the information.

Different organisations have different information needs

The type of organisation will have an effect on the type and style of information that it uses on a regular basis. A **public-sector** organisation is concerned with transparency of information as they are accountable to many external entities, such as various facets of the government and the general public. A **private organisation** will be foremost accountable to its **shareholders** and may also be accountable to some external legal bodies, as well as other **stakeholders**.

Payslips show lots of information

Stakeholder

A stakeholder is any party with an interest in an organisation, e.g. employees, customers, suppliers or the local community. They have a 'stake' due to the effect that the organisation's activities will have on them, even though they may not be part of the organisation.

Shareholder

A shareholder holds one or more shares in a company. Shareholders get an invitation to the company's annual meeting, and have the right to vote for the members of the board of directors and on other company matters.

Public sector

The public sector is a term for the parts of the economy that are not controlled by individuals, voluntary organisations or private companies. This includes national and local government, and government-owned firms.

Public limited company (PLC)

A PLC is a company which offers its shares to the wider public (unlike a limited company). The company must have a minimum share value of £55,000. Some PLCs are listed on the London Stock Exchange.

Private company

A private company is a limited liability company in the UK, and must have between two and 50 shareholders. The shares cannot be transferred without the consent of other shareholders, and cannot be offered to the general public.

The scale of the organisation will also have an effect on the information required.

A small organisation that is on one site may use less formal methods of passing information round than a large multi-national organisation, so reducing the need for copious formal reports being produced. If the owner of a business is involved on a day-to-day basis in the operations of the business, they are less likely to need daily progress or sales reports from the sales team. Verbal reports, followed up by weekly summary information, are more likely to be adequate for purpose.

However, a large organisation, with a head office in one city or country and branches spread out geographically, will need more formal reporting mechanisms in place, to keep control of the information from all corners of the business. There will be more people using the information and each will require the information pertinent to their own role in the organisation.

The nature of the organisation will also have an influence on the type of information that is required to run its operation. A charity may need information about its regular donors, the monies taken and given out, and whatever is legally necessary for it to keep its charitable status, but may not require detailed information about customers or volunteers in its shops or collecting at events. However, a bank, for instance, will need copious amounts of information about its customers, investments, its product sales and so on, and different departments will use this information for varying purposes.

Different activities within organisations have different information needs

Internal departments will have a self-imposed style of information requirements. External activities will have to conform to the external entity's requirements for style, format and delivery method.

Customer support systems will have to show a sympathetic interface for the customers. If the customer is supplying data to an internal business system, then the information presented back to the customer must be accurate, up-to-date, complete and relevant. The success of the organisation may rest on customer reactions to the information provided to them by the organisation. The customer relations department may require a combination of internal systems to work together to ensure that the customer gets the right information.

Ordering systems rely on accurate information – what needs ordering and how much, the price, and so on – so that orders sent to the suppliers are in the right format and with the right information.

Activities such as payroll, personnel and finance, using personal and corporate data, require validated formal information from the organisation's systems to ensure that all functions are working accurately and within the laws that govern such systems.

Different levels of task have different information needs

There are three levels of personnel within an organisation, which have specific information requirements and which are served by different types of information system. Using a large supermarket as an example, the levels are:

- **operational (management)** (at the 'sharp end' e.g. check-out operators – they are still 'managing' the information and could be making small decisions at an item level)
- **tactical management** (middle management, e.g. Head of Bakery)
- **strategic management** (in charge of all stores in the north-west, or the Managing Director, based at head office.)

Operational management is performed by line managers and supervisors and is concerned with ensuring that the day-to-day operations of the organisation are performed correctly. An operational-level information system will have to facilitate and keep track of the basic activities and transactions of the organisation. Information systems that serve this level of the organisation are called **Transaction Processing Systems (TPS)**.

Middle management, including department managers and functional managers (such as sales managers), performs tactical management. It is concerned with the setting of strategic objectives and mid- to long-term planning. Decisions at this level will be based on information that attempts to predict the future of the organisation and its environment. **Management information systems (MIS)** concentrate on the regular reporting of the transactions of the organisation, therefore facilitating monitoring and control. They are commonly used at this level, and are also used at the strategic level.

Strategic management is performed by the senior management of the organisation, such as the board of directors, and is concerned with the setting of strategic objectives and long-term planning. Decisions at this level will be based on information that attempts to predict the future of the organisation and its environment. Information may come from within the business or from external agencies, such as government, competitors or environmental agencies.

There are three levels of personnel within an organisation

Choose an organisation that you are familiar with or have been studying, and identify the people at each of the three levels of task. Do the following for each of them:

- Identify the role that they perform.
- Identify information that they would need to perform this role.
- Describe how the information would help them fulfil their role.

Different personnel have different information needs

As well as the internal information requirements, external personnel also require information from an organisation. External personnel include customers, suppliers and official and legal bodies.

Customers need information from an organisation if they are purchasing goods or services. This information can be presented in many ways: for example, on paper, on the organisation's website, using email or via telecommunications systems, as sound or via SMS.

Many organisations offer the customer choices of method of delivery and customers can choose the method that suits them best. The information is likely to be to do with the order that the customer has made, so contents of the order, progress of any customised order and expected delivery dates and methods might all be useful information for the customer. Customers are unlikely to be interested in knowing the internal details of how the goods were put together or from which store room they were picked or by whom. Also, the customer isn't normally interested in internal codes, just the ones that agree with what they have ordered.

Likewise, suppliers require only the precise ordering information from the organisation. They do not need to know the reorder level for an item or even how many are still in stock at the organisation, just the items required, how many, the delivery address and payment details. Many large organisations have automated reordering that is electronically sent from organisation to the supplier, without much need for human intervention.

Automatic Ordering

Accurately ordering replacement stock for an independent pharmacy is a difficult and time-consuming task. If you don't order enough of a popular product, you will run out of stock and alienate your best customers. On the other hand, if you order too much of a slow-moving item, you waste your money and shelf space on product you will never sell. Many independent pharmacies hire a full-time skilled employee whose primary responsibility is to manually calculate order quantities each business day. A crisis can develop for the store if this employee decides to seek employment elsewhere!

Incorporated into TSS is an advanced automatic ordering system that handles this important yet cumbersome task for your store effortlessly and accurately. Utilizing a variety of different automatic ordering algorithms, the TSS automatic ordering system prepares consistently accurate orders on specified days of the week. Store personnel have the opportunity to manually review and adjust the order quantities prior to the ordering cut-off time. Ordering information can be printed and, armed with an RF gun, employees can correct perpetual inventory data and adjust order quantities, all in real time while walking the aisles of the store. These orders are electronically transmitted to the appropriate vendor or vendors using the integrated WAN or internet-based data communication system.

Intelligent ordering requires three pieces of data for each product to be ordered: the average weekly movement for the product, the number of pieces of the product currently in stock, and the number of pieces of the product currently on order but not yet delivered.

Armed with this collection of data, the TSS automatic ordering system calculates an order quantity intended to keep the store in stock with the product for two to eight weeks, depending upon system configuration.

Unfortunately, a perfect world does not exist inside a retail store. When new products are stocked, or when the TSS is newly installed, products will not have accurate or meaningful item movement data. A variety of real-world store situations can result in inaccuracies in the perpetual inventory quantities for a number or products. When any of these situations arise, the TSS automatic ordering system drops into one of several recovery modes of operation, and it generates a more conservative order for the affected products. Over time, these smaller orders will lead to meaningful item movement data for the new products, resulting in accurate item movement history after a few ordering cycles.

When orders are shipped to the store by the vendor, an Advance Ship Notice, or ASN, is electronically transmitted into the TSS store system. This ASN document plays a critical role in driving the receiving process. Using a wireless RF gun, the store's receiver is able to quickly receive the entire order, without counting the individual products contained in the order. As a result, the store's perpetual inventory levels are accurately maintained with a minimum of employee labour. And, due to the quality of the perpetual inventory management system data, future automatic orders are calculated accurately.

The TSS automatic ordering system enables the storeowner to easily maintain the correct in stock levels, keeping the customers happy without diluting profits on expensive labour or excessive overstocks.

A link to this website is available at www.heinemann.co.uk/hotlinks (express code 2349P)

In the retail example on the previous page, identify the steps in the process and who is involved in them.

- What benefits does this approach have for the retailer?
- What benefits does this have for the customers?
- What benefits does this have for the supplier of the goods?
- What drawbacks are there in using this approach?

Official and legal bodies have information requirements from all organisations: from income tax and purchase tax bodies, to Customs and Excise if goods are being imported or exported, to various government departments (such as the Department for Children, Schools and Families or the Departments for Health and for Work and Pensions), student loans companies, professional bodies, financial regulators and so on. The nature of this information might be personal in some cases, corporate in others. In all cases, though, it is likely that the information provided will have to be in a set format, and using the set mechanisms, from all organisations, so that it is useful to the external organisation. To this end, any internal systems that are feeding into information to be provided externally will be affected by any changes that are made to the requirements by the external organisation.

Likewise, any information entering an organisation from an official or legal body will have to be assimilated into the organisation's systems in the format provided, and collected using the mechanisms given.

The implications of exchanging data and information with external bodies are vast in terms of the privacy of the information, its security and the legal requirements. Personal data is covered under Data Protection legislation, and all organisations are required to register and to abide by its rules, when holding and sending or receiving such data. Sensitive corporate data may not be bound under such stringent rules, but the organisation is likely to want to ensure its privacy also. One way to do this is by

encrypting the in-transit data. There are many ways of doing this and more and more complex and secure commercial methods are being developed all the time.

Encryption
Encryption is the process of applying a mathematical transformation to data to keep it private and secure. The data can only be decrypted and used by someone with the password-key.

Likewise, the security of transmitted data is of paramount importance to an organisation. Again, there are many methods of ensuring that no unauthorised person can get hold of the in-transit data, some of which are crypto-security, transmission security, emission security, traffic-flow security and physical security.

For this activity, break into groups and each take one method.

1. For one of the methods of communication security (crypto-security, transmission security, emission security, traffic-flow security and physical security):
   - investigate what it means
   - find some example situations where it might be used
   - find a commercial example.
2. Write up your findings.
3. Discuss the findings as a group.

Organisations must comply with relevant legislation when transmitting information. One way is to make sure that the personnel responsible for security within the organisation and the personnel responsible for protecting personal and sensitive data work together to ensure that all measures are taken to protect all information being transmitted. In order to ensure that the correct information is being sent out or received, organisations should have in place secure data- and information-handling procedures that are tried and tested and checked regularly, together with auditing and monitoring software to detect any unusual activity within the workplace. Network security, such as firewalls, should help to ensure the information's safety within the organisation's network, but once it has left the controlled zone, it is a matter of choosing the best encryption methods and the best routing methods.

Systems

ICT systems are used by organisations solely for the purpose of making their business run more smoothly and efficiently, to support the business processes. Most large organisations have a stringent decision process to go through before a new ICT system gets the go-ahead and then there are many more steps before development of any system starts.

Most organisations will have a corporate information strategy aligned to their business plan that has guidelines for hardware and software procurement, for instance, among many other items. This will detail timelines and budgets and may have an outline plan of the ways in which the use of ICT will be implemented within the organisation.

Common ICT systems

There are some ICT systems that are used by most organisations these days – for instance payroll systems, personnel records, pension systems and accounting systems. Only the very smallest organisation attempts to perform these functions manually.

The choice of whether these are 'off-the-shelf' packages, bespoke systems made specifically for the organisation, or part of bigger enterprise-wide systems, is largely dependent on the demands of the organisation, its style and its size.

Some external agencies may determine the choice of ICT system that an organisation installs. This may be for compatibility reasons or simply because choosing the same package as one of their external interfaces will make information exchange less troublesome. Small businesses without knowledgeable internal ICT advisors may end up with complex hardware and software systems that are not used to full capacity because of this.

A simple supply chain can go from manufacturer to retailer to customer

Organisations involved in a **supply chain** tend to make sure that the ICT systems they use interface and exchange data and information with other organisations in the supply chain with as little fuss as possible. They are likely to invest in the same technologies and ICT systems as their partners wherever possible.

Supply chain

A supply chain (also known as a logistics network or supply network) is the system of organisations, events and resources that forms the process by which a product or service is moved from supplier to customer.

Enterprise Resource Planning (ERP)

Enterprise Resource Planning is the process of attempting to unify the data and processes within an organisation (see page 192).

Return On Investment (ROI)

The RIO is the ratio of the profit made on an investment relative to the amount invested.

Investigate examples of the use of ICT systems in the supply chain.

Write an essay of 300–400 words on the effects of being or not being part of a supply chain for an organisation that manufactures a product.

When organisations introduce new ICT systems, perhaps to extend their customer base to new platforms, or to administer new products, it is probable that the new ICT system will have to get data from, or send data to, existing (legacy) ICT systems.

Organisations that have been around since the 1970s may have some very old systems that are still working. Examples of this can be found in the finance industry where, typically, some products, such as life insurance policies, pensions or mortgages are 'live' for many years. Also, as companies take over other companies, many

Some organisations may have some very old ICT systems in place

different but similar ICT systems need to be run to maintain the business operations. These may be on different hardware and software and so it is then a matter of deciding whether to try to bring the systems together or to keep them apart.

Back office systems

Back office systems are the internal ICT systems that are needed by most organisations to keep the business operational. They may be batch-processing systems which collect data from online and web-based systems that are working throughout the day, updating master files and databases, then generating the reports that are required by staff and managers to carry out their daily work.

Back office systems include the human resources, telephony, administration and accounting systems that keep the business running. If the business has a data warehouse storing the vast amount of data held, for instance, in a bank or insurance company, then one of the back office systems will be the management and security of this data store.

Transaction processing systems

A transaction processing system is a computer-based **data processing** system employed at the operational level of an organisation. The sequence of events is normally: data is collected and input; data is processed; the result of the transaction is output as information.

> ### Data processing
> Data processing is the precise, low level, day-to-day, electronic capturing of data, which is used for repetitive business operations, such as Electronic Point of Sales (EPOS) systems in shops, where each item is entered into the system until all items are complete, then a total is calculated.

Typical examples of transaction processing systems are ticket booking systems, Automatic Teller Machine (ATM) systems at cash points, EPOS and DVD rental systems. They may be run as batch-processing systems or as interactive processing systems, depending on the requirements of the business for speed of output.

Case study

East Herts Council

'Many councils have spent a great deal of money putting in brand new back office and web-based systems to meet e-Government targets. At East Herts we didn't have the budget to do this – and we didn't want to do it. Our existing legacy systems which handle core tasks such as benefits claims and revenue collection work very well. We wanted to utilise their proven capability, integrate them with a new CRM system and move towards a flexible, web-based environment.'

To achieve this, East Herts has installed a Lagan CRM system and then used software solutions from integration specialist ndl-metascybe and Ebase Technology to integrate and present data across the Council.

A link to this website is available at www.heinemann.co.uk/hotlinks (express code 2349P)

> ### Customer Relationship Management (CRM)
> The capture, storage and management of information about the relationships that organisations have with their customers (see page 193).

activity

1 Make a list of **five** transaction processing systems that you have used or studied.

2 For each, find out which type of processing (batch or interactive) it uses.

3 Write a short description of each system, the organisation it is in and the users of the system, incorporating your findings about processing.

Workflow and document management systems

Workflow and document management systems help in the struggle to achieve the paperless office. Any paperwork used in the business is scanned, using OCR methods, into the system and put into a folder for the designated worker or team to open up and deal with. These systems are used in many different industries that deal with paper documents arriving. They can greatly reduce the paperwork and administrative costs of running a business and improve business performance by reducing the time and cost of processing information. Workflow management systems help ensure that established policies, procedures and timeliness are observed by tracking the status of a workflow and spotting bottlenecks. As part of the statistics offered, they will also keep track of average completion times, so that management can keep an eye on productivity.

activity

Discuss the implications for BUPA in moving to workflow systems such as the one described in the following case study. Research other areas that are now making use of these document management systems.

If possible, visit an organisation that uses a workflow system and observe how it works.

case study

BUPA Hospitals Invoice Processing

OCR software recently launched onto the market from software manufacturers such as Paradatec and Neurascript can read unsorted documents in their original format, whatever that may be, and includes the capability to read numeric tables. This makes it eminently suitable to read invoices, prior to routing them automatically into a workflow system.

The accounts department is also an ideal candidate for automation, for another reason; the fact that so much of its activity is purely routine data entry and clerical work. With many businesses under pressure to cut costs, projects are driven by the need for efficiency and users are looking for a swift payback. Document imaging systems are reducing routine clerical work and are delivering exactly this kind of bottom line benefit.

One company that has just converted its processing of accounts payable is BUPA Hospitals (which) has just installed Prosar-AIDA from Paradatec, as part of a complete solution provided by systems integrators Digital Vision. Having identified the pinch points in their business process, the company was seeking

a more efficient way to process its invoices but was not entirely happy with the option of outsourcing the process. 'We decided that we could maintain much better relations with our suppliers if we managed the work ourselves,' said John Brazell, Head of Finance and Information Systems for BUPA Hospitals. 'Ownership of the work makes a great difference to the quality of the work performed.' BUPA's new invoicing system is delivering consistently accurate results already, only weeks after the project was completed and is on target to deliver a payback in 10 months.

On the continent, where wages for clerical work are relatively higher than in the UK, the Germans have taken the concept further – to create fully automated digital mailrooms where all of the mail arriving for a company in the morning is read and captured by intelligent OCR that will also route it to its destination department for processing. While UK users may find it difficult to believe that this is feasible, corporate companies in Germany have at least 30 such installations, and many of these have been operational for as long as six years.

A link to this website is available at www.heinemann.co.uk/hotlinks (express code 2349P)

Collaborative working systems

Collaborative working is enabled by the use of collaborative technology, a '**collaboration** platform', which is a unified electronic platform that supports synchronous and asynchronous communication through a variety of devices and channels.

> **Collaboration**
> ICT-supported collaboration is the facility for multiple users simultaneously to view and modify a shared document or to use a shared application.

Collaboration platforms offer a set of software components and software services that enable individuals to find each other and the information they need and to be able to communicate and work together to achieve common business goals. The core elements of a collaboration platform are as follows:

- messaging, e.g. email, calendaring and scheduling
- team collaboration using real-time collaboration and communication, e.g. instant messaging, web conferencing, application or desktop sharing, voice, audio and video conferencing
- social computing tools (e.g. blog, wiki, tagging, RSS, shared bookmarks).

Management Information Systems (MIS)

An MIS is designed to assist management, at all levels of the organisation, to control the functions for which they are responsible. It can generally achieve this through the regular production of summarised reports of the transactions which have taken place in the organisation.

A definition of an MIS is a 'system to convert data from internal and external sources into information, which is communicated in an appropriate form to managers at different levels, to enable them to make effective decisions, directing and controlling the activities for which they are responsible'.

An MIS usually relies on existing internal data, generated by transaction-processing systems (TPS), to produce information. Only occasionally does it use information obtained from external sources (e.g. asking people if certain adverts make them more likely to shop at a particular store).

Multiple users can simultaneously view and modify a shared document

Adidas SAP® E-Commerce for SAP R/3® Enables Online Store for Retailers

'Our new order and information service on the Internet has really struck a chord with our customers,' says Thomas Wiesel, business project leader at Adidas. The company – headquartered in Herzogenaurach, Germany – has received plenty of positive feedback from the some 1,000 retailers that have been using its electronic sales channel since May 2005. The channel is based on the SAP® E-Commerce for SAP R/3® application. The application's high-performance functionality enabled Adidas to enhance service, increase customer satisfaction, and improve efficiency. SAP Consulting provided comprehensive support throughout the project, which was completed on time and within budget.

The legacy system that the company had integrated into its sales processes in a number of western European countries was no longer performing sufficiently. Nor did it provide an online availability check. In addition, many customers were submitting orders by telephone, fax, or by way of an order office. Each of these options involved a considerable amount of follow-up effort by Adidas. With the functionality found in SAP software, the situation has changed fundamentally.

A link to this website is available at www.heinemann.co.uk/hotlinks (express code 2349P)

Here are two examples of an MIS:

- A college register/attendance system is used to record each student's attendance or otherwise at each lesson (the TPS); this information is used to provide reports showing attendance over a term for each student or each class, or to show patterns of attendance, for tutors or senior managers to see trends.
- A supermarket uses the data collected in its point of sales systems to produce sales reports showing performance of different items in the store, or across the country.

The information that is produced by an MIS may be used by management for a number of purposes, including:

- to control the operations of the organisation
- to assist with decision making at the different levels of management
- to assist with planning at the senior management level
- to be used along with external or other information sources for decision making at the strategic level.

Some MIS reports are only produced when exceptional conditions occur. This is known as **exception reporting**. For example, a student's parent is coming into college, or the teacher wonders where all the students are on Friday afternoon, or a supermarket finds that at certain times it is left with too much fresh fruit and it goes bad.

In the past, the Fresh Produce Manager would need to get an IT specialist to produce such an exception report, but now many MIS provide facilities for managers to perform ad hoc enquiries on data and to produce their own reports whenever necessary. This area is known as **end-user computing** and refers to users being able to build their own information systems, in this case an MIS, without referring to systems analysts or programmers. End-user computing tools include reporting packages, spreadsheet packages, database packages, and database query languages such as SQL (Structured Query Language) – in fact any tool that enables users to manipulate or query data that is held electronically.

Enterprise Resource Planning (ERP)

ERP systems support enterprise-wide or cross-functional requirements, rather than a single department or group within the organisation. They cover a range of business needs, including accounting and financial activities, operations and distribution activities (including sales, purchasing and production planning), administration and reporting activities (including human resources), and customer relationship management activities.

These packages can be bought a module at a time and adapted to fit the organisation's needs. It is usual to hire an IT consultancy firm to help with the introduction of the enterprise system, aiding with data migration from existing systems. The major producers of enterprise systems have also produced scaled-down versions for small businesses.

Customer Relationship Management (CRM) systems

CRM systems have modules to manage the entire interface with customers, using many diverse methods. Typically the modules will cover marketing, sales opportunity handling, sales, customer service and support, call centres and field service, service and contracts management, web interfaces and so on. Again, the major producers will have a different option for small businesses and the normal method of acquiring such a system is modular and by using an IT consultancy firm.

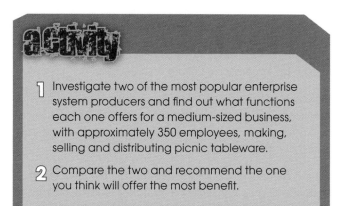

activity

1 Investigate two of the most popular enterprise system producers and find out what functions each one offers for a medium-sized business, with approximately 350 employees, making, selling and distributing picnic tableware.

2 Compare the two and recommend the one you think will offer the most benefit.

Decision Support Systems / Executive Information Support systems (DSS/EIS)

A DSS is a computerised system for helping make decisions. A decision is the choice between alternatives based on estimates of the values of those alternatives. DSS help people working alone, or in a group, gather information, generate the alternative solutions and make their choices. They support non-routine decision making for which information requirements may not be clear. They are used widely, though not exclusively, at the strategic level.

A DSS is an interactive, flexible, and adaptable computer-based information system, especially developed for supporting the solution of a non-structured management problem for improved decision making. It utilises data, provides an easy-to-use interface, and allows for the decision maker's own insights.

A DSS is a computerised system for helping make decisions

There are many fields where DSS are used, the most common example being in the field of medicine, where clinical diagnosis is often supported by a DSS. However, other areas, such as farming (land planning, livestock control), the finance industry (stock market predictions), veterinary medicine and many others, make regular use of such systems.

Case study

Land Allocation Decision Support System – Climate Change

Climate change represents a significant source of risk to the future viability of marginal agricultural systems. The ability of these systems to adapt can often be constrained by their biophysical resources or their ability to invest in new infrastructure required by alternative land uses. While frequently marginal in terms of financial viability such agricultural systems perform a vital stewardship function, maintaining rural communities, landscapes and important habitats. It is important that the implications of climate change are explored for these systems and that strategies are developed to ameliorate the effects of climate change on their financial, social and environmental viability. One approach to these questions is to test the impacts of climate change scenarios for exemplar management units.

The Macaulay Institute has, for 10 years, been developing computer-based decision support systems (DSS) to assist land-managers with strategic, farm-scale, land-use planning decisions. These DSS provide a framework within which it is possible to conduct a wide range of counterfactual analyses assessing the financial, social and environmental impacts of changes to the land management context. The DSS have been particularly successful in allowing exploration of the structure of trade-offs between multiple objectives. Since the individual land-management unit, or farm, is one of the fundamental units within the agri-ecosystem, understanding the impacts of change on these units may also be used to better inform policy makers.

A link to this website is available at www.heinemann.co.uk/hotlinks (express code 2349P)

E-commerce

Typical **e-commerce** activities for an organisation might be selling on a website, automatic reordering of products (perhaps via email or direct to the supplier's network), simply advertising themselves on the World Wide Web, paying official body membership fees, paying for other services and goods and, by using an intranet, keeping remote employees in touch and able to upload and download commercial data when necessary. In fact, carrying on their regular operations using technology.

> **E-commerce**
> E-commerce is the use of electronic media to conduct business. It is most likely to refer to the ability to buy and sell products or services using Internet technology and the everyday use of the World Wide Web.

Typical e-commerce activities for an individual are buying goods online, ticket reservations, applications for licences and official documents (driving licence, passport, car tax, visas, birth certificates, etc.).

An e-commerce site typically requires the fusion of many systems – a shopping cart system linked to stock control, a customer records system, a payments system and a delivery system. Not all these systems will be obvious to the user of the e-commerce site, but they are necessary for the site to function. There may be further links to various back-office systems that are recording monies, organising picking lists for the warehouse, arranging deliveries and so on.

Activity

Spend 10–15 minutes trying out the following activities on different e-commerce sites, making notes:

- buying a CD or DVD
- booking a concert ticket
- applying for a passport
- finding a personalised number plate.

For each one, try to identify what processes you have used and if you can identify what system those processes would most likely to be a part of.

Practice exam questions

1. A high-street building society uses a data processing system to record receipts and withdrawals from its customers' accounts. The data from branches is sent once a day up to the ICT systems at head office in Yorkshire to update all master accounts, and all data is then input into various information systems.

   (a) For each of the following users, state the level of information that is needed by:
   - (i) a Customer Service Clerk in a local branch (1)
   - (ii) a Branch Manager (1)
   - (iii) the Managing Director of the building society. (1)

   (b) For each of the following individuals, name a suitable output, state how it may be used, and give a typical item of data that it may contain:
   - (i) a Customer Service Clerk in a local branch (3)
   - (ii) a Branch Manager (3)
   - (iii) the ICT Manager, controlling all ICT systems within the building society (3)
   - (iv) the Managing Director of the building society (3)

   (c) Explain why the information used by the Customer Service Clerk is not appropriate for the Managing Director. (3)

   (June 2006)

2. Managers at the highest, or strategic, levels of an organisation have particular requirements from an information system. Give **one** example of an information system that would be useful to managers at this level, and explain how they would use it. (3) (June 2005)

3. Information produced by ICT systems may be required both within (internal) and outside (external) organisations such as schools and supermarkets.

   (a) Describe **two** examples of internal information requirements, stating for each:
   - who needs the information
   - what information they require
   - what it is to be used for. (6)

   (b) Describe **two** examples of external information requirements, stating for each
   - who needs the information
   - what information they require
   - what it is to be used for. (6)

   (June 2005)

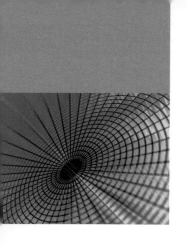

3.3 Managing ICT

Organisation size

Many companies use organisation charts to show their structure. These can help to show communication problems and allow individuals to see their position in the company.

Hierarchical structures

Organisations with a hierarchical structure operate with different levels of authority and responsibility. Line managers or heads of department are often responsible to directors or senior managers, who are in turn responsible to the chairman and shareholders. The structure can be said to appear to be in a pyramidal form with seniority within the organisation progressing towards the top of the structure.

is necessary in any type of organisation that information flows in any direction required; this is especially relevant to hierarchical structures. Here information should flow both ways (up and down) through the structure. Information is passed in the organisation by moving it through each of the layers of responsibility.

Information going **up** the chain becomes more **summarised** as the 'general' at the top just needs an overview situation.

Information going **down** the chain becomes more **detailed** as every 'soldier' needs to know exactly what to do.

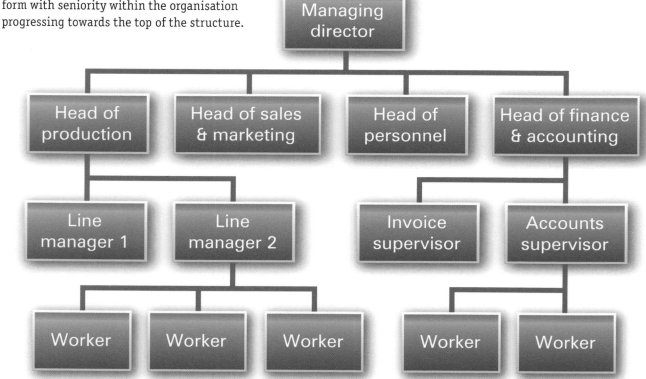

A typical hierarchical structure

Flat structures

A flat structure usually has a single layer of management. Very few organisations have a flat structure. Those that do are usually very small. Those organisations that want to keep their levels of management to a minimum often follow a flat structure. Examples of organisations that follow this type of structure include small law practices and accountancy firms.

Management style has an influence on the information required in an organisation. A relaxed, entrepreneurial style may allow for a mixture of formal and informal information to be considered when making decisions about the organisation.

In an **entrepreneurial** structure one or two key people take central decisions. This is found mostly in small businesses, although there are one or two large organisations that are famously entrepreneurial in style, if not now in structure.

In a **matrix** structure people are organised into teams that work independently, making their own decisions, yet working alongside each other, exchanging information only when it is deemed necessary for the organisation.

The way in which an organisation is structured can determine whether or not management is **centralised** or **decentralised**.

Centralisation

Centralisation is where senior management have more control and apply more standardisation. This type of structure can be extremely stressful for managers.

Decentralisation

Decentralisation gives subordinates more job satisfaction and uses their local knowledge. Decision-making is often quicker with no need to pass decisions up and down the chain of command. It also makes it easier to groom staff replacements by delegation of responsibility.

It is important to remember that there are often very good reasons for an organisation to have a certain structure, such as:

- the size of the business
- views of the leaders of the business
- the objectives of the business

Business aims and objectives

Business aims and objectives drive the approach to the use of ICT within the organisation. An aim is where the business wants to go in the future. It is a statement of purpose, such as 'we want to grow the business into Europe'. Business objectives are the stated, measurable targets of how to achieve the business aims. For instance, 'we want to achieve sales of £5 million in European markets in the next financial year'. A corporate mission statement sets out the business vision and values that enable employees, managers, customers and even suppliers to understand the underlying basis for the actions of the business.

Objectives give the business a clearly defined target. Plans can then be made to achieve these targets. This can motivate the employees and enables the business to measure the progress towards to its stated aims. Objectives can be short-term or long-term. Profit maximisation might be one objective, or sales growth. For a smaller business, profit satisfaction (i.e. just enough to make the owner a comfortable living without having to work long hours) may be the objective.

Not all businesses seek profit or growth. Some organisations have alternative objectives, such as ethical and socially responsible objectives – organisations like the Co-op or the Body Shop have objectives that are based on their beliefs on how one should treat the environment and people who are less fortunate.

Different types of organisation might have different objectives.

- Public sector corporations are run to not only generate a profit but also to provide a service to the public e.g. a cheap and accessible transport service.

- Public sector organisations that monitor or control private sector activities have objectives to ensure that the business they are monitoring complies with the laws laid down.

- Healthcare and education establishments have objectives to provide a service. Most private schools, for instance, have charitable status. Their aim is the enhancement of their pupils through education.

- Charities and voluntary organisations have aims and objectives led by the beliefs that they stand for.

A link to this website is available at www.heinemann.co.uk/hotlinks (express code 2349P)

- changes in technology, e.g. IT reducing administration.

Whatever the aims and objectives of the organisation, its use of ICT needs to support them. The management of ICT use within an organisation is of paramount importance to the success or failure of the organisation to meet its objectives, and so should not be underestimated in its strategic decision-making.

A corporate ICT strategy should be in place for every organisation if it is to manage the use of ICT properly and in the most effective way.

ICT policies will need to be written to outline how the corporate ICT strategy would be put into effective operation.

The importance of getting the use of ICT right in organisations is reflected by the fact the most medium to large organisations now appoint a Chief Information Officer (CIO) to oversee the management of the ICT within the organisation.

This post within many organisations has come about as the importance of ICT has grown. The CIO normally reports directly to the Chief Executive Officer (CEO) of the company and often sits on the executive board, or board of directors.

ICT strategy

Some factors that might influence a corporate information strategy are as follows.

- The business goals – one might be to ensure that the organisation keeps up with its rivals technologically, or that it moves into electronic data interchanges with suppliers.
- Finance might be a factor – it depends how much

CIO at AstraZeneca

Countless reports and column inches in IT publications have debated the difference between the IT director and the CIO. The latter is generally seen as the more prestigious role, implying a seat on the board, or at least easy access to it. But Paul Burfitt, global CIO at pharmaceuticals giant AstraZeneca, does not agonise over his job title or who he reports to.

'It is very difficult to generalise what a CIO does, as there is no general CIO definition,' he says. 'It's what you do to add value to your business that counts.

'I am not saying it is irrelevant who you report to – it is important. Not because of their label, but whether that person actually gives you the support, energy and inspiration to help you deliver. If I reported to someone who did not do that, I would want out.'

Nor does Burfitt focus on the hands-on running of IT, either in day-to-day or larger operations. The reason is a practical one: with a company the size of AstraZeneca, monitoring all IT operations would be virtually impossible.

'I am the global CIO for AstraZeneca but I don't have direct, hands-on control of all the company's IT resources. It would be impractical to have direct control over IT in every country where the company operates. My role is to see the overall framework of IS policies, standards and strategies, and to empower people to deliver and contribute locally within that.'

Instead, as an executive board member, Burfitt focuses on what most other company directors do: setting targets for IT within AstraZeneca.

'I spend most of my time on the IS vision: the priorities, objectives and targets, and how IS contributes to deliver value to business. I have difficulty with the term 'IT strategy' because it separates IT strategy from business strategy.

'I meet with members of the executive team three or four times a year. These meetings are a challenging debate, to steer the IS function towards the company's goals. I am very clear about our business objectives and our vision for IS, and so is the executive team.'

A link to this website is available at www.heinemann.co.uk/hotlinks (express code 2349P)

budget can be given to expanding hardware or software or developing new ICT solutions, all relative to the overall finances of the organisation.

- The style of the organisation – its structure, its management methods; functions that exist in the organisation and how information flows around the organisation, in a set formal method, or in a more informal way.

- The size and type of organisation – whether to have an in-house development department, to outsource to a third party and just have business managers in charge of the process of commissioning and maintaining systems, or to have a small IT department who organises things for the business.

- Where its customers are – if worldwide, then communication methods might be a factor as technological advances are made all the time and new ways to communicate become available.

- The ethos of the organisation – if a formal business, then a formal information flow is likely and formal methods will be in place. More modern businesses, with different less formal management styles, might be more relaxed and expecting a more collective approach where many people have some responsibility rather than just those at the top having it all. The more modern style of organisation is more likely to have staff and managers who are better able to adapt to change, especially the kind of change that happens as more and more facets of the business become more technologically reliant and technically advanced year on year.

- The hardware and general purpose software in use around the organisation, plus staff skills in using the ICT facilities available.

- Compliance with external organisations with which its ICT systems have to communicate.

- Compliance with legislation – depending on the type of business, there may be many legal and mandatory audit constraints , e.g. if the primary function is financial then the organisation would be confined by many pieces of legislation and regulations that would have to be incorporated in all its practices and procedures as well as all its ICT systems.

With any new organisation introducing new ICT systems, one of the issues during the design is to estimate how much data will need to be stored, and for how long.

Long-established systems within organisations can hold many millions of records, possibly stored in many large data stores. The management of these assets over time is another factor when considering the ICT strategy, and several questions must be answered.

- Who is responsible for managing our data and **information assets**?
- What is going to be kept?
- Where is it going to be kept?
- How will we keep it secure?
- How will the information be accessed?
- Who will be allowed to access it?
- What else can be done with it?

Personal data and information would, of course, be covered under the Data Protection legislation, but much public information is now covered under the Freedom of Information legislation that gives the public certain rights to see certain information. Many public bodies publish an Information Asset Register to enable the public to see what is available, with instructions on how to access the information.

Information assets

Information assets are any resources associated with information systems. All types of information can be regarded as assets, including all forms of electronic and paper-based information and the hardware, software and infrastructure necessary to access the information.

activity

1. Investigate, using the Internet, the Information Register from a public body. List some of the assets and find out how to access these, how long it takes and if there is a cost involved.

2. Discuss your findings with a group of classmates and decide if there is an approved approach to laying out the information for public scrutiny.

Strategy for technology

Information technology policies are unique to an organisation and form part of the overall ICT strategy.

Areas that may be addressed in the technology aspects include:

- current hardware and software provisions
- future hardware and software provisions
- security and user procedural issues
- backup
- general rules and conditions of technology usage.

By having such a policy, all users within an organisation should be able to see what is expected of them in terms of ICT usage and their responsibilities for adhering to certain rules, the Code of Practice and legislation such as Data Protection.

It may also outline current and future hardware and software provisions so that users, especially at the tactical and strategic levels, can see how these provisions currently support the infrastructure of the organisation and the changes (if any) required for the future.

All users within an organisation will have a range of needs. Some of these will be generic (applying to all) such as access to certain resources, such as appropriate hardware and software, that is:

- fast and powerful
- up-to-date
- easy to use (for inexperienced end users)
- compatible with existing systems.

Other needs may be more specialist and unique depending upon the job role, for example, a specific platform to run a specific piece of software.

As technology changes and hardware and software become more sophisticated, faster and more powerful, an organisation must upgrade. Hardware and software upgrades can be as a result of on-going hardware or software development and change, or as part of an organisation's culture where corporate policy may dictate that every six months or year an overhaul takes place. An upgrade may also be task-driven, where higher-specification hardware or software is required to meet a specific objective.

In general an organisation may decide to upgrade to:

- ensure and sustain compatibility with existing systems
- maintain competitiveness
- ensure continued support from suppliers/vendors.

Not all organisations have the financial resources to upgrade their hardware and software provisions periodically. One way to address this is to 'future-proof' systems. Future-proofing attempts to overcome the need to upgrade at a later date by estimating requirements needed in terms of storage, speed, functionality, etc. A system is then purchased that incorporates a higher specification than that which is currently required.

Decisions for technology may be based on various considerations such as:

- the data that is stored
- the information that circulates around the organisation
- the people that will be using the information and the technology.

Standards that affect strategic choices

Various 'industry standards' have arisen through the years that may affect the technology chosen within an organisation.

The standard desktop computer for general purpose use now tends towards the PC (Personal Computer) standard as introduced by IBM towards the end of the 1980s. Although the Apple Mac was once the only choice for CAD (Computer-Aided Drawing) technicians, most commercially used CAD packages will now run on standard PC desktop and laptop machines. It is still difficult to transfer data from one platform to the other without some manipulation and possible loss of accuracy, so it is a brave organisation that will choose to decide on something different to that used by other organisations with which they might be exchanging data.

An early IBM computer

Likewise, on the software front, there is an accepted standard for general office applications and only the brave will choose to differ from this for their corporate platform choice. Files of data that are exchanged between platforms, even using some of the non-prescriptive formats that are available, tend to lose some accuracy, formatting of the original and so on.

Strategically, the options open to the decision-makers may be few, if they are to keep their interfaces simple when dealing with others. Also, their own staff may be familiar with the standards from previous employment or personal use and be averse to swapping and changing too often.

So the strategy then becomes one of deciding when, where and how to upgrade both hardware and general software as well as how to procure it. Choices for procurement of hardware fall into two categories: buy or lease. Within these, there may be other choices with ways to pay and so on.

For general software, there are many options to consider – again buying and leasing are the main categories. In addition, the decision has to be made about licensing –

how many staff will be using a particular piece of software? Some software companies have site licence options; others have different pricing structures depending on how many copies are bought.

For specialist software, the choices could include buying a package off the shelf or having it developed especially for the organisation, either in-house or by an outside company known as a software house.

For operations and systems software, there is a market leader GUI for desktops. Some other operating systems still find favour in large organisations where their ICT networks are not solely based on the PC platform.

New versions of both systems software and application software are released every year or two and one of the strategy choices is how often and how quickly to move to newer versions. With such a fast-changing field, it is sometimes necessary to make ad hoc off-strategy decisions.

ICT policies

To try to create some order in a corporate ICT strategy, there needs to be set of ICT policies that will cover all the items in the strategy, to give procedures that the staff of the organisation can follow to ensure that the strategy is upheld.

Procurement policy

Procurement is the acquisition of goods or services at the best possible total cost of ownership, in the right quantity, at the right time, in the right place for the direct benefit or use of an organisation. There could be separate procurement policies for:

- hardware
- communication technology
- systems and generic application software
- specific, specialist and bespoke software
- office supplies
- staff services (e.g. help desk).

Security policy

An ICT systems security policy will cover a myriad of topics relating to keeping the organisation's ICT systems secure from unauthorised access. It will cover the prevention of misuse of the ICT systems, detection of misuse, investigation of misuse, acceptable use, staff responsibilities, procedures for ensuring security and disciplinary procedures.

There will also be a series of Acceptable Use Policies, either as part of security policy or as separate documents. For example, there might be documentation covering Internet acceptable use, email acceptable use, file/records/data acceptable use, alongside procedures that ensure compliance with appropriate legislation such as the Data Protection legislation.

Other sections of the security policy may pertain to risk analysis and consideration of threats and counter-measures to these threats.

Related to security, backup policies and contingency planning/disaster recovery procedures will also need to be in place. These are considered in more detail in Section 3.5.

Training policy

An organisation will only be successful if it has well-trained staff. An on-going and planned training schedule will produce well-motivated and competent employees who fulfil their tasks to the highest standards. Any new or amended ICT system that is introduced, or any new or amended rules and regulations that they must abide by will require some training.

The training policy must stipulate what the baseline level of skills and knowledge is for each staff role, what training is required at the induction of new employees, and must allow for job changes and promotions. It should also state what developmental training is required. It should cover not only training in ICT skills, but also in all the policies and regulations that a particular job role requires the person to be aware of when doing their job.

The training policy is turned into a training plan that should be owned by the staff member and administered by the Human Resources function in the organisation, and reviewed at regular intervals as part of the personal development plan for the employee.

Legislation

There are many pieces of legislation concerning ICT compliance. Each will have some impact on how an organisation makes use of ICT and the policies that need to be in place and the procedures that need to be followed within that organisation.

Legislation concerning software

The **Copyright, Designs and Patents Act 1988** protects, amongst other things, software. Copyright is the most important intellectual property right – a right not to be copied. It is the primary means of protecting software. There is no need to register; the right arises automatically once the original software is written. Duration of the copyright is up to 70 years. Remedies include damages, seizure and criminal sanctions. Both a company and its managers (usually directors) and individuals may be criminally liable for copyright infringement, for which there are fines and, depending on the offence and facts, a maximum of 10 years' imprisonment.

Software licensing comprises the permissions, rights and restrictions imposed on software (whether a component or a free-standing program) which form part of the 'software ecosystem'. Use of software without a license could constitute infringement of the owner's intellectual property rights, and allow the owner to sue the infringer.

Statements in the ICT Security Policy will inform employees what they can and cannot do with software – no bringing in of unlicensed software, no taking copies for home use, etc. There should be a person responsible for ensuring that all software licences are adequate and up-to-date for use within the organisation; there may be automatic controls on the network, restricting the number of users simultaneously using a piece of software to the number of licences held, and there may be automatic auditing and accounting for software usage.

Legislation concerning hardware and networks

The **Computer Misuse Act 1990** created three new offences.

- The basic hacking offence, where criminals just attempt to access data where they shouldn't, which is punishable by a fine of up to £5,000 and/or 6 months imprisonment.

- Criminal sanctions where the criminal has committed the hacking offence but with the intent to commit or facilitates the commission of further offences, maybe by selling the data on to a third party – industrial espionage. Here sanctions include a 5-year prison sentence and an unlimited fine.
- A tampering criminal offence, where someone who is unauthorized modifies computer material. 'Modifications' include impairing the operation of any computer, preventing access to any data or program, or impairing the reliability of a program or any such data.

To prosecute under this act, it must be shown that 'unauthorised' access has occurred. Organisations should therefore clearly define the limits of an employee's right to access the computer system. This would normally be in the ICT Code of Practice or Acceptable Use Policy.

The Regulation of Investigatory Powers Act 2000 was introduced to put in place a clear framework governing the interception of private communications networks, setting out the circumstances in which it may be authorised and the safeguards which should apply. Primarily, this Act prohibits any interception of a communication in the course of transmission where the private telecommunications system is connected to a public telecommunications system.

Interception also includes checking an employee's email inbox where messages are stored. Monitoring or recording of business communications (including email and telephone calls) is unlawful unless they fall within the provisions of the Act.

Compliance with the Data Protection Act usually means getting the consent of the data subject and observing the eight data protection principles. Such data when lawfully recorded under the act must be handled in accordance with the Data Protection Act.

From this Act came **The Telecommunications (Lawful Business Practice) (Interception of Communications) Regulations 2000**, which allow businesses to intercept communications in the course of lawful business practice and in specific circumstances without the express consent of either the sender or the recipient. Organisations may intercept communications such as emails without consent for the purposes of detecting crime. However, they first must inform users that interceptions may take place. This would normally be in the security policy or the acceptable use policies pertaining to communications.

The Electronic Commerce (EC Directive) Regulations 2002 aims to guarantee the free movement of 'information society services' ('ISS') across the European Community and to encourage the use of e-commerce by clarifying the obligations of businesses and the rights of consumers. The regulations will apply to commercial activities carried out online, which involve the use of ISS. ISS includes advertising and selling goods online; promotion of goods or services online; transmission or storage of electronic communications or, if providing the means to access, a communication network.

The following information must be 'easily, directly and permanently accessible' online: the name of the organisation, geographical address and contact details (including email), clear and unambiguous prices, stating whether tax and delivery is included and the VAT number (where applicable). Members of trade associations and regulated professions, such as accountants and solicitors, are required to provide additional information.

These regulations will obviously have an effect on the design procedures for any website in use by the organisation.

Legislation concerning data and information

The Data Protection Act 1998 protects data that identifies a living individual who can be identified from the data. It governs what may be lawfully done with such data. The 1998 Act requires that all personal data must be 'processed' in accordance with the eight data protection principles of good practice. Personal data covers both facts and opinions about the individual. Personal data must not be 'processed' unless one of six specific conditions applies.

If you are deemed to be a 'data controller' who is 'processing' data under the 1998 Act, the organisation must register, unless you are 'exempt'. Not registering if you are required to is a criminal offence.

If there is a breach of the basic principles (which concern the security and accuracy of the data, and ensure it is used only for the specified purpose and kept no longer than necessary) then the Information Commissioner can investigate, which may lead to prosecution. Furthermore, an individual who has suffered damage due to the data controller's contravention of the 1998 Act may seek compensation.

Access controls, allowing only authorised people to see and use the data concerned, form the simplest way of keeping the data secure. Procedures for checking the accuracy of the data, for ensuring it is still required and for ensuring that it is not being used for other purposes are required and need managing.

The Freedom of Information Act 2003 provides people with rights of access to the information held on them. It applies only to public sector bodies. The Act promotes a culture of accountability and openness so the public may have a clearer understanding of how public authorities perform their duties and how public money is spent. The Act applies to all recorded information held by public authorities and usually access to personal data will be under the Data Protection Act 1998.

For these public organisations, there will need to be procedures in place for handling requests for information, with clear guidelines as to how the information requested will be disseminated.

The Copyright and Rights in Databases Regulations 1997 introduced a new special property right called a **database right**. The right may exist whether or not the database or its contents is a copyright work. A database right will subsist in a database 'if there has been a substantial investment in obtaining, verifying or presenting the contents of the database'. 'Substantial' is in terms of quantity or quality. The general rule is that the database rights last for 15 years, but this period starts again if substantial changes and updates or other sufficient amendments are made to the contents of the database.

This has implications for an organisation that is building a data warehouse containing a mass of organisational data to be used in multiple ways by multiple departments. It means that their data held in such a database is safe from others wanting to use it.

Legislation concerning health and safety

This topic was discussed in Section 1 at some length. An organisation has to provide a safe working environment for all employees. Each circumstance may be different – it depends on the working environment, whether the worker is inside an office, outside on a building or work site, travelling in a car or working remotely at home. The procedures for working safely will be different in each case and it is up to the organisation to consider the needs of all staff when drawing up policies and writing procedures. The organisation has a duty of care to its employees, but the employee also has a duty to follow safe practice when working with the organisation's ICT.

Practice exam questions

1. Many organisations employ a Health and Safety Officer to enforce health and safety legislation for all users of their ICT systems. Give **five** ways that this officer could help to ensure that health and safety legislation is being enforced. (5)
   (AQA June 2006)

2. What is meant by formal information flow? Give an example of a formal information flow mechanism. (3)
   (AQA June 2006)

3. Protecting its information systems and the data that they contain is a major concern for an organisation. Discuss the aspects of system security and data security that an organisation needs to consider, paying particular attention to:
   • risk analysis
   • security policy
   • audit requirements
   • disaster recovery management. (16)
   (AQA June 2006)

4. Information System Security Policies cover issues to do with the secure use of information systems, as well as issues surrounding the security of the data held within them.
   a) A typical Information System Security Policy includes the procedures needed to protect the systems and data. Give **three** procedures, explaining how each one is used to protect systems and data. (6)
   b) Name **two** pieces of legislation that should be considered when writing an Information System Security Policy. (2)
   c) State **four** factors that should be considered when writing an Information System Security Policy. (4)
   (AQA January 2006)

5. A long-standing national chain of shoe shops has built up its information systems one at a time, and without an overall plan. It is now having difficulty in getting these systems to work together effectively and has therefore decided to create a Corporate Information Systems Strategy. Discuss the influence of the following factors when planning a Corporate Information Systems Strategy.
   • The structure of the organisation.
   • Information flow around the organisation.
   • Personnel in the organisation. (16)
   (AQA January 2006)

3.4 System development

Developing ICT solutions

ICT systems are merely the solutions to problems that occur in an organisation. It may be that an existing process, currently done manually, is not now efficient or producing information fast enough for the staff needing to use that information. It is possible that the volumes of transaction now taking place are overwhelming for the staff handling them. These are problems and an ICT system might be the answer.

ICT projects are created to develop a solution to a problem. Many projects are a great success and the users of the system wonder how they managed without their ICT system. A project manager is normally appointed to oversee the development of the system and the team of people involved in the development.

What makes a project a success?

- The project manager ensuring that all requirements – strategic, tactical and operational – are met and that the project does not get bogged down in the technical and lower layers, if the system is to deliver information at all levels in the organisation.
- Having a professional development team, who work as a team and who use standards so that the system they produce is completed to a high level and will be easily maintainable after it is installed.
- Keeping all parties informed about progress at regular intervals.
- Making sure the analysis is done thoroughly, talking to the business managers and users about their requirements, so that it meets everyone's needs.
- Making sure that business managers and users' representatives have a say in the design of the system and give it approval.

- Ensuring that the business managers and users are aware of the capabilities and limitations of ICT and are not expecting miracles of the system.
- Making sure that the system is tested thoroughly, in all circumstances and on all the platforms and configurations that it will be used on when operational.
- Ensuring the changeover method chosen is the right one for this organisation and this system, so that no unexpected obstacles appear, and that all operational procedures are in place ready for the new system.
- Providing good user documentation, so that there is a reference for new users of the system.
- Writing good technical documentation, so that the people responsible for running and maintaining system have all the information they require, for instance space required to run the system, space required to hold the data, when and how the output is produced.
- Ensuring that all staff are trained and prepared to use the new system.

A new ICT system will almost certainly fail adequately to deliver if there is:

- inadequate analysis, design or testing
- lack of management and end-user involvement in design
- emphasis on computer system (hardware/software) rather than the functions it needs to perform
- concentration on low-level data processing, rather than the needs of the users of the information
- lack of management knowledge of ICT systems and their capabilities, wanting the systems to do things that are not technically feasible
- inappropriate or excessive management demands on time, budget or functionality
- lack of teamwork between the development team, the business sponsors of the system and the end-users

- lack of professional standards being used by the developing team
- the Project Manager loses control of the project plans and allows the scope of the system to slip, or the development team to go off and 'do their own thing'.

Development methods

ICT systems need to be developed in stages if they are to be successful and meet the requirements of the organisation's management and users.

The systems development life cycle has been formulated over the many years that ICT systems have been developed and, despite there being numerous methodologies, the same stages have to be performed at some stage in each.

The main stages in software development are project definition, analysis, design, constructing the solution, and testing.

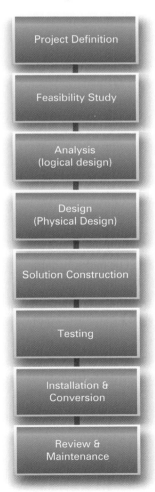

Systems development life cycle

Project definition and feasibility study

The project definition stage is mainly concerned with analysing the organisation at a strategic level (top level of management) and defining the information systems that are needed in order for the organisation to meet its aims and objectives. Some reasons for initiating a systems development might be:

- to meet some new requirements of the business
- a new 'ethos' for the business
- to solve problems in an area where a system is not functioning effectively
- because technology has moved on so fast that current systems hardware, software or facilities are out of date or not maintainable.

The objectives and scope of the new system will be defined, along with 'ball park' estimates as to its duration, complexity and cost.

A **feasibility study** is conducted before any major expenditure is undertaken to determine whether or not a project should proceed. The study should address:

- the problems with the existing system
- the objectives of the proposed system
- an evaluation of a number of options for a new system and the recommendation of one for development.

Feasibility studies often include some or all of the following, although they may also appear in the Systems Specification produced in the Systems Analysis phase.

- An overview of the current system.
- Performance criteria for the new system.
- The scope of the new system – what it will cover, what it won't.
- The benefits which the new system will bring (compared to the expected costs).
- Consideration of hardware and software – what exists now, what might be needed for the future development.
- A recommendation for the new system.
- A plan for developing the new system, with priorities for what are the most important functions.
- Time scales for the development.

- The skills required to carry out the development and whether or not staff have these skills and what training might be required.
- A budget for the cost of developing and running the new system.

When the new system is introduced, a good feasibility study should have resulted in:

- savings in staff costs
- savings in operating costs
- increase in sales revenue
- greater customer satisfaction
- improved information for more effective decision making.

The final step of the feasibility study stage is to produce the feasibility study report, which should include:

- a definition of the current problem
- an outline of various possible solutions
- the reason for choosing the preferred solution including the cost/benefit analysis
- a specification of the preferred solution including its technical and operational implications.

The feasibility report will have to be approved and 'signed-off' by the organisation's senior management before detailed systems analysis can begin.

Analysis (logical design)

One or more **systems analysts**, working in close co-operation with the users, carry out the analysis. The principal objective of this stage is for the analyst to produce a detailed specification of the business requirements for the new system. In order to achieve this objective the systems analyst must perform a number of tasks including:

- understand the current system
- identify the user's requirements for the new system
- interpret the user's requirements for the new system
- define the user's requirements for the new system.

Systems analysts are rarely experts in the business area in which they are required to work. However they must at least have a working understanding of the business area.

For a systems analyst assigned to develop an information system in an unfamiliar business area, a first step towards acquiring this understanding would be to read around the subject area using journals, textbooks and other reference materials.

As the majority of information-gathering during the analysis stage will involve some form of interaction between the analyst and the user, it is important that the analyst is able to communicate effectively with the end user about the business. For example, the analyst should be able to understand the use of appropriate business terminology.

The main methods of gathering information include:

- interview
- questionnaire
- observation of the current system in operation
- analysis of existing documentation.

All of the information gathered during the systems analysis stage will allow the systems analyst to answer two key questions.

- What needs to be done by the new system?
- What data does the new system need to hold?

The output (or deliverable) from the analysis stage will normally be a logical system specification with a clear recommendation for what input forms, output forms and reports will be needed, along with what processes will be required to turn input data into output information, and also what data will be need to be held to effect the conversion of data to information. This may take the form of a list of functions, forms and reports, plus a data dictionary showing how the data will be logically held, with relationships between entity data stores.

Design (physical design)

While systems analysis is concerned with defining what a system should do, in the design stage the analysts concentrate on how the system will operate. In order to be successful, the design phase requires the analyst or designer to have specialist computer expertise and a clear understanding of the business requirements.

The following areas must be addressed during systems design.

- Report design – considering the hard output from the system.
- Screen design – considering how information should be presented on screen.
- Dialogue design – considering how language/interfaces are used to communicate.
- Database design – considering the structure of the database to be created.
- Procedure design – considering what underlying procedures the system needs to perform.

The outputs from the design stage will be a set of specifications that give detailed instructions as to what the inputs and outputs will look like, how the data will be held (files, tables, records, fields) and step-by-step process definitions. Designs for forms and reports must be exact. Validation for every input data field must be included. The data design must be accurate in every detail. There should be nothing left for the constructor to decide.

Design is often the longest stage of the development life cycle because it is imperative that every detail is specified and checked back with the client and the users to ensure that the construction will produce exactly what they require. Technical aspects cannot be inaccurate and the technology that is being used needs to be capable of running the system effectively and efficiently.

Constructing the solution

The construction stage can take many forms – it could be taking a ready-made package and customising it to suit the purposes of this organisation, it could be using a generic software package such as a database application and creating tables, forms, reports and queries to produce a customised application, or it could be writing specific code. Sometimes it is a combination of the latter two.

If code is to be written (**programming**), then each module needs to be specified at code level. Design process specification may be sufficient, or a further more detailed specification may be required, known as program specification. It depends on the complexity of the function. The most commonly used approach to program design is **structured programming**. With this approach the overall problem is broken down into sub-problems, and each sub-problem is successively refined until it can be easily translated into a programming language. In other words, each small routine like 'Add a New Client' or 'Calculate Bill' is perfected, and then the individual sub-routines are linked together, rather than trying to solve the whole problem in one whole program.

In any case, it is important that each customised function, or each newly written function, is tested thoroughly with test data to make sure each path in the logic is tested. This is known as **unit testing** and is the responsibility of the person who has written or customised that module. It may involve checking validation on a series of input fields, for instance.

Integration testing ensures that all discretely written pieces of code work together as a whole, so that the complete function works.

In an object oriented language such as Visual Basic, for instance, unit testing is the checking that the code behind each button works as it is meant to, whereas integration testing would make sure that a whole form works as it is meant to. Integration testing may further check that the data stored by one function is readable by another.

The coding or construction teams usually perform unit and integration testing.

Testing

Once it has been established that each individual function works as it should, the whole application should then be subject to various across-system tests. These fall into three distinct types: systems testing, user testing and operational testing.

Systems testing (also known as alpha testing)

Systems testing is normally performed by the coders under the supervision of the Systems Analyst, who will provide a system test plan and adequate data to test all paths through the complete system. There will be enough data to create a full range of combinations of fields and to check that report paging is tested, for instance. The data will be realistic, without being taken from the live data held by the organisation. Any interfaces to other systems must also be tested at this stage.

Testing may show up anomalies and coding bugs. These will have to be resolved before testing can continue or be signed off. Tests may have to be repeated numerous times before the analyst is convinced that the system is working to the user's requirements.

User testing (also known as beta testing)

Often the Systems Analyst will work in conjunction with the users to provide a test plan and to advise on data that would be useful to use as test data. The data used is normally 'live' data, i.e. real company data, so that any misunderstandings in the meaning of user requirements can be sorted out here. In an ideal world, the users themselves should be involved in actually performing the tests; this has the advantage of giving these testers a chance to become familiar with the system before it is installed, and to feel that they have some ownership of the system. In reality, it is often the case that the users are too busy doing their jobs to take time out to become involved in the testing, and so the development team do it using the real data, reporting back any anomalies.

Often, the use of real data shows up some combinations that weren't catered for in the original design. Sometimes this can mean that functions must be re-specified, re-designed and re-written, all adding time and cost to the development. Other times, if it is just the odd case or two, a compromise will be made and these cases treated as special cases and flagged up to be dealt with in some other way, outside of the system.

Operational testing

Operation testing is performed after user testing to ensure that the system will actually work when and where it is installed. If it will be used on more than one platform or in more than one configuration then it must be test-installed and some of the system tests re-run on each to ensure it will work once operational.

One of the other forms of testing that should be performed at this stage is **volume testing**. This can be to do with the number of users expected to be entering data, or 'hitting' a website simultaneously, or it could be to do with the number of transactions occurring in the system at once, or it could be to do with the number of records being added per hour, or the number of records having to be held.

Most of these aspects would have been considered as part of the design stage, but it might be that the implications of the number crunching were not realised. Operational testing is the most important type of all as it would be no use having a wonderful system with all the functionality required if it seized up as soon as the 101st person pressed the 'send' button.

Installation and conversion

This stage of the System Development Life Cycle consists of the steps that need to be taken to put the new system into operation. The main steps are hardware and software installation, staff training, documentation, file conversion and system changeover.

Hardware and software installation

Any hardware or network installation must be planned. This may involve office moves or a refurbished working environment and could be a major activity, involving many people and agencies. On the other hand it may be that no new hardware is required and the new system will merely be loaded onto a central server and accessible by all immediately.

Software installation could be as simple as the description above, or it could mean a technician visiting every desktop and laptop in a company to install the new system. Some companies send software out on a CD with instructions for users to load it themselves. Others could put it on their intranet and send out an email to all staff concerned, telling them to download it onto their own machines.

Staff training

If the new system is completely different from what was being used previously, the staff who are going to use it will need training. This training could be a formal course lasting many days or a series of hands-on training sessions, both before the system is installed, or a quick talk and guide given on or just before the day of changeover. It all depends on the changes to the person's job caused by the system.

The systems analyst will work alongside business managers to come up with the optimum training schedule for the new system. Having staff who are prepared is the best way of ensuring acceptance of the new system. Staff will lose motivation and become restless if they are presented with a complex new ICT system that they are suddenly expected to work out for themselves, and it could cause misuse (accidental or deliberate) of the system.

Production of technical and user documentation

The teams who may be involved in either supporting or maintaining the new system need the technical documentation. It should cover all the technical aspects from the design phase, plus copies of all the test plans, lists of code, library modules used, where data is held and so on; in fact everything a designer, coder or tester might need so they can amend the system, plus everything a help desk technician might need to answer user queries.

It is normal to provide some form of user guide. This could be in the form of a training manual (tied in with staff training above) with a series of exercises to familiarise the user with the system. More usually, it would be a guide to using the system, step-by-step, function-by-function, in the most logical way for the majority of the users. Each function will have instructions as to what data to put in each field, what data/information will be shown and how to save, print, delete etc.

A good user guide will be well illustrated with screen-shots of what to expect at every major step taken. There should also be a troubleshooting section that spells out some common problems that may occur; for example, 'What to do if the record you're looking for is not found?' or 'What if the system says I can't delete an entry?'. Finally, there should be instructions on how to get support.

File conversion

Most organisations will already have data stored electronically. It may not be in the format required for this new or amended system and so will need converting. This can be a lengthy process and would need to be planned out right from the start.

Firstly there would be a mapping process of matching data fields from the old files to the new. Some new fields may be combinations of data in the old files or derived from old fields. There may be some new data fields that will need populating in other ways – sourcing the data from other systems, perhaps, or creating default values that will get amended over time by processing.

Either way, a method of converting the old to the new will have to be specified – this may mean special one-off programs will need to be written if the conversion is complex. These programs would have to go through all the normal stages (design, code and test) before they are ready for use in this final life cycle stage. The actual date for the conversion of data to take place will have to be planned carefully and is tied in with the next step in the stage, changeover.

System changeover

How to make the change from the old system to the new is a matter for careful thought and planning. It depends on many factors, including how many staff will be affected, where they are situated geographically and how important the continuity of the tasks is.

For the customers of the organisation there needs to be either a seamless changeover that makes no difference to their interactions with the organisation, or, if they are going to be affected in any way, a communication period so that they know what to expect.

There are four main methods of changeover from an old system to a new system.

- **Direct changeover.** New system starts on Monday morning. Staff may find this very stressful, and there is no fallback position if the new system crashes.
- **Parallel running.** Old and new systems are run side by side. This is safer than direct changeover, but is twice as much work for staff.
- **Pilot operation.** A few members of staff try the new system, or a single branch. These 'guinea pigs' report any problems, then are also available to train the rest of the staff.
- **Phased implementation.** Part I (e.g. transferring names from cards to computer) is completed before Part II (e.g. addressing bills). This is safer, but it may take a long time before the new system is in full operation.

Formal methods

Project management methods are used to control the process of initiating, planning, executing, and closing down a project. Project Management is both a process and a set of tools and techniques concerned with defining the project's goal, planning all the work to reach the goal, leading the project and support teams, monitoring progress and seeing to it that the project is completed in a satisfactory way to meet customer requirements.

Normally, there will be a Project Manager in charge of the development team. The job of this person is to ensure that the project runs smoothly, delivering on time the system that is required. If the project is large, there may be a number of different teams involved in the development, each led by a team leader. A project plan will have been drawn up at the start of the project, showing deadline dates for each project stage, with a list of milestones and deliverables, so that all parties know what is being delivered and when.

PRINCE is a generic, tailorable, simple to follow project management method. It covers how to organise, manage and control your projects. It is aimed at enabling you to successfully deliver the right products, on time and within budget. As a Project Manager you can apply the principles of PRINCE2 and the associated training to any type of project. It will help you to manage risk, control quality and change effectively, as well as make the most of challenging situations and opportunities that arise within a project.

A PRINCE2 project has the following characteristics:

- A finite and defined life cycle
- Defined and measurable business products
- A corresponding set of activities to achieve the business products
- A defined amount of resources
- An organisation structure, with defined responsibilities, to manage the project.

PRINCE2 does not cover all aspects of project management. Certain aspects of project management (such as leadership and people management skills, detailed coverage of project management tools and techniques) are well covered by other existing and proven methods and are therefore excluded from PRINCE2.

A link to this website is available at www.heinemann.co.uk/hotlinks (express code 2349P)

1 Find out more about PRINCE2, then research another project management methodology and compare the two.

2 List **five** similarities and **five** differences between the two methodologies.

3 Discuss in class the reasons for the similarities.

Having a clear time plan (which might change during the course of the project), with agreement from all parties, makes the project's progress easier to monitor. Regular progress meetings with the business managers and the users will also ensure that the functionality matches the users' expectations.

There are several methodologies in existence, but the one used by most UK government departments, among many other organisations, is **PRINCE2**.

Some of the main themes running through all formal methodologies are the need for **milestones**, **agreed deliverables**, **sign-off** and **approval to proceed**.

The project plan is the tool used for controlling the project. This plan may be re-drawn many times through the life of the project, at the very least at the completion of each stage and at every milestone if they are different. The plan should contain each task to be completed, with the resource or resources expected to undertake them, and the amount of time it is expected to take (in hours or days, where a day is defined as, for example, 7 or 7.5 hours) plus expected start and end dates. A good plan will show these tasks logically, within the life cycle stage they are expected to take place in, and also show dependencies of tasks.

Milestones will be shown on the plan – these may be a meeting arranged for a particular date, the delivery of a document, or an externally imposed deadline date (for example, a date when new legislation comes into force). These form the overall deadlines that all project members must meet.

Other milestones can be added. For instance, if a developer is going on holiday for two weeks, they may have imposed a deadline that their tasks must be fully completed two days before they go away, so that the next task can be under way without problems using their output.

At the start of any project, a set of deliverables will have been agreed with the client, business managers or users. These could be documents such as the System specification, the Design specification, the Test plan, a list of modules from the construction phase, the user guide and so on. These items will be slotted into the project plan by adding the tasks required to produce the content, plus time for producing the document, printing, binding and reviewing it.

Once a document is delivered, then the business managers and users will have an opportunity to review and approve it before giving the go-ahead for the project to carry on (approval to proceed with the next stage of the project). Normally there is a space for an approval signature (the sign-off), which ensures that the project manager knows that the project is on track to produce the system that meets user requirements.

Large projects are often broken down into sub-tasks and allocated to teams. This break-down could be stage-based for a linear development method, so there would be teams of analysts to do the analysis, teams of designers to do the design work, teams of developers to do the coding and so on. Alternatively, a functional breakdown could be used for an iterative development method, where there is one team to do overall analysis, one team to produce functions 1–4 from detailed analysis and design through to test, another to do functions 5–12 and so on.

The reasons for this sub-division are many, but are mostly to do with splitting the management and control over a number of leaders. These teams may be specialised so that the managers could allocate the right set of tasks to the most appropriate team. This would make the project easier to control and testing more manageable. It would have the additional benefit of allowing non-dependant sub-projects to run simultaneously, which would bring down the elapsed timescale (make the end date earlier than it would have been if all tasks were done in a linear way).

Development methodologies

There are two basic types of development methodology – linear and iterative – and most of the methodologies fall into these two types.

Linear methodologies

The most well known linear methodology is the **Waterfall model**, which is the earliest method of structured system development. Although it has come under attack in recent years for being too rigid and unrealistic when it comes to quickly meeting customer's needs, it is still widely used. It is attributed with providing the theoretical basis for other process models because it most closely resembles a 'generic' model for software development.

The steps normally associated with the Waterfall method are as follows.

- **System Conceptualisation**, which refers to the consideration of all aspects of the targeted business function or process, how each of those aspects relates to the others and which of the aspects are needed to be included in the system. This is the step that relates to the Project definition and feasibility stages of the life cycle.
- **Systems Analysis** refers to the gathering of system requirements and how these requirements will be met by the system. Extensive communication between the customer and the developer is essential.
- **System Design**. Once the requirements have been collected and analysed, it is necessary to identify in detail how the system will be constructed to perform the necessary tasks. More specifically, the System Design phase is focused on the data requirements (what information will be processed in the system?), the software construction (how will the application be constructed?), and the interface construction (what will the system look like and what standards will be followed?).
- **Coding**. Also known as **programming**, this step involves the creation of the system software. Requirements and systems specifications from the System Design step are translated into machine-readable computer code. Nowadays, this does not solely apply to the writing of new code, but can mean the customising of existing package code (which can be by using a friendly not-too-technical customising interface).
- **Testing**. As the software is created and added to the developing system, testing is performed to ensure that it is working correctly and efficiently. Testing is generally focused on two areas: internal efficiency (to make sure

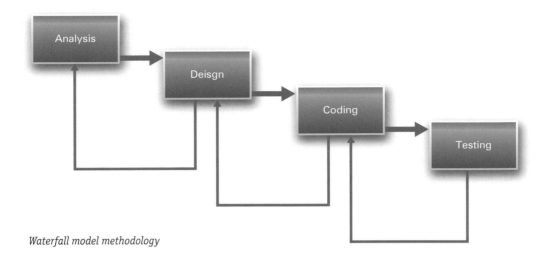

Waterfall model methodology

that the computer code is efficient, standardised, and well documented) and external effectiveness (to verify that the software is functioning according to system design, and that it is performing all necessary functions or sub-functions). Testing can be a labour-intensive process, due to its iterative nature.

Although the Waterfall model has been used extensively over the years in the production of many quality systems, it is not always the best solution. In recent years it has been criticised, due to its rigid design and inflexible procedure. Criticisms fall into the following categories.

- Real projects rarely follow the sequential flow that the model proposes.
- At the beginning of most projects there is often a great deal of uncertainty about requirements and goals, and it is therefore difficult for customers to identify these criteria on a detailed level. The model does not accommodate this natural uncertainty very well.
- Developing a system using this model can be a long, painstaking process that does not yield a working version of the system until late in the process.

Iterative methodologies

The problems with the Waterfall model created a demand for a new method of developing systems that could provide faster results, require less up-front information, and offer greater flexibility. With Iterative Development, the project is divided into small parts. This allows the development team to demonstrate results earlier on in the process and to obtain valuable feedback from system users. Often,

each iteration is actually a mini-Waterfall process with the feedback from one phase providing vital information for the design of the next phase. In a variation of this model, the software products that are produced at the end of each step (or series of steps) can go into production immediately as incremental releases. This is also known as Rapid Application Development (RAD) technique.

Problems associated with RAD methods include the following.

- The user community needs to be actively involved throughout the project. While this involvement is a positive for the project, it is demanding on the time of the staff and can add project delay.
- Communication and coordination skills take centre stage in project development.
- Informal requests for improvement after each phase may lead to confusion – a controlled mechanism for handling substantive requests must be developed.
- The Iterative Model can lead to 'scope creep', since user feedback following each phase may lead to increased customer demands. As users see the system develop, they may realise the potential of other system capabilities that would enhance their work.

One well-known RAD methodology is Dynamic Systems Development Method (DSDM). DSDM was developed in the United Kingdom in the 1990s by the DSDM Consortium of vendors and experts in the field of Information System (IS) development by combining their best-practice experiences. The DSDM Consortium is a non-profit, vendor independent organisation, which owns and administers the framework. As an extension of rapid application development, DSDM focuses on IS projects that are characterized by tight schedules and budgets. DSDM addresses the common reasons for IS project failure, including exceeding budgets, missing deadlines and lack of user involvement and management commitment.

DSDM consists of three phases: pre-project phase, project life-cycle phase, and post-project phase. The project life-cycle phase is subdivided into five stages: feasibility study, business study, functional model iterations, design and build iterations, and implementation. For the design and build iterations, each iteration will have a subset of the overall functionality required by the project – in effect, a list of requirements will have been drawn up and prioritised. The categories for prioritising are known as **MoSCoW**: Must-have functions (what we cannot do without), Should-have functions (what we should have to make the system work well), Could-have functions (what we could have to make it work efficiently) and Would-have functions (what would be nice to have but we could live without).

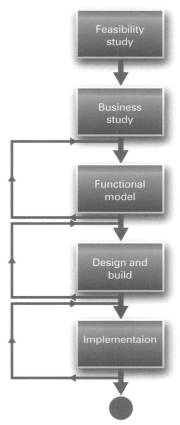

Each iteration is normally time-bound (for example, six weeks for a team of five developers and two users), and will cover a number of functions from the list. The Must-haves are the most important functions, so some of these will be included in each iteration until they are complete, then the Should-haves will be included, and so on. The list of planned funtions is normally longer than it will be possible to complete in the iteration. Any incomplete, or not yet started, functions return to the list to be planned into the next iteration.

Dynamic Systems Development Method

For instance, suppose a project has the following functions.

- Must-haves – 5 large, 3 medium, 3 small
- Should-haves – 4 large, 2 medium, 5 small
- Could-haves – 5 medium, 10 small
- Would-haves – 3 medium, 5 small.

Iteration 1 may look like this.

- Must-haves – 2 large, 1 medium, 3 small – all completed
- Should-haves – 2 large, 1 medium, 2 small – the large and mediums completed
- Could-haves – 1 medium – not done.

Iteration 2 may look like this.

- Must-haves – 2 large, 2 medium – all completed
- Should-haves – 2 large, 1 medium, 2 small – the large and medium completed
- Could-haves – 1 medium – not done.

Iteration 3 may look like this.

- Should-haves – 5 small – all completed
- Could-haves – 5 medium, 5 small – mediums done, 2 small done
- Would-haves – 3 medium – 1 completed.

Iteration 4 may look like this.

- Could-haves – 8 small
- Would-haves – 2 mediums, 5 small.

In some circumstances, it is possible to integrate practices from other methodologies, such as **Rational Unified Process (RUP)**, **Extreme Programming (XP)**, and **PRINCE2**, as complements to DSDM.

1 Research further into Rapid Application Development and read more about DSDM.

2 Investigate the **Spiral model** and compare its philosophy with DSDM – is it similar?

3 What conclusions can you reach as to why these methods of development are more popular nowadays than the traditional linear methods?

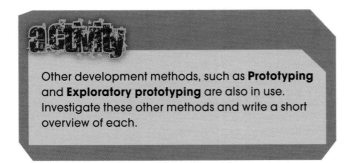

Other development methods, such as **Prototyping** and **Exploratory prototyping** are also in use. Investigate these other methods and write a short overview of each.

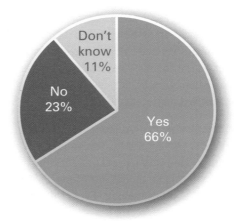

Responses for new function: automatic saves

Techniques and tools for systems development

Investigation and recording techniques

The four basic methods of investigation – Interview, Questionnaire, Observation and Document Analysis – have been covered already in this book Section 1, so the techniques discussed here will be concerned with how to show the results of these investigations.

Interviews

Once an interview is over and the answers have been taken down (normally on paper, but occasionally by sound recording), then the interview transcript must be written or typed up, including both questions and answers, and sent to the interviewee for confirmation that this is a true reflection of what was said. This ensures that the interviewer had not misheard factual answers or misconstrued anything said during the interview.

Questionnaires

If a questionnaire has been sent out to a number of people, it is customary to collate all the answers together in a report. This report will be useful to inform further analysis decisions. Quantitative answers (those that have a limited number of possible answers, including yes/no questions) can be reported back in numeric ways – e.g. '65% said they would like function x in their system'. For more choices, graphs can be used to show the results, if the report is going to be used by a variety of people. For the analyst, it may be enough to identify where the problems in the current system are and what potential users want from any new system by using the simple 'x% said this, and y% said that' approach.

Observation

One way to observe is to video one or more users doing their jobs, seeing how they interact with the current ICT system and use it to complete their daily tasks. The only problem with this is that the analyst will still need to re-watch the tape and analyse it. An alternative is to write down each step taken by the observed person, noting the time, what the task is, how long it takes, who else was involved, what happens next and so on.

Observation can be a time-consuming investigative method as there will be more than one type of user for any given system within an organisation and to do the investigation completely it may be necessary to observe many different people interacting with the data and information involved in the process. However, observation

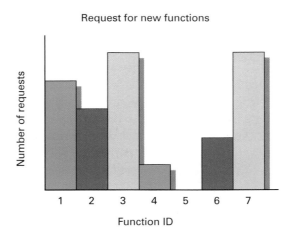

Presentation of quantitative responses

is sometimes the only way to truly analyse the processes that take place – people often do so many of their routine tasks without thought that they can fail to mention actions taken when asked in interview or questionnaire.

Document analysis

Looking at current documentation is not just looking at order forms and current system reports; it is also getting copies of procedures that are followed, lists of instructions for doing particular tasks, user and technical documentation that may be part of any current ICT system and guides and manuals that may be part of the business process that the system supports.

If the documentation has data fields, then making a list of these is a start to the data analysis that will be required later on. Any fields that do not correspond to the data fields need noting down for later investigation into where they come from. Written procedures give a clue to the functionality required of the system if it is to enable staff to perform their jobs.

Although always put at the bottom of the list of investigation techniques, document analysis is often the activity that should be done first, as there are many questions that arise from looking at existing documentation that would be best answered directly when interviewing the users.

Business Process Modelling tools

The results of investigation into business processes and current systems are often shown diagrammatically.

Information flow diagrams

Information flow diagrams are used to demonstrate the flow of information via activities within an organisation and to show the external people and systems that interact with the information. Diagrammatically, these people and systems are known as **entities**. An activity, which could also be a series of activities within a department of the organisation, is known as a **process**, and the flow of information is known as an **information flow**.

The example below is for a basic production company that sells goods directly to its customers, for example

a PC manufacturer. The company's sales team receive orders directly from the clients. The order details are sent to the production line in the form of requisitions. The production team order any necessary raw materials from external suppliers, and pass on the purchase details to the accounts department. On delivery of the raw materials the suppliers send delivery notes to the production team and invoices to the accounts team. The accounts department send payments to the suppliers for the raw materials. When the production line has manufactured the goods and delivered them to the clients, a despatch note is sent to the accounts department. The accounts department then send an invoice to the client and await payment.

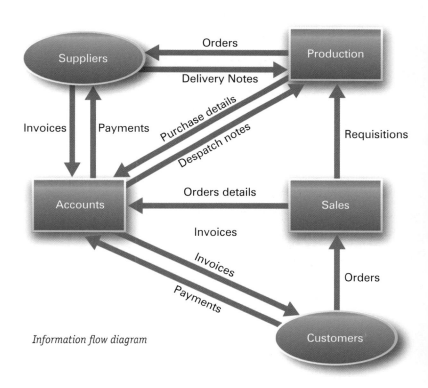

Information flow diagram

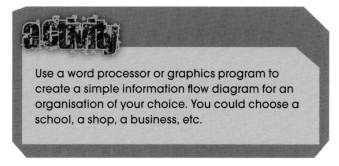

Use a word processor or graphics program to create a simple information flow diagram for an organisation of your choice. You could choose a school, a shop, a business, etc.

Data flow diagrams and entity-relationship diagrams are also used to describe what has been found out by the analyst and are explained further below.

This area of topics is also often referred to as Business Process Analysis (BPA) or Business Process Modelling and is used with object-oriented development methods.

A simple business process diagram using BPMN (Business Process Modelling Notation) is a clear diagrammatic representation of a set of events and activities. The circles are events, the rectangles are activities, diamonds are gateways (decisions) and arrows show the sequence of activities.

Draw a diagram using BPMN to show the process of renting a film from a DVD rental shop.

Modern methods use the Unified Modelling Language (UML) where these diagrams are replaced by use case, activity and class diagrams.

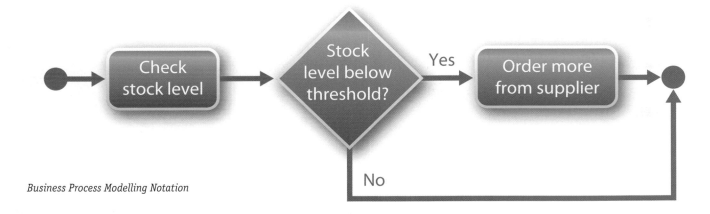

Business Process Modelling Notation

BALTIC Shipping is an international shipping company that specializes in transporting shipments from the U.S. to Eastern Europe. It seeks to create a mechanism for tracking shipments from its headquarters in New York to its regional offices such as the one in Tallinn, Estonia. When products are shipped, the head office sends information electronically in XML about the shipment. Once the shipment has reached its destination, the confirmation is electronically sent back to headquarters.

All the order and confirmation data is exchanged in XML documents and schemas have to be designed to outline the structure of the documents. The business constructs used to model shipping orders are also used to exchange information with the Inventory Tracking System, which knows which packages the company is holding for delivery at any time.

business concepts of the domain. You could make some rough sketches on paper, but UML provides a better formal methodology for modelling these concepts with diagrams and notations.

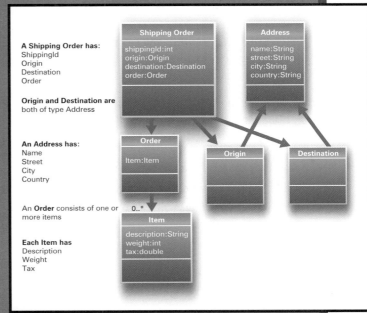

UML diagram

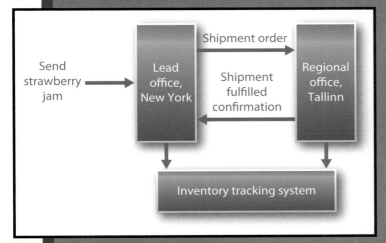

Baltic shipping workflow

Imagine that the business manager of BALTIC Shipping comes to you and asks you to model the XML schema that will formalize the information that is transmitted between different systems in the company. He sits down with you to discuss the

In the UML diagram the business definition of a Shipping Order is outlined. BALTIC Shipping defines a Shipping Order as consisting of a Shipping Id, an Origin, a Destination, and an Order. It considers this imperative information whenever any data regarding a Shipping Order is exchanged. In addition, the UML diagram is used to represent what constitutes an Origin or an Order. Origin and Destination types are shown to be the same as type Address, and BALTIC Shipping stores an Address in its database with the following characteristics: Name, Street, City, and Country. These are business concepts and they have been used in the database models, in the software programs, and in the documents that are read by managers and business partners.

A link to this website is available at www.heinemann.co.uk/hotlinks (express code 2349P)

Data modelling tools

Entity relationship diagrams (E-R diagrams) are used to identify how sets of data relate to one another. They can be used to describe data currently in use and data to be used in the new system.

Essentially, an **entity** is a thing of significance, either real or conceptual, about which the business or system being modelled needs to hold information. Examples are STUDENT, SUBJECT, TEACHER and so on. Each entity in an E-R diagram tends to correspond to a physical table in the database, once it is designed.

For example, suppose the logical analysis has produced various 'business rules'.

- A student can study many different subjects.
- Many students can take the same subject.
- Teachers can teach more than one subject.
- There are many teachers who can teach a particular subject.

So the E-R diagram created might look like this:

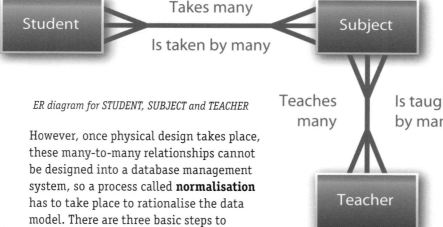

ER diagram for STUDENT, SUBJECT and TEACHER

However, once physical design takes place, these many-to-many relationships cannot be designed into a database management system, so a process called **normalisation** has to take place to rationalise the data model. There are three basic steps to normalisation.

1. Remove repeating groups.
2. Remove partial key dependencies.
3. Remove non-key dependencies.

The ability to understand in any detail the normalisation process is not part of this specification, so it is sufficient to know just the bare details and the reasons.

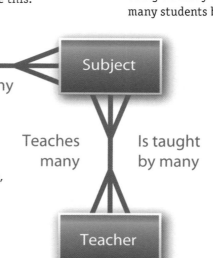

E–R diagram in first normal form

The aim of physical data design is to rationalise the data to make as efficient a data structure as possible. It is done to reduce data duplication, data inconsistency and redundancy.

An E-R diagram to first normal form, based on the SUBJECT, STUDENT, TEACHER example, would look like the one above. (Notice that the many-to-many relationships have been replaced by 'linking' entities and one-to-many relationship).

By inserting the linking entities, the business rules are still followed – e.g. a student can take many subjects, by being on many subject registers; subjects can be taken by many students by having one or more subject registers.

Without adding the data fields to the E-R diagram, a technique that is used when it comes to detailed database design, it is hard to go further with the normalising process, as the next steps require keys to be identified – the primary key, any secondary keys, plus foreign keys which link one entity to another.

Once the data has been modelled, using the normalisation process and E-R diagrams, then a **data dictionary** is drawn up. Remember that a data dictionary is a description of the data in the system – an example can be found earlier in the book in Section 1.

The next data modelling technique to look at is the use of Data Flow Diagrams (DFDs) to illustrate how processes in the current or proposed system link together. Traditionally, the Level 0 DFD is the highest level of conceptual DFD; it is also known as the Context Diagram and serves merely to put the current or proposed system in its context, showing only interfaces with external entities.

Here is a sample context diagram for a simple appointment booking system.

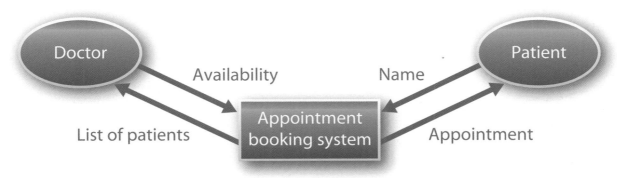

Sample context diagram

The context diagram clearly shows the interfaces between the system under investigation and the external entities with which it communicates. Therefore, while it is often conceptually trivial, a context diagram serves to focus attention on the system boundary and can help in clarifying the precise scope of the analysis.

The notation used in one structured analysis technique is as follows.

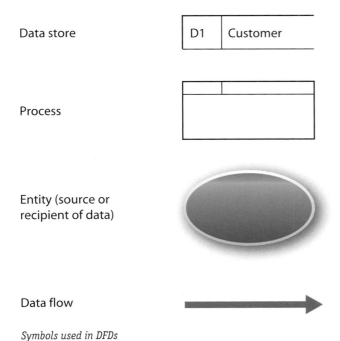

Symbols used in DFDs

Data stores are any places where data is held – in a manual system this may be in an address book, a directory, a pile of invoices stuck on a spike; in a computer it is generally a file of some sort.

Processes are any actions that cause something to happen to some data, causing a change or converting it into information. In a manual system this could be looking up a phone number in a directory, writing a phone number down in an address book, calculating a total and putting it at the bottom of an invoice; in a computer it could be automatic calculation of the total or producing a list of patient and appointment times. All processes have input and output – something going in and something coming out. With DFDs, it is processes involving data that are included.

Data flow is used to show how data moves into, between and out of processes, and between sources and recipients of data, both of which may be a person, an institution or another system. Data flow is not the physical article but the data that accompanies it – not the actual physical stock item, but the order, the picking list, the delivery note, the bill or the receipt.

Sources of data are those external entities that provide data for the system. These may be customers, who provide order details, or suppliers, who provide delivery notes and invoices, or other systems, for example, an ordering system may provide data for an internal accounting system.

Recipients (destinations) of data are those external entities who receive output from the system, but are not directly using it. For example, government departments receive tax returns from payroll systems and the board of governors at a school receives performance reports, but neither entity directly uses the system.

Data flow diagrams can be drawn at different levels, to show levels of process. If a process is not a single step,

then a further DFD is required to show the breakdown. Each process is numbered (so the system is numbered 0).

DFDs may be useful for documenting the current system, but they are especially useful when designing the proposed system.

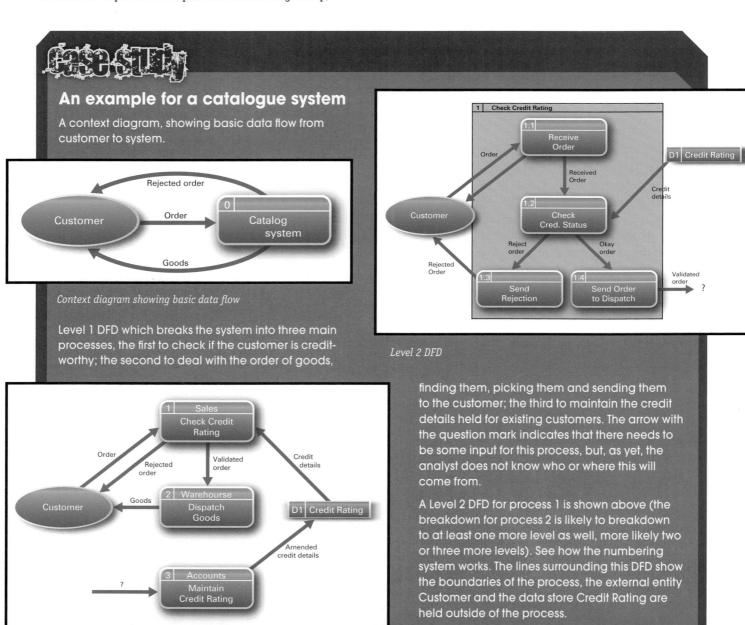

Case study

An example for a catalogue system

A context diagram, showing basic data flow from customer to system.

Context diagram showing basic data flow

Level 1 DFD which breaks the system into three main processes, the first to check if the customer is credit-worthy; the second to deal with the order of goods,

Level 2 DFD

finding them, picking them and sending them to the customer; the third to maintain the credit details held for existing customers. The arrow with the question mark indicates that there needs to be some input for this process, but, as yet, the analyst does not know who or where this will come from.

A Level 2 DFD for process 1 is shown above (the breakdown for process 2 is likely to breakdown to at least one more level as well, more likely two or three more levels). See how the numbering system works. The lines surrounding this DFD show the boundaries of the process, the external entity Customer and the data store Credit Rating are held outside of the process.

Level 1 DFD

Techniques for testing

In the traditional linear development model, testing comes right at the end, sometimes too late to catch bugs that should have been fixed back in the design phase, causing great cost and delays to the project.

Life cycle testing or **V testing** aims at catching the defects as early as possible and thus reduces the cost of fixing them. It achieves this by continuously testing the system during all phases of the development process rather than just limiting testing to the last phase. The life cycle testing can be best accomplished by the formation of a separate test team.

When the project starts, both the system development process and system test process begin. The team that is developing the system begins the systems development process and the team that is conducting the system test begins planning the system test process. Both teams

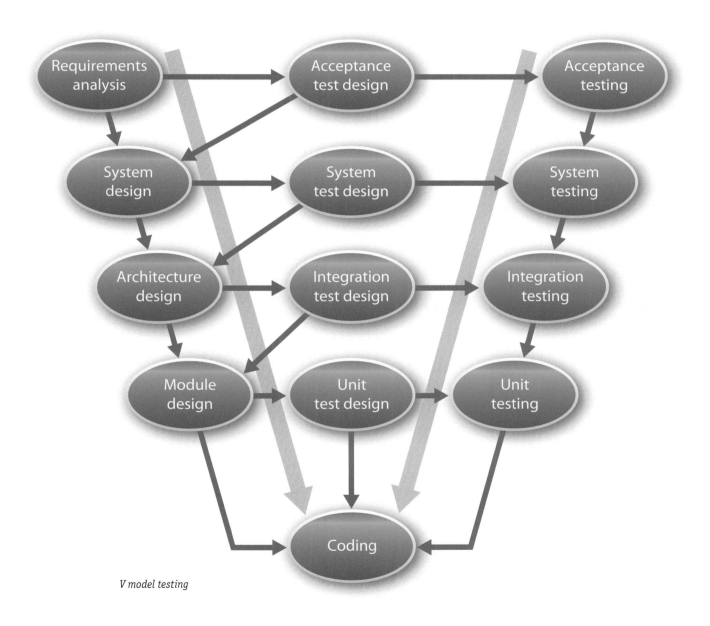

V model testing

start at the same point using the same information. The systems development team documents the requirements for developmental purposes. The test team will use those same requirements, but for the purpose of testing the system.

At appropriate points during the development process, the test team will test the development process in an attempt to uncover defects. For example, at the analysis stage, the test team will check that the requirements captured are true user needs that are complete, unambiguous, accurate and not conflicting with each other.

There are several types of testing, including black box testing, white box testing and volume testing.

Black box testing is not based on any knowledge of the internal design or code. Tests are based on requirements and functionality, so it is also known as User or Beta testing, i.e. simulating reality.

White box testing is based on knowledge of the internal logic of an application's code. Tests are based on coverage of code statements, branches, paths and conditions. White box testing is also known as Unit or Module testing. A unit or module is typically the work of one coder/constructor. This unit is tested in isolation with the help of a **test harness**.

Test harness

A test harness is a piece of code which encompasses the modules under test, and acts as the channel for data into the code. It typically contains a simple call-return process for each unmatched procedure call in the code. It is used for the dynamic testing of an incomplete module or part of the application.

Volume testing is used to make sure that the system will run under stress, in terms of:

- the **number of users** accessing the same data at the same time – for example, when tickets for a popular band go on sale at 9am on Friday, thousands of people try and book on the website, keeping on hitting the refresh button until they connect to the ordering page

- the **number of transactions** passing through the system in an hour – for example, the ATM system between 6pm and 7pm on Saturday as people go out on the town

- the **amount of data** or number of records being stored per hour – for example, the take-up of a new product or half-price offer might be higher than expected.

In the first case, often there are testing centres, where many testers sit, entering test data at a pace and volume set by the test plan. If testing an Internet-based system, they are likely to be 'hitting' the system many times an hour and from different browsers to test the system's capability in coping with the load. Failure to anticipate take-up and volume of interest can lead to some high-level embarrassment.

case study

1901 census site

The 1901 census website is now running successfully and problems originally encountered when the Public Record Office and QinetiQ implemented the site in January 2002 have been overcome. Moreover, according to today's report to Parliament by NAO head Sir John Bourn, the lessons learned will be valuable to government and other public sector bodies planning to make services available on the Internet.

The Public Record Office had planned a low key launch for the website which provides online access to the results of the 1901 census. However, press coverage on the day the website was launched was more extensive than expected and resulted in overwhelming demand. By noon on the launch day, 2 January 2002, 1.2 million users an hour were attempting to access the site, which had been designed to cope with a peak of 1.2 million users in a 24 hour period.

The site was withdrawn on 7 January 2002 and QinetiQ instigated technical reviews. Agreement on the changes required to launch a working website was achieved with the assistance of the Office of the e-Envoy. The site was made available with restricted access on 27 August 2002. And, in November 2002, full access, 24 hours a day, seven days a week, was restored. The site now receives between 8,000 and 10,000 visitors a day and has generated some 4.5 million (hits) up to 31 October 2003.

A link to this website is available at www.heinemann.co.uk/hotlinks (express code 2349P)

The scalability of an ICT system is checked so that, in the future, its data capacity, or its number of users, could be increased without any impact on performance. In testing terms, this might mean benchmarking (measuring) performance with a fixed number of users, perhaps by recording response times, then trying it with, say, 10 times as many users and measuring performance again, and so on. However, the larger numbers of users might have to be simulated. This is true of any kind of design for expansion – it can only be tested so far realistically, so any further figures quoted are likely to be theoretical ones only.

Prototyping is a proven form of testing – the prototype is produced, in conjunction with one or more users, to 'paint' the interface, manipulating it until the user is happy with the outcome. This is self-checking design. Once they have agreed the design, or outline functionality of the prototype, the developers can continue, safe in the knowledge that they are producing exactly what the user wants.

Multi-**platform** testing is just common sense – it is necessary to test a commercial package on as many different platforms and configurations as can be thought of so the package can be confidently sold in many arenas. If the multi-platform testing has not occurred, then it is likely that the package will fail. If all platforms are known, for example if the system is being written in-house for one organisation, then there is no problem as the system can be tried out on them all before being installed.

Platform
In IT, a platform means any combination of hardware or software on which other software will run. For example, a Pentium 4 PC with 2GB RAM running Windows XP could be considered to be a platform.

The use of simulated environments is also a testing technique. Not dissimilar to test harnesses, a simulated environment uses computer-generated inputs to the processes. It will simulate the behaviour of functionality being tested given various inputs and outputs; these can then be compared to the actual results and adjustments made. It can also be used to simulate the actions of external entities so that the modules or functions being tested can cope with realistic data.

Practice exam questions

1. Give **three** reasons why projects are often sub-divided into tasks and allocated to teams. (3)
    (AQA June 2006)

2. Formal development methods have distinct phases. For the following development phases:
    • state **one** activity that is undertaken
    • state **one** deliverable that is a typical output.
    (a) Analysis (2)
    (b) Design (2)
    (c) Implementation/Programming (2)
    (d) Testing (2)
    (AQA June 2006)

3. When developing ICT systems, project teams should follow a formal method. Give **three** reasons for using a formal method. (3)
    (AQA January 2006)

4. Within ICT projects, describe the need for:
    (a) agreed deliverables (2)
    (b) clear timescales (2)
    (c) approval to proceed. (2)
    (AQA June 2005)

5. The development of an effective new information system, and its successful introduction into an organisation, can be due to a combination of factors such as formal development methods and teamwork. Discuss these factors, paying particular attention to:
    • the possible methods of acquiring, developing and
    • implementing a new information system
    • the people involved in the development
    • the role of the organisation's management in the development and introduction of a new system. (16)
    (AQA January 2007)

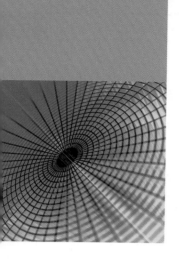

3.5 Introducing large ICT systems into organisations

Scale

A large system may be introduced into a single organisation or across a range of different ones. We consider the two options separately.

A large system, such as an ERP system (mentioned in Section 3.2), may be customised and introduced into a single organisation. These systems are sometimes bought in as packages and customised by, or with the help of, consultants who are experts in their use; or sometimes they are developed specially for the organisation, either by their own IS department or by a software house employed by the organisation.

In contrast, some large systems are used by many organisations, which can vary from small, single-owner businesses to medium or large multi-personnel operations. Examples of these systems include Smiths News Connect2U newspaper and magazine ordering system, used by many small and large businesses across the world, and the NHS Connect systems, used by hospitals, clinics and GP surgeries across the UK.

Smiths News

What is Connect2U?

Connect2U is an easy-to-use website that enables retailers to manage their Smiths News orders online. It is also a valuable source of information designed to keep retailers up-to-date with all the latest product news for newspapers and magazines. The only cost to retailers is the price of a local telephone call. All that is needed is a PC and an Internet connection.

Advantages to retailers

Connect2U offers an efficient and cost-effective way to manage customer supplies. It saves time and money, makes stock management easier and helps decision-making. Advantages include:

1. Quicker order management – retailers can make changes to their account 24 hours a day. They don't have to compete with other retailers for a limited number of phone lines or operators.

2. Greater convenience – because retailers can manage their supplies at any time, they are free to concentrate on customers during busy periods.

As well as being an easy-to-use order management tool for Smiths News customers, the site is a great source of valuable information. There is a wide range of features to help retailers run their businesses, including:

1. Industry news.

2. Magazine information.

3. Title ranking reports.

4. New launches and promotions.

5. Smiths News customer information.

6. A discussion forum.

Connect2U provides advice on industry issues and offers the chance to swap hints and tips with other retailers across the country. Our discussion group is always buzzing with debate.

What services does Connect2U offer?

Connect2U makes life easier in many ways. It's the most convenient way to keep track of orders and it is much more efficient than spending time and money chasing orders over the phone. With Connect2U retailers can:

1. View net sales history for the last six issues and identify sell-outs at a glance.

2. Claim for magazines that were invoiced but not received.

3. Receive early morning updates on local deliveries.

4. Order back issues of partworks.

5. Access sales promotional and HND support from newspaper publishers.

6. Contact their local Customer Service Manager direct.

A link to this website is available at www.heinemann.co.uk/hotlinks (express code 2349P)

NHS connecting for health

Programmes for IT

Accountability for the delivery of National Programme for IT (NPfIT) transferred to strategic health authorities (SHAs) on 1 April 2007, as part of the NPfIT Local Ownership Programme (NLOP).

NHS Connecting for Health has been working closely with the 10 strategic health authorities (SHAs) to help with the transition and the subsequent transfer of activities.

These activities were previously carried out by the former NHS CFH Clusters. SHA Chief Information Officers and their teams have been fully involved throughout the process.

To ensure relationships with Local Service Providers (LSPs) continue effectively, NHS Programme for IT Management Boards have been established in three geographic areas to:

- act as a forum for Chief Executive discussion and decision making, in line with the SHA mandate and provide strategic direction within a defined geographic area

- ensure a joined-up approach in implementing NPfIT across constituent SHAs

- ensure the effective engagement of NHS CFH and other key regional stakeholders.

A link to this website is available at www.heinemann.co.uk/hotlinks (express code 2349P)

Investigate the NHS Connecting for Health site at **www.connectingforhealth.nhs.uk** and research how hospitals, clinics, GP surgeries and individuals can make use of these IT systems. **Systems and Services** and **Programmes for IT** are two areas where the use of ICT is explored.

Assign each individual one element from one of the two areas to research further and produce a presentation of the main features of that element, from an ICT perspective, for the rest of the class.

http://www.connectingforhealth.nhs.uk

Analysing and Testing of Large-Scale Software Systems

With the increase of applications of large-scale software systems, software quality and assurance have become a main challenge in software industry, since it is complex and difficult to organise, develop, analyse and test the systems with millions of elements that interact to achieve the system functionality. New software development methods, such as component-based software, middleware, web-service, etc., are helpful to managing and represent the complexity involved in the interaction of system elements. However, there is still a lack of effective automation and formal techniques to assure the large-scale system's quality.

Software analysing and testing is one of the most important methods to assure software quality, which is critical and expensive, especially when time, expenses and human resources are limited. Also, the traditional techniques can hardly manage the complexity and scale of most large-scale software systems. Therefore, there is an urgent demand for effective and efficient software analysing and testing methods for large-scale software systems.

A link to this website is available at www.heinemann.co.uk/hotlinks (express code 2349P)

Reliability and testing

When testing a simple application, such as one developed by a student as part of their coursework, it is fairly simple to construct a test plan that covers all pathways through the system, to check the navigation and validation works and the workings of, say, about 10 functions. However, when the system has taken a year to develop, with 25 or more development staff, an e-commerce aspect, hundreds of functions, thousands of potential users, and millions of lines of code, then the testing task is a little more complicated!

On many occasions, software and IT project costs spiral out of control and some projects never get completed. This has disastrous effects for the customer and also leads to a bad reputation and negative publicity for the company producing the product. In many cases, the project is just too big for the requirements to be pinned down with enough confidence to get the go-ahead for development; in other cases it is the lack of control over development, and especially the testing, that causes the failure.

Papers have been written and methodologies set up concerning the requirements for testing large-scale systems. A call for academic know-how, shown in the case study above, sets the scene for the problem.

A Framework for Testing Distributed Systems

Thorough testing of distributed systems, particularly peer-to-peer systems can prove difficult due to the problems inherent in deploying, controlling and monitoring many nodes simultaneously. This problem will only increase as the scale of distributed systems continues to grow. This framework implements a test bed environment using a semi-centralized peer-to-peer network as a substrate for sharing resources made available from standard PCs. This framework automates the process of test-case deployment using a combination of Reflection and Aspect Oriented Programming. This allows 'point-and-click' publishing of software onto the test-bed. Our framework also provides a common monitoring, control and logging interface for all nodes running on the network. Together, these features greatly reduce deployment-time for real-world test scenarios. Automated insertion and removal of test code also ensures that the testing process does not compromise the correctness of the final system.

A link to this website is available at www.heinemann.co.uk/hotlinks (express code 2349P)

IEEE 829 testing standard

One of the challenges facing software testers has been the availability of an agreed set of document standards and templates for testing. The IEEE 829 provides an internationally recognised set of standards for test planning documentation.

IEEE 829 has been developed specifically with software testing in mind and is applicable to each stage of the testing life cycle including system and acceptance testing.

Types of Document

The IEEE 829 standard covers 8 document types.

Test specification

Test Plan: Covers how the testing will be managed, scheduled and executed.

Test Design Specification: Defines logically what needs to be tested by examining the requirements or features. Then these requirements can be converted into test conditions.

Test Case Specification: Converts the test conditions into test cases by adding real data, pre-conditions and expected results.

Test Procedure: Describes in practical terms how the tests are run.

Test Item Transmittal Report: Specifies the items released for testing.

Test execution

Test Log: Is an audit trail that records the details of tests chronologically.

Test Incident Report: Records details of any unexpected events and behaviours that need to be investigated.

Test reporting

Test Summary Report: Summarises and evaluates tests.

A link to this website is available at www.heinemann.co.uk/hotlinks (express code 2349P)

Some methods have been put forward and there are numerous special interest groups, including the British Computer Society's Special Interest group in Software Testing. There are even specialist testing certification exams (ISEB qualifications) that can be taken by professional systems testers, which cover all types of testing.

Large-scale system testing involves many people – project managers, business and systems analysts, developers, specialist testing personnel, system users, operations staff and, sometimes, remote testers. Types of testing that go beyond the normal modular, functional, systems and user acceptance testing include volume testing, regression testing and performance testing.

Volume testing, as its name implies, is testing that purposely subjects a system (both hardware and software) to a series of tests where the volume of data being processed is the subject of the test. Such systems can be transaction processing systems capturing real-time sales, or could be database updates or data retrieval systems.

Volume testing will try to find the physical and logical limits to the system's capacity and then judge whether these limits are acceptable to meet the projected capacity of the organisation's business processing.

Regression testing is a process which tests a system once again to ensure that it still functions as expected, usually after a major change has occurred to the system. For example, if a software vendor releases a new version of its database, a comprehensive regression test plan needs to be developed and completed to ensure that the reports, screen, scripts, remote procedure calls, user options and so on are all functioning as expected. If they don't work completely as expected, then certain aspects of the configuration may need to change – perhaps new hardware.

Regression testing must also test the revised software by simulating its operational environment to ensure that all systems and interfaces still operate as expected.

Performance testing is performed to determine how fast some aspect of a system performs under a particular workload. It can also serve to validate and verify other quality attributes of the system, such as scalability and reliability.

Performance testing can serve different purposes. It can demonstrate that the system meets performance criteria.

It can compare two systems to find which performs better. Or it can measure what parts of the system or workload cause the system to perform badly. Benchmarking is one activity that is used to measure how a system performs.

It is critical to the cost-performance of a new system that performance test efforts begin at the start of the development project and extend through to implementation. The later a performance defect is detected, the higher the cost of rework. This is true in the case of functional testing, but even more so with performance testing, due to the end-to-end nature of its scope.

In performance testing, it is best for the test conditions to be similar to the expected actual use. This is, however, not entirely possible in practice because running systems have a random workload; while the tests do their best to mimic what may happen in the real environment, it is impossible to exactly replicate this workload variability, except in the most simple system.

Loosely-coupled architectural implementations (e.g. client-server systems) create additional complexities with performance testing. Enterprise services or assets (which share common infrastructure or platform) require coordinated performance testing (with all consumers creating production-like transaction volumes and load on shared infrastructures or platforms) to truly replicate production-like states. Due to the complexity and financial and time requirements around this activity, some organisations now employ tools that can monitor and create production-like conditions (also referred to as 'noise') in their performance testing environments (PTE) to understand capacity and resource requirements and to verify and validate quality attributes.

Testing network-based systems

By their very nature, network-based systems pose particular problems for testers. The reality of having many hundreds of people sat at terminals at many locations, some geographically remote, all trying to use (test) the system at once to see if it can cope with throughput and give an acceptable response time, would be a logistical nightmare and probably totally unmanageable. Instead, it is necessary to use specialist environments, which are set up to simulate the effects.

Performance testing technology employs one or more PCs or Unix servers to act as injectors – each emulating the presence of numbers of users and each running an automated sequence of interactions (recorded as a script, or as a series of scripts to emulate different types of user interaction) with the host whose performance is being tested. Usually, a separate PC acts as the test conductor, coordinating and gathering metrics from each of the injectors and collating performance data for reporting purposes. The usual sequence is to ramp up the load – starting with a small number of virtual users and increasing the number over a period to some maximum. The test results show how the performance varies with the load, given as number of users against a response time. Sometimes the results can reveal oddities, such as a few key transactions that take considerably longer to complete – something that might be caused by inefficient database queries, etc.

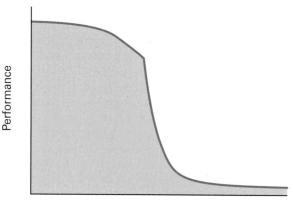

The usual sequence is to ramp up the load

Performance testing can be combined with stress (or volume) testing, in order to see what happens when an acceptable load is exceeded. Does the system crash? How long does it take to recover if a large load is reduced? Does the system fail in a way that causes collateral damage?

Post Office systems, testing outsourced to Acutest

In 2003, the Post Office decided to outsource their technical testing. The demand for these services was intermittent and there was not the critical mass to create a career path in this area and retain and grow staff. Acutest were selected because of their proven ability in providing non-functional testing services and their virtual team solution.

Response

Acutest set up the testing service to cover four key areas:

- Test strategy and implementation
- Performance testing and monitoring
- Security testing and security reviews
- Business continuity and disaster recovery testing.

Acutest provide a managed service within a controlled budget. For each project with a requirement for business driven testing, the Acutest service manager works closely with the client side project team to devise the most cost effective testing solution, Acutest then provide skilled resources to deliver the solution, sometimes on individual assignments but more typically in mixed teams of Acutest staff, Post Office staff and staff from third party suppliers of the system under test. The approach, processes and techniques used in this outsourced testing service were built from a combination of Post Office existing practices and best practice introduced by Acutest. These processes have continued to evolve as the Post Office's business operations have changed. For example, Acutest have helped bring testing forward into the earlier stages of the lifecycle, with a beneficial impact on costs and timescales.

Outcome

By combining continuity of approach and understanding with a flexible resourcing levels, Acutest have been able to meet the Post Office's testing needs and help assure the successful introduction of new applications and business processes.

Acutest have supported the Post Office in delivering 8 major releases based around its Horizon system. These activities included:

- Network Banking – on line cash withdrawals, balance enquiries and cash deposits
- Debit Cards
- Smart Post – intuitive postal application that embeds business rules
- Driver and Vehicle Licensing Agency (DVLA) automation
- E top-ups
- National Savings & Investment product re-engineering
- Bureau on Horizon
- DVLA additions
- IMPACT programme first release including improved cash management
- PAF
- AP-ADC (a generic application that gives time to market measured in weeks for in-payment products)
- EMV Chip & Pin
- Replacement of Network Banking Engine
- IMPACT programme full launch including new SAP based system for back end branch and product accounting, new Branch Trading and new MI.

All the above were delivered on cost and on time.

A link to this website is available at www.heinemann.co.uk/hotlinks (express code 2349P)

Installation

Again, installation of a large scale-system is, essentially, no different from that of any other ICT system – it still has to be introduced in a planned and methodical way, making sure that existing or new hardware is in place and compatible, that existing software works with the new system, that both documentation and people are ready for its use. It is just that all these things may well be on a much larger scale – more machines to set up, more machines for the software to be installed on, more existing data to be converted and transferred, more users to train, more functions to document, generally just more of everything. In fact, all these things may not even be in the same location. Imagine trying to install a new stock control system simultaneously in 350 stores and warehouses across Europe – it takes some planning to achieve such a feat.

Whichever method of changeover is chosen – Pilot, Parallel or Direct ('big bang') – there is a need for a vast amount of planning. All methods will involve both technical and non-technical staff. Depending on the situation, builders, electricians and so on may become involved.

For instance, many outside contractors may be involved in installing and testing new hardware and network communication systems. Any new equipment will need to be purchased and delivered in time for the changeover. Any communication systems may need installing or connecting and testing. Any new security features will have to be installed and tested.

Teams of technical staff may be sent off to different locations to install and test software on local servers. For example in a banking system upgrade, each branch may need new software to be installed on the same weekend.

Each PC in a system may need adjusting or upgrading, and certainly testing, to make sure that it is recognised by the network and can access the new system.

The existing database may need converting from the old format to the new. In some cases this exercise can be a large-scale project in its own right. Special one-off programs are often written to make these changes happen and a different development team assigned to this task. The only time-saving element of this is that, as it is a one-off process, little or no documentation is required beyond the 'data field matching' exercise and the analysis of where any missing data is to be found or calculated from. After the program has been run, it can, effectively, be thrown away.

Both technical and user documentation must be ready before the system is due to be implemented. There may be different versions of both technical and user documentation, depending on the system, its functions and its usage. Local operating procedures may also be introduced or amended as a result of this system, and these also require documenting.

If the system is completely new or represents a significant change to previous systems, then training documentation will also be required and training sessions set up to ensure that all staff will be familiar and confident using the new system from day one. Again, these may need to be held at numerous locations, so a team of trainers may be required. Appropriate training methods must be

Electricians may become involved

employed for each identified group of users of the system. Consideration must be given to the level of business or technical knowledge required by these trainers.

The changes that occur as a result of introducing such a system need managing carefully, as they may affect both the organisation and its employees:

- The new system may automate some tasks, resulting in staff being redeployed or losing their jobs. For instance, where a clerk used to manually collate figures from various sources and input them into a management accounting system, perhaps this is now done automatically.

- The new system may require more IT skills than staff currently have. For example, the need to be able to get ad-hoc reports from the new database using a report-generation application would result in the requirement for training or re-skilling.

- The organisation may have centralised its operations in a new location, resulting in staff being told to relocate if they want to keep their jobs.

- 24-hour working may have been introduced, for example for an online store's ordering service, meaning that staff may have to work unsociable hours, or that new staff need to be employed.

Piloting e-procurement at Wellingborough council

Where was the authority starting from?

The Borough Council of Wellingborough is a small authority which until recently did not have the resources for a procurement officer. The procurement policy was not clearly defined or accessible to all its users, despite such measures being part of the financial standing orders. The ordering system was paper-based and de-centralised, orders were sometimes faxed or phoned but most often sent by post. All orders were manually authorised before sending, but were not necessarily checked for completeness or accuracy. This led to random use of commitment accounting and the use of suppliers was not controlled, other than by financial regulations. Overall, there was limited control over the budgetary expenditure.

What were the drivers for implementing e-procurement?

Following several audit reports, including a specially commissioned Best Value Audit, two requirements were identified. Firstly, there was a need for closer budgetary control to prevent overspending and maverick and fraudulent purchases. Secondly, it was necessary to ensure that orders were completed accurately and authorised using correct procedures.

What system was selected?

Following a tendering process, the Borough Council of Wellingborough selected Radius Orbit as the most appropriate solution to meet our needs.

What approach to rollout/implementation was decided upon?

A phased approach was adopted, starting with a small pilot group of users. Further phases would extend the system to additional business units within the Council one at a time. The group of pilot users were selected on the basis of:

- their confidence with IT

- their 'empathy' with the aims and objectives of the project

- their accessibility to the Project Management Team to facilitate support and problem solving. (i.e. they were on the same site).

In addition, to keep staff aware of the coming changes and to help us identify any potential issues with these users, we decided to adopt an approach that would keep the users updated and where possible involved in the decision-making processes.

A link to this website is available at www.heinemann.co.uk/hotlinks (express code 2349P)

- The new system may produce improved management information automatically which means that some current levels in the hierarchy may not be needed, causing some management to become surplus to requirements. For operational staff, this might mean a change in department or supervisor and could lead to disgruntled staff.

In conclusion, the management of the installation of a large-scale system is very complex and is one of the most important factors in ensuring a successful system implementation.

Direct changeover has its own set of obstacles. It is often the case that completely new hardware is required for the new system, which makes a direct changeover the only choice to make, as the old hardware needs to be uninstalled. If this is the case, the development may well not have been carried out on customer premises. In these cases, one approach is to dummy run an entire month with live data at the developer's location, trying to match results with the current system still running at the organisation's own premises, and to emulate special reports such as end-of-year figures, to prove as far as is possible that the new system will run successfully. There is often a 'changeover weekend' where all systems are shut down, the new hardware and software are installed and tested and the new system goes ahead on Monday, in the hope that all will run smoothly.

Read the case study on pilot changeover and answer the following questions:

1 What did the borough council want from an e-procurement system?

2 Why did they choose to implement it with a pilot changeover?

3 What were their reasons for choosing who would pilot the new system?

Both this method and parallel running will involve a lot of work while the two systems are running side-by-side. Two sets of data entry might be required, maybe slightly different from one another, and there will be two sets of reports to be checked. However, this crossover period is extra training for those involved, giving them confidence in the new software and a chance to see how it will make their day-to-day tasks run more smoothly.

Backup and recovery

The main issues and choices to do with backing up of data are dealt with earlier in this book, on page 111. However, it is paramount that an appropriate method of backing up is used for large-scale systems. Obviously, a manual backup of a 10-terabyte database cannot be achieved using CD-ROMs! In large-scale systems, the backup is more likely to be to a second machine of the same, or slightly smaller, size as the operational one, so that there is enough space to hold all the necessary data and programs.

When organisations are setting up or reviewing their backup and recovery choices, most will undertake a risk analysis. Security risk analysis, otherwise known as risk assessment, is fundamental to the security of any organisation. It is essential in ensuring that controls and expenditure are fully equal to the risks to which the organisation is exposed.

Backup options depend on the material to be stored

However, many conventional methods for performing security risk analysis are becoming more and more unsustainable in terms of usability, flexibility, and critically in terms of what they produce for the user.

P		S	E	V	E	R	I	T	Y
R		9	8	7	6	5	4	3	2	1
O	9	81	72	63	54	45	36	27	18	9
B	8	72	64	56	48	40	32	24	16	8
A	7	63	56	49	42	35	28	21	14	7
B	6	54	48	42	36	30	24	18	12	6
I	5	45	40	35	30	25	20	15	10	5
L	4	36	32	28	24	20	16	12	8	4
I	3	27	24	21	18	15	12	9	6	3
T	2	18	16	14	12	10	8	6	4	2
Y	1	9	8	7	6	5	4	3	2	1

Probability	Severity
9. Almost Certain	9. Total business loss - bankruptcy
8. Very likely	8. 50-75% business loss - rebuild in years
7. Probably	7. 25-50% business loss - rebuild in months
6. More than even chance	6. 10-25% business loss - up to 2 months to recoup
5. Even chance	5. Significant delay - some profits gone
4. Less than even chance	4. Some delay - lose old customer
3. Improbable	3. Slight delay
2. Very improbable	2. Minor - annoyed customers
1. Almost impossible	1. No real effect

An example of a risk grid

Security in any system should be proportionate to its risks. However, determining which security controls are appropriate and cost effective is quite often a complex and sometimes a subjective matter. One of the prime functions of security risk analysis is to put this process on a more objective basis.

Below is an example of a risk grid, where a number is given to each threat to each element using the probability of it occurring combined with the severity of its impact on the business. These figures are then added up to give an overall risk factor.

Risk evaluation – either look at each threat individually or take an average risk factor (points/no. of threats assessed):

- an average of 30 points and above = high risk
- an average of 10–28 points = medium risk
- an average 1–9 points = low risk.

There are a number of distinct approaches to risk analysis. However, these essentially break down into two types: quantitative and qualitative.

Quantitative risk analysis

This approach employs two fundamental elements; the probability of an event occurring and the likely loss should it occur.

Quantitative risk analysis makes use of a single figure produced from these elements. This is called the **annual loss expectancy (ALE)** or the **estimated annual cost (EAC)**. This is calculated for an event by simply multiplying the potential loss by the probability. It is thus theoretically possible to rank events in order of risk (ALE) and to make decisions based upon this.

The problems with this type of risk analysis are usually associated with the unreliability and inaccuracy of the data. Probability can rarely be precise and can, in some cases, promote complacency. In addition, controls and countermeasures often tackle a number of potential events and the events themselves are frequently interrelated.

Notwithstanding the drawbacks, a number of organisations have successfully adopted quantitative risk analysis.

Qualitative risk analysis

This is by far the most widely used approach to risk analysis. Probability data is not required and only estimated potential loss is used. This approach does rely on the knowledge and skills of the risk analyst.

Most qualitative risk analysis methodologies make use of a number of interrelated elements: threats, vulnerabilities and controls.

Threats are things that can go wrong or that can 'attack' the system. Examples might include fire, natural disaster, terrorist attack, external hackers or fraud. Threats are ever-present for every system.

Vulnerabilities make a system more prone to attack by a threat or make an attack more likely to have some success or impact. For example, for fire a vulnerability would be the presence of inflammable materials (e.g. paper).

Controls are the countermeasures for vulnerabilities. There are four types:

- **Deterrent controls** reduce the likelihood of a deliberate attack. For example, having access restrictions might deter a potential fraudster.

- **Preventative controls** protect vulnerabilities and make an attack unsuccessful or reduce its impact. For example, having a firewall will identify and block hackers trying to access the system from outside the organisation.

- **Corrective controls** reduce the effect of an attack. For example, having an audit trail on the system transactions and monitoring audit controls on network usage can highlight unauthorised file access and enable roll-back of the system to before the attack occurred.

- **Detective controls** discover attacks and trigger preventative or corrective controls, such as those described above. An example is an anti-virus detection program that not only identifies the virus, but also deletes it and repairs any damage.

> ## Contingency plan
> The **contingency plan** deals with what happens before the disaster – the processes that have to take place to ensure that recovery is possible.
>
> ## Disaster recovery plan
> The **disaster recovery plan** is the set of procedures detailing what will take place when the worst happens.

Once the organisation has identified the elements of its systems that are vulnerable and has organised a suitable backup strategy, it is part way to producing its **contingency** and **disaster recovery** plans. Disaster recovery planning is the term that encompasses the activities taken both before and after the disaster.

It is now generally recognised that business continuity planning and disaster recovery planning are vital activities. However, the creation of (and maintenance of) sound plans is a complex undertaking, involving a series of steps.

Prior to creation of the contingency plan itself, it is essential to consider the potential impacts of disaster and to understand the underlying risks: these are the foundations upon which a sound contingency and disaster recovery plans should be built. Following these activities the plan itself must be constructed – no small task. The plans must then be maintained, tested and audited to ensure that they remain appropriate to the needs of the organisation.

It is not only the hardware and software that need to be considered; the support infrastructure and services are also required – anything, in fact, that the organisation needs to carry on running as normal in the eyes of its customers, suppliers and anyone else externally.

Sound contingency and disaster recovery plans are essential to protect the well-being of an organisation. This cannot really be over-emphasised, yet many enterprises still side-step the issue or hold plans that are clearly out of date or inadequate. These plans need reviewing on a regular basis, at least annually whenever any new IT-related element is added to the organisation's portfolio,

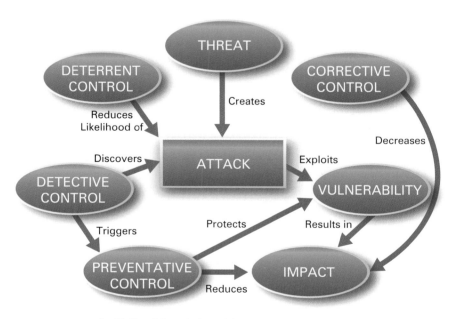

Qualitative risk analysis model

It is not only the hardware and software that need to be considered

or if it suddenly finds that its location is newly prone to natural disaster, such as the sudden heavy flooding in Gloucestershire and Oxfordshire in 2007.

Part of the reason for organisations not wanting to spend time creating or updating these plans is the complexity of the task. This is not helped by some vendors selling planning products that are extremely difficult to master. There is now, however, a growing trend to address this head on: to use a quality template with forms and a guide to create the plans directly. There are many commercial disaster and contingency planning consultancies that will help organisations to do their planning, and they will provide these templates.

Policies underpin an organisation's whole approach to contingency and disaster recovery. They determine the fundamental practices and culture throughout the enterprise and are usually linked closely with information security policies, both addressing the basic defence requirements to ensure the stability and continuity of the organisation. It is essential, therefore, that these policies exist, are up to date and are comprehensive in their coverage.

ISO 17799 requires appropriate business continuity and disaster recovery planning, and compliance with this internationally-recognised standard is growing in importance.

Having created the contingency and recovery plans, it is important to ensure that they remain up to date and workable. Equally, it is essential to monitor contingency practices on the ground to ensure that they are appropriate.

Factors that need considering when drawing up the contingency plan are:

- the scale of the organisation and its ICT systems, the volume of data that is held and the size of the system
- the nature of the operation, whether it runs in real-time, online or is a system that only runs weekly
- the importance of the data held – personnel data, customer data, order data, etc.
- the timescale until the system is up and running – how important it is to be active within an hour, a day, a week
- the costs of recovery options relative to the 'value' of systems
- the perceived likelihood of disaster, based on the risk analysis.

The plan will include details of backup procedures, contingency site planning and staff responsible for various day-to-day activities (to ensure that data and systems are safe, secure and backed up should a disaster occur).

Choose a small to medium organisation that you know or have studied and perform a risk analysis using the steps below:

Step 1 – Identify all ICT elements in your organisation, including hardware, communications equipment, software (bespoke and application packages, data and information) – try to find 10.

Step 2 – Give each element an estimated monetary value in pounds (<£100, £101–£500, £501–£1,000, £1,001–£5,000, and >£5,000, coded as 1,2,3,4 and 5 respectively).

Step 3 – Identify one or two threats possible against each element.

Step 4 – Give each threat a likelihood factor of 1 to 5, where 1 is not very likely, 3 is might happen and 5 is probably will happen.

Step 5 – Using the grid below, transcribe the value code and the likelihood figures, then multiply one by the other for each element. Add up the 10 risk figures to get a total and compare to the severity of the potential problems.

Element	Value	Likelihood	Elemental risk factor
1			
2			
3			
4			
5			
6			
7			
8			
9			
10			
		TOTAL	

Risk severity

The severity can be calculated from the total risk as follows:

- 10–50   Very low
- 51–100   Low
- 101–150   Medium
- 151–200   High
- 201–250   Very high.

A very high severity means that immediate action is required to avoid disaster!

	Element	Value		Threats	Likelihood
No.	Title	£	Code		
1					
2					
3					
4					
5					
6					
7					
8					
9					
10					

Threats

The recovery plan is a document that is used starting on day one of a disaster. It needs to contain all the information that is required to get the business back up and running as soon as possible. For example, it must include who to contact, where to go, what people should do, and the steps to be taken to recover data, systems and communications, possibly in an alternative location.

It will have sections with actions to be taken:

- immediately
- in the next 3 hours
- in the next 24 hours
- in the next month.

There may be an Emergency Management Team already set up with roles laid out. Many organisations hold disaster drills to see how the plan works and if it is successful. If any problems arise, then the plans may need adjustment.

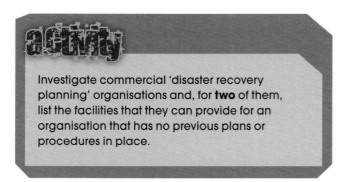

activity

Investigate commercial 'disaster recovery planning' organisations and, for **two** of them, list the facilities that they can provide for an organisation that has no previous plans or procedures in place.

Maintenance

It is impossible to produce software that does not need to be maintained. Over the lifetime of any software system or package, maintenance will be required for a number of reasons:

- Errors may be discovered in the software.
- The original requirements may be modified to reflect changing needs.
- Hardware developments may give scope for advances in software.
- New legislation may be introduced which impacts upon software systems (e.g. the introduction of a new tax).

There are three types of maintenance:

- **Perfective maintenance** continually improves the system so that it gets better and better (tries to make it 'perfect').
- **Adaptive maintenance** adapts the software to changing hardware capabilities or to meet the changing aims of the company (e.g. producing new reports).
- **Corrective maintenance** as users report bugs, the company corrects them, and issues an updated version of the software.

Maintenance releases

New versions of software attempt to include all the above types of maintenance. Minor changes in software systems are often released with version numbers like Version 3.0, 3.1 etc. Major new releases may be given numbers like 4.0, 5.0 etc., or a completely new name.

Most large-scale systems have a team of people dedicated to maintaining the software for the first few months, or sometimes years of its life. If it is a package sold to a number of similar organisations, such as insurance companies, then the software developer may be in constant touch with its customers, updating and upgrading the software and fixing bugs for as long as has been negotiated when the software was purchased. The best maintenance teams will have one or more of the development team among their number, as these will have the most intimate knowledge of the system. System documentation, if comprehensive, should allow the maintenance team to become familiar with the nuances of the code.

Many large organisations will have a specialist maintenance team looking after a number of their systems once the systems have been in service for a while and are mostly stable in operation, reacting to requests for adaptive changes or to any problems as and when they arise. Sometimes, systems that have been running for years suddenly crash due to, for instance, a numerical field overflowing its boundary size, or a previously unused combination of data causing the logic to follow a pathway that has not been used before and which has a bug.

Practice exam questions

1. Explain what is meant by the term risk analysis. (3)
   (AQA January 2007)

2. All organisations are advised to have a contingency plan to guide them in case a disaster strikes their computerised operations.
   (a) State **three** of the criteria that should be considered when drawing up a contingency plan for recovery after a disaster. (3)
   (b) Discuss what should be included in the plan. (6)
   (AQA January 2006)

3. Describe **four** topics that should be included in an organisation's backup strategy. (8)
   (from AQA January 2007)

4. A software house produces a maintenance release for its spreadsheet software. Explain **three** reasons why this maintenance release may have been needed. (3)
   (AQA January 2007)

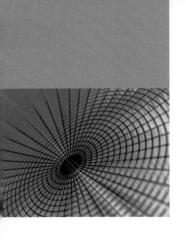

3.6 Training and supporting users

Introduction

New products, new technology, new software and new personnel pass through every business and school each year. Technology has changed the way people work and play. To gain the full benefits of new technology it is necessary to train users in how it all works. By training staff, children and personal computer users how to best use new technology, companies become more efficient, school children leave school familiar with the skills required for the workplace and individuals get more for their money at home.

Training

Training can come in many forms but is best delivered according to the learning style of the individual. The classic school approach is to stand and deliver content to rows of pupils behind desks and hope the information penetrates the young minds and stays stored until it is all let out at exam time. This method does not suit everyone and experts have acknowledged this as failing practice.

The world of commerce has slowly warmed to the idea that people learn best by listening, seeing, saying, reading and doing whatever the skills are to be learnt. Walking is learnt by walking, proficiency at sport is achieved by long hours of practice and learning a new job is best achieved by doing it. It is these principles which promote effective learning. Each individual will be stronger in one of these areas than the others, but good training combines them all. A course that appeals to all the senses is probably going to promote better learning and recall.

There are many options used to convey information about new technology. Training should be ongoing and relevant to the users' needs, with everybody involved. There is a need for training in response to any of the following events:

- new hardware is introduced
- new software is purchased
- an entire new system replaces a long-standing model
- a workforce is restructured
- company policies change
- laws relating to the companies dealings and handling of data change
- a promotion is taken or sought after
- somebody starts an entirely new career.

Methods of training

There is a range of training methods available in order to get the best out of individuals. Failure to train staff adequately can be more costly and time-consuming than the actual training process and certainly less productive in the long term.

Computer-based training (CBT)

CBT can involve a number of computer-based resources. Software with interactive activities can be loaded onto a system and worked through. Alternatively, similar courses can be accessed online and used in the same way. This type of delivery is popular for some learners because it allows them to work at their own pace, in short bursts or in long sessions. It can easily be built into the normal working day if the learner usually sits in front of a computer. The software often has an index that allows users to hyperlink past sessions they are confident with or have already completed, and to repeat sections that may require more support and repetition.

Some people do not like being lectured, lose concentration quickly or may not have the time to be at a pre-scheduled class due to other work commitments. The CBT option provides the learner with an attractive and flexible alternative, which can provide feedback related to progression and allow their progress to be compared to that of other learners. Those commissioning the learning can track the progress and identify areas for reinforcement and strengths, then assign work accordingly or recommend further training.

Training books and manuals

Should the need arise, and if they are available, books and manuals are a possible training option. Some people are more comfortable selecting appropriate literature and working their way through a step-by-step course by making notes after reading. This is the traditional university model and still popular among many learners. This method is flexible in that it can be performed at home, on the train and at the office desk.

Usually a range of training manuals is supplied with the new system. These will be presented in different ways and can be selected by the learner according to their preference. Commercial package manuals and specific training guides may also have reference sections, contents pages and an index to allow the reader to locate the exact information they want.

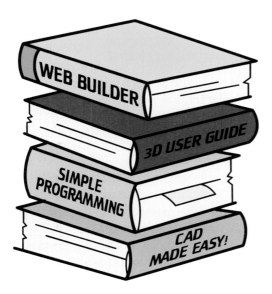

Books and manuals are a possible training option

This method can support those who have an instant need to learn something new, such as how to create a logical function in a spreadsheet or how to search a database. In cases like this there is no need to enrol on a course, pay tuition fees or attend classes, making it much more informal, which again may appeal to the learner.

Structured training courses

To avoid purchasing CBT or books that may go out of date quickly, some companies send employees to official classes or training days. Some people prefer this method, as it is delivered by experts to groups of people who have the opportunity to interact with the speaker and ask questions. Any areas of doubt can be clarified and good courses will allow the group to see any new hardware, software or system in action and have the opportunity to use it in a controlled environment.

Some people do not like this method because they find concentrating on long lectures difficult and the chance to see what they are being taught in action may be omitted. Often, structured courses require some form of written evidence from the attendees to demonstrate they understand the new theory; some people are happy to do this, whereas others are not so confident about producing essays.

Structured courses could be delivered, depending on the content and value, in an hour, a day, a week or over a period of weeks at a set time. Higher professional qualifications take longer to achieve and require a mixture of different materials, whereas some policy training can be achieved within the space of half a day.

One-to-one/hands-on training

In certain specialised instances it may be appropriate to offer training on a one-to-one basis. This could be because only one person requires the training, for example, if they are new or they are the only person to whose job the skill relates. One-to-one training allows for full clarification on particular processes, a demonstration, and could be more suitable for someone who is not comfortable learning in a group or class-based environment.

People may learn a lot faster using this model or they may go and share what they have learnt with hundreds of others (cascade training, see below).

When training takes place on a one-to-one basis, it can have an element of flexibility, as it does not involve gathering a group of busy people at one time, which could cause disruption and may not have full attendance. One-to-one sessions are good for demonstrations and monitoring how somebody uses what they have learnt. For example, learning how to use the point-of-sale and electronic payment systems in a shop is often done in a one-to-one environment.

Videos and DVDs

Videos and DVDs are ideal for quick, sharp instructions and clear illustrations of how to do something. A well-organised audiovisual resource can be used by everybody, when convenient, within the same organisation. Such a resource places little demand on learners and the reduced stress level is thought to be comforting. The ability to rewind and skip sections also appeals, as well as the option of having several people view the same training scene at the same time.

Forward-thinking organisations produce their own motion resources and the very act of producing a learning resource like this is a very effective way of learning. The limitation of such resources, like many others, is that they need replacing when new systems are brought in. Videos in particular are being superseded by DVDs and online tuition.

Paper help sheets and emails

The use of printed reminder sheets or emailed instructions is a very simple method of training and would usually be used to provide quick, simple details about a change to a procedure or simple instructions about how to perform a task that is likely to need a walk-through and is repetitive.

Winslade and Clifford run a small publishing company. Produce a 'How to Use' double-sided document to show them how to incorporate graphics into articles in DTP software.

A physical online file can store handouts and develop into a historical resource that can be passed around to other staff and new joiners. Handouts can be emailed as attachments or the training can be typed straight into the body of a message, depending on its content. Handouts and email messages are not likely to be very appropriate for extensive courses, although when combined with a range of training methods, they can be useful for adding personal notes and references.

Induction training

Induction training is given to new employees when they join a new organisation. This usually involves an introduction to company procedures, policies and how to use the IT resources. Such training will ensure the new member of staff becomes familiar with everyday operations and feels more confident when they start to perform their job.

Induction training may be delivered by a department manager, or by a specialist who deals with all new employees regardless of their position. The delivery method chosen should best reflect the company structure and the likely requirements of new personnel. Part of the induction training might be to plan what other training is required. This would be personalised to the new employee, depending on what their job was going to entail.

Off-site courses or boot camps

Boot camp training is intensive, often off-site and specialised. It may involve packing a bag and leaving home for several days or weeks and spending every waking moment training with people from other companies with similar training needs. This type of training does not appeal to everyone, but is often chosen because it significantly reduces the time taken to complete the courses.

Boot camps provide the opportunity to learn a lot in a short space of time, to perform practical activities and to leave qualified (provided the necessary standards have been reached). This option can be quite expensive but means that new and emerging theories and technology can be absorbed quickly and implemented at company level at a time when it is required.

Many people do not like the idea of being away from home or being bombarded with masses of information in short spaces of time. Therefore, it is crucial that those sent know what to expect and are those most likely to benefit from such an approach.

The following case study describes boot camps designed for IT professionals trying to achieve Microsoft Certified Systems Engineer (MCSE) status.

Cascade training

Cascade training is when one or a few members of a company are trained to do something new or perhaps learn a new business technique and share it with others in the company.

For example, suppose one member of the graphics team is sent to learn about a new powerful animation tool for 3 days at a boot camp. On return, he or she delivers the same course to the rest of the department. The company will only have to fund the boot camp once, which will save them money and reduce the amount of absent personnel at any one time.

Getting Your MCSE Certification: The Difference between Real Boot Camps and Cheat Camps

A technical training school that provides accelerated instruction leading to MCSE certification is typically referred to as an MCSE boot camp. From my experience, having taught boot camps for five years, the name is fitting. It is an experience that can make or break you. It is at times painful, and at times one of the most rewarding experiences imaginable. And when I say rewarding, the last thing that comes to mind is the four-letter title at the end of your name when you pass all of the MCSE certification exams. The reward from an MCSE boot camp is in what you learn, how you learn it, and how the overall experience affects your life.

Involvement in an MCSE boot camp is an immersion experience. Students seeking MCSE certification are dunked – head first – into the technology, and learn to swim in the binary waters with an urgency born out of a will to survive. They develop buddies quickly, and learn to trust the instructor who has charted the waters before. And the students develop greater self-respect, as they tackle a mountain of knowledge and put it to task.

This type of learning is the right way to achieve MCSE certification for folks who have experience in the IT industry and those with sufficient preparation.

A real MCSE boot camp only accepts qualified students. At least one year of experience in the networking field, managing users and dataflow, is an acceptable standard. Sales people at a real MCSE boot camp are required to turn down job-changers and folks that are not adequately prepared.

A true MCSE boot camp requires highly customised training materials. Be wary of schools that solely use a vendor's official curriculum or some bookstore purchased self-paced training materials for MCSE certification. These both provide excellent instructional support in the right environment, but they are incompatible with an accelerated boot camp experience.

Boot camps use highly customised materials that teach key concepts and skills with exam objectives in mind. The best MCSE boot camp makes its own materials, improving them based on appropriate feedback.

For most that are planning on attending accelerated training, some pre-training is essential. A real MCSE boot camp provides materials, practice tests, and guidelines for study to be completed before coming to class. They provide their students with contact to instructors before they attend class, to ensure that they are on target with their preparation.

A link to this website is available at www.heinemann.co.uk/hotlinks (express code 2349P)

The company will only have to fund the boot camp once, which will save them money and reduce the amount of absent personnel at any one time

The fact that nobody apart from the person who went on the initial training will be officially certified will not be a factor in some companies, who may only need the new information to be disseminated to the relevant people. This may suit an organisation, but some employees will want to gain the certificate or award as it will add to their employability should they decide to change jobs.

The person sent on the original training must be chosen carefully. It is no use sending someone who is fantastic at passing exams and makes great notes on the course if they struggle to teach what they have learnt upon their

return. Cascade training needs to be performed by those who understand the best methods of delivery and can hold attention, otherwise time and money will have been wasted. Finally, those delivering cascade training have the option to drop what was not effective and use any of the above techniques in their delivery.

All learners become more effective when they share and discuss ideas with others training in a similar context. By talking to colleagues and exchanging experiences, much of the content learnt can be validated and enhanced. Not all training is followed by a test that provides a grade. The reality is that it is those who keep themselves up-to-date and have developed their own learning style who add value to a company and to their own employability. Those who can take what they have learnt and demonstrate sound benefits from training are those who will be in high demand in the modern, more flexible employment market.

Support

After training, there will still be occasions when IT users will need support with a specific process, application or system. Support differs from training in that it is short term and helps users to move from a position of being stuck to where they can get going again.

For example, a computer may keep crashing. The computer's user could be trained to deal with this, but the causes may be wide ranging and numerous – the user will probably only be interested in fixing their specific problem. In such cases, somebody previously trained to sort out the problem will be required to make the machine productive again. This

The Caston Sports Academy hires its sports hall, five-a-side pitches, gym and other facilities to members. Coaches or instructors are required to attend sessions when bookings are made. The academy has decided to switch its paper-based booking system to an online system, which customers can access from home to make their bookings. Staff will be able to check online what they have been booked for and how many clients to expect each session.

You have been asked to produce a short report to the manager describing and giving reasons for the most appropriate methods of training that should be used to introduce staff to the new system.

type of support means that a company can be filled with many personnel who all have different skills and are able to support one another when required. Technical staff will keep the systems running and provide user support.

Methods of support

This type of support can be accessed in a variety of ways and, just like training, will be selected based on individual needs and will also be dependent on the nature of the problem.

Phone help desk

A phone help desk consists of one or more experts who are contacted with queries and give verbal feedback until the problem is solved. If the problem is not solved, they may send someone to the area where the problem exists.

Experts are contacted with queries and give verbal feedback until the problem is solved

Call-out support

A support engineer may be sent to the location of the problem. Crashing machines, complex software fixes and simple instructions are best dealt with this way so that the person who made the original request can see how to solve the problem in the future.

User guides

User guides can be referred to at any time when using the specific software or hardware. The index or contents page will provide directions to the pages most likely to help solve the problem. This will require some reading and experimentation but is effective in many cases.

Bulletin boards and discussion forums

Bulletin boards and discussion forums provide online access to people who use similar systems. Like-minded people will use this resource to communicate with one another and it is an excellent support option when direct and specific responses are needed. Answers to problems can be found and users can also gain credibility by giving answers and sharing experience.

Online technical support

When new ICT system products are released, the supplier may provide a specialist online resource which can be accessed by customers who have bought the product. Experts who would have been involved with the product development can field queries and piece together a valuable picture of common problems, which will aid the development of the next version.

On-screen help

Most software has a built-in help facility. In some packages, this feature can be accessed by pressing **F1**. To access this support feature, users may need to enter one or two carefully selected words relating to the query. The system will then search for the most likely response and display it on screen. Alternatively, it will recommend websites where the solution to the problem can be found.

Some software provides context-sensitive help. This may take the form of a 'tip' appearing when the cursor or mouse is passed over a label or data entry field, or it may be that, if a data entry field is active, pressing the **F1** key brings up a box with help or instructions.

ICT Hub

The ICT Hub is a partnership of national Voluntary and Community Organisations (VCOs) providing a range of services to assist organisations in the voluntary and community sector to access the benefits of ICT.

The partners collaborate to provide a range of services to help voluntary and community organisations benefit from ICT. They also collaborate using ICT to provide these services and to enable others to collaborate and share learning. The partners bring together their different skills and expertise to collaborate on some projects as a whole partnership and some just with one or two other partners.

The ICT Hub collaborates to provide a range of services to raise awareness of the strategic understanding of the importance of ICT and to support and co-ordinate the provision of hands-on ICT support.

Within the ICT Hub's website www.icthub.org.uk are two other websites: a knowledge base of good practice materials and a directory of local support including trainers and circuit riders searchable by postcode. The ICT Hub website publishes its own research and publications about the take up and use of ICT in the sector as well as signposting to others resources.

The ICT Hub is developing models of ICT support including volunteers. IT volunteers are an effective way of supporting organisations and the Hub can offer a wide range of volunteers all over the country.

The ICT Connect scheme enables voluntary and community organisations to explore their ICT needs by visiting another organisation.

A link to this website is available at www.heinemann.co.uk/hotlinks (express code 2349P)

Supervisors and superiors

It would not be wise to discount the human element in support. The option of talking to someone who has experience and expertise can often be comforting and informative. Digital resources do not provide reassurance on a personal level and cannot come back later to check that the problem is truly solved. Management and supervisors should embrace the responsibility to ensure that their workforce is happy at work and that they have the tools required to perform their jobs properly.

Customers

Customers will also need training and support if they are to operate new products and take advantage of new systems.

Failure to make training resources known to buyers may result in dissatisfied customers, mystified as to how to make something work properly. Customers should have access to email support, leaflets, user manuals and downloadable training programmes that are customised for their use.

Designers of any new equipment need to consider the human interaction and provide clear and easy to follow instructions.

For some organisations, providing a training or support system for existing customers might be straightforward, perhaps an extension of the training or support already provided. However, if, for instance, a business has launched a new online ordering website (and therefore their customers could be anyone worldwide), then any training or, more likely, support, must be designed for the lowest level of ICT skill and knowledge.

Practice exam questions

1. Why would it be appropriate to combine a range of training methods when a new system is introduced to staff? (3)

2. A new application suite is introduced to a company of accountants. What **three** methods could be used to train them to use the new software? Give reasons for your answer. (9)

3. What are the limitations associated with using DVDs and videos for training? (2)

4. Give **three** advantages of training on a one-to-one basis and when it would be the appropriate method to use. (4)

5. What objections would some people have to attending a day-long class-based structured training session and why would they have these objections? (4)

3.7 External and internal resources

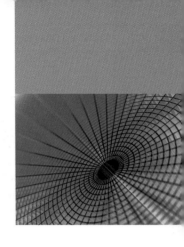

Using external ICT services and business support

Very few businesses are able to internally satisfy all of their own business requirements. They might have staff that are trained and qualified in a particular field of expertise – such as law, graphic design, catering or real estate – but the business may require assistance beyond company personnel in order to meet its business objectives.

It would be unreasonable to expect a team of master chefs in a medium-sized catering company to be able to network its IT resources, produce and manage an online presence and implement backup procedures and disaster recovery plans! The same applies to many companies which prefer to trade and operate in the business they know best and leave their IT needs in qualified hands.

Some businesses are better off outsourcing their IT needs

Outsourcing

Outsourcing is when one business contracts another to carry out a particular task for it. For example, a law firm may ask an IT company to manage its network facilities so that the lawyers can concentrate on legal matters and do not have to worry about repairing machines or installing software.

There are many companies who specifically support the IT needs of non-IT companies. IT is a feature of most organisations and heavily relied upon in daily operations. Customer details need storing, applications need to run smoothly, and equipment needs to be maintained, as well as a host of other IT-related issues. By outsourcing, companies are buying the confidence and peace of mind that comes with knowing that all the IT equipment is secure and running as requested.

Some companies may choose to employ a team to take care of their systems, while others prefer to outsource. The decision will be based on the most affordable and cost-effective option. Specialist IT companies that outsource their services will be aware of the latest technological developments and may be able to recommend cost-saving technology. All of their staff should be competent in a range of IT skills and will be able to exploit successful strategies and experience from previous clients. These outsourcing companies may offer a rolling replacement system of stock, which means that at specified times they replace a company's hardware for new equipment and rotate the old stock to another part of the company or sell it on behalf of their client. They may even provide a team or individual who is permanently based at the client's office. This means immediate support and assistance is on site when it is most likely to be required.

Offshore support

Some companies are large enough to have sites in more than one country. They may have a head office in one country, a call centre in another and production facilities somewhere else. In this situation it is crucial that the company has excellent communication channels so that each site knows what the rest are doing.

Head office needs to know how much is being produced and whether they can meet demand. The call centre will need to be confident that what they are telling clients over the phone can be delivered and the production outlet will need to know how much to produce. If the communication between any of these areas is not precise, expensive mistakes could be made.

At the turn of the millennium, many UK-based firms shifted their production to developing countries because the labour costs are significantly cheaper than in the UK. As a result, production costs fell, which meant better profit margins or a reduction in sale prices. Call centres also grew in stature in countries like India, where most call centre workers are graduates.

Many large IT specialist companies (software houses) work in this way – there is a mainland presence of managers and high-level analysts who liaise with the client face-to-face, but there are one or more large offshore offices where teams of developers and testers work assigned to one project or client at a time.

Find a case study of an organisation that has used offshore ICT development or services (you might try going to the website of one of the big software companies, such as CapGemini, EDS or IBM Consulting to find the case study).

- Make notes on how the offshore-onshore communication works.
- How does the client feel about having offshore workers doing its development?
- Discuss the relative merits of outsourcing and offshoring in terms of the client's business.
- Share your findings with your class and discuss them.

Offshore value and local control - experience the best of both worlds

With a presence in India dating back to the 1980s, Xansa was one of the first UK outsourcing and technology companies to bring UK clients the benefits of a full portfolio of integrated onshore and offshore solutions.

This heritage gives us a unique combination of local knowledge and cultural understanding enabling us to wholly integrate UK and Indian operations. We deliver the cost-effectiveness of offshore, balanced with the comfort of onshore control and management rigour. This greatly reduces the risk involved in taking critical processes offshore while still realising the visible commercial benefits to be derived from outsourcing.

Our clients across public and private sectors are enjoying the advantages of India – harnessing global sourcing as a highly effective means of accelerating their performance.

A link to this website is available at www.heinemann.co.uk/hotlinks (express code 2349P)

Obtaining ICT services

Organisations who do not have IT as their primary focus need to turn to those who can offer IT support. There are many firms who can take on this role on behalf of others. People can be contacted to upgrade network requirements or be called out when a problem is encountered. A large network may need someone constantly on site, whereas half a dozen machines will probably only need minimal supervision once the network is up and running and its basic operations are established.

As well as general support, non-IT organisations may prefer to leave the purchasing of equipment in the hands of experts. A local travel agency could phone or email an IT company, explain what it needs, accept a quote for the work and equipment and wait for the technology to arrive and be installed. This equipment could be bought outright and owned by the travel agency or it could lease it. Leasing is a popular option as it allows the company leasing to replace and upgrade equipment at appropriate times, normally for a set fee which may be more affordable than buying a new range of equipment every few years. The company's corporate ICT strategy will dictate whether a company will lease or buy equipment outright and the decision will usually be based on economic issues or the desire for control and flexibility.

Additional IT services

Employees must be paid for their time and efforts. Automated systems which link business accounts to staff accounts transfer funds at specified times, weekly or monthly, from one account to another. The software is designed to calculate variables entered by the management. This could include details relating to commission, number of hours worked, bonuses, national insurance number and tax code. With this information, the payroll software will calculate the gross (before tax) and net (after tax) pay, national insurance contribution and tax payments. This task may be performed by the accounts department or a contracted agency that deals with this type of procedure.

Further IT services may include employing a firm or individual to produce a company website and to maintain its presence on the web. This will include keeping all the data that is displayed online accurate and up-to-date

as well as presenting it in an appropriate manner for the intended audience (caterers and accountants will have different expectations of what their websites should do and show). Some companies who deal in web development can also assist with pre-launch promotion and e-marketing.

Caterers and accountants will have different expectations of what their websites should do and show

Home worker access

Not all company employees work at the company premises. External technical assistance may be required to allow staff who work from home to access the company network. It is possible for a home worker to gain the same IT benefits as if they were in the office, but setting this up is best left to experts, who will be able to advise on appropriate equipment and software. Access to a central calendar, email, key applications and VOIP technology can all be arranged and managed externally whilst offering a secure connection and flexibility for the worker.

External IT traders will be able to offer backup, disaster recovery and security services. This could take the form of a place to work should the original office burn down, or the installation of an automated backup system that streams data to remote sites and keeps it secure. Firewalls, anti-virus software, wireless and remote access security may all need to be deployed.

A global pharmaceutical company frees up IT resources to focus on strategic initiatives

Driven to speed product development and patent approval while competing against other brands and lower-cost generics, pharmaceuticals are under pressure to streamline operations, increase efficiencies and improve results. A major pharmaceutical company in the United States Midwest works to address these imperatives through a commitment to supporting strategic IT initiatives internally – and using a world-class partner to deliver routine computing services.

Initially, the relationship centered on the company's data center operations, with Unisys providing support for a collection of multi-vendor mainframe and midrange platforms running administrative and back-office applications.

Having demonstrated solid technical capabilities – along with high degrees of flexibility and client focus – Unisys was asked to extend the contract for an additional five years. The new contract reflected the dynamic nature of the pharmaceutical company's IT environment, while still holding Unisys accountable for delivering established service levels. It also marked the beginning of a fast-expanding business relationship between the two firms.

This client has turned to Unisys for increasing levels of service and support. With a team of more than 100 employees on site, (Unisys) provides support for Lotus Notes and manages a Remote Access Center of Excellence (COE). In all, Unisys outsourcing services support some 15,000 employees.

The ongoing success of this outsourcing relationship can be attributed to a true partnership between Unisys and the pharmaceutical company. Unisys Program Manager Jeff Hayhow explains, 'We strive to be flexible and walk in every day with a can-do attitude. We leverage our company-wide resources to deliver more for less – without compromising the quality or level of service.'

For instance, the organization initially asked Unisys to provide service-desk support Monday through Friday, from 6 a.m. to 6 p.m. The client gave Unisys just one month to make this transition. By making the best possible use of resources, Unisys was able to deliver the needed levels of support within the required timeframe.

In addition, Unisys now manages this organization's remote computing operations. From handling employee requests to managing installations and providing ongoing telephone support, Unisys has complete responsibility for the client's Remote Access. As more employees telecommute, the demands placed on this COE continue to grow. 'Having us handle this important but highly tactical function frees up the in-house staff to focus on more strategic projects,' Hayhow says.

One thing is certain: By leveraging Unisys resources, infrastructure and expertise, this pharmaceutical giant has been able to control and avoid costs while redeploying in-house resources to more strategic IT initiatives.

A link to this website is available at www.heinemann.co.uk/hotlinks (express code 2349P)

Managing internal resources

All organisations rely on managing their resources as efficiently as possible. Efficient management involves many aspects, which are usually broken down into discrete responsibilities and delegated accordingly.

Hardware resource management will be the particular responsibility of specialists who know and understand the company's computing requirements. They will be involved in purchasing the most appropriate equipment for each member of the company and replacing systems when they are no longer fit for purpose. They should be able to report and recommend alternative hardware options and ensure that what is purchased is good value for money while allowing the company to achieve its business aims.

Software is another key factor that needs proficient management. Application suites tend to encompass most of the software requirements of many firms but it may be prudent to look beyond the basics. Software can be purchased or commissioned to achieve most business aims. The decision to buy, make or customise one's own software will depend on the level of expertise available, the costs involved and the required timescales.

The most important aspect of software management is to achieve full understanding of what the software is required to do. If packaged software is bought and installed but lacks some of the functionality required by the client, then problems will persist and a new solution will have to be considered. A good understanding of what tasks are to be performed and by whom will help software managers make informed decisions about their software needs before making a purchase.

Efficient software management also involves making sure that the exchange of data is fluid and supported across the company's systems. Diligent purchasing means that a company does not spend money on licensing for 300 copies of a package when only 50 users need to use it. A big saving can be made if the purchasing and management of software is carried out by experienced staff who have a broad understanding of the options on the market and how best to deploy new solutions.

Good communication is the bedrock of any successful business and is an attribute required of most employees. The way information is transferred around huge organisations, from person to person and from system to system, is often a big investment. Management of communication resources encompasses issues such as:

- who has a phone on their desk and who has a phone in their car
- the size of email accounts and the availability of distribution lists
- access to VOIP and video conferencing technology and equipment
- maintenance of the company network and bulletin board facilities
- printing requirements and distribution of internal reports and memos
- channels from shop floor to boardroom.

The role and position of each employee will determine their communication needs, which a good organisation will attempt to satisfy as far as possible. The result of good communication is that customers will have all the information they need, management will be able to make decisions based on full and up-to-date information and personnel will understand what tasks have been done and what needs doing. Slow or poorly communicated decision-making can seriously affect the motivation of staff who rely on timely decisions in order to perform their jobs properly.

The management of IT **consumables**, at a basic level, involves making sure that printers have toner in them and that paper is available for printing on when required. It is incredibly frustrating when a simple 5-minute job takes 45 minutes because it was not possible to print. It would be poor business if estate agents could not print out house details or banks could not provide receipts for cash deposits.

Consumables
Consumables are materials consumed during a production process, such as the toner and paper used up when printing. Other consumables include cleaning materials, batteries for mobile technology and simple stationery.

There is network software available that communicates to a central area (IT support) and displays a message when toner is running low or the printer is jammed. This allows a support engineer to arrive and fix the problem before it becomes a nuisance.

Consumables may all seem like fairly low-level concerns in the fast-moving IT industry, but it is amazing how quickly the lack of them can bring a business to a sudden halt. Good management will provide all the consumables a company needs when they are most expected.

Prior to converting or using any space to support ICT equipment, it is wise to make sure that it has adequate power sockets, phone sockets, lighting and network points. An office to accommodate 20 workers is no use if it only has a couple of power sockets. Each worker may require at least three sockets for their own equipment. Planning and investigation should ensure that whatever equipment is due to be installed can all be turned on and fits in the available space.

It is important to have enough power sockets for the workers' requirements

The room temperature and furniture will also need to be measured to satisfy legal requirements. In order to maximise productivity within the physical space, various factors must be considered: the choice of which rooms are to be offices, the location of the printers, provision of quiet areas for concentrating, which team members sit near each other, which department goes on which floor, and the number of windows and exits.

Buildings and equipment are a significant part of any business. However, it is people who make a business what it is, and it is people that work, sell and build reputations. For this reason the management of people is crucial. Management can expect the best from all their physical resources, which can be bought after recommendations and reviews. Unlike electrical equipment, humans do not perform to an exact specification every time. They have moods and emotions, which fluctuate on a daily basis and contribute to a person's behaviour.

The ability to get the best out of each individual in a workforce is a skill and is dependent on understanding people's strengths, weaknesses and moods. By matching people to tasks that suit their natural abilities, experience and qualifications, management are more likely to witness success and satisfaction.

If staff are aware that they are appreciated, paid a fair rate, given opportunities to develop, progress and carry out responsibilities, they may perform better, show initiative and want to raise the profile of the company. Staff who are expected to carry out the same mundane task each day, which offers little challenge, change or scope, are not being managed well.

It is important to match people to tasks that suit their natural abilities

You have been asked by Hunt and Arnold Educational Atmosphere Developers to look at your current classroom and come up with a new plan to make it a more productive working environment. Every decision you make regarding the location and type of furniture and hardware will need to be documented and explained. Produce a design on A3 paper and present it to the rest of your group.

Practice exam questions

1. Describe **three** advantages to a leisure centre of outsourcing its IT requirements. (6)

2. What is the advantage of leasing hardware from a supplier? (3)

3. Why would a personal trainer ask a specialist web developer to produce a website instead of attempting to do it themself? (4)

4. Describe **two** tasks a software manager needs to perform before recommending software for purchase. (4)

5. Foakes and Howndes TransCom intend to move their call centres to overseas facilities. Explain **two** advantages and **two** disadvantages this move may have. (8)

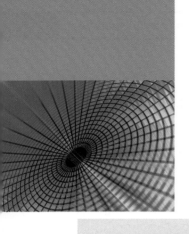

3.8 Section 3 topic round-up

Future developments

Emerging technologies

- Remote working
- Mobile working

Future uses

Impact of future developments

- On society
- On the way organisations are run
- On individuals as consumers and as workers
- Social, cultural, legal, technical, ethical, economic and environmental issues

Types of organisation

Nature and management style of organisations

Information and systems

Information requirements

- Activities within organisations – ordering systems, customer support systems
- Levels of task – strategic, tactical and operational
- Types of task – managing, operating
- People using ICT systems – suppliers, customers, official bodies, legal bodies
- External information exchange – privacy, security, legal compliance implications.

Role of ICT systems to support business processes

Common ICT systems – payroll, personnel, accounting

Demands on systems – internal, external, supply chain, interfaces with legacy systems

Types of ICT systems

- Back office systems
- Transaction processing systems
- Workflow and document managing systems
- Collaborative working systems
- Management information systems
- Decision support systems
- E-commerce systems, e.g. online sales, ticket reservations, licence applications

Managing ICT

Formal and informal systems

ICT strategy to match business aims

ICT policies to support the strategy

Chief Information Officer role

ICT strategy

- Influencing factors – business goals, available finance, legacy systems, geography of clients and business fulfilment, external factors, compliance, legislation
- Management of assets, volume of data to be held and used
- Corporate technology strategy, future-proofing technology choices, procurement, information management, people
- Standards.

ICT policies

- Security
- Training
- Procurement

Legislation – impact on ICT policies and procedures

Developing ICT solutions

Factors for successful development

- Management involvement at appropriate times, e.g. feasibility, requirements
- User involvement at appropriate times e.g. requirements, design, testing
- Effective teamwork

Factors that cause failure

- Excessive demands or constraints (unreasonable expectations)
- Inadequate analysis
- Losing control of the project plan

Systems development life cycle

- Problem analysis and proposed solution
- Design and specification
- Construction of the solution, writing code, customising a package
- Testing at module level, functional level, systems, user acceptance, operational acceptance
- Installation and conversion, including documentation, training of users, handover to support/maintenance and operations teams
- Review and maintenance

Formal methods

- Project management
- Agreed deliverables
- Milestones
- Sign-off and approval to proceed

Development methodologies

- Linear methods
- Iterative methods

Techniques and tools

- For investigating and recording findings
- For business process modelling – context or scope diagrams, information flow diagrams
- For data modelling – E-R diagrams, data flow diagrams
- For testing – test harnesses, simulated environments, volume testing, prototyping, scalability, multi-platform testing

Large ICT systems

Scale – single organisation or multiple small organisations

Reliability and testing

- Scale
- Volume
- Geography and linking
- Network-based

Installation

- Methods
- Hardware installation and testing
- Software installation and testing
- Documentation
- Training

Backup and recovery

- Risk analysis
- Scale
- Procedures for recovery
- Disaster recovery/contingency planning
- Options for recovery
- Training in procedures

Maintenance

- Adaptive
- Corrective
- Perfective
- How to roll out updates and upgrades
- Maintenance teams
- Handover

Training and support

Levels of staff and choices to suit

External user consideration

Training methods, relative merits for the organisation and for the individual

Support methods, relative merits

How an organisation would chose a support system

Customer interfaces

- Choices of type of interface
- Support for the customer
- Managing the customer interface

External and internal resources

ICT services, outsourcing, offshore, bulk processing (payroll, billing)

Obtaining ICT services – contracting, purchasing, leasing

Managing internal resources – hardware, software, communication, consumables, facilities and power, people

Exam Café

Relax, refresh, result!

Relax and prepare

What other students wish they had known before the exam...

Shaheen

Enzo

I spent last summer in an organisation's IT department and saw some of the interaction between development teams and the business at first hand, so when this topic came up in class I was able to relate it in part to what I'd seen, which made it easier to learn. I am quite a positive person, so I found it quite easy to see positive actions for the managers to take and the effect they'd have on the project.

I think I did quite well with the questions although I got fazed by one section. If I had taken time to think about what it really meant I am sure I could have managed to get the marks. At the end of the exam I wasted 20 minutes doing nothing rather than checking what I had written. The comment I gave was not very sophisticated for A level.

How can you learn from Jamie's, Shaheen's and Enzo's comments as you prepare for your A2 exam? What do you need to do differently?

Getting started...

For this section the first thing to remember is that it is a **synoptic** section.

What does this mean?

Well, it means that the questions asked can expect the candidate sitting the exam to have studied all the other parts of the specification and so can ask them to apply their knowledge to a given situation.

So, what do I have to revise?

Everything – that is, all the topics that are in the AS sections as well as all the topics in Section 3.

What's the best way to do this?

- You should have a quick look at the topic round-up sections of this book for Section 1 and Section 2, plus a glance through the section headings, stopping to read any topic you may have forgotten.

- Remember that this is an A2 section – you are expected to be a year more mature than when taking the AS exams, have an extra year's understanding, and so be able to apply your matured knowledge and understanding of all things ICT to the broader questions that might appear on the exam paper.

- The real difference in this exam is all of the questions are based upon the case study that has been published before the exam. The questions will not test simple comprehension of the given scenario, but require more in-depth knowledge where you will be expected to answer questions about, for instance, people's roles or system testing within the context of the information that you have been given. Section 3.1 (see page 170) gives some advice for working with the case study to give you the best chance of understanding any questions asked – read this again as part of your exam preparation.

Refresh your memory

Revision checklist

Use the following checklist and refer back to pages 256–259 to remind yourself of the sections within the following main topics; check them off when you've refreshed your memory on them. Use the Exam Café CD-ROM for a bigger checklist.

- [ ] Future developments
- [ ] Information and systems
- [ ] Managing ICT
- [ ] Developing ICT solutions

- [ ] Large ICT systems
- [ ] Training and support
- [ ] External and internal resources

Quality of written communication

Don't forget you'll be given marks for your written communication, so make sure your skills are up to scratch!

▷ **4 marks.** The candidate has expressed complex ideas clearly and fluently. Sentences and paragraphs follow on from one another smoothly and logically. Arguments will be consistently relevant and well structured. There will be few, if any, errors of grammar, punctuation and spelling.

▷ **3 marks.** The candidate has expressed moderately complex ideas clearly and reasonably fluently through well-linked sentences and paragraphs. Arguments will be generally relevant and well structured. There may be occasional errors of grammar, punctuation and spelling.

▷ **2 marks.** The candidate has expressed straightforward ideas clearly, if not always fluently. Sentences and paragraphs may not always be well connected. Arguments may sometimes stray from the point or be weakly presented. There may be some errors of grammar, punctuation and spelling.

▷ **1 mark.** The candidate has expressed simple ideas clearly, but may be imprecise and awkward in dealing with complex or subtle concepts. Arguments may be of doubtful relevance or obscurely presented. Errors in grammar, punctuation and spelling may be noticeable and intrusive, suggesting weaknesses in these areas.

Get the result!

Model answers

Exam question

Management's understanding and involvement can play an important part in the introduction of a Management Information System (MIS).

Give **three** actions that managers could take to increase the chances of a MIS being successful. For each action state how it would help ensure success. (6)

Examiner says:

Lizzie's first two answers make good points about how managers (of the business) can contribute towards a successful MIS introduction, although the extensions do not really go far enough to properly describe how the action ensures success. The second extension is just about enough to get the mark. The third response goes off the point a bit. It would not be a business manager's place to interfere in the working of an ICT team – that is the Project manager's job. She scored just 3 marks.

Student answer (Lizzie)

1. Managers could make sure that they understand what ICT is capable of, so they are not making unreasonable demands on the development team.

2. They could make sure that both they and the end users of the new system are involved in the design process and are a part of the development so that they will be happy with the MIS when it is installed.

3. They could check that the team are working properly together and sort out any squabbles that occur.

Student answer (Enzo)

1. By allowing the development team to have adequate time to do their jobs properly by agreeing the time-scales at the start, which will help ensure the best quality and properly tested MIS for them to use.

2. By keeping all parties involved with each other, so that the best people are available for interview during analysis, the right people are given time to help with design and user testing and regular meetings are held for all parties to discuss progress. This will help ensure that the new system meets everybody's requirements and will do its job properly.

3. By having a training schedule for the users of the system drawn up and implemented, so that the users are fully prepared to use the system when it is introduced and there is no resistance, which is one of the reasons that MIS systems fail.

Examiner says:

Enzo has given three good answers to the actions that managers could take, with clear signposts in answers 1 and 2 to how these actions will help ensure success. In his third answer, the second mark was not as well signposted, but gets the mark as having fully prepared staff does help ensure the success of a newly installed ICT system. Enzo scored all 6 marks here.

Examiner's tips

Questions often ask you to 'describe' or 'explain' something. If part of a question asks you for the 'effect' of something, or 'how' it happens, it is useful to write that bit out. It helps point the examiner to the mark and also clarifies in your head the response you need to make.

A2 Section 4

Practical Issues Involved in the Use of ICT in the Digital World

This is the coursework section for A2. It is assessed by a piece of coursework that provides evidence of your ability to undertake a realistically sized project that involves a real user with a need for a solution to an ICT-related issue. This project will take place over an extended period of time. The objective for this section is to provide an opportunity for enhancing transferable practical skills in:

- investigation
- analysis
- defining requirements
- designing effective solutions to meet a requirements specification, including the methods to be used for testing and installation
- selecting and using appropriate technologies
- implementation
- testing
- documentation
- evaluation of solutions and own performance.

The section is designed so that it can be taught either alongside or after INFO3, as many of the topics covered in INFO3 may provide the foundation for work in this section; however, you can explore new areas of ICT if you so wish.

Whatever project is chosen – be it producing a system, a policy, a plan or some training materials – it should involve the use of applications software for a variety of purposes and should also introduce the fundamentals of project management. Although there is no requirement to use dedicated project-management software, you may consider this so you can better manage your own project or your part in a bigger project. This takes further the knowledge of a variety of application software packages learnt at AS, providing the opportunity to enhance practical skills or to develop new ones.

The report that you produce must be of the highest quality, as expected of an A2 student, so full use of the functionality of word-processing software is required. If collaborative working is involved, it is even more important to know how to keep control of shared documents and files.

This section is worth 35% of the A2 marks, so time spent on the project must be kept in proportion to the time allocated to the study of INFO3.

The work consists of six parts and marks are allocated as follows.

1.	Background and investigation	14 marks
2.	Analysis and deliverables	15 marks
3.	Design and planning for implementation	14 marks
4.	Testing and documentation of implementation	13 marks
5.	Evaluation of the implemented solution	7 marks
6.	The project report	7 marks
		Total 70 marks

This section is useful as a teaching and learning resource, but can also be used as a companion while the project is underway, to ensure that nothing is missed. An interpretation of the specification content is given for each phase of the project, together with guidelines as to how the marks are allocated.

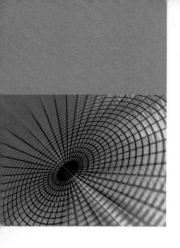

4.1 Coursework introduction

The first thing to remember for this section is that there are many ICT-related topics that do not involve simply creating a database system. For many years, through school, it seems that the term ICT is synonymous with using generic applications packages to create little systems.

By this stage, you will have created many practical systems and gained many skills. An advanced level course is not simply trying to teach you more of those skills for the sake of it; it is in place to try to teach the contexts in which ICT is used: how and why it is used, plus all the associated procedures that ensure safe and successful use of ICT. This then is the focus of the whole of the AS part of this qualification – to enable you to understand the use of ICT in organisations: the **what**, **where**, **when**, **why**, **who** and **how.**

The What

Most organisations make use of ICT for storage, processing and communications. For this they need hardware, software and communications media. There may be **internal systems** (such as payroll and personnel), **production systems** (such as order control and stock control) or **external systems** (such as direct customer ordering using the Internet).

The Where

An organisation may be in one location or in many. Decisions have to be made as to where to locate the hardware, how many computers are needed and where to store the data (centrally or distributed over many servers, for instance).

The When

An organisation may run an automated system that runs continuously, or may collect transactions up over a period of time to process all in one go weekly, monthly and annually. A new business may be able to run without the aid of ICT for a while, until the time is right to invest in hardware and software to streamline their processes. An ICT strategy may dictate the timings of upgrades and investment in ICT. Timing can be important to match ICT strategy with the organisation's business objectives.

The Why

An organisation makes use of ICT for various purposes, such as for internal financial and resource controls, for production control, for customer and supplier interfaces, for sales and marketing systems and for tracking and controlling.

The Who

The people in an organisation are the most important resource and it is their information needs that drive many of the requirements for the use of ICT. Someone permanently in an office, entering data, might need a desktop PC attached permanently to a server. Some job roles may need non-standard ICT equipment; for instance, a meter reader or delivery driver may need a lightweight, handheld ICT device. Not everybody needs to have continual access to ICT to complete their jobs.

The How

How ICT is used is also aligned to the requirements of job role of the person using it. Hardware, software and communication requirements can vary from role to role. The way in which each person uses the ICT available to them can also vary.

- An architectural design technician may need a powerful graphics processor so they can use a 3-D computer-aided-design package to create or amend detailed multi-level technical drawings of buildings, which are then sent to an A1 printer attached to their machine.

- A fee earner in a solicitor's office may use a communications package as a work-flow system to open up and process claims, coding, amending, sorting and filing all within the same package and forwarding completed claims on to the next person to process, while needing to use the Internet for specific research and sending emails to gather information.

- A teacher may use a desktop or laptop to prepare lesson plans and notes, using a word processing package, a presentation package to provide visual lesson material, a spreadsheet or database to track student marks and progress, and a whiteboard in the classroom to view the presentation and to access interactive stimulus material either self-prepared or from other sources such as the Internet.

- The examinations officer at a school or college may access an examination board's website to download exam timetables, then gain access to its protected extranet site to input examination entries or to receive results to download, to print locally.

- Anyone in an organisation who wishes to invite other staff members to a meeting can use communications software to send out the invitations and update diary entries over the intranet.

Approaches to this section

There are many different approaches to the section. There is very little content that can be taught specifically for the section that hasn't already been covered in the other three sections of the qualification.

For the practically minded, who wish to produce a software solution for a user using a generic package, the first thing to do is to find someone who has a real problem for which a new ICT system is the best solution.

For those whose greatest fear is having to write 'yet another database solution', there are plenty of alternatives. The ICT-related solution does not have to be an input-process-output type system at all. Organisational use of ICT has many aspects, from requirements for training staff, through providing a user support system, to backup and recovery and disaster planning.

There is plenty of scope for work to be tailored to each student's needs and interests and for a wide-range of ICT-related systems to be created. Groups of students can work together for the same organisation while producing individual solutions for various problems, so fulfilling the QCA's (Qualification and Curriculum Authority, who oversee all exam-based qualifications in the UK) requirement that all level-3 students partake in collaborative working.

The specification provides some ideas for projects:

- a software solution such as an e-commerce or multimedia system

- a training system including training materials for a client, for example a course for someone working from home

- a user support system such as for a user help desk in a company or school/college, or a fault logging system

- a system for ensuring the security of an organisation's ICT systems. (e.g. formulate a policy to specify appropriate use of a company or school/college's laptop computers and other mobile devices, or a database to record usage)

- a system for communication within an organisation. (e.g. a system allowing schools to use technology to communicate with students within the school, or a communal diary system)

- a system for evaluating new software to be purchased or for a new system to be installed, including hardware, software, communications, consumables and services

- a backup and recovery system and a disaster recovery plan for an organisation

- a system for managing relationships with customers

- a website, intranet or extranet.

However, anything that is ICT-related and is causing a problem for a small-to-medium sized organisation with which the student has a relationship might be suitable. There will be a coursework advisor assigned to the school or college who will be able to say if the project being considered is suitable for the level required.

Choosing a project

- Split into groups of four or five people, each with a scribe to record the outcome of the discussion.
- Discuss the types of problems that might be suitable subjects for projects. Look through the whole specification to find possible topics.
- Feed back from your group to the whole class and get the teacher to eliminate any ideas that are unsuitable and to add any that have not been considered by the groups.
- As an individual, write down three or four ideas for projects that might interest you and prioritise them. This will then give some choice after finding a client.

There are many possibilities for projects

The next step is to find a real client with one or more ICT-related problems that need solving. Look around family, friends, clubs and societies to which you belong. In fact any small-to-medium organisation where there is a need for an ICT-related solution.

Most large organisations are unlikely to be able to provide a problem requiring a software solution, but they may have other ICT-related problems. For example, their security or disaster recovery planning systems may be out-of-date or inadequate, or they may have recently installed a new system and need plans for staff training or a user support system. None of these necessarily involve you having to learn their software systems, as the implementation may be carried out by the organisation's own staff; it is the planning and setting up of systems and procedures that are involved that would be the INFO4 project.

Be wary of assuming that multi-site organisations, for instance supermarkets and chain stores, will need any ICT-related systems for a local branch. A project that purports to be for, say, Derby's branch of NEXT would have to have real client evidence. A project done for a pretend or assumed client will never be as good a quality as one that is for a smaller organisation where the real client has been involved with the student at all stages of the project.

Most schools and colleges already have many of the suggested projects in place, but some systems and procedures may well be out of date. For instance, the ICT security policy may have been written before there were items for students and staff to borrow, or there may be a need to revamp the website for prospective students to include new courses or application procedures. There may be an opportunity to provide evaluation criteria for some new ICT equipment or software that is required by a particular department and even to help perform the evaluation and write the evaluation report. There may be a need to install and set up hardware, software and communications in a new area for which you could plan and oversee the implementation.

Other organisations that could be approached include charities (they are often in need of many of the ideas suggested, especially if they are local), sports clubs, drama societies or just a group of people trying to organise an event. Approaching the local council to see if they know of any of these organisations and if they might want some help could be one way to find a project, or a series of projects.

Allow time to find the ideal client. If an organisation that you approach has a problem that you personally don't want to solve, then pass it on to someone who might – not everybody wants to build a website, not everybody wants to set up a network, not everybody wants to evaluate financial software packages, and not everybody wants to write training plans or security policies. But someone else might, and they may have the found exact type of problem that you want to base your project on.

Working together

The important thing to remember is that one person does not have to do it all – if you approach an organisation with a list of problems they might have that you'd be able to solve for them, they are unlikely to turn you away if they think they are going to get solutions to all their problems.

For instance, if there is a new software system required, then not only does that need to be analysed, designed, and implemented, it may need specialist testing, the users may need training, a backup and recovery system may be required, new procedures and security measure may be involved and user support may need planning. There are numerous project opportunities from just the one organisation such as:

- analysis, design and creation of the online system
- test planning and execution of the online system
- changeover and installation planning and implementation
- planning user training, writing documentation, producing materials
- planning and writing backup and recovery procedures
- writing and implementing security policy and procedures
- user support planning and documentation
- writing technical documentation.

It is quite acceptable to work in teams if that is what is required for the work being undertaken. The team could consist of one or more students working in conjunction with one or two members from the client organisation. This approach is a good idea as it allows you to become involved in larger more realistic projects where each student can work on a part of a system.

For an organisation that wants a website or intranet setting up, each student could produce the part that is required for one department in an organisation, working collaboratively to establish house styles and consistency of the end product and sharing skills in the use of a variety of applications software needed to create the end product.

Another project might involve producing training materials for a course within your centre or for an external organisation where the materials may be needed in a variety of formats for the different people requiring training. Different formats may need a variety of software for their production and a variety of media for their dissemination. Individual students could work on one aspect, while the whole group has to adopt consistent styles and approaches to the material development. The training could be for a new software system, new machinery being introduced, new legislation that needs implementing or new organisational procedures.

For a new user support system in an organisation, there may be differing needs for support by different levels or departments, and individual students could work with a different group of users, producing support materials to best support their own group of users, some of whom may have specialist needs. Another student could produce a system to record and catalogue problems and their solutions.

If the requirement is for a multimedia solution then, as these are often quite large projects, the work could be broken down into more manageable chunks. Separate students could work on parts of the overall solution. See the specification for an idea of how to break down the work for an interactive map that might be used in a tourist information office.

There are no marks allocated for evidencing collaborative working, as it is not a compulsory element of this section; however, sometimes it is hard to find an individual project of the right size at the right level to enable you to show your investigatory, analysis, design and evaluation skills.

Final approach

It is not the end product that gains the marks in this section, it is the process that is involved and the maturity of the project report in showing your knowledge and understanding of the process of implementing a solution from scratch. This is why the traditional 'major project' approach of producing a complex database software system, where most of the time is spent creating and testing the software to the detriment of the surrounding processes, especially evaluation, is not the best approach. There are now no marks for using 'advanced features' of any one software package, although it is expected that advanced word processing skills will be shown in the final report (for instance, using the automatic Table of Contents feature).

There is no requirement to provide any evidence at all of actual implementation. The evidence will be provided through a plan for implementation, the test strategy and plan, plus evidence of testing the final solution by the student, the end user and the client (not all testing has to be practical evidence – taking the requirements back to the client for checking and getting them to sign-off the list is classed as testing and should be in the plans) and the evaluation, where the final implemented solution will be tested against the requirements and test results referred to.

4.2 Preparing to produce the coursework

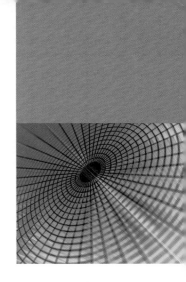

There are many books and guidelines about how to develop a software system following the systems development life cycle, and most students have already been down the route of software solution analysis, design and testing as part of the AS for this course. Guidance has already been given about the importance of accurate designs, good functional testing and so on. Because of this, most of the examples included in this section are from the alternative types of project that are available for INFO4.

Section 3.4 in this book describes the methods, tools and techniques that could be used during the project's life cycle. This section of the book is not going to repeat the information and advice given there, so it is important to refer to that section when producing your coursework.

Section 1.4 of this book gives some advice about preparing a project plan. An **outline plan** is what is required at the very start of this project. Obviously, the only detailed tasks that can be put down on the plan initially are those required to prepare and plan the investigation phase. To these tasks you can add the known milestone dates that are set by your teacher, who may want the analysis and deliverables phase to be completed by a certain date, the design and planning by another and so on.

Only by having tasks at a detailed level can proper monitoring and control of the project take place. The ability to break work down into such small chunks becomes easier with practice – try the activity.

In groups of three or four, produce a list of tasks with estimates in seconds or minutes for the following activity (give a total time, then identify tasks that can be done at the same time and work out an elapsed time as well).

How to make a cup of tea

Allow 5 minutes for the group, then compare the lists and estimates. Discuss.

(One possible solution is at the end of this section on page 291.)

Once you have chosen an organisation and have a rough idea of what their problem is, you can start to plan the background and investigation phase. An example plan, together with 'ball park' estimates for the remaining phases, follows.

Task ID	Task	Estimated hours	Where to be done - Class/ On-site/ Home
1	Identify contact within chosen organisation, phone and arrange interview	0.5	H
2	Read up on organisation	1.0	C
3	Prepare a list of questions	1.0	C
4	Interview	1.0	O
5	Write-up interview notes	0.5	C
6	Document analysis	2.0	O
7	Write notes on findings	0.5	C
8	Observation of current system	2.0	O
9	Write observation report	0.5	C
10	Check back with interviewee for accuracy	0.5	H/O
11	Write report section introducing the organisation, identifying contact name and role	1.0	C/H
12	Write description of current system, identifying people and departments involved	1.0	C/H
13	Write list of client and potential users of any new system, with roles	0.5	C/H
14	Write a justification for the new system	1.0	C/H
15	Write up how investigative techniques have been used and why	1.0	C/H
16	Identify all client requirements in detail	1.0	C/H
17	Arrange client meeting	0.1	H
18	Prepare for meeting and send requirement list to client for checking	0.5	C/H
19	Client meeting	1.0	O
20	Re-work and re-check	0.5	C/H
	Contingency time in case of slippage @ 10%	1.8	
	MILESTONE: Requirements agreement	*	Target date dd/mm/yy

Analysis phase Review plan, update analysis phase Scope Description of proposed system Documenting processes Description of users Evaluation criteria List of deliverables Complete detailed project plan for all other phases	21		
MILESTONE: Scope, evaluation criteria and deliverables agreed with client	*	Target date dd/mm/yy	
Draft design phase Investigating alternative solutions Draft design	15		
MILESTONE: Draft design discussion	*	Target date dd/mm/yy	
Design and planning phase Final design work Implementation, test and installation plan Training requirements Testing strategy Test plan Review project plan	10		
Contingency analysis/design 10%	4.6		
MILESTONE: Agree design with client	*	Target date dd/mm/yy	
Implementation phase (including contingency)	22		
Testing phase Testing following plan Client/user test preparation Client/user testing Write technical documentation Write user documentation	22		
Contingency @ 10%			
MILESTONE: Get test and project sign-off from client	*	Target date dd/mm/yy	
Evaluation phase Write evaluation of solution Write self-evaluation	6		
Produce project report Collate all separate documents into one Format it to a professional standard (sections/outline numbering, page formatting etc.) Verify spelling and grammar Insert table of contents Print and bind	6		
MILESTONE: Hand in project report	*	Target date dd/mm/yy	

The following two activities follow a similar cycle to the project life cycle – you will need to state your requirements, analyse them, create a design and implement it.

activity

Produce a list of tasks with estimates for your Christmas shopping, starting with making a list of people to buy for (requirements).

activity

Produce a list of tasks with estimates and dependencies for decorating your bedroom from the state it is in now to when you can move back into it.

The benefit of having detailed plans is that it is much easier to track progress and to amend the plans as necessary. The first estimated total may well frighten you, but it is important to know how much time you might need to set aside for the work that has to be done. It is better to over-estimate than under-estimate to start with. At each milestone, the plan should be reviewed and the estimates amended in line with how things have gone so far, plus the following phase can be broken down into more digestible tasks.

If the project is being done by a group of people, then an overall outline plan is a good idea, especially to highlight milestone dates that more than one person needs to meet. This will highlight important tasks and events that are client-related – for instance a meeting schedule may be agreed with a busy client at the start of the project and it is important that everyone involved knows what needs to be achieved before each meeting.

A **project diary** is also a good idea. It is not necessary to include it in the project report (if you do, add it as an appendix), but it will give you useful information to feed into the evaluation of own performance, such as:

- any reasons why a task took more or less time than you had estimated
- any problems that occurred, perhaps in locating and using software, or information that had to be researched
- if you had to draw up a questionnaire because there were lots of users from whom you needed information that could not be got from anyone else.

This overall planning and control will form the basis of a well-run project.

Background and investigation

Most of the evidence for this part of the report will come from the investigation that you undertake: the interviews with your client and other people in the organisation, observation of how they currently work, any documents that are currently used, any previous similar exercises that they have done and, if necessary and appropriate, questionnaires.

One note of caution: constructing a questionnaire that is going to produce answers of value is a long and hard task. There should be more than one draft and you must trial it with a few respondents before giving it out to everyone else. If there are many users for your system, it might be easier to ask a representative group of them to a **round-table interview** so that you can get their opinions at one time – this still needs preparing and organising, but the results are instantaneous and can normally be achieved more quickly and with less effort than by using questionnaires. This group interview should never take longer than 2 hours and is often a much better option.

> ## Round-table interview
> A round-table interview is a discussion in which all participants are treated as equals (i.e. nobody is sitting at the 'head' of the table controlling things). In such an interview, everyone should feel comfortable to express their opinions.

Investigation is not just about gathering information, it is about examining and analysing it. The skill is to find the important information and to ignore the rest. When looking at the background to the organisation, it is not necessary to know all the ins and outs of who, what and when – a quick summary of those facts is enough. It is the current organisation that needs describing.

When describing the current system and environment, only describe in detail the bits that are pertinent to your project – so if there is a group working for the same organisation, each student's description should be different. The same goes for the descriptions of client and users and the reasons for the organisation wanting this solution.

A write-up of how the investigation has been carried out, and why the methods chosen were appropriate forms the main body of the report, but any interview transcripts, filled-in questionnaires, questionnaire analysis, documents seen, observation notes and so on should be put in an appendix, with the results included in the write-up in the main body.

Round-table discussion

What is required for this phase

Item in the project report	Amplification (as given in the specification)	What you need to write
1 An introduction to the organisation	1.1 Type and purpose, size and scale, contact identified	1.1.1 Name of organisation 1.1.2 Type (public, private etc.) 1.1.3 Purpose (what do they do?) 1.1.4 How big they are (no. of sites, no. of employees, etc.) 1.1.5 Scale (local small business, small-medium, national, international) 1.1.6 Name of contact and/or client (could be two different people)
2 A description of the current system (or existing situation) and the environment	2.1 Current system, existing situation, departments and people	2.1.1 If there is a current system, a one-page description of its purpose, who uses it, what functionality it has, what data it contains, what information it produces and what shortcomings it has 2.1.2 If there is no system, or you are producing an brand new item (e.g. training materials), then a good description of what happens now, including the context etc.
3 Identification of client and users	3.1 Likely to be one client and many users	3.1.1 Name and role of client and their involvement in the project 3.1.2 Names and roles of all potential users for what you produce (e.g. for training materials this could be both trainers and trainees). If there are multiple users in one department, then group them together. Remember both operational and tactical staff (and possibly strategic staff).
4 A business case for change	4.1 Why the project is needed by the organisation	4.1.1 A reason for wanting this problem to be solved (could be legal, economical, technical or operational, e.g. 'want to have a streamlined web presence', or 'need to make sure that all staff are aware of new procedures')
5 Evidence of investigation	5.1 Evidence of planning, conducting, documenting and evaluating meetings with clients, interviews, observation, questionnaires and research, as appropriate	5.1.1 Emails or phone transcripts arranging meetings and interviews 5.1.2 Lists of questions and meeting agendas 5.1.3 Interview transcripts or meeting notes 5.1.4 Empty and filled (sample of) questionnaires 5.1.5 Samples of documents 5.1.6 Observation notes 5.1.7 Samples of research done 5.1.8 Write-ups of findings 5.1.9 Narrative of possible methods of investigation, which were chosen and why they were appropriate
6 Client requirements	6.1 What is the system supposed to provide?	6.1.1 List of deliverables – in terms of functionality and documents required. For the functionality, explain what the client wants the system to do or contain (e.g. for a training system, they may want a training presentation, training manuals, exercises, teacher notes, session timings and training plans for the user. Explain the who, when and what of the deliverables. 6.1.2 Qualitative requirements, such as house style, format, usability, visual factors and readability 6.1.3 Quantifiable benefits, such as speed, cost savings and timing 6.1.4 Any constraints

Report item	1 mark	2 marks	3 marks	4 marks
Introduction to the organisation	Brief	Full	-	-
Description of current system/situation	Brief	Shows understanding	-	-
Identification of client and users	Client only	Client and ALL users	-	-
Reasons for change	Suggested	Clear justification	-	-
Use of investigation techniques	One technique and basic understanding	Two or more with understanding	Two or more and appropriate use	Two or more and clear understanding of appropriateness
Client requirements	Some identified	Full understanding	-	-

Mark grid for background and investigation stage

The more you write, the more likely you are to get the higher marks on each row. A full description is likely to be 400–600 words, whereas a brief description may be only around 100 words. However, it is what you write that is important, not how much, so even a short description can show some understanding.

Analysis and deliverables

The analysis phase produces, in a usable form, all the information you have gathered and analysed, and sets out what is to be done and the benefits to the organisation of this work. It also produces a set of evaluation criteria, gleaned from the client requirements of the last phase, and a set of deliverables. This is the point that means milestones can be set on your plan – each deliverable will need checking back with the client and the sooner those

Feasibility report
A **feasibility report** examines a proposed project and explains whether it is technically possible and recommends whether or not the work should go ahead.

Systems specification
A **systems specification** describes the requirements of a proposed system.

Logical data model
The **logical data model** shows all fields and some relationships between entities, specifying validation rules, types of field, length and so on. The design phase takes this further, once the technical route has been decided, and maps the logical data model onto the target file-handler/language.

deadline dates for meetings are put into the plan, the more controlled your project will be.

The deliverable that is produced at this phase is sometimes a **feasibility report**, sometimes a **systems specification** (or logical analysis) or it can be a hybrid of the two. It really depends on what the project is based on. If there is data involved, then the logical analysis will need to cover data analysis, producing a **logical data model** that can be passed through to the design phase.

If the project is for setting up training, then part of the analysis would be looking at the possibilities, location, facilities, timings, costs, availability of trainers, training content and so on. You may not be required to actually produce the training materials, just to do the organising of the group – maybe a member of the organisation's staff is briefed to produce the content, which you are then tasked with reproducing and you must then ensure that there is a system to get the materials to the right place at the right time for courses or self-training to take place.

The scope of the project must be defined – a descriptive list of what is going to be included in the project, and what is not. There may be some things that might be included if there is time. You will need to state any other systems, sets of procedures and external organisations that will be impacted by the project or that have their own requirements – especially if these relationships cause constraints on the proposed system. Internal constraints must also be identified and a discussion of the impact that they may have on the approach to the project would gain marks. The scope needs to cover the current position and required position in terms of the technologies that the organisation has: hardware, systems software (including operating systems), application software (both generic packages and any bespoke systems), and communications links, both internal and external. Staffing and environmental factors also need discussing. What kind of impact will the new system have on staff and the environment? What are the benefits for the organisation and its staff of going ahead with the project?

At this stage you must describe the proposed system. It may be that a decomposition exercise would be a good step. This is where the requirements are broken down logically into functions or processes, depending on the project. This technique can also be used when investigating the organisation in the first place. The

overall system is the first level, then the major sets of functions or processes are the next level, then each of those is broken down until the bottom level, which may be different for each thread, is a single function or process.

There are two ways of laying the decomposition diagram out, from top to bottom like a hierarchy chart, or from left to right, which enables multi-page diagrams to be followed. A combination of both can be used. See the example below for a website for an example travel agency macro navigation structure modelled in the modelling tool ARIS. There are other similar drawing toolsets available.

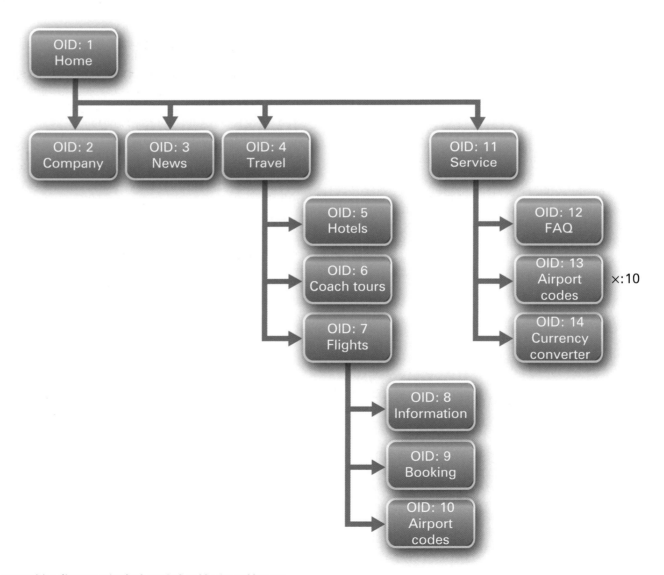

Decomposition diagram using both vertical and horizontal layouts

From this it is easy to see the overall design of the end system (a website in this case) and it also provides ideas for a menu system if the project is a software system. Note that there are apparently two functions called Airport codes, but the cross-reference notation means that the function would only be developed once, just available to be chosen from two different routes through the website.

This method still works if the proposed system is not a software solution. For example, for a training plan for a new system, the diagram might look something like the unfinished one below.

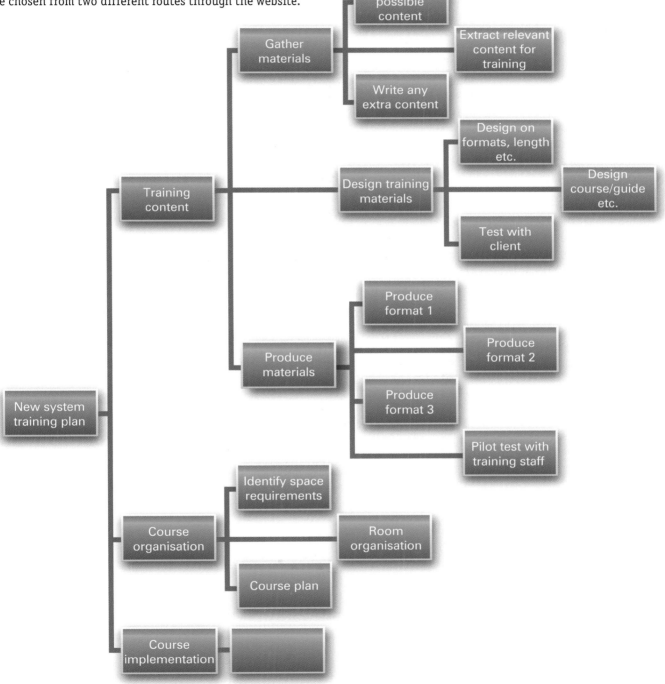

Partially completed training plan

Each process, even at the lower level, may be broken into many tasks, but the more levels there are in the decomposition, the clearer the overall project becomes. Finding the logical order of events is sometimes the hardest part on the way to understanding the overall problem and solution. Notice that in the above example, even two and three layers down there is still a pattern of investigate, design, produce, test – this cycle of events can recur throughout the processes.

From the decomposition diagram, it becomes simpler to create Data Flow Diagrams (DFDs), explained in Section 3, to add in the entities and data stores to the identified processes, if applicable. Not every solution has data, so not every solution will need DFDs. However, a flow diagram of how the pieces fit or flow together may be a good idea. In fact anything that clarifies and explains what is in the proposed solution will potentially gain higher marks.

Each process must be described and documented. If it is logical, the best way is to try to use the **input-process-output** rule: describe what goes into the process (data, people, information), what happens to these inputs during the process and what is the result. Sources of inputs and recipients of outputs should be identified.

There needs to be a discussion about the potential users of the system. These users were those identified during investigation time, plus any others that have come to light since. Their skill levels should be assessed – not assumed – and comments made about any training required against the proposed system. For example, if the project is to produce a disaster recovery planning system for the organisation, then there may be different training needs for the key personnel identified in the plan to those for the majority of the staff, who may just need to be made aware that such documents exist and where they should go in case of a major disaster.

Having created a comprehensive list of client requirements for the solution during the investigation phase, you must write the evaluation criteria in a clear manner, so that it is then straightforward to write the test strategy and plan in the design phase, and you will have a list of criteria against which to write the evaluation of the solution.

Once all this has been written, it is most important that the analysis is taken back to the client for their approval. This may mean sending them your analysis document prior to a meeting. One idea is to produce a sheet describing the work that has been done, including scope, proposed system and evaluation criteria, and, once they are satisfied that you can solve the problem in the manner that you are suggesting, they can sign it to indicate agreement. Keep this document very safe, as it forms a major piece of evidence for your project report. If possible, scan it in so it can be incorporated electronically into the final report.

Each phase of the project requires a similar sign-off, which should be titled and personalised – an example is shown below.

Amazing Grace Appointment Booking System - Analysis and Deliverables sigh-off

I, _____ (please insert name in Capital letters), give approval
for _____ (student name) to proceed with the design work on the
new system.

I have read, agreed and understood the
- Scope of the system
- Processes that will be included in the system, including inputs and outputs
- Deliverables that will be produced
- Evaluation criteria that will be used to test the success of the system

Further comments:

Signed: _____   Date: _____

Titled: _____

Example of sign-off form

Choosing a car

Suppose you have a client who says: 'I want a reliable car that will take me and my family on holiday to Cornwall in the summer and to our ski chalet in Scotland in the winter.'

After interviewing the client, you may come up with a list of requirements as follows. The car must:

- be big enough to take five people plus luggage
- be able to take ski equipment
- be able to take bicycles
- be reliable
- be comfortable for long journeys
- have CD player/radio
- be under £10,000
- be new registration
- be a nice colour: not too bright, but not black or white.

From these, a set of evaluation criteria can be deduced and the start of ideas for testing can also be jotted down at the same time, forming the start of the test strategy.

Client requirement	Evaluation criteria	Type	Notes
Five people + luggage	Does it have five or more seats?	Quantitative	Yes/No answer, easy to test
	Is there enough luggage capacity?	Qualitative	Without precise dimensions, hard to test accurately – can only measure a supposed volume and test against that
Ski equipment	Can it carry ski equipment?	Quantitative	Look for accessories
Bicycles	Can we add a bicycle rack?	Quantitative	Rack capacities testing
Reliable	Does it start in all conditions?	Quantitative	Test under different temperatures, different terrains etc.
Comfort	Is it comfortable?	Qualitative	Can only be tested and passed by client and family
CD player/radio	Does it have a CD player and a radio?	Quantitative	Yes/No, but may be variations
Cost under £10,000	Is the price under £10,000?	Quantitative	Yes/No
New reg.	Is it new reg.?	Quantitative	Yes/No
Colour	Is it a colour other than black or white?	Quantitative	Yes/No
	Is it a bright colour?	Qualitative	Can't be precise as one person's perception of 'bright' could be different from another's
	Is it a nice colour?	Qualitative	Only the client can decide this

What is required for this phase

Item in the project report	Amplification (as given in the specification)	What you need to write (extra to notes above)
1 Statement of scope	1.1 Internal or external constraints 1.2 Hardware, software, communication technologies 1.3 Format of external information requirements 1.4 Staffing 1.5 Environmental factors	1.3.1 For example, official and legal bodies have rigid formats for information whether hard or soft copy
2 Description of the proposed system	2.1 Benefits 2.2 Impact on organisation	2.1.1 Include soft benefits such as improved customer satisfaction; costs are not necessary at this level, but major outlays or savings could be mentioned 2.2.1 Could be major reorganisation, location move and so on
3 Documentation of processes		3.1.1 Cannot give advice, as it depends on the project
4 Description of the users of the proposed system	4.1 Details of skills appropriate to the system	4.1.1 A quick skills audit may be needed 4.1.2 What is required for users to (continue to) do their job efficiently and confidently
5 Evaluation criteria	5.1 Quantitative 5.2 Qualitative	5.1.1 You can make a list for each – remember, these are the objective yes/no questions (closed) 5.2.1 These are subjective criteria – only the client can definitively say if the system has met them, although they may appoint representatives to do it. Testing for qualitative criteria may take longer than for quantitative ones as usability may be need to be assessed over a few weeks.
6 Agreed deliverables	6.1 What is being handed over to the client? It could be a prototype or partial system.	6.1.1 List the deliverables, with dates when they will be delivered
7 Evidence of checking the findings with the client	7.1 Findings must be understandable	7.1.1 Start as you mean to go on – keep all work neat, organised and in the right format for collating into one report at the end. Try to be professional in what is produced – use a draft watermark if necessary to ensure you don't include old paper versions at the end. Watermarks can be attached to the header of a page in a word-processed document and are printed out with every page. Always make sure watermarks are faint and behind the text.

Report item	1 mark	2 marks	3 marks	4 marks
Statement of scope	Brief statement	Clear statement plus constraints	-	-
Description of proposed system	Just description of system	And some benefits	And the impact on the organisation	-
Documentation of processes	Processes identified	All processes described	All processes clearly documented with inputs and outputs	-
Description of the users	Skills identified	Clearly identified skills and an explanation of how users will be using the system	-	-
Evaluation criteria	List of evaluation criteria	Split into quantitative and qualitative	And matching the client requirements	-
Agreed deliverables	Description of agreed deliverables	-	-	-
Evidence of checking with client	Evidence of agreement	-	-	-

Mark grid for analysis and deliverables stage

Design and planning for implementation

When designing a solution to a problem, the first thing to do is to sit back and consider all the possible ways of approaching the solution. This could be a group exercise, done in one of the meetings, with suggestions from the client. Research any tools that could be used, such as ways of training, ways of producing policies and procedures, software available for creating web pages or multimedia applications and equipment available for setting up a network. Any alternative approaches to the solution should be written up and the pros and cons of each method properly considered before deciding which option(s) to choose.

The next step is to draft the design and take it back to the client for their approval. Anything visual must be as accurate as possible, annotated with notes explaining what each section, part or element is for, how it will be used and so on. Another agreement meeting will produce ideas to update and finalise the design (it may be necessary to get more input from the client – each case will be different). To get the highest marks, the detail on the final design must have all the necessary accurate and detailed information for a third party to take and implement.

There needs to be a detailed plan for implementation, testing and installation. If there is already a plan in place,

then this is an updated version, with more detailed tasks. Each type of project will have different sets of tasks, and even similar projects may have different needs for volume and depth of task. The list of deliverables for the system will drive this plan – each has to be implemented, each may need drafting and testing, then finalising. Testing may be simple and involve only one or two people, or it might be multi-functional and multi-user. Installation may be as simple as handing over a document to one person, or it could be installation of software at multiple locations.

For most systems, including training systems, there is likely to be some kind of training or awareness required. For a training system, the trainers and their manager may still need to be talked through the end product, to become familiar with it and agree its level and content.

The test strategy and test plan have been discussed earlier in the book. Obviously, for any solution that has data entry, testing of whole functions or processes is required and the whole system needs to have data run through it from end to end, plus the users should have an opportunity to test it with real data. For solutions without data, testing will vary, but some form of verification of the product, by the author, the client and others, will be necessary. If possible, get an expert and some potential users in the field to look at the product and give their opinions. Try the solution out for a period of time, and then ask the users if it is successfully working or not.

To summarise, the 'design and planning for implementation' phase is the mechanical and physical design. From this point on, anyone should be able to take the deliverables produced here – the design, the implementation plan, the test strategy and plan – and produce the solution exactly as it is required by the client, without having to ask any fundamental questions.

What is required for this phase

Item in the project report	Amplification (as given in the specification)	What you need to write (extra to notes above)
1 Evidence of investigating alternative design solutions	1.1 For all elements appropriate to the project	1.1.1 Could be software alternatives, other technology alternatives, alternative approaches, evidence of research, meeting notes etc.
2 Draft design work	2.1 Enough to discuss with client	2.1.1 Accurate, not free-hand, probably a word-processed document or samples etc.
3 Final design work	3.1 From which to implement	3.1.1 Third party implementable – accurate, detailed, annotated etc.
4 Plan for implementation, testing and installation, including proposed timescales		4.1.1 New version of project plan
5 Training requirements for the new system	5.1 May include training/user documentation	5.1.1 Even for a training system! New security policy – awareness session required; might need different format for memory joggers or induction of new employees later
6 Testing strategy	6.1 Set out what is necessary and who will do it. List any constraints that mean a simulated environment is required	6.1.1 The strategy should be clearly laid out in a logical order, stating who will be involved in a particular stage of testing and a broad description of what is being tested and how
7 Test plan	7.1 Tests to be undertaken, what is being tested and the order in which they will be performed	7.1.1 Also, if appropriate, what data will be used (and use data sets for end-to-end testing), and the expected results

The allocation of marks to this part of the report is as follows.

Report item	1 mark	2 marks	3 marks	4 marks
Alternative design solutions; draft and final designs	Alternative solutions have been investigated plus a first draft design	Draft design has been shown to client and amended	Final design has been produced	Final design is explained and client has signed it off.
Implementation, testing and installation plan	Plan is present	Plan has timescales	-	-
Training requirements	Training implications identified	Training needs also included in plan above	-	-
Test strategy	Some ideas present	A strategy present	Strategy also justified	-
Test plan	Is brief	Shows clear understanding of testing against evaluation criteria or client needs	Shows clear understanding of testing against evaluation criteria and client needs	-

Between this design phase of the report work and the next phase it is necessary to actually implement the solution. There are no marks for this work directly – they are awarded for the design and planning, then the testing and documentation. There is no need to produce step-by-step explanations of how the deliverables were produced – test evidence and any user documentation will prove that the work has been done.

Testing and documentation of the implemented system

As there is the option of producing a non-software solution, and to even out the kind of testing evidence required at this level, there is no requirement to test individual fields for validation. All the testing done for a software solution should be of complete processes or end-to-end testing.

It is important that there is evidence that the client and some potential end users have been involved in the testing. If the test strategy and plan are comprehensive, then this shouldn't be hard – screen-shot evidence is acceptable if there is a software solution, otherwise signed confirmation from the client, or completed questionnaires from a selection of users may be used. The questions on the questionnaires must be well planned (and belong as part of the test plan).

If what has been produced is a procedure, for example a contingency plan as part of disaster recovery planning, then it might be impossible to test it for real – earthquakes can hardly be called up to order! However, a simulation exercise is acceptable, so that it can be seen if the procedures for recovery work as smoothly as was planned. The actions that take place could be recorded by an impartial observer, then checked to see if these actions were as expected and the results compared. If this route is being followed, then make sure that it matches what is said in the test strategy and plan.

Some testing should only be simulated

Exactly what documentation is required very much depends on the type of solution being produced. If there is a software solution of any kind, then there should be some technical documentation, lists of objects such as forms and tables, or programs and any image, sound or video files used on a website for instance, and the hardware and software required to run the solution. There should also be some kind of user guide, appropriate for the users of the system. The user guide should contain function-by-function usage instructions, with screen-shots of what the user should expect.

If the solution is procedural, the agreed deliverables should be included – perhaps as a set of self-explanatory procedures. If in doubt, introduce what is being presented as documentary evidence of the implemented solution. The more explanations you include throughout the report, the more understanding you are showing.

What is required for this phase

Item in the project report	Amplification (as given in the specification)	What you need to write (extra to notes above)
1 Evidence of testing	1.1 Simulated environment acceptable 1.2 Testing should be of complete processes and the system as a whole	1.1.1 Don't use this as an excuse not to do it in the real situation – the testing will only be comprehensive if (a) there is a real client and (b) the solution has been produced 1.2.1 No individual field or button testing or validation testing is required – that has been done at AS level
2 Evidence of client and end-user testing	2.1 Client may also be the end user	2.1.1 Client and users should match those identified in the analysis phase
3 Comprehensive documentation	3.1 User documentation 3.2 Technical documentation	3.1.1 This could be the actual solution (if a procedure or plan) 3.2.1 For maintaining or further developing the solution. For example, this could be installation instructions for a multimedia application or inventory lists

The allocation of marks to this part of the report is as follows.

Report item	1 mark	2 marks	3 marks	4 marks
Evidence of testing	Some testing has been carried out	Testing of processes has been carried out	Whole solution has been tested	-
Client/user involvement in testing	Candidate only	Candidate and client	Client and potential users	-
Documentation	Some documentation of the implemented solution	Comprehensive documentation of the implemented solution	… that is appropriate to the project	-
	Some technical documentation is present	Comprehensive technical documentation, allowing further development	-	-
	Documentation is understandable by candidate	Is appropriate for the identified client and users	-	-

Evaluation of the implemented system

This is not just a section to pat yourself on the back, but is an occasion to be fully critical of what has been produced. It carries 10% of the marks for the project.

If you produced a good evaluation criteria list in the analysis, then the evaluation should be fairly easy – just go through each item in turn saying how you met or failed to meet that criterion. The purpose is to critically evaluate the solution to see if it will 'allow the solution to be used/maintained or developed further which is appropriate to the client/user'.

Evaluation is all about assessing what was successful and how the solution could be improved. Look at the original client objectives. Make a note of which were achieved and which weren't. You'll need to look at the testing to find evidence that you actually fulfilled these objectives. Make a note of where there is evidence.

Try and evaluate why some objectives weren't achieved and make notes on why not. You don't need to know the solution, but try to explain how your solutions failed. Be honest!

If appropriate, have an end-user questionnaire. The end users may be the best people to evaluate the system.

They should have evaluated your system already. Try and get the client to complete a summary evaluation (cross-referenced to the original requirements list) printed or written on company notepaper. A simple letter praising your efforts is **not** sufficient.

Keeping a diary or log book will help

As well as evaluating the solution, there is a requirement to look critically at your own performance. This is where the diary you have been keeping comes into its own – it will jog your memory about where you had problems, when you had to wait for a response from the client, when you had to stop and learn a new skill, the time you had to wade through tons of research material that took twice as long as estimated and so on. These are the descriptive elements.

To be truly critical of your own performance, you may have needed to set some personal objectives before you started – perhaps to improve your communication skills, your note-taking skills or to be less shy in picking up the phone and asking an adult questions. Now you can look at how your knowledge, understanding and skills have improved over the course of the project. If nothing else, and assuming that you have followed the suggestions for keeping control of your project, your time management and estimating skills will have improved!

The strengths and weaknesses you have shown during the project should be identified and described, plus any areas for improvement for future projects.

What is required for this phase

Item in the project report	Amplification (as given in the specification)	What you need to write (extra to notes above)
1 Critical evaluation of the solution to allow it to be used/ maintained or further developed	1.1 Identifying strengths/weaknesses in the solution and any areas for improvement	1.1.1 Evaluation against criteria, citing testing evidence 1.1.2 Evaluation against client requirements and the original problem 1.1.3 Strengths/weaknesses of the solution. How has the company benefited? Are there any negative implications? 1.1.4 Any areas for future development? What else could it do?
2 Evaluation of student's own performance	2.1 Identifying strengths/weaknesses in the approach and how to improve their performance	2.1.1 Starting objectives 2.1.2 Description of how the project has been approached in terms of personal characteristics 2.1.3 Evaluation of how you got to this end point, and what strengths and weaknesses you have shown. This has to be more than a GCSE student, or even an AS student would write – think critically about what you have done and what you failed to do. 2.1.4 Describe what you would change in yourself if you had to do it all over again

The allocation of marks to this part of the report is as follows.

Report item	1 mark	2 marks	3 marks	4 marks
Evaluation of solution	Solution evaluation present	And is critical with strengths, weaknesses, areas for improvement	-	-
	Evaluated against evaluation criteria or client requirements	Against evaluation criteria and client requirements	-	-
Evaluation of own performance	Own performance evaluated	With identified strengths and weaknesses	… and how they would improve on a similar project in the future	

The project report

The trouble with deadlines is that sometimes it is just easier to throw all the bits of paper you already have together, hand number them and stick a treasury tag through the lot, then hand it in.

That way you would lose most of the 10% of the marks for your Section 4 coursework!

Keep your file tidy

For very little effort – possibly only about an hour or two, depending on the pace of your printer, those 7 marks are yours for the taking. As long as you have been keeping files and folders in a systematic fashion and you know which is the latest version of any files, then it is a simple job to gather all the work into a single document for printing.

If you have not already done so, create the project report outline in a word-processing package, then:

- collate all files and bring them into one main document in the right order, with section/phase title pages as separators
- check for completeness – use the grids in this section to check that all items are present
- rework anything that requires it – it could be that an image size means it cannot be read easily, so change it
- put everything into a logical order – double-check this
- do headers, footers, sections and appendices
- make sure your report is page-numbered from front to back
- create a table of contents
- save it!
- spell-check the whole document, then print it
- read it out loud or get someone else to read it – this is invaluable for spotting grammatical mistakes or wrong spellings that are correct words (like **form** and **from**)
- reprint those pages that you have amended
- punch holes in the left-hand side of the report
- add a signed candidate record form
- use two long treasury tags to keep the work together
- hand in your report – an envelope-style document wallet can be used, but no other binding is required, and especially no plastic wallets.

The allocation of marks to this part of the report is as follows.

Report item	1 mark	2 marks	3 marks	4 marks
Project report	Has some structure	Well-structured and makes good use of software facilities	Professional-standard document	-
	Written expression with some specialist language	Used suitable specialist vocabulary to organise and interpret information	-	-
	All illustrative material is readable	Appropriate use of diagrams and/or illustrations to enhance the clarity of the report to the reader	-	-

Solution to cup of tea activity in 4.2

To make a cup of tea.

ID	Task	Estimate (seconds)	Can run alongside
1	Fill kettle with water	30	
2	Put kettle on to boil	2	
3	Fetch cup and spoon	5	7
4	Fetch teabags and sugar	5	7
5	Put teabag in cup	2	7
6	Put teabags away	3	7
7	Kettle boils	150	
8	Pour boiling water over teabag	5	
9	Steep	30	
10	Fetch milk from fridge	8	9
11	Take teabag out and throw away	5	
12	Add milk and sugar and stir	10	
13	Put away sugar and milk	10	
*	**MILESTONE**: Tea ready to drink	*	

Total time = 265 seconds (4 minutes 25 seconds)

Elapsed time = 240 seconds (4 minutes)

Glossary

Applications software Applications software can include general packages for text, number, image and sound manipulation, as well as software that is written for a specific purpose, such as accounting software or stock control.

Bespoke software Bespoke software is made to perform a particular specified task like producing invoices for an international shipping company or keeping a register of parts for NASA. As NASA and a shipping company will have slightly different operating needs from their competitors they are likely to require software specifically designed to perform tasks that match their business aims.

Centralisation Centralisation is where senior management have more control and apply more standardisation. This type of structure can be extremely stressful for managers.

Collaboration ICT-supported collaboration is the facility for multiple users simultaneously to view and modify a shared document or to use a shared application.

Communications software Communications software can include electronic mail, network connection software, browser software and search engine software.

Consumables Consumables are materials consumed during a production process, such as the toner and paper used when printing. Other consumables include cleaning materials, batteries for mobile technology and simple stationery.

Contingency plan This deals with what happens before the disaster – the processes that have to take place to ensure that recover is possible.

CPU The processor, or central processing unit (CPU), is an integrated circuit which consists of an instruction set, a control unit that manages the execution of instructions and a set of registers which are used while processing instructions, either for controlling the order of instructions or for holding results of calculations.

Customer Relationship Management (CRM) This is the capture, storage and management of information about the relationships that organisations have with their customers.

Data dictionary This is typically a table containing information about the data held in the system. The columns will normally hold the following: item name (that will be used on implementation); description; data or file type; size or length; any validation rules associated with the item; any relationships to other data items; any special properties of that item; any other information about the item (e.g.default value).

Data processing Data processing is the precise, low level, day-to-day, electronic capturing of data, which is used for repetitive business operations, such as Electronic Point of Sales (EPOS) systems in shops, where each item is entered into the system until all items are complete, then a total is calculated.

Data warehousing Data warehousing is the storage of large amounts of historical data in a structured way.

Decentralisation Decentralisation gives subordinates more job satisfaction and uses their local knowledge. Decision-making is often quicker with no need to pass decisions up and down the chain of command. It also makes it easier to groom staff replacements by delegation of responsibility.

Disaster recovery plan The set of procedures detailing what will take place when the worst happens.

Duplex Duplex (double-sided printing) means that both sides of a page can be printed without intervention whereas ink-jet printers would need the user to reverse the page and feed it back into the printer to achieve the same result.

E-commerce E-commerce is the use of electronic media to conduct business. It is most used to refer to the ability to buy and sell products or services using Internet technology and the everyday use of the World Wide Web.

Encryption Encryption is the process of applying a mathematical transformation to data to keep it private and secure. The data can only be decrypted and used by someone with the password-key.

Enterprise Resource Planning (ERP) Enterprise Resource Planning is the process of attempting to unify the data and processes within an organisation.

Expert system An expert system is a computer program about a specific subject, set up by experts in that subject to provide answers to questions about it. Simple expert systems use a sequence of yes/no questions to guide the user to an answer to their question, although more advanced techniques can be used.

External threats External threats to an ICT system come from people who do not work for the company and who want to infiltrate the system for financial gain or simply to destroy the data.

Feasibility report This examines a proposed project, and explains whether it is technically possible and recommends whether or not the work should go ahead.

Generic software Generic software is an applications package that can be used by many people for many purposes.

Global Positioning System (GPS) GPS is a global navigation system using microwave signals sent from an arrangement of satellites. A GPS receiver can use these signals to determine its location and velocity.

Hardware Hardware is all the physical components that make up the computer system that the ICT system is based upon. It consists of the processors that perform the manipulations and obey control instructions from the software, storage devices, and input and output peripherals, including communications devices and communication media.

ICT system An ICT system is defined as a complete set of components – hardware, software, peripherals, power supplies and communication links – that makes up a computer installation, with the addition of the data that is input, the information that is output, the procedures that it uses to process and the people that are involved.

Information assets Information assets are any resources associated with information systems. All types of information can be regarded as assets, including all forms of electronic and paper-based information and the hardware, software and infrastructure necessary to access the information.

Input Input is any method of entering data into a system. Input methods can be manual or automatic. Manual methods include the use of a keyboard, a scanning device, a mouse-click, a touch-screen and a microphone. Automatic methods include electronic file exchange, and downloading from other sources, for instance a digital camera.

Internal threats Internal threats are threats to data where the threats originate within the organisation itself.

Internet and World Wide Web The Internet is not the same as the World Wide Web. It is a series of interconnected networks that communicate with each other. The World Wide Web is the content and services that are available by using the Internet connections.

Iteration Steps that are repeated a fixed number of times or until some condition becomes true.

Key-to-disk A method of keying in data and saving it directly to disk, typically used with mainframe computers.

Logical data model This shows all fields and some relationships between entities, specifying validation rules, types of field, length and so on. The design phase takes this further, once the technical route has been decided, and maps the logical data model onto the target file-handler/language.

Logistics Logistics is the process of controlling the movement of resources in a supply chain.

Loyalty card A loyalty card is issued to a customer, who presents it at the till when they are paying for goods. The more the customer spends, the more rewards they receive. The rewards can come in the form of discount vouchers, which can be used to reduce the monthly shopping bill or put towards larger purchases. In return for the reward, the outlet is making a record of everything that the customer has bought from their first purchase to the current day of trading.

Milestone A fixed point in a plan, often connected with a delivery to the client.

Modem A modem (**mod**ulator-**dem**odulator) is an electronic device used to convert digital output from a computer system into an analogue signal, suitable for transmission over a non-digital public telephone system. It also converts the analogue signals from the telephone into digital input into a computer system.

Output Output is when the processed data is formed into meaningful information. It can be produced in many ways, including hardcopy (printed), softcopy (on an electronic device) or through speakers.

Phishing Phishing schemes use email messages to lure unwitting consumers to websites by masquerading as home pages of trusted banks and credit card issuers. Online visitors are induced to reveal passwords as well as bank account, social security and credit card numbers.

PIN PIN stands for Personal Identification Number, typically a 4-digit number. Most cards allow users to change the PIN to something more memorable than the random PIN initially assigned to the card.

Platform In IT, a platform means any combination of hardware or software on which other software will run. For example, a Pentium 4 PC with 2GB RAM running Windows XP could be considered to be a platform.

Port A port is a real (hardware) or virtual (software) connection point between two computers.

Private company A private company is a limited liability company in the UK, and must have between two and 50 shareholders. The shares cannot be transferred without the consent of other shareholders, and cannot be offered to the general public.

Processing Processing is the element of ICT that turns the input data (whether directly input or from storage) into the output information by performing some calculation or manipulation.

Public limited company (PLC) A PLC is a company which offers its shares to the wider public (unlike a limited company). The company must have a minimum share value of £55,000. Some PLCs are listed on the London Stock Exchange.

Public sector The public sector is a term for the parts of the economy that are not controlled by individuals, voluntary organisations or private companies. This includes national and local government, and government-owned firms.

Radio-Frequency Identification (RFID) RFID uses low-power transponders in RFID tags attached to products to send signals identifying those products. RFID tags may be passive (powered by the incoming signal) or active (with an internal power supply).

Return On Investment (ROI) The RIO is the ratio of the profit made on an investment relative to the amount invested.

RFID tag RFID tags are a radio-frequency identification chips that store data identifying whatever they have been built into. They are incredibly small and can be placed into almost any product. They could also be built into payment cards. The information on the RFID tag is read by radio wave technology.

Round-table interview A discussion in which all participants are treated as equals (i.e. nobody is sitting at the 'head' of the table controlling things). In such an interview, everyone should feel comfortable to express their opinions.

Selection Steps that will only be taken if some condition is true.

Sequence A series of steps, one following another from start to finish.

Shareholder A shareholder holds one or more share in a company. Shareholders get an invitation to the company's annual meeting, and have the right to vote for the members of the board of directors and on other company matters.

Software Software is all the programs that make up an ICT system and the data held within it.

Stakeholder A stakeholder is any party with an interest in an organisation, e.g. employees, customers, suppliers or the local community. They have a 'stake' due to the effect that the organisation's activities will have on them, even though they may not be part of the organisation.

Storage Storage is any method of holding data either temporarily or permanently; for instance, random access memory (RAM) is temporary storage, whereas a hard drive, DVD-ROM or pen drive is permanent storage. Permanent storage holds the data when the computer is switched off.

Supply chain A supply chain (also known as a logistics network or supply network) is the system of organisations, events and resources that form the process by which a product or service is moved from supplier to customer.

Systems software Systems software can include the operating system, which controls how the ICT system's hardware components work together, software to protect the system from outside attack, for example, firewall and anti-virus software, peripheral driver software to enable the various hardware components to 'talk' to the processor, and software to organise and control file usage.

Systems specification This describes the requirements of a proposed system.

Test harness A test harness is a piece of code which encompasses the modules under test, and acts as the channel for data into the code. It typically contains a simple call-return process for each unmatched procedure call in the code. It is used for the dynamic testing of an incomplete module or part of the application.

USB Universal Serial Bus – a standard interface for connecting peripherals to a PC.

Validation This is the automatic or computerised checking of the validity of the data entering a system. It can detect unreasonable or incomplete data, but cannot check its accuracy. For instance, a date of birth may be input as 10/10/1985 which would pass the validation check for a correct and reasonable date; however, only verifying that this is the actual date of birth of the subject will ensure it is accurate. Validation checks include range check, presence check, check digit check, type check, format check, length check, list or lookup check, cross-field check and, on batch systems, control totals and batch totals checks.

Verification This is the term given to the double-checking of data being entered and processed in a computerised system to help ensure accuracy. At the point of manual data entry, there are two ways of doing this. The first is to visually check that the data on screen matches the data on the physical data capture form. In this age of details being taken over the phone, this is often done by the data inputter double-checking with the caller before sending the data off to be stored. The second way is to enter the data twice – either by two people entering the same data and the two versions being automatically compared, or by the same inputter double-entering. An example of this is when a form asks for a new password to be entered twice. If the data is being entered into a system automatically from a remote source or another internal system, there may have to be a retroactive form of verification – perhaps sending out the stored details to the subject or owner of those details and getting them to verify their accuracy. One way to automatically verify electronic input is to check some details with data already held that is known to be accurate – for example, stock items and prices entered from a remote source could be verified by checking them against your own stock file.

Voice over Internet Protocol (VoIP) VoIP is a technology for encoding speech as data and sending it across a network (typically the Internet) in real time. This technology allows people to speak to one another for free, even if they are in different countries, as long as each is on an Internet-connected computer with a headset and the appropriate software.

Index

Your Exam Café CD-ROM

In the back of this book you will find an Exam Café CD-ROM. This CD contains advice on study skills, interactive questions to test your learning and many more useful features. Load it on to your computer to take a closer look.

Among the files on the CD are editable Microsoft Word documents for you to alter and print off if you wish.

Minimum system requirements:
- Windows 2000, XP Pro or Vista
- Internet Explorer 6 or Firefox 2.0
- Flash Player 8 or higher plug-in
- Pentium III 900 MHZ with 256 Mb RAM

To run your Exam Café CD, insert it into the CD drive of your computer. It should start automatically; if not, please go to My Computer (Computer on Vista), click on the CD drive and double-click on 'start.html'.

If you have difficulties running the CD, or if your copy is not there, please contact the helpdesk number given below.

Software support
For further software support between the hours of 8.30–5.00 (Mon–Fri), please contact:
Tel: 01865 888108
Fax: 01865 314091
Email: software.enquiries@pearson.com